English Skills

Seventh Edition

John Langan

Atlantic Cape Community College

Boston   Burr Ridge, IL   Dubuque, IA   Madison, WI   New York   San Francisco   St. Louis
Bangkok   Bogotá   Caracas   Lisbon   London   Madrid
Mexico City   Milan   New Delhi   Seoul   Singapore   Sydney   Taipei   Toronto

McGraw-Hill Higher Education

A Division of The **McGraw-Hill** *Companies*

ENGLISH SKILLS

Published by McGraw-Hill, an imprint of The McGraw-Hill Companies, Inc., 1221 Avenue of the Americas, New York, NY, 10020. Copyright © 2001, 1997, 1993, 1989, 1985, 1981, 1977 by The McGraw-Hill Companies, Inc. All rights reserved. No part of this publication may be reproduced or distributed in any form or by any means, or stored in a database or retrieval system, without the prior written consent of The McGraw-Hill Companies, Inc., including, but not limited to, in any network or other electronic storage or transmission, or broadcast for distance learning. Some ancillaries, including electronic and print components, may not be available to customers outside the United States.

This book is printed on acid-free paper.

5 6 7 8 9 0 FGR/FGR 0 9 8 7 6 5 4 3

ISBN 0-07-238127-2

Editorial director: *Phillip A. Butcher*
Senior sponsoring editor: *Sarah Touborg*
Developmental editor II: *Alexis Walker*
Marketing manager: *Thayne Conrad*
Senior project manager: *Pat Frederickson*
Senior production supervisor: *Lori Koetters*
Designer: *Jennifer Hollingsworth*
Cover illustration: *Paul Turnbaugh*
Supplement coordinator: *Carol A. Bielski*
Compositor: *Electronic Publishing Services, Inc., TN*
Typeface: *11/13 Times Roman*
Printer: *Quebecor Printing Book Group/Fairfield*

Library of Congress Cataloging-in-Publication Data

Langan, John (date)
    English skills / John Langan.—7th ed.
        p.   cm.
    Includes index.
        ISBN 0-07-238127-2 (student ed) — ISBN 0-07-238128-0 (annotated instructor's ed)
        1. English language—Rhetoric. 2. English language—Grammar. 3. College readers. 4. Report writing. I. Title.

PE1408.L3178 2000
808'.0427—dc21   00-024280

http://www.mhhe.com

About the Author

John Langan has taught reading and writing at Atlantic Cape Community College near Atlantic City, New Jersey, for over twenty years. The author of a popular series of college textbooks on both subjects, he enjoys the challenge of developing materials that teach skills in an especially clear and lively way. Before teaching, he earned advanced degrees in writing at Rutgers University and in reading at Glassboro State College. He also spent a year writing fiction that, he says, "is now at the back of a drawer waiting to be discovered and acclaimed posthumously." While in school, he supported himself by working as a truck driver, machinist, battery assembler, hospital attendant, and apple packer. He now lives with his wife, Judith Nadell, near Philadelphia. Among his everyday pleasures are running, working on his Macintosh computer, and watching Philadelphia sports teams on TV. He also loves to read: newspapers at breakfast, magazines at lunch, and a chapter or two of a recent book ("preferably an autobiography") at night.

Praise for *English Skills*

"There can be no legitimate comparison between John Langan's McGraw-Hill developmental composition text series and any other texts available. Other texts are simply not as clear, precise, interesting, or comprehensive as *English Skills,* especially with the improvements made in the 7th edition."

Candace C. Mesa, Dixie College

"It is an outstanding text, good for discussion, individual work, or collaborative activities."

Patsy Krech, University of Memphis

'This text has great examples and activities [. . .]. The writing is clear, the format appealing. I think it's a very useful textbook that students would enjoy using and that they would learn much from."

Janice S. Trollinger, Fort Valley State University

"The greatest strength of the sixth edition of Langan's text is its organization and voice. I have found few [other] texts that offer the right combination of common-sense advice AND helpful, sophisticated examples and exercises. The seventh edition is even better. The topics are clear and up-to-date, and the new arrangement of important concepts [. . .] makes the book easier to use than ever."

Kevin R. McGarvey, Cumberland County College

"The text is thorough, useful, well conceived, and well written."

Kurt Neumann, William Rainey Harper College

"The greatest strengths of this text are its flexibility for the instructor, accessibility for the student, and clear focus on the writing needs of developmental students."

Michael A. Orlando, Bergen Community College

"The strength of the entire text is its comprehensiveness: it has qualities of a skills text and English handbook, of a composition and research and library guide."

Russell J. Gaudio, Gateway Community College

Contents

Grammar

Mechanics

Punctuation

To the Instructor

Key Features of the Book

English Skills will help students learn and apply the basic principles of effective composition as well as master important skills of grammar, punctuation, and usage. It is a nuts-and-bolts book based on a number of assumptions or beliefs about the writing process:

- *First of all,* English Skills *assumes that four principles in particular are keys to effective writing:* **unity, support, coherence, and sentence skills.** These four principles are highlighted on the inside front cover and reinforced throughout the book.

  - Part One focuses on the first three principles and to some extent on sentence skills; Part Five serves as a concise handbook of sentence skills.
  - The rest of the book shows how the four principles apply in different types of paragraph development (Part Two), in several-paragraph essays (Part Three), and in specialized types of writing (Part Four).

  The ongoing success of *English Skills* is evidence that the four principles are easily grasped, remembered, and followed by students.

- *The book also reflects a belief that, in addition to these four principles, there are other important factors in writing effectively.* The second chapter discusses *prewriting, rewriting, and editing.* Besides encouraging students to see *writing as a process,* the chapter also asks students to examine their *attitude toward writing,* to *write on what they know* about or can learn about, to consider keeping a *writing journal,* and to make *outlining* a part of the writing process.

- English Skills *assumes that the best way to begin writing is with personal experience.* After students have learned to support a point by providing material from their own experience, they are ready to develop an idea by drawing on their own reasoning abilities and on information in reports, articles, and books. In Parts Two and Three, students are asked to write on *both experiential and objective topics.* Part Four offers guidance in many practical writing situations*: exam essays, summaries, reports, the job application letter, and the research paper.*

- *The book also assumes that beginning writers are more likely to learn composition skills through lively, engaging, and realistic models than through materials remote from the common experiences that are part of everyday life.* For example, when a writer argues that proms should be banned, or catalogs ways to harass an instructor, or talks about why some teenagers take drugs, students will be more apt to remember and follow the writing principles that are involved.

- *A related assumption is that students are especially interested in and challenged by the writing of their peers.* After reading vigorous papers composed by other students and understanding the power that good writing can have, students will be more encouraged to aim for similar honesty, realism, and detail in their own work.

- *Another premise of* English Skills *is that mastery of the paragraph should precede work on the several-paragraph essay.* Thus Part One illustrates the basic principles of composition writing using paragraph models, and the assignments in Part Two aim at developing the ability to support ideas within a variety of paragraph forms. The essential principles of paragraph writing are then applied to the several-paragraph essays in Part Three.

- *Part Four in particular reflects the belief that an English text should provide help in a variety of specific writing situations.* Among the skills covered are *writing reports and summaries, using the library and the Internet,* and *writing and documenting a research paper.*

- *The grammar, punctuation, and usage skills that make up Part Five are explained clearly and directly, without unnecessary technical terms.* Here, as elsewhere, *abundant exercise material* is provided, especially for the mistakes that are most likely to interfere with clear communication.

- *A final assumption is that, since no two people will use an English text in exactly the same way, the material should be organized in a highly accessible manner.* Because each of the five parts of the book deals with a distinct area of writing, instructors can turn quickly and easily to the skills they want to present. At the same time, ideas for sequencing material are provided in a section titled "Using This Text" at the end of Chapter 1. And a detailed syllabus is provided in the Instructor's Manual.

I am very grateful for the ongoing popularity of *English Skills.* Instructors continue to say that the four bases really do help students learn to write effectively. And they continue to comment that students find the activities, assignments, and model passages especially interesting and worthwhile.

Changes in the Seventh Edition

Here is an overview of what is new in the seventh edition of the book:

- The most substantial change in the book is its *far greater emphasis on prewriting and revising*.

  - A new opening chapter titled "The Writing Process" uses a model student essay to demonstrate how prewriting and revising are essential parts of the act of writing. The opening chapter of the book helps students see writing right from the start as both a skill and a process of discovery.
  - While Part One of the text continues to focus on four bases of effective writing—unity, support, coherence, and sentence skills—students also learn how prewriting and revising will help them achieve the four bases.
  - Some of the skills that deal with writing effective sentences (parallelism, consistent point of view, the use of specific and concise language, and sentence variety) have been moved from Part Five to a major new section on revising sentences in Part One, Chapter 5.
  - Detailed prewriting and revising strategies are now part of many writing assignments that accompany the nine rhetorical patterns of essay development in Part Two.

- The book includes a *new model research paper* that examines a contemporary topic and that follows the latest MLA guidelines, including the citation of sources found on the Internet.
- A revised and updated chapter—Chapter 24—provides a *highly practical guide to the library and the Internet.* The chapter illustrates how the author of the model research paper was able to draw upon the resources of the traditional library and of the Internet in doing research.
- An entirely new Chapter 52 presents *pointers and brief activities for ESL students*.
- As part of the book's *new design*, chapters are now numbered, making the text even easier to use.
- Throughout the book, particularly in Part Five, *student models and practice materials have been updated and revised*.
- Finally, a new and more comprehensive *Instructor's Edition* consists of the student text complete with answers to all the activities and tests, followed by a helpful Instructor's Guide.

Helpful Learning Aids Accompany the Book

Supplements for Instructors

- An *Instructor's Edition* (ISBN 0-07-238128-0) consists of the student text complete with answers to all activities and tests, followed by an Instructor's Guide featuring teaching suggestions and a model syllabus.

- The *Instructor's Manual and Test Bank* (ISBN 0-07-238129-9) includes the Instructor's Guide along with thirty-two supplementary activities and tests.

- An *Online Learning Center* (**www.mhhe.com/langan**) offers a host of instructional aids and additional resources for instructors, including a comprehensive computerized test bank, the Instructor's Manual and Test Bank, online resources for writing instructors, and more.

- An *Instructor's CD-ROM* (0-07-245104-1) offers all of the above supplements and M.O.R.E. (McGraw-Hill Online Resources for English, also available online at **www.mhhe.com/english**) in a convenient offline format.

- *PageOut!* helps instructors create graphically pleasing and professional web pages for their courses, in addition to providing classroom management, collaborative learning, and content management tools. PageOut! is **FREE** to adopters of McGraw-Hill textbooks and learning materials. Learn more at **www.mhhe.com/pageout.**

- *WebWrite!* is an interactive peer-editing program that allows students to post papers, read comments from their peers and instructor, discuss, and edit *online*. To learn more, visit the online demo at **www.metatext.com/webwrite.**

Supplements for Students

- An *Online Learning Center* (**www.mhhe.com/langan**) offers a host of instructional aids and additional resources for students, including self-correcting exercises, writing activities for additional practice, a PowerPoint grammar tutorial, guides to doing research on the Internet and avoiding plagiarism, useful web links, and more.

- A *Student CD-ROM* (0-07-245105-X) offers all of the resources of the Student's Online Learning Center and M.O.R.E. (McGraw-Hill Online Resources for English, also available online at **www.mhhe.com/english**) in a convenient offline format.

- *AllWrite! 2.0* is an interactive, browser-based tutorial program that provides an online handbook, comprehensive diagnostic pre-tests and post-tests, plus extensive practice exercises in every area.

You can contact your local McGraw-Hill representative or consult McGraw-Hill's web site at **www.mhhe.com/english** for more information on the supplements that accompany *English Skills, 7th Edition.*

Acknowledgments

Reviewers who have contributed to this edition through their helpful comments include

David Basena, Bowie State University
Gail C. Caylor, Mesa Community College
Lillian Dailey, Cuyahoga Community College
Judith Rae Davis, Bergen Community College
Doug Dickston, Mt. Hood Community College
Michael M. Dinielli, Chaffey College
Ann D. Ecoff, Lambuth University
Francis N. Elmi, Borough of Manhattan Community College/City University of New York
Russell J. Gaudio, Gateway Community College
Patsy Krech, University of Memphis
Anneliese Homan, State Fair Community College
Nancy Kolk, Clinton Community College
Donna Lenhoff, Butte Community College
Kevin R. McGarvey, Cumberland County College
Candace C. Mesa, Dixie College
Robin Morris, Eastern Shore Community College
Kurt Neumann, William Rainey Harper College
Michael A. Orlando, Bergen Community College
Rebecca Peterson, Asbury College
Lola M. Richardson, Paine College
Barbara L. Tosi, Community College of Allegheny County – Boyce Campus
Janice S. Trollinger, Fort Valley State University

I am also grateful for help provided by Janet M. Goldstein, Beth Johnson, Carole Mohr, Susan Gamer, Pat Frederickson, Eliza Comodromos, and Paul Langan, as well as for the support of my McGraw-Hill editors: Sarah Touborg and Alexis Walker.

John Langan

Part One

Basic Principles of Effective Writing

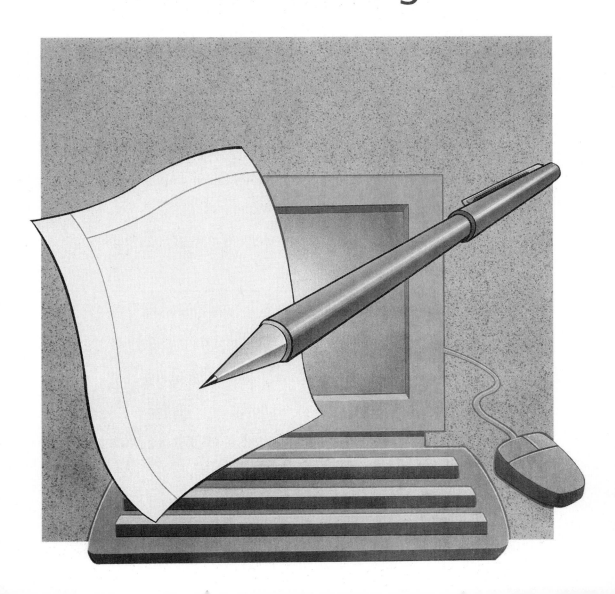

Preview

Part One, "An Introduction to Writing," begins, in Chapter 1, by introducing you to the basic principles of effective writing. You learn that what is most important in writing is to make a point and support that point. This chapter next provides an overview of how the book is organized. It then goes on to discuss the benefits of paragraph writing and two key ideas about writing. The first key idea is that writing is a skill that anyone can learn with practice. The second key idea is that one can often discover a subject in the very process of writing about it. Finally, the chapter presents journal writing and offers some suggestions on how to use the text.

Chapter 2, "The Writing Process," explains and illustrates the sequence of steps in writing an effective paragraph. You learn how prewriting, revising, and editing will help with every paper that you write.

Chapter 3, "The First and Second Steps in Writing," shows you, in detail, how to begin your paper with a point and provide specific evidence to support that point.

Chapter 4, "The Third Step in Writing," shows you how to organize and connect the specific evidence in a paper.

Chapter 5, "The Fourth Step in Writing," shows you how to revise so that your sentences flow smoothly and clearly and how to edit so that your sentences are error-free.

Chapter 6, "Four Bases for Evaluating Writing," explains how four bases—unity, support, coherence, and sentence skills—will help you evaluate and revise papers.

1 An Introduction to Writing

This chapter will

- introduce you to the basic principles of effective writing
- ask you to write a simple paragraph
- explain how the book is organized
- suggest a sequence for using the book

This chapter will also

- present writing as both a skill and a process of discovery
- suggest keeping a journal

English Skills grows out of experiences I had when learning how to write. My early memories of writing in school are not pleasant. In the middle grades I remember getting back paper after paper on which the only comment was "Handwriting very poor." In high school, the night before a book report was due, I would work anxiously at a card table in my bedroom. I was nervous and sweaty because I felt out of my element, like a person who knows only how to open a can of soup being asked to cook a five-course meal. The act of writing was hard enough, and my feeling that I wasn't any good at it made me hate the process all the more.

Luckily, in college I had an instructor who changed my negative attitude about writing. During my first semester in composition, I realized that my instructor repeatedly asked two questions about any paper I wrote: "What is your point?" and "What is your support for that point?" I learned that sound writing consists basically of making a point and then providing evidence to support or develop that point. As I understood, practiced, and mastered these and other principles, I began to write effective papers. By the end of the semester, much of my uneasiness and bad feelings about writing had disappeared. I knew that competent writing is a skill that I or anyone can learn with practice. It is a nuts-and-bolts process consisting of a number of principles and techniques that can be studied and mastered. Further, I learned that while there is no alternative to the work required for competent writing, there is satisfaction to be gained through such work. I no longer feared or hated writing, for I knew I could work at it and be good at it.

English Skills explains in a clear and direct way the four basic principles you must learn to write effectively:

1 Start with a clearly stated point.
2 Provide logical, detailed support for your point.
3 Organize and connect your supporting material.
4 Revise and edit so that your sentences are effective and error-free.

Part One of this book explains each of these steps in detail and provides many practice materials to help you master them.

Understanding Point and Support

An Important Difference between Writing and Talking

In everyday conversation, you make all kinds of points, or assertions. You say, for example, "I hate my job"; "Sue's a really generous person"; or "That exam was unfair." The points that you make concern such personal matters as well as, at times, larger issues: "A lot of doctors are arrogant"; "The death penalty should exist for certain crimes"; "Tobacco and marijuana are equally dangerous."

The people you are talking with do not always challenge you to give reasons for your statements. They may know why you feel as you do, or they may already agree with you, or they simply may not want to put you on the spot; and so they do not always ask "Why?" But the people who *read* what you write may not know you, agree with you, or feel in any way obliged to you. If you want to communicate effectively with readers, you must provide solid evidence for any point you make. An important difference, then, between writing and talking is this: *In writing, any idea that you advance must be supported with specific reasons or details.*

Think of your readers as reasonable people. They will not take your views on faith, but they *are* willing to consider what you say as long as you support it. Therefore, remember to support with specific evidence any statement that you make.

Point and Support in a Paragraph

Suppose you and a friend are talking about jobs you have had. You might say about a particular job, "That was the worst one I ever had. A lot of hard work and not much money." For your friend, that might be enough to make your point, and you would not really have to explain your statement. But in writing, your point would have to be backed up with specific reasons and details.

Below is a paragraph, written by a student named Gene Hert, about his worst job. A *paragraph* is a short paper of 150 to 200 words. It usually consists of an opening point called a *topic sentence* followed by a series of sentences supporting that point.

My Job in an Apple Plant

Working in an apple plant was the worst job I ever had. First of all, the work was physically hard. For ten hours a night, I took cartons that rolled down a metal track and stacked them onto wooden skids in a tractor trailer. Each carton contained twenty-five pounds of bottled apple juice, and they came down the track almost nonstop. The second bad feature of the job was the pay. I was getting the minimum wage at that time, $3.65 an hour, plus a quarter extra for working the night shift. I had to work over sixty hours a week to get a decent take-home pay. Finally, I hated the working conditions. We were limited to two ten-minute breaks and an unpaid half hour for lunch. Most of my time was spent outside on the loading dock in near-zero-degree temperatures. I was very lonely on the job because I had no interests in common with the other truck loaders. I felt this isolation especially when the production line shut down for the night, and I spent two hours by myself cleaning the apple vats. The vats were an ugly place to be on a cold morning, and the job was a bitter one to have.

Notice what the details in this paragraph do. They provide you, the reader, with a basis for understanding *why* the writer makes the point that is made. Through this specific evidence, the writer has explained and successfully communicated the idea that this job was his worst one.

The evidence that supports the point in a paragraph often consists of a series of reasons followed by examples and details that support the reasons. That is true of the paragraph above: three reasons are provided, with examples and details that back up those reasons. Supporting evidence in a paper can also consist of anecdotes, personal experiences, facts, studies, statistics, and the opinions of experts.

Activity 1

The paragraph on the apple plant, like almost any piece of effective writing, has two essential parts: (1) a point is advanced, and (2) that point is then supported. Taking a minute to outline the paragraph will help you understand these basic parts clearly. Add the words needed to complete the outline.

Point: Working in an apple plant is the worst job I ever had.

Reason 1: _____

    a.   Loaded cartons onto skids for ten hours a night

    b.   _____

Reason 2: _____

    a.   _____

    b.   Had to work sixty hours for decent take-home pay

Reason 3: _____

    a.   Two ten-minute breaks and an unpaid lunch

    b.   _____

    c.   Loneliness on job

        (1) No interests in common with other workers

        (2) By myself for two hours cleaning the apple vats

Activity 2

See if you can complete the statements below.

1. An important difference between writing and talking is that in writing we absolutely must _____ any statement we make.

2. A _____ is made up of a point and a collection of specifics that support the point.

Activity 3

An excellent way to get a feel for the paragraph is to write one. Your instructor may ask you to do that now. The only guidelines you need to follow are the ones described here. There is an advantage to writing a paragraph right away, at a point where you have had almost no instruction. This first paragraph will give a quick sense of your needs as a writer and will provide a baseline—a standard of comparison that you and your instructor can use to measure your writing progress during the semester.

Here, then, is your topic: Write a paragraph on the best or worst job you have ever had. Provide three reasons why your job was the best or the worst, and give plenty of details to develop each of your three reasons.

Notice that the sample paragraph, "My Job in an Apple Plant," has the same format your paragraph should have. The author:

- states a point in his first sentence
- gives three reasons to support the point
- introduces each reason clearly with signal words (*First of all, Second,* and *Finally*)
- provides details that develop each of the three reasons

Write your paragraph on a separate sheet of paper. After completing the paragraph, hand it in to your instuctor.

An Overview: How the Book Is Organized

English Skills is divided into five parts. Each part will be discussed briefly below. Questions appear, not to test you but simply to introduce you to the book's central ideas and organization. Your instructor may ask you to fill in the answers or just to note the answers in your head.

Part One (Pages 1–157)   A good way to get a quick sense of any part of a book is to look at the table of contents. Turn back to the contents at the start of this book (pages v–ix) to answer the following questions:

• What is the title of Part One? _____

• "An Introduction to Writing" is the opening chapter of Part One. How many

  subheads are included in this chapter? _____

• Chapter 2 describes the steps in the writing process. Fill in the two missing
  steps:

  Step 1: _____

  Step 2: Writing a First Draft

  Step 3: _____

  Step 4: Editing

• The title of the third chapter in Part One is "The First and Second Steps in Writing." What are the first and second steps in writing?

  _____

  _____

• The title of the fourth chapter in Part One is "The Third Step in Writing." What is the third step in writing?

  _____

• The next chapter introduces the fourth step in writing, which includes all the skills involved in writing clear, error-free sentences. Most of these sentence skills are covered later in the book, where they can be easily referred to as needed. In which part of the book are sentence skills treated?

  _____

- The title of the final chapter in Part One is "Four Bases for Evaluating Writing." Fill in the first four subheads following the title.

  Subhead 1. _____

  Subhead 2. _____

  Subhead 3. _____

  Subhead 4. _____

Inside Front Cover   Turn now to the inside front cover. You will see there a (*fill in the missing word*) _____ of the four bases of effective writing. These four standards can be used as a guide for every paper that you write. They are summarized on the inside front cover for easy reference. If you follow them, you are almost sure to write effective papers.

Part Two (Pages 159–290)   The title of Part Two is

_____

Part Two, as the title explains, is concerned with different ways to develop paragraphs. Read the preview on page 160 and record here how many types of paragraph development are explained: _____.

Turn to the first method of paragraph development, "Providing Examples," on page 171. You will see that the chapter opens with a brief introduction followed by several paragraphs written by students. Then you will see a series of six (*fill in the missing word*) _____ to help you evaluate the descriptive paragraphs in terms of unity, support, and coherence. Finally, there is a series of writing topics that can be developed by means of description. The same format is used for each of the other methods of paragraph development in Part Two.

Part Three (Pages 291–318)   The title of Part Three is

_____

As the preview notes, in Part Two you were asked to write single paragraphs; in Part Three, you are asked to write papers of more than one (*fill in the missing word*) _____.

Part Four (Pages 319–402)   The title of Part Four is

_____

Part Four gives you advice on a number of important skills that are related to writing. You can refer to this part of the book whenever the need arises.

- Which chapter will help you write effective answers to essay questions?

  _____

- Which chapters will help you prepare papers on books or articles you must read for other classes?

  _____

  _____

  _____

Part Five (Pages 403–626)   The title of Part Five is

_____

Part Five is the longest part of the book. It gives you practice in skills needed to write clear and effective sentences. You will note from the table of contents that it contains a diagnostic test, the skills themselves, mastery tests, editing tests, and an achievement test. The skills are grouped into four sections:

"Grammar," "Mechanics," (*fill in the missing word*) "_____," and "Word Use."

Inside Back Cover   On the inside back cover is an alphabetical list of (*fill in the missing words*) _____.
Your instructor may use these symbols in marking your papers. In addition, you can use the page numbers in the list for quick reference to a specific sentence skill.

Charts in the Book   In addition to the guides on the inside front and back covers, several charts have been provided in the book to help you take responsibility for your own learning.

- What are the names of the charts on pages 632–635?

  _____

  _____

  _____

Benefits of Paragraph Writing

Paragraph writing offers at least three benefits. First of all, mastering the structure of the paragraph will help make you a better writer. For other courses, you'll often do writing that will be variations on the paragraph form—for example, exam answers, summaries, response papers, and brief reports. In addition, paragraphs serve as the basic building blocks of essays, the most common form of writing in college. The basic structure of the traditional paragraph, with its emphasis on a clear point and well-organized, logical support, will help you write effective essays and almost every kind of paper that you will have to do.

Second, the discipline of writing a paragraph will strengthen your skills as a reader and listener. You'll become more critically aware of other writers' and speakers' ideas and the evidence they provide—or fail to provide—to support those ideas.

Most important, paragraph writing will make you a stronger thinker. Writing a solidly reasoned paragraph requires mental discipline and close attention to a set of logical rules. Creating a paragraph in which there is an overall topic sentence supported by well-reasoned, convincing evidence is more challenging than writing a free-form or expressive paper. Such a paragraph obliges you to carefully sort out, think through, and organize your ideas. You'll learn to discover and express just what your ideas are and to develop those ideas in a sound and logical way. Traditional paragraph writing, in short, will train your mind to think clearly, and that ability will prove to be of value in every phase of your life.

Writing as a Skill

A sure way to wreck your chances of learning how to write competently is to believe that writing is a "natural gift" rather than a learned skill. People with such an attitude think that they are the only ones for whom writing is unbearably difficult. They feel that everyone else finds writing easy or at least tolerable. Such people typically say, "I'm not any good at writing" or "English was not one of my good subjects." They imply that they simply do not have a talent for writing, while others do. The result of this attitude is that people try to avoid writing, and when they do write, they don't try their best. Their attitude becomes a self-fulfilling prophecy: their writing fails chiefly because they have brainwashed themselves into thinking that they don't have the "natural talent" needed to write. Unless their attitude changes, they probably will not learn how to write effectively.

A realistic attitude about writing must build on the idea that *writing is a skill.* It is a skill like driving, typing, or cooking, and like any skill, it can be learned. If you have the determination to learn, this book will give you the extensive practice needed to develop your writing skills.

Many people find it difficult to do the intense, active thinking that clear writing demands. (Perhaps television has made us all so passive that the active thinking necessary in both writing and reading now seems harder than ever.) It is frightening to sit down before a blank sheet of paper or a computer screen and know that an hour later, nothing on it may be worth keeping. It is frustrating to discover how much of a challenge it is to transfer thoughts and feelings from one's head into words. It is upsetting to find that an apparently simple writing subject often turns out to be complicated. But writing is not an automatic process: we will not get something for nothing—and we should not expect to. For almost everyone, competent writing comes from plain hard work—from determination, sweat, and head-on battle. The good news is that the skill of writing can be mastered, and if you are ready to work, you will learn what you need to know.

Activity

To get a sense of just how you regard writing, read the following statements. Put a check (✓) beside those statements with which you agree. This activity is not a test, so try to be as honest as possible.

1. A good writer should be able to sit down and write a paper straight through without stopping.

2. Writing is a skill that anyone can learn with practice.

3. I'll never be good at writing because I make too many mistakes in spelling, grammar, and punctuation.

4. Because I dislike writing, I always start a paper at the last possible minute.

5. I've always done poorly in English, and I don't expect that to change.

Now read the following comments about the five statements. The comments will help you see if your attitude is hurting or helping your efforts to become a better writer.

Comments

- Statement 1: *"A good writer should be able to sit down and write a paper straight through without stopping."*

  Statement 1 is not true. Writing is, in fact, a process. It is done not in one easy step but in a series of steps, and seldom at one sitting. If you cannot do a paper all at once, that simply means you are like most of the other people on the planet. It is harmful to carry around the false idea that writing should be easy.

- Statement 2: *"Writing is a skill that anyone can learn with practice."*

  Statement 2 is absolutely true. Writing is a skill, like driving or word processing, that you can master with hard work. If you want to learn to write, you can. It is as simple as that. If you believe this, you are ready to learn how to become a competent writer.

  Some people hold the false belief that writing is a natural gift, which some have and others do not. Because of this belief, they never make a truly honest effort to learn to write—and so they never learn.

- Statement 3: *"I'll never be good at writing because I make too many mistakes in spelling, grammar, and punctuation."*

    The first concern in good writing should be content—what you have to say. Your ideas and feelings are what matter most. You should not worry about spelling, grammar, or punctuation while working on content.

    Unfortunately, some people are so self-conscious about making mistakes that they do not focus on what they want to say. They need to realize that a paper is best done in stages, and that applying the rules can and should wait until a later stage in the writing process. Through review and practice, you will eventually learn how to follow the rules with confidence.

- Statement 4: *"Because I dislike writing, I always start a paper at the last possible minute."*

    This is all too common. You feel you are going to do poorly, and then behave in a way that ensures you *will* do poorly! Your attitude is so negative that you defeat yourself—not even allowing enough time to really try.

    Again, what you need to realize is that writing is a process. Because it is done in steps, you don't have to get it right all at once. If you allow yourself enough time, you'll find a way to make a paper come together.

- Statement 5: *"I've always done poorly in English, and I don't expect that to change."*

    How you may have performed in the *past* does not control how you can perform in the *present.* Even if you did poorly in English in high school, it is in your power to make English one of your best subjects in college. If you believe writing can be learned and then work hard at it, you *will* become a better writer.

In conclusion, your attitude is crucial. If you believe you are a poor writer and always will be, chances are you will not improve. If you realize you can become a better writer, chances are you *will* improve. Depending on how you allow yourself to think, you can be your own best friend or your own worst enemy.

Writing as a Process of Discovery

In addition to believing that writing is a natural gift, many people believe, mistakenly, that writing should flow in a simple, straight line from the writer's head onto the page. But writing is seldom an easy, one-step journey in which a finished paper comes out in a first draft. The truth is that *writing is a process of discovery* that involves a series of steps, and those steps are very often a zigzag journey. Look at the following illustrations of the writing process:

Very often, writers do not discover just what they want to write about until they explore their thoughts in writing. For example, Gene Hert had been asked to write about a best or worst job. Only after he did some freewriting on good and bad jobs did he realize that the most interesting details centered on his job at an apple plant. He discovered his subject in the course of writing.

Another student, Rhonda, talking afterward about a paper she wrote, explained that at first her topic was how she relaxed with her children. But as she accumulated details, she realized after a page of writing that the words *relax* and *children* simply did not go together. Her details were really examples of how she *enjoyed* her children, not how she *relaxed* with them. She sensed that the real focus of her writing should be what she did by herself to relax, and then she thought suddenly that the best time of her week was Thursday after school. "A light clicked on in my head," she explained. "I knew I had my paper." Then it was a matter of detailing exactly what she did to relax on Thursday evenings. Her paper, "How I Relax," is on page 80.

The point is that writing is often a process of continuing discovery. As you write, you may suddenly switch direction or double back. You may be working on a topic sentence and realize suddenly that it could be your concluding thought. Or you may be developing a supporting idea and then decide that it should be the main point of your paper. Chapter 2 will treat the writing process directly. What is important to remember here is that writers frequently do not know their exact destination as they begin to write. Very often they discover the direction and shape of a paper during the process of writing.

Keeping a Journal

Because writing is a skill, it makes sense that the more you practice writing, the better you will write. One excellent way to get practice in writing, even before you begin composing formal paragraphs, is to keep a daily or almost daily journal. Writing a journal will help you develop the habit of thinking on paper and will show you how ideas can be discovered in the process of writing. A journal can make writing a familiar part of your life and can serve as a continuing source of ideas for papers.

At some point during the day—perhaps during a study period after your last class of the day, or right before dinner, or right before going to bed—spend fifteen minutes or so writing in your journal. Keep in mind that you do not have to plan what to write about, or be in the mood to write, or worry about making mistakes as you write; just write down whatever words come out. You should write at least one page in each session.

You may want to use a notebook that you can easily carry with you for on-the-spot writing. Or you may decide to write on loose-leaf paper that can be transferred later to a journal folder on your desk. No matter how you proceed, be sure to date all entries.

Your instructor may ask you to make journal entries a specific number of times a week, for a specific number of weeks. He or she may have you turn in your journal every so often for review and feedback. If you are keeping the journal on your own, try to make entries three to five times a week every week of the semester. Your journal can serve as a source book of ideas for possible papers. More important, keeping a journal will help you develop the habit of thinking on paper, and it can help you make writing a familiar part of your life.

Activity

Following is an excerpt from one student's journal. (Sentence-skills mistakes have been corrected to improve readability.) As you read, look for a general point and supporting material that could be the basis for an interesting paper.

October 6

Today a woman came into our department at the store and wanted to know if we had any scrap lumber ten feet long. Ten feet! "Lady," I said, "anything we have that's ten feet long sure as heck isn't scrap." When the boss heard me say that, he almost canned me. My boss is a company man, down to his toe tips. He wants to make a big impression on his bosses, and he'll run us around like mad all night to make himself look good. He's the most ambitious man I've ever met. If I don't transfer out of Hardware soon, I'm going to go crazy on this job. I'm not ready to quit, though. The time is not right. I want to be here for a year and have another job lined up and have other things right before I quit. It's good the boss wasn't around tonight when another customer wanted me to carry a bookcase he had bought out to his car. He didn't ask me to help him—he <u>expected</u> me to help him. I hate that kind of "You're my servant" attitude, and I told him that carrying stuff out to cars wasn't my job. Ordinarily I go out of my way to give people a hand, but not guys like him. . . .

- If the writer of this journal is looking for an idea for a paper, he can probably find several in this single entry. For example, he might write a narrative supporting the point that "In my sales job I have to deal with some irritating customers." See if you can find another idea in this entry that might be the basis for an interesting paragraph. Write your point in the space below.

- Take fifteen minutes to prepare a journal entry right now on this day in your life. On a separate sheet of paper, just start writing about anything that you have said, heard, thought, or felt, and let your thoughts take you where they may.

Using This Text

Here is a suggested sequence for using this book if you are working on your own.

1   After completing this introduction, read the remaining five chapters in Part One and work through as many of the activities as you need to master the ideas in these chapters. By the end of Part One, you will have covered all the basic theory needed to write effective papers.

2   Turn to Part Five and take the diagnostic test. The test will help you determine what sentence skills you need to review. Study those skills one or two at a time while you continue to work on other parts of the book. These skills will help you write effective, error-free sentences.

3   What you do next depends on course requirements, individual needs, or both. You will want to practice at least several different kinds of paragraph development in Part Two. If your time is limited, be sure to include "Providing Examples," "Explaining a Process," "Comparing or Contrasting," and "Arguing a Position."

4   After you develop skill in writing effective paragraphs, go on to practice writing one or more of the several-paragraph essays described in Part Three.

5   Turn to Part Four as needed for help with study skills and the types of writing you will do in college: exam essays, summaries, reports, the résumé and job application letter, and the research paper.

Remember that, for your convenience, the book includes the following:

- On the inside front cover, there is a checklist of the four basic steps in effective writing.
- On the inside back cover, there is a list of commonly used correction symbols.

Get into the habit of referring to these guides on a regular basis; they'll help you produce clearly thought-out, well-written papers.

English Skills will help you learn, practice, and apply the thinking and writing skills you need to communicate effectively. But the starting point must be your determination to do the work needed to become a strong writer. The ability to express yourself clearly and logically can open doors of opportunity for you, both in school and in your career. If you decide—*and only you can decide*—that you want such language power, this book will help you reach that goal.

2 The Writing Process

This chapter will explain and illustrate

- **the sequence of steps in writing an effective paragraph**
- **prewriting**
- **revising**
- **editing**

Chapter 1 introduced you to the paragraph form and some basics of writing. This chapter will explain and illustrate the sequence of steps in writing an effective paragraph. In particular, the chapter will focus on prewriting and revising—strategies that can help with every paper that you write.

For many people, writing is a process that involves the following steps:

1 Discovering a point—often through prewriting.

2 Developing solid support for the point—often through more prewriting.

3 Organizing the supporting material and writing it out in a first draft.

4 Revising and then editing carefully to ensure an effective, error-free paper.

Learning this sequence will help give you confidence when the time comes to write. You'll know that you can use prewriting as a way to think on paper and to discover gradually just what ideas you want to develop. You'll understand that there are four clear-cut goals to aim for in your writing—unity, support, organization, and error-free sentences. You'll realize that you can use revising to rework a paper until it is strong and effective. And you'll be able to edit a paper so that your sentences are clear and error-free.

Prewriting

If you are like many people, you may have trouble getting started writing. A mental block may develop when you sit down before a blank sheet of paper. You may not be able to think of an interesting topic or a point to make about your topic. Or you may have trouble coming up with specific details to support your point. And even after starting a paper, you may hit snags—moments when you wonder "What else can I say?" or "Where do I go next?"

The following pages describe five techniques that will help you think about and develop a topic and get words on paper: (1) freewriting, (2) questioning, (3) making a list, (4) clustering, and (5) preparing a scratch outline. These prewriting techniques help you think about and create material, and they are a central part of the writing process.

Technique 1: Freewriting

When you do not know what to write about a subject or when you are blocked in writing, freewriting sometimes helps. In *freewriting,* you write on your topic for ten minutes. You do not worry about spelling or punctuating correctly, about erasing mistakes, about organizing material, or about finding exact words. You just write without stopping. If you get stuck for words, you write "I am looking for something to say" or repeat words until something comes. There is no need to feel inhibited, since mistakes *do not count* and you do not have to hand in your paper.

Freewriting will limber up your writing muscles and make you familiar with the act of writing. It is a way to break through mental blocks about writing. Since you do not have to worry about mistakes, you can focus on discovering what you want to say about a subject. Your initial ideas and impressions will often become clearer after you have gotten them down on paper, and they may lead to other impressions and ideas. Through continued practice in freewriting, you will develop the habit of thinking as you write. And you will learn a technique that is a helpful way to get started on almost any paper.

Freewriting: A Student Model

Gene Hert's essay "My Job in an Apple Plant" on page 5 was written in response to an assignment to write a paper on the best or worst job he ever had. Gene began by doing some general freewriting and thinking about his jobs. Here is his freewriting:

> I have had good and bad jobs, that's for sure. It was great earning money for the first time. I shoveled snow for my neighbor, a friend of mine and I did the work and had snowball fights along the way. I remember my neighbor reaching into his pocket and pulling out several dollars and handing us the money, it was like magic. Then there was the lawnmowing, which was also a good job. I mowed my aunts lawn while she was away at work. Then I'd go sit by myself in her cool living room and have a coke she left in the refrigarator for me. And look through all her magazines. Then there was the apple plant job I had after high school. That was a worst job that left me totaly wiped out at the end of my shift. Lifting cartons and cartons of apple

juice for bosses that treated us like slaves. The cartons coming and coming all night long. I started early in the evening and finished the next morning. I still remember how tired I was. Driving back home the first time. That was a lonely job and a hard job and I don't eat apples anymore.

At this point, Gene read over his notes, and as he later commented, "I realized that I had several potential topics. I said to myself, 'What point can I make that I can cover in a paragraph? What do I have the most information about?' I decided to narrow my topic down to my awful job at the apple plant. I figured I would have lots of interesting details for that topic." Gene then did a more focused freewriting to accumulate details for a paragraph on his bad job:

> The job I remember most is the worst job I ever had. I worked in an apple plant, I put in very long hours and would be totaly beat after ten hours of work. All the time lifting cartons of apple juice which would come racing down a metal track. The guy with me was a bit lazy at times, and I would be one man doing a two-man job. The cartons would go into a tracter trailer, we would have to throw down wooden skids to put the cartons on, then wed have to move the metal track as we filled up the truck. There is no other job I have had that even compares to this job, it was a lot worse than it seems. The bosses treated us like slaves and the company paid us like slaves. I would work all night from 7 p.m. and drive home in the morning at 5 a.m. and be bone tired. I remember my arms and sholders were so tired after the first night. I had trouble turning the steering wheel of my father's car.

Comment

Notice that there are problems with spelling, grammar, and punctuation in Gene's freewriting. Gene was not worried about such matters, nor should he have been. At this stage, he just wanted to do some thinking on paper and get some material down on the page. He knew that this was a good first step, a good way of getting started, and that he would then be able to go on and shape that material.

You should take the same approach when freewriting: explore your topic without worrying at all about being "correct." Figuring out what you want to say and getting raw material down on the page should have all of your attention at this early stage of the writing process.

Activity

To get a sense of the freewriting process, take a sheet of paper and freewrite about different jobs you have had and what you liked or did not like about them. See how much material you can accumulate in ten minutes. And remember not to worry about "mistakes"; you're just thinking on paper.

Technique 2: Questioning

In *questioning*, you generate ideas and details by asking as many questions as you can think of about your subject. Such questions include *Why? When? Where? Who? How? In what ways?*

Here are questions that Gene Hert asked while further developing his paper:

Questioning: A Student Model

Questions	Answers
<u>What</u> did I hate about the job?	Very hard work. Poor pay. Mean bosses.
<u>How</u> was the work hard?	Nonstop cartons of apple juice. Cartons became very heavy.
<u>Why</u> was pay poor?	$3.65 an hour (minimum wage at the time). Only a quarter more for working the second shift. Only good money was in overtime—where you got time-and-a-half. No double time.
<u>How</u> were the bosses mean?	Yelled at some workers. Showed no appreciation. Created bad working conditions.
<u>In what ways</u> were working conditions bad?	Unheated truck in zero-degree weather. Floor of tractor trailer was cold steel. Breaks were limited—only two of them. Lonely job.

Comment

Asking questions can be an effective way of getting yourself to think about a topic from different angles. The questions can help you generate details about a topic and get ideas on how to organize those details. Notice how asking questions gives Gene a better sense of the different reasons why he hated the job.

Activity

To get a feel for the questioning process, use a sheet of paper to ask yourself a series of questions about your best and worst jobs. See how many details you can accumulate in ten minutes. And remember again not to be concerned about "mistakes," because you are just thinking on paper.

Technique 3: Making a List

In *making a list,* also known as *brainstorming*, you create a list of ideas and details that relate to your subject. Pile these items up, one after another, without trying to sort out major details from minor ones, or trying to put the details in any special order, or even trying to spell words correctly. Your goal is to accumulate raw material by making up a list of everything about your subject that occurs to you.

After freewriting and questioning, Gene made up the following list of details.

Making a List: A Student Model

Apple factory job—worst one I ever had

Bosses were mean

Working conditions were poor

Went to work at 5 P.M., got back at 7 A.M.

Lifted cartons of apple juice for ten hours

Cartons were heavy

Only two ten-minute breaks a night

Pay was only $3.65 an hour

Just quarter extra for night shift

Cost of gas money to and from work

No pay for lunch break

Had to work 60 hours for good take-home pay

Loaded onto wooden skids in a truck

Bosses yelled at some workers

Floors of trucks ice-cold metal

Nonstop pace

Had to clean apple vats after work

Slept, ate, and worked—no social life

No real friends at work

Comment

One detail led to another as Gene expanded his list. Slowly but surely, more details emerged, some of which he could use in developing his paragraph. By the time he had finished his list, he was ready to plan an outline of his paragraph and then to write his first draft.

Activity

To get a sense of making a list, use a sheet of paper to list a series of details about one of the best or worst jobs you ever had. Don't worry about deciding whether the details are major or minor; instead, just get down as many details as you can think of in five or ten minutes.

Technique 4: Clustering

Clustering, also known as *diagramming* or *mapping*, is another strategy that can be used to generate material for a paper. This method is helpful for people who like to think in a visual way. In clustering, you use lines, boxes, arrows, and circles to show relationships among the ideas and details that occur to you.

Begin by stating your subject in a few words in the center of a blank sheet of paper. Then, as ideas and details occur to you, put them in boxes or circles around the subject and draw lines to connect them to each other and to the subject. Put minor ideas or details in smaller boxes or circles, and use connecting lines to show how they relate as well.

Keep in mind that there is no right or wrong way of clustering. It is a way to think on paper about how various ideas and details relate to one another. Below is an example of what Gene might have done to develop his ideas:

Clustering: A Student Model

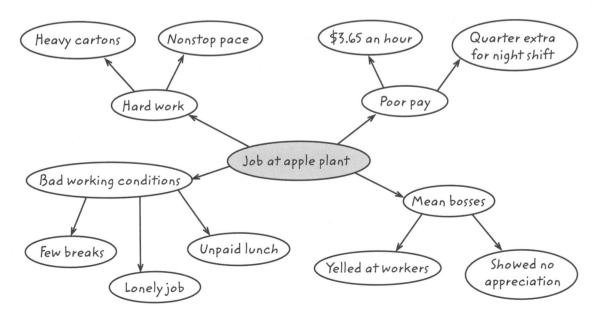

Comment

In addition to helping generate material, clustering often suggests ways to organize ideas and details.

Activity

Use clustering or diagramming to organize the details about a best or worst job that you created for the previous activity (page 20).

Technique 5: Preparing a Scratch Outline

A scratch outline can be the *single most helpful technique* for writing a good paper. A scratch outline often follows freewriting, questioning, making a list, or clustering, but it may also gradually emerge in the midst of these strategies. In fact, trying to make a scratch outline is a good way to see if you need to do more prewriting. If you cannot come up with a solid outline, then you know you need to do more prewriting to clarify your main point and its several kinds of support.

In a scratch outline, you think carefully about the point you are making, the supporting items for that point, and the order in which you will arrange those items. The scratch outline is a plan or blueprint to help you achieve a unified, supported, and well-organized composition.

Scratch Outline: A Student Model

In Gene's case, as he was working on his list of details, he suddenly realized what the plan of his paragraph could be. He could organize many of his details into one of three supporting groups: (1) the job itself, (2) the pay, and (3) the working conditions. He then went back to the list, crossed out items that he now saw did not fit, and numbered the items according to the group where they fit. Here is what Gene did with his list:

> Apple factory job—worst one I ever had
>
> ~~Bosses were mean~~
>
> 3 Working conditions were poor
>
> ~~Went to work at 5 P.M., got back at 7 A.M.~~
>
> 1 Lifted cartons of apple juice for ten hours

1 Cartons were heavy

3 Only two ten-minute breaks a night

2 Pay was only $3.65 an hour

2 Just quarter extra for night shift

~~Cost of gas money to and from work~~

2 Had to work 60 hours for good take-home pay

1 Loaded onto wooden skids in a truck

~~Bosses yelled at some workers~~

3 Temperature zero outside

~~Floors of trucks ice-cold metal~~

1 Nonstop pace

3 No pay for lunch break

3 Had to clean apple vats after work

~~Slept, ate, and worked—no social life~~

3 No real friends at work

Under the list, Gene was now able to prepare his scratch outline:

The apple plant was my worst job.

1. Hard work

2. Poor pay

3. Poor working conditions

Comment

After all his prewriting, Gene was pleased. He knew that he had a promising paper—one with a clear point and solid support. He saw that he could organize the material into a paragraph with a topic sentence, supporting points, and vivid details. He was now ready to write the first draft of his paragraph, using his outline as a guide. Chances are that if you do enough prewriting and thinking on paper, you will eventually discover the point and support of your paragraph.

Activity

Create a scratch outline that could serve as a guide if you were to write a paragraph on your best or worst job experience.

Writing a First Draft

When you write a first draft, be prepared to put in additional thoughts and details that did not emerge during prewriting. And don't worry if you hit a snag. Just leave a blank space or add a comment such as "Do later" and press on to finish the paper. Also, don't worry yet about grammar, punctuation, or spelling. You don't want to take time correcting words or sentences that you may decide to remove later. Instead, make it your goal to state your main idea clearly and develop the content of your paper with plenty of specific details.

Writing a First Draft: A Student Model

Here is Gene's first draft, done in longhand:

> 1. ~~The apple plant job was my worst.~~ Working in an apple plant was the worst job I ever had. The work was physicaly hard. For ~~a long time~~ ten hours a night, I stacked cartons that rolled down a metal track in a tracter trailer. Each carton had cans or bottles of apple juice, and they were heavy. At the same time, I had to keep a mental count of all the cartons I had loaded. The pay for the job was a bad feature. I was getting the minamum wage at that time plus a quarter extra for night shift. I had to work a lot to get a decent take-home pay. Working conditions were poor at the apple plant, we were limited to ~~short breaks~~ two ten-minute breaks. The truck-loading dock where I was most of the time was a cold and lonely place. Then by myself cleaning up. DETAILS!

Comment

After Gene finished the first draft, he was able to put it aside until the next day. You will benefit as well if you can allow some time between finishing a draft and starting to revise.

Activity

See if you can fill in the missing words in the following explanation of Gene's first draft.

1. Gene presents his ___The apple plant job was my worst___ in the first sentence and then crosses it out and revises it right away to make it read smoothly and clearly.

2. Notice that he continues to accumulate specific supporting details as he writes the draft. For example, he crosses out and replaces "a long time" with the more specific ___time___; he crosses out and replaces "short breaks" with the more specific ___time___.

3. There are various misspellings—for example, ___details.___ Gene doesn't worry about spelling at this point. He just wants to get down as much of the substance of his paper as possible.

4. There are various punctuation errors, especially the run-on and the fragment near the (*beginning, middle, end*) ___end___ of the paragraph.

5. Near the close of his paragraph, Gene can't think of added details to insert, so he simply prints "___Details.___" as a reminder to himself for the next draft.

Revising

Revising is as much a stage in the writing process as prewriting, outlining, and doing the first draft. *Revising* means that you rewrite a paper, building upon what has already been done, in order to make it stronger. One writer has said about revision, "It's like cleaning house—getting rid of all the junk and putting things in the right order." It is not just "straightening up"; instead, you must be ready to roll up your sleeves and do whatever is needed to create an effective paper. Too many students think that a first draft *is* the paper. They start to become writers when they realize that revising a rough draft three or four times is often at the heart of the writing process.

Here are some quick hints that can help make revision easier. First, set your first draft aside for a while. You can then come back to it with a fresher, more objective point of view. Second, work from typed or printed text, preferably double-spaced so you'll have room to handwrite changes later. You'll be able to see the paper more impartially if it is typed than if you were just looking at your own familiar handwriting. Next, read your draft aloud. Hearing how your writing sounds will help you pick up problems with meaning as well as with style. Finally, as you do all these things, write additional thoughts and changes above the lines or in the margins of your paper. Your written comments can serve as a guide when you work on the next draft.

There are two stages to the revision process:

- Revising content
- Revising sentences

Revising Content

To revise the content of your paper, ask the following questions:

1 Is my paper **unified?**

- Do I have a main idea that is clearly stated at the beginning of my paragraph?
- Do all my supporting points truly support and back up my main idea?

2 Is my paper **supported?**

- Are there separate supporting points for the main idea?
- Do I have *specific* evidence for each supporting point?
- Is there *plenty of* specific evidence for the supporting points?

3 Is my paper **organized?**

- Do I have a clear method of organizing my paper?
- Do I use transitions and other connecting words?

The next two chapters (Chapters 3 and 4) will give you practice in achieving **unity, support,** and **organization** in your writing.

Revising Sentences

To revise individual sentences in your essay, ask the following questions:

1 Do I use *parallelism* to balance my words and ideas?
2 Do I have a *consistent point of view*?
3 Do I use *specific* words?
4 Do I use *active* verbs?

5   Do I use words effectively by *avoiding slang, clichés, pretentious language,* and *wordiness*?

6   Do I *vary my sentences* in length and structure?

Chapter 5 will give you practice in revising sentences.

Revising: A Student Model

For his second draft, Gene used a word-processing program on a computer. He then printed out a double-spaced version of his paragraph, leaving himself plenty of room for handwritten revisions. Here is Gene's second draft plus the hand-written changes and additions that became his third draft:

First of all
Working in an apple plant was the worst job I ever had. The work was

physicaly hard. For ten hours a night, I stacked cartons that rolled down a

25 pounds of bottled
metal track in a tracter trailer. Each carton contained ~~bottles of~~ apple juice,

down the track
and they came nonstop. ~~At the same time, I had to keep a mental count of~~

~~all the cartons I had loaded.~~ The second bad feature ~~that made the job a~~

~~worst one~~ was the pay. I was getting the minamum wage at that time, $3.65

just   *over sixty hours a week*
an hour. Plus a quarter extra for night shift. I had to work ~~a lot of hours~~ to

Finally
get a decent take-home pay. I hated the working conditions. We were

an unpaid half hour for lunch
limited to two ten-minute breaks and ~~the half hour for lunch was not paid~~.

loading   near-zero-degree
Most of my time was spent outside on the dock in ~~cold~~ temperatures. And

because
I was very lonely on the job, I had nothing in common with the other

I
workers. ~~You~~ felt this isolation especially when the production line shut

, and   *an ugly*
down for the night I had to clean the apple vats. The vats were ~~a bad~~ place

bitter
to be on a cold morning and the job was a ~~bad~~ one to have.

Comment

Gene made his changes in longhand as he worked on the second draft. As you will see when you complete the activity below, his revision serves to make the paragraph more unified, supported, and organized.

Activity

Fill in the missing words.

1. To clarify the organization, Gene adds at the beginning of the first supporting point the transitional phrase "_____," and he sets off the third supporting point with the word "_____."

2. In the interest of (*unity, support, organization*) _____, he crosses out the sentence "_____." He realizes that this sentence is not a relevant detail to support the idea that the work was physically hard.

3. To add more (*unity, support, organization*) _____, he changes "a lot of hours" to "_____"; he changes "on the dock" to "_____"; he changes "cold temperatures" to "_____."

4. In the interest of eliminating wordiness, he removes the words "_____" from the sixth sentence.

5. To achieve parallelism, Gene changes "the half hour for lunch was not paid" to "_____."

6. For greater sentence variety, Gene combines two short sentences, beginning the second part of the sentence with the subordinating word "_____."

7. To create a consistent point of view, Gene changes "You felt this isolation" to "_____."

8. Finally, Gene replaces the somewhat vague "bad" in "The vats were a bad place to be on a cold morning, and the job was a bad one to have" with two more precise words: "_____" and "_____."

Editing

The last major stage in the writing process is editing—checking a paper for mistakes in grammar, punctuation, usage, and spelling. Editing as well as proofreading (checking a paper for typos and other careless errors) is explained in detail on pages 114–116.

Editing: A Student Model

After typing into his word-processing file all the revisions in his paragraph, Gene printed out another clean draft of the paper. He now turned his attention to editing changes, as shown below:

My Job in an Apple Plant

Working in an apple plant was the worst job I ever had. First of all, the

work was ~~physicaly~~ *physically* hard. For ten hours a night, I took cartons that rolled

down a metal track and stacked them onto wooden skids in a ~~tracter~~ *tractor* trailer.

Each carton contained ~~25~~ *twenty-five* pounds of bottled apple juice, and they came

down the track almost nonstop. The second bad feature of the job was the

pay. I was getting the ~~minamum~~ *minimum* wage at that time, $3.65 an hour. *,* ~~P~~lus just

a quarter extra for working the night shift. I had to work over sixty hours a

week to get a decent take-home pay. Finally, I hated the working conditions.

We were limited to two ten-minute breaks and an unpaid half hour for

lunch. Most of my time was spent outside on the loading dock in near-zero-

degree temperatures. And I was very lonely on the job because I had no

interests in common with the other workers. I felt this isolation especially

when the production line shut down for the night, and I ~~had to clean~~ *spent two hours by myself cleaning* the

apple vats. The vats were an ugly place to be on a cold morning, and the

job was a bitter one to have.

Comment

Once again, Gene made his changes in longhand right on the printout of his paper. To note these changes, complete the activity below.

Activity

Fill in the missing words.

1. As part of his editing, Gene checked and corrected the _____ of three words, *physically, tractor,* and *minimum.*

2. He added _____ to set off an introductory phrase ("First of all") and an introductory word ("Finally") and also to connect the two complete thoughts in the final sentence.

3. He corrected a fragment ("_____") by using a comma to attach it to the preceding sentence.

4. He realized that a number like "25" should be _____ as "twenty-five."

5. And since revision can occur at any stage of the writing process, including editing, Gene makes one of his details more vivid by adding the descriptive words "_____."

All that remained for Gene to do was to enter his corrections, print out the final draft of the paper, and proofread it for any typos or other careless errors. He was then ready to hand it in to his instructor.

Review Activities

You now have a good overview of the writing process, from prewriting to first draft to revising to editing. The remaining chapters in Part One will deepen your sense of the four goals of effective writing: unity, support, organization or coherence, and sentence skills.

To reinforce much of the information about the writing process that you have learned in this chapter, you can now work through the following activities:

1 Taking a writing inventory

2 Prewriting

3 Outlining

4 Revising

1 Taking a Writing Inventory

Activity

To evaluate your approach to the writing process, answer the questions below. This activity is not a test, so try to be as honest as possible. Becoming aware of your writing habits can help you make helpful changes in your writing.

1. When you start work on a paper, do you typically do any prewriting?

   _____ Yes   _____ Sometimes   _____ No

2. If so, which of the prewriting techniques do you use?

   _____ Freewriting   _____ Clustering

   _____ Questioning   _____ Scratch outline

   _____ List making   _____ Other (please describe)

3. Which prewriting technique or techniques work best for you or do you think will work best for you?

4. Many students have said they find it helpful to handwrite a first draft and then type that draft on a computer. They then print the draft out and revise it by hand. Describe your own way of drafting and revising a paper.

5. After you write the first draft of a paper, do you have time to set it aside for a while, so you can come back to it with a fresh eye?

6. How many drafts do you typically write when doing a paper?

7. When you revise, are you aware that you should be working toward a paper that is unified, solidly supported, and clearly organized? Has this chapter given you a better sense that unity, support, and organization are goals to aim for?

8. Do you revise a paper for the effectiveness of its sentences as well as for its content?

9. What (if any) information has this chapter given you about prewriting that you will try to apply in your writing?

10. What (if any) information has this chapter given you about revising that you will try to apply in your writing?

2 Prewriting

Activity

Below are examples of how the five prewriting techniques could be used to develop the topic "Inconsiderate Drivers." Identify each technique by writing F (for freewriting), Q (for questioning), L (for listing), C (for clustering), or SO (for the scratch outline) in the answer space.

_____

High beams on
Weave in and out at high speeds
Treat street like a trash can
Open car door onto street without looking
Stop on street looking for an address
Don't use turn signals
High speeds in low-speed zones
Don't take turns merging
Use horn when they don't need to
Don't give walkers the right of way
More attention to cell phone than the road

_____

What is one example of an inconsiderate driver?	A person who turns suddenly without signaling.
Where does this happen?	At city intersections or on smaller country roads.
Why is this dangerous?	You have to be alert and slow down yourself to avoid rear-ending the car in front.
What is another example of inconsideration on the road?	Drivers who come toward you at night with their high beams on.

_____   Some people are inconsiderate drivers.
    1. In city:
       a.   Stop in middle of street
       b.   Turn without signaling
    2. On highway:
       a.   Leave high beams on
       b.   Stay in passing lane
       c.   Cheat during a merge
    3. Both in city and on highway:
       a.   Throw trash out of window
       b.   Pay more attention to cell phone than to road

_____

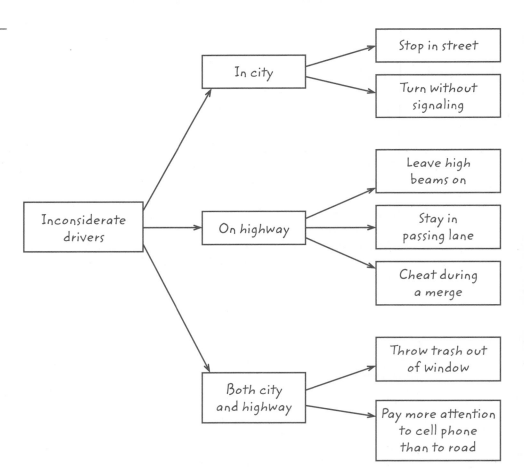

_____   I was driving home last night after class and had three people try to blind me by coming at me with their high beams on. I had to zap them all with my high beams. Rude drivers make me crazy. The worst are the ones that use the road as a trash can. People who throw butts and cups and hamburger wrappings and other stuff out the car windows should be tossed into a trash dumpster. If word got around that this was the punishment maybe they would wise up. Other drivers do dumb things as well. I hate the person who will just stop in the middle of the street and try to figure out directions or look for a house address. Why don't they pull over to the side of the street? That hardly seems like too much to ask. Instead, they stop all traffic while doing their own thing. Then there are the people who keep what they want to do a secret. They're not going to tell you they plan to make a right- or left-hand turn. You've got to figure it out yourself when they suddenly slow down in front of you. Then there are all the people on their cell phones yakking away and not paying attention to their driving.

3 Outlining

As already mentioned (see page 23), outlining is central to writing a good paragraph. An outline lets you see, and work on, the bare bones of a paper, without the distraction of cluttered words and sentences. It develops your ability to think clearly and logically. Outlining provides a quick check on whether your paper will be *unified*. It also suggests right at the start whether your paper will be adequately *supported*. And it shows you how to plan a paper that is *well organized*.

The following series of exercises will help you develop the outlining skills so important to planning and writing a solid paragraph.

Activity 1

One key to effective outlining is the ability to distinguish between general ideas and specific details that fit under those ideas. Read each group of specific ideas below. Then circle the letter of the general idea that tells what the specific ideas have in common. Note that the general idea should not be too broad or too narrow. Begin by trying the example item, and then read the explanation that follows.

Example   *Specific ideas:* runny nose, coughing, sneezing, sore throat

The general idea is:

a. cold symptoms.

b. symptoms.

c. throat problems.

Explanation: It is true that the specific ideas are all symptoms, but they have in common something even more specific—they are all symptoms of the common cold. Therefore, answer *b* is too broad; the correct answer is *a*. Answer *c* is too narrow because it doesn't cover all the specific ideas; it covers only the final item in the list ("sore throat").

1. *Specific ideas:* leaking toilet, no hot water, broken window, roaches
   The general idea is:
   a.   problems.
   b.   kitchen problems.
   c.   apartment problems.

2. *Specific ideas:* count to ten, take a deep breath, go for a walk
   The general idea is:
   a.   actions.
   b.   ways to calm down.
   c.   ways to calm down just before a test.

3. *Specific ideas:* putting sticky tape on someone's chair, putting a "kick me" sign on someone's back, putting hot pepper in someone's cereal
   The general idea is:
   a.   jokes.
   b.   practical jokes.
   c.   practical jokes played on teachers.

4. *Specific ideas:* going to bed earlier, eating healthier foods, reading for half an hour each day, trying to be kinder
   The general idea is:
   a.   resolutions.
   b.   problems.
   c.   solutions.

5. *Specific ideas:* money problems, family problems, relationship problems, health problems
   The general idea is:
   a.   poor grades.
   b.   causes of poor grades.
   c.   effects of poor grades.

Activity 2

In the following items, the specific ideas are given but the general ideas are unstated. Fill in each blank with a general heading that accurately describes the list provided.

Example
  General idea: __Household Chores__

  Specific ideas: washing dishes
            preparing meals
            taking out trash
            dusting

1. *General idea:* _____
   Specific ideas: convenient work hours
            short travel time to job
            good pay
            considerate boss

2. *General idea:* _____
   Specific ideas: greed
            cowardice
            selfishness
            dishonesty

3. *General idea:* _____
   Specific ideas: order the invitations
            get the bride's gown
            rent the tuxedos
            hire a photographer

4. *General idea:* _____
   Specific ideas: "Your mother stinks."
            "Your father's a bum."
            "You look like an ape."
            "Your car is a real junk heap."

5. *General idea:* _____
   Specific ideas: "I like your dress."
            "You look great in red."
            "Your new haircut looks terrific."
            "You did very well on the exam."

Activity 3

Major and minor ideas are mixed together in the two paragraphs outlined below. Put the ideas in logical order by filling in the outlines.

1. *Topic sentence:* People can be classified by how they treat their cars.

Seldom wax or vacuum car
Keep every mechanical item in top shape
Protective owners
Deliberately ignore needed maintenance
Indifferent owners
Wash and polish car every week
Never wash, wax, or vacuum car
Abusive owners
Inspect and service car only when required by state law

a. _____

    (1) _____

    (2) _____

b. _____

    (1) _____

    (2) _____

c. _____

    (1) _____

    (2) _____

2. *Topic sentence:* Living with an elderly parent has many benefits.

Advantages for elderly person
Live-in baby-sitter
Learn about the past
Advantages for adult children
Serve useful role in family
Help with household tasks

Advantages for grandchildren
Stay active and interested in young people
More attention from adults

a. _____
   (1) _____
   (2) _____
b. _____
   (1) _____
   (2) _____
c. _____
   (1) _____
   (2) _____

Activity 4

Again, major and minor ideas are mixed together. In addition, in each outline one of the three major ideas is missing and must be added. Put the ideas in logical order by filling in the outlines that follow (summarizing as needed) and adding a third major idea.

1. *Topic sentence:* Extending the school day would have several advantages.

Help children academically
Parents know children are safe at the school
More time to spend on basics
Less pressure to cover subjects quickly
More time for extras like art, music, and sports
Help working parents
More convenient to pick up children at 4 or 5 P.M.
Teachers' salaries would be raised

a. _____
   (1) _____
   (2) _____

    b. _____

        (1) _____

        (2) _____

    c. _____

        (1) _____

        (2) _____

2. *Topic sentence:* By following certain hints about food, exercise, and smoking, you can increase your chances of dying young.

Don't ever walk if you can ride instead.

Choose foods such as bacon and lunch meats that are laced with nitrites and other preservatives.

Be very selective about what you eat.

If you begin to cough or feel short of breath, keep smoking.

If a friend invites you to play an outdoor sport, open a beer instead and head for your La-Z-Boy recliner.

Resist the urge to exercise.

Choose foods from one of four essential groups: fat, starch, sugar, and grease.

Smoke on a regular basis.

    a. _____

        (1) _____

        (2) _____

    b. _____

        (1) _____

        (2) _____

    c. _____

        (1) _____

        (2) _____

Activity 5

Read the following two paragraphs. Then outline each one in the space provided. Write out the topic sentence in each case and summarize in a few words the primary and secondary supporting material that fits under the topic sentence.

1.   **Why I'm a Stay-at-Home Baseball Fan**

       I'd much rather stay at home and watch ball games on television than go to the ballpark. First of all, it's cheaper to watch a game at home. I don't have to spend twelve dollars for a ticket and another eight dollars for a parking space. If I want some refreshments, I can have what's already in the refrigerator instead of shelling out another six dollars for a limp, lukewarm hot dog and a watery Coke. Also, it's more comfortable at home. I avoid a bumper-to-bumper drive to the ballpark and pushy crowds who want to go through the same gate I do. I can lie quietly on my living-room sofa instead of sitting on a hard stadium seat with noisy people all around me. Most of all, watching a game on television is more informative. Not only do I see all the plays that I might miss from my twelve dollar seat, but I see some of them two and three times in instant replay. In addition, I get each play explained to me in glorious detail. If I were at the ballpark, I wouldn't know that the pitch our third baseman hit was a high and inside slider or that his grand-slam home run was a record-setting seventh in his career. The other fans can spend their money; put up with traffic, crowds, and hard seats; and guess at the plays. I'll take my baseball lying down—at home.

Topic sentence: _____

_____

a. _____

    (1) _____

    (2) _____

b. _____

    (1) _____

    (2) _____

c. _____

    (1) _____

    (2) _____

2.   **Why Teenagers Take Drugs**

There are several reasons why teenagers take drugs. First of all, it is easy for young people to get drugs. Drugs are available almost anywhere, from a school cafeteria to a movie line to a football game. Teens don't have to risk traveling to the slums or dealing with shady types on street corners. It is also easy to get drugs because today's teens have spending money, which comes from allowances or earnings from part-time jobs. Teens can use their money to buy the luxuries they want—records, makeup, clothes, or drugs. Second, teens take drugs because the adolescent years are filled with psychological problems. For a teenager, one of these problems is the pressure of making important life decisions, such as choosing a career path. Another problem is establishing a sense of self. The teen years are the time when young people must become more independent from their parents and form their own values. The enormous mental pressures of these years can make some people turn to drugs. A final, and perhaps most important, reason why teenagers take drugs is peer pressure to conform. Teens often become very close to special friends, for one thing, and they will share a friend's interests, even if one interest is drugs. Teenagers also attend parties and other social events where it's all-important to be one of the crowd, to be "cool." Even the most mature teenager might be tempted to use drugs rather than risk being an outcast. For all these reasons, drugs are a major problem facing teenagers.

Topic sentence: _____

_____

a.   _____

    (1) _____

    (2) _____

b.   _____

    (1) _____

    (2) _____

c.   _____

    (1) _____

    (2) _____

4 Revising

Activity 1

Listed in the box below are five stages in the process of composing a paragraph titled "Dangerous Places."

---

1. Prewriting (list)

2. Prewriting (freewriting, questioning, list, and scratch outline)

3. First draft

4. Revising (second draft)

5. Revising (final draft)

The five stages appear in scrambled order below and on the next page. Write the number 1 in the blank space in front of the first stage of development and number the remaining stages in sequence.

_____   There are some places where I never feel safe. For example, public rest rooms. The ~~dirt and graffiti~~ dirt on the floors and the graffiti scrawled on the walls ~~make the room seem dangerous~~ create a sense of danger. I'm also afraid in parking lots. ~~Late at night, I don't like walking in the lot After class, I don't like the parking lot.~~ When I leave my night class or the shopping mall late the walk to the car is scary. ~~Most parking lots have large lights which make me feel at least a little better.~~ I feel least safe in our laundry room. . . . It is a depressing place . . . Bars on the windows, . . . pipes making noises, . . . cement steps the only way out. . . .

_____   Dangerous Places

Highways

Cars—especially parking lots

Feel frightened in our laundry room

Big crowds—concerts, movies

Closed-in places

Bus and train stations

Airplane

Elevators and escalators

Dangerous Places

_____   There are some places where I never feel completely safe. For example, I seldom feel safe in public rest rooms. I worry that I'll suddenly be alone there and that someone will come in to mug me. The ugly graffiti often scrawled on the walls, along with the grime and dirt in the room and crumpled tissues and paper towels on the floor, add to my sense of unease and danger. I also feel unsafe in large, dark, parking lots. When I leave my night class a little late, or I am one of the few leaving the mall at 10 P.M., I dread the walk to my car. I am afraid that someone may be lurking behind another car, ready to mug me. And I fear that my car will not start, leaving me stuck in the dark parking lot. The place where I feel least safe is the basement laundry room in our apartment building. No matter what time I do my laundry, I seem to be the only person there. The windows are barred, and the only exit is a steep flight of cement steps. While I'm folding the clothes, I feel trapped. If anyone unfriendly came down those steps, I would have nowhere to go. The pipes in the room make sudden gurgles, clanks, and hisses, adding to my unsettledness. Places like public rest rooms, dark parking lots, and the basement laundry room give me the shivers.

_____   There are some places where I never feel completely safe. For example, I never feel safe in public rest rooms. If I'm alone there, I worry that someone will come in to rob and mug me. The dirt on the floors and the graffiti scrawled on the walls create a sense of danger. I feel unsafe in large, dark parking lots. When I leave my night class a little late or I leave the mall at 10 P.M., the walk to the car is scary. I'm afraid that someone may be behind a car. Also that my car won't start. Another place I don't feel safe is the basement laundry room in our apartment building. No matter when I do the laundry, I'm the only person there. The windows are barred and there are steep steps. I feel trapped when I fold the clothes. The pipes in the room make frightening noises such as hisses and clanks. Our laundry room and other places give me the shivers.

_____   Some places seem dangerous and unsafe to me. For example, last night I stayed till 10:15 after night class and walked out to parking lot alone. Very scary. Also, other places I go to every day, such as places in my apartment building. Also frightened by big crowds and public rest rooms.

Why was the parking lot scary?	What places in my building scare me?
Dark	Laundry room (especially)
Only a few cars	Elevators
No one else in lot	Lobby at night sometimes
Could be someone behind a car	Outside walkway at night
Cold	

2 Parking lots

3 Laundry room

1 Public rest rooms

Activity 2

The author of "Dangerous Places" in Activity 1 made a number of editing changes between the second draft and the final draft. Compare the two drafts and, in the spaces provided below, identify five of the changes.

1. _____

2. _____

3. _____

4. _____

5. _____

3 The First and Second Steps in Writing

This chapter will show you how to

- begin a paper by making a point of some kind
- provide specific evidence to support that point
- write a simple paragraph

Chapter 2 emphasized how prewriting and revising can help you become an effective writer. This chapter will focus on the first two steps in writing an effective paragraph:

1 Begin with a point.

2 Support the point with specific evidence.

Chapters 4 and 5 will then look at the third and fourth steps in writing:

3 Organize and connect the specific evidence (pages 79–96).

4 Write clear, error-free sentences (pages 97–130).

Step 1: Begin with a Point

Your first step in writing is to decide what point you want to make and to write that point in a single sentence. The point is commonly known as a *topic sentence*. As a guide to yourself and to the reader, put that point in the first sentence of your paragraph. Everything else in the paragraph should then develop and support in specific ways the single point given in the first sentence.

Activity

Read the two student paragraphs below about families today. Which paragraph clearly supports a single point? Which paragraph rambles on in many directions, introducing a number of ideas but developing none of them?

Paragraph A

Changes in the Family

Changes in our society in recent years have weakened family life. First of all, today's mothers spend much less time with their children. A generation ago, most households got by on Dad's paycheck, and Mom stayed home. Now many mothers work, and their children attend an after-school program, stay with a neighbor, or go home to an empty house. Another change is that families no longer eat together. In the past, Mom would be home and fix a full dinner—salad, pot roast, potatoes, and vegetables, with homemade cake or pie to top it off. Dinner today is more likely to be takeout food or TV dinners eaten at home, or fast food eaten out, with different members of the family eating at different times. Finally, television has taken the place of family conversation and togetherness. Back when there were meals together, family members would have a chance to eat together, talk with each other, and share events of the day in a leisurely manner. But now families are more likely to be looking at the TV set than talking to one another. Many homes even have several TV sets, which people watch in separate rooms. Clearly, modern life is a challenge to family life.

Paragraph B

The Family

Family togetherness is very important. However, today's mothers spend much less time at home than their mothers did, for several reasons. Most fathers are also home much less than they used to be. In previous times, families had to work together running a farm. Now children are left at other places or are home alone much of the time. Some families do find ways to spend more time together despite the demands of work. Another problem is that with parents gone so much of the day, nobody is at home to prepare wholesome meals for the family to eat together. The meals Grandma used to make would include pot roast and fried chicken, mashed potatoes, salad, vegetables, and delicious homemade desserts. Today's takeout foods and frozen meals can provide good nutrition. Some menu choices offer nothing but high-fat and high-sodium choices. People can supplement prepared foods by eating sufficient vegetables and fruit. Finally, television is also a big obstacle to togetherness. It sometimes seems that people are constantly watching TV and never talking to each other. Even when parents have friends over, it is often to watch something on TV. TV must be used wisely to achieve family togetherness.

Complete the following statement: Paragraph _____ is effective because it makes a clear, single point in the first sentence and goes on in the remaining sentences to support that single point.

Paragraph A starts with a point—that changes in our society in recent years have weakened family life—and then supports that idea with examples about mothers' working, families' eating habits, and television.

Paragraph B, on the other hand, does not make and support a single point. At first we think the point of the paragraph may be that "family togetherness is very important." But there is no supporting evidence showing how important family togetherness is. Instead, the line of thought in paragraph B swerves about like a car without a steering wheel. In the second sentence, we read that "today's mothers spend much less time at home than their mothers did, for several reasons." Now we think for a moment that this may be the main point and that the author will go on to list and explain some of those reasons. But the paragraph then goes on to comment on fathers, families in previous times, and families who find ways to spend time together. Any one of those ideas could be the focus of the paragraph, but none is. By now we are not really surprised at what happens in the rest of the paragraph. We are told about the absence of anyone "to prepare wholesome meals for the family," about what "the meals Grandma used to make" would be like, and about nutrition. The author then goes on to make a couple of points about how much people watch TV. The paragraph ends with yet another idea that does not support any previous point and that itself could be the point of a paragraph: "TV must be used wisely to achieve family togetherness." No single idea in this paragraph is developed, and the result for the reader is confusion.

In summary, while paragraph A is unified, paragraph B shows a complete lack of unity.

Step 2: Support the Point with Specific Evidence

The first essential step in writing effectively is to start with a clearly stated point. The second basic step is to support that point with specific evidence. Consider the supported point that you just read:

Point

Changes in our society in recent years have weakened family life.

Support

(1) Mothers
    (a) Most stayed home a generation ago
    (b) Most work now, leaving children at an after-school program, or with a neighbor, or in an empty house

(2) Eating habits
    (a) Formerly full homemade meals, eaten together
    (b) Now prepared foods at home or fast food out, eaten separately
(3) Television
    (a) Watching TV instead of conversing
    (b) Watching in separate rooms instead of being together

The supporting evidence is needed so that we can *see and understand for ourselves* that the writer's point is sound. The author of "Changes in the Family" has supplied specific supporting examples of how changes in our society have weakened family life. The paragraph has provided the evidence that is needed for us to understand and agree with the writer's point.

Now consider the following paragraph:

Good-Bye, Tony

I have decided not to go out with Tony anymore. First of all, he was late for our first date. He said that he would be at my house by 8:30, but he did not arrive until 9:30. Second, he was bossy. He told me that it would be too late to go to the new Jim Carrey comedy that I wanted to see, and that we would go instead to a new action film with Arnold Schwarzenegger. I told him that I didn't like violent movies, but he said that I could shut my eyes during the bloody parts. Only because it was a first date did I let him have his way. Finally, he was abrupt. After the movie, rather than suggesting a hamburger or a drink, he drove right out to a back road near Oakcrest High School and started necking with me. What he did a half hour later angered me most of all. He cut his finger on a pin I was wearing and immediately said we had to go right home. He was afraid the scratch would get infected if he didn't put Bactine and a Band-Aid on it. When he dropped me off, I said, "Good-bye, Tony," in a friendly enough way, but in my head I thought, "Good-bye <u>forever,</u> Tony."

The author's point is that she has decided not to go out with Tony anymore. See if you can summarize in the spaces below the three reasons she gives to support her decision:

Reason 1: _____

Reason 2: _____

Reason 3: _____

Notice what the supporting details in this paragraph do. They provide you, the reader, with a basis for understanding why the writer made the decision she did. Through specific evidence, the writer has explained and communicated her point successfully. The evidence that supports the point in a paragraph often consists of a series of reasons introduced by signal words (the author uses *First of all, Second,* and *Finally*) and followed by examples and details that support the reasons. That is true of the sample paragraph above: three reasons are provided, followed by examples and details that back up those reasons.

Activity

Both of the paragraphs that follow resulted from an assignment to "Write a paper that details your reasons for being in college." Both writers make the point that they have various reasons for attending college. Which paragraph then goes on to provide plenty of specific evidence to back up its point? Which paragraph is vague and repetitive and lacks the concrete details needed to show us exactly why the author decided to attend college?

Hint: Imagine that you've been asked to make a short film based on each paragraph. Which one suggests specific pictures, locations, words, and scenes you could shoot?

Paragraph A

Reasons for Going to College

I decided to attend college for various reasons. One reason is self-respect. For a long time now, I have had little self-respect. I spent a lot of time doing nothing, just hanging around or getting into trouble, and eventually I began to feel bad about it. Going to college is a way to start feeling better about myself. By accomplishing things, I will improve my self-image. Another reason for going to college is that things happened in my life that made me think about a change. For one thing, I lost the part-time job I had. When I lost the job, I realized I would have to do something in life, so I thought about school. I was in a rut and needed to get out of it but did not know how. But when something happens that is out of your control, then you have to make some kind of decision. The most important reason for college, though, is to fulfill my dream. I know I need an education, and I want to take the courses I need to reach the position that I think I can handle. Only by qualifying yourself can you get what you want. Going to college will help me fulfill this goal. These are the main reasons why I am attending college.

Paragraph B

Why I'm in School

There are several reasons I'm in school. First of all, my father's attitude made me want to succeed in school. One night last year, after I had come in at 3 A. M., my father said, "Mickey, you're a bum. When I look at my son, all I see is a good-for-nothing bum." I was angry, but I knew my father was right in a way. I had spent the last two years working at odd jobs at a pizza parlor and luncheonette, taking "uppers" and "downers" with my friends. That night, though, I decided I would prove my father wrong. I would go to college and be a success. Another reason I'm in college is my girlfriend's encouragement. Marie has already been in school for a year, and she is doing well in her computer courses. Marie helped me fill out my application and register for courses. She even lent me sixty-five dollars for textbooks. On her day off, she lets me use her car so I don't have to take the college bus. The main reason I am in college is to fulfill a personal goal: for the first time in my life, I want to finish something. For example, I quit high school in the eleventh grade. Then I enrolled in a government job-training program, but I dropped out after six months. I tried to get a high school equivalency diploma, but I started missing classes and eventually gave up. Now I am in a special program where I will earn my high school degree by completing a series of five courses. I am determined to accomplish this goal and to then go on and work for a degree in hotel management.

Complete the following statement: Paragraph _____ provides clear, vividly detailed reasons why the writer decided to attend college.

Paragraph B is the one that solidly backs up its point. The writer gives us specific reasons he is in school. On the basis of such evidence, we can clearly understand his opening point. The writer of paragraph A offers only vague, general reasons for being in school. We do not get specific examples of how the writer was "getting into trouble," what events occurred that forced the decision, or even what kind of job he or she wants to qualify for. We sense that the feeling expressed is sincere; but without particular examples we cannot really see why the writer decided to attend college.

The Importance of *Specific* Details

The point that opens a paper is a general statement. The evidence that supports a point is made up of specific details, reasons, examples, and facts.

Specific details have two key functions. First of all, details *excite the reader's interest*. They make writing a pleasure to read, for we all enjoy learning particulars about other people—what they do and think and feel. Second, details *support and explain a writer's point;* they give the evidence needed for us to see and understand a general idea. For example, the writer of "Good-Bye, Tony" provides details that make vividly clear her decision not to see Tony anymore. She specifies the exact time Tony was supposed to arrive (8:30) and when he actually arrived (9:30). She mentions the kind of film she wanted to see (a new Jim Carrey movie) and the one that Tony took her to instead (a violent movie). She tells us what she may have wanted to do after the movie (have a hamburger or a drink) and what Tony did instead (went necking); she even specifies the exact location of the place Tony took her (a back road near Oakcrest High School). She explains precisely what happened next (Tony "cut his finger on a pin I was wearing") and even mentions by name (Bactine and a Band-Aid) the treatments he planned to use.

The writer of "Why I'm in School" provides equally vivid details. He gives clear reasons for being in school (his father's attitude, his girlfriend's encouragement, and his wish to fulfill a personal goal) and backs up each reason with specific details. His details give us many sharp pictures. For instance, we hear the exact words his father spoke: "Mickey, you're a bum." He tells us exactly how he was spending his time ("working at odd jobs at a pizza parlor and luncheonette, taking 'uppers' and 'downers' with my friends"). He describes how his girlfriend helped him (filling out the college application, lending money and her car). Finally, instead of stating generally that "you have to make some kind of decision," as the writer of "Reasons for Going to College" does, he specifies that he has a strong desire to finish college because he dropped out of many schools and programs in the past: high school, a job-training program, and a high school equivalency course.

In both "Good-Bye, Tony" and "Why I'm in School," then, the vivid, exact details capture our interest and enable us to share in the writer's experience. We see people's actions and hear their words; the details provide pictures that make each of us feel "I am there." The particulars also allow us to understand each writer's point clearly. We are shown exactly why the first writer has decided not to see Tony anymore and exactly why the second writer is attending college.

Activity

Each of the five points below is followed by two attempts at support (*a* and *b*). Write S (for *specific)* in the space next to the one that succeeds in providing specific support for the point. Write X in the space next to the one that lacks supporting details.

1. My two-year-old son was in a stubborn mood today.

_____ a. When I asked him to do something, he gave me nothing but trouble. He seemed determined to make things difficult for me, for he had his mind made up.

_____ b. When I asked him to stop playing in the yard and come indoors, he looked me square in the eye and shouted "No!" and then spelled it out, "N . . . O!"

2. The prices in the amusement park were outrageously high.

_____ a. The food seemed to cost twice as much as it would in a supermarket and was sometimes of poor quality. The rides also cost a lot, and so I had to tell the children that they were limited to a certain number of them.

_____ b. The cost of the log flume, a ride that lasts roughly three minutes, was ten dollars a person. Then I had to pay four dollars for an eight-ounce cup of Coke and six dollars for a hot dog.

3. My brother-in-law is accident-prone.

_____ a. Once he tried to open a tube of Krazy Glue with his teeth. When the cap came loose, glue squirted out and sealed his lips shut. They had to be pried open in a hospital emergency room.

_____ b. Even when he does seemingly simple jobs, he seems to get into trouble. This can lead to hilarious, but sometimes dangerous, results. Things never seem to go right for him, and he often needs the help of others to get out of one predicament or another.

4. The so-called "bargains" at the yard sale were junk.

_____ a. The tables were filled with useless stuff no one could possibly want. They were the kinds of things that should be thrown away, not sold.

_____ b. The "bargains" included two headless dolls, blankets filled with holes, scorched potholders, and a plastic Christmas tree with several branches missing.

5. The key to success in college is organization.

_____ a. Knowing what you're doing, when you have to do it, and so on is a big help for a student. A system is crucial in achieving an ordered approach to study. Otherwise, things become very disorganized, and it is not long before grades will begin to drop.

_____ b. Organized students never forget paper or exam dates, which are marked on a calendar above their desks. And instead of having to cram for exams, they study their clear, neat classroom and textbook notes on a daily basis.

Comments: The specific support for point 1 is answer *b*. The writer does not just tell us that the little boy was stubborn but provides an example that shows us. In particular, the detail of the son's spelling out "N . . . O!" makes his stubbornness vividly real for the reader. For point 2, answer *b* gives specific prices (ten dollars for a ride, four dollars for a Coke, and six dollars for a hot dog) to support the idea that the amusement park was expensive. For point 3, answer *a* vividly backs up the idea that the brother-in-law is accident-prone by detailing an accident with Krazy Glue. Point 4 is supported by answer *b*, which lists specific examples of useless items that were offered for sale—from headless dolls to a broken plastic Christmas tree. We cannot help agreeing with the writer's point that the items were not bargains but junk. Point 5 is backed up by answer *b*, which identifies two specific strategies of organized students: they mark important dates on calendars above their desks, and they take careful notes and study them on a daily basis.

In each of the five cases, the specific evidence enables us to *see for ourselves* that the writer's point is valid.

The Importance of *Adequate* Details

One of the most common and most serious problems in students' writing is inadequate development. You must provide *enough* specific details to support fully the point you are making. You could not, for example, submit a paragraph about your brother-in-law being accident-prone and provide only a single short example. You would have to add several other examples or provide an extended example of your brother-in-law's accident-proneness. Without such additional support, your paragraph would be underdeveloped.

At times, students try to disguise an undersupported point by using repetition and wordy generalities. You saw this, for example, in paragraph A ("Reasons for Going to College") on page 51. Be prepared to do the plain hard work needed to ensure that each of your paragraphs has full, solid support.

Activity

The following paragraphs were written on the same topic, and each has a clear opening point. Which one is adequately developed? Which one has few particulars and uses mostly vague, general, wordy sentences to conceal the fact that it is starved for specific details?

Paragraph A

Abuse of Public Parks

Some people abuse public parks. Instead of using the park for recreation, they go there, for instance, to clean their cars. Park caretakers regularly have to pick up the contents of dumped ashtrays and car litter bags. Certain juveniles visit parks with cans of spray paint to deface buildings, fences, fountains, and statues. Other offenders are those who dig up and cart away park flowers, shrubs, and trees. One couple were even arrested for stealing park sod, which they were using to fill in their lawn. Perhaps the most widespread offenders are the people who use park tables and benches and fireplaces but do not clean up afterward. Picnic tables are littered with trash, including crumpled bags, paper plates smeared with ketchup, and paper cups half-filled with stale soda. On the ground are empty beer bottles, dented soda cans, and sharp metal pop-tops. Parks are made for people, and yet—ironically—their worst enemy is "people pollution."

Paragraph B

Mistreatment of Public Parks

Some people mistreat public parks. Their behavior is evident in many ways, and the catalog of abuses could go on almost without stopping. Different kinds of debris are left by people who have used the park as a place for attending to their automobiles. They are not the only individuals who mistreat public parks, which should be used with respect for the common good of all. Many young people come to the park and abuse it, and their offenses can occur in any season of the year. The reason for their inconsiderate behavior is known only to themselves. Other visitors lack personal cleanliness in their personal habits when they come to the park, and the park suffers because of it. Such people seem to have the attitude that someone else should clean up after them. It is an undeniable fact that people are the most dangerous thing that parks must contend with.

Complete the following statement: Paragraph _____ provides an adequate number of specific details to support its point.

Paragraph A offers a series of detailed examples of how people abuse parks. Paragraph B, on the other hand, is underdeveloped. Paragraph B speaks only of "different kinds of debris," while paragraph A refers specifically to "dumped ashtrays and car litter bags"; paragraph B talks in a general way of young people abusing the park, while paragraph A supplies such particulars as "cans of spray paint" and defacing "buildings, fences, fountains, and statues." And there is no equivalent in paragraph B for the specifics in paragraph A about people who steal park property and litter park grounds. In summary, paragraph B lacks the full, detailed support needed to develop its opening point convincingly.

■ ## Review Activity

To check your understanding of the chapter so far, see if you can answer the following questions.

1. It has been observed: "To write well, the first thing that you must do is decide what nail you want to drive home." What is meant by *nail?*

2. How do you drive home the nail in the paper?

_____

3. What are the two reasons for using specific details in your writing?

    a. _____

    b. _____

Practice in Making and Supporting a Point

You now know the two most important steps in competent writing: (1) making a point and (2) supporting that point with specific evidence. The purpose of this section is to expand and strengthen your understanding of these two basic steps.

You will first work through a series of activities on *making* a point:

  1 Identifying Common Errors in Topic Sentences
  2 Understanding the Two Parts of a Topic Sentence
  3 Selecting a Topic Sentence
  4 Writing a Topic Sentence: I
  5 Writing a Topic Sentence: II

You will then sharpen your understanding of specific details by working through a series of activities on *supporting* a point:

  6 Recognizing Specific Details: I
  7 Recognizing Specific Details: II
  8 Providing Supporting Evidence
  9 Identifying Adequate Supporting Evidence
10 Adding Details to Complete a Paragraph
11 Writing a Simple Paragraph

1 Identifying Common Errors in Topic Sentences

When writing a point, or topic sentence, people sometimes make mistakes that undermine their chances of producing an effective paper. One mistake is to substitute an announcement of the topic for a true topic sentence. Other mistakes include writing statements that are too broad or too narrow. Following are examples of all three errors, along with contrasting examples of effective topic sentences.

Announcement

My Ford Escort is the concern of this paragraph.

The statement above is a simple announcement of a subject, rather than a topic sentence expressing an idea about the subject.

Statement That Is Too Broad

Many people have problems with their cars.

The statement is too broad to be supported adequately with specific details in a single paragraph.

Statement That Is Too Narrow

My car is a Ford Escort.

The statement above is too narrow to be expanded into a paragraph. Such a narrow statement is sometimes called a *dead-end statement* because there is no place to go with it. It is a simple fact that does not need or call for any support.

Effective Topic Sentence

I hate my Ford Escort.

The statement above expresses an opinion that could be supported in a paragraph. The writer could offer a series of specific supporting reasons, examples, and details to make it clear why he or she hates the car.

Here are additional examples:

Announcements

The subject of this paper will be my apartment.

I want to talk about increases in the divorce rate.

Statements That Are Too Broad

The places where people live have definite effects on their lives.

Many people have trouble getting along with others.

Statements That Are Too Narrow

I have no hot water in my apartment at night.

Almost one of every two marriages ends in divorce.

Effective Topic Sentences

My apartment is a terrible place to live.

The divorce rate is increasing for several reasons.

Activity 1

For each pair of sentences below, write A beside the sentence that only *announces* a topic. Write OK beside the sentence that *advances an idea* about the topic.

1. _____ a. This paper will deal with flunking math.

   _____ b. I flunked math last semester for several reasons.

2. _____ a. I am going to write about my job as a gas station attendant.

   _____ b. Working as a gas station attendant was the worst job I ever had.

3. _____ a. Obscene phone calls are the subject of this paragraph.

   _____ b. People should know what to do when they receive an obscene phone call.

4. _____ a. In several ways, my college library is inconvenient to use.

   _____ b. This paragraph will deal with the college library.

5. _____ a. My paper will discuss the topic of procrastinating.

   _____ b. The following steps will help you stop procrastinating.

Activity 2

For each pair of sentences below, write TN beside the statement that is *too narrow* to be developed into a paragraph. Write OK beside the statement in each pair that could be developed into a paragraph.

1. _____ a. I do push-ups and sit-ups each morning.

   _____ b. Exercising every morning has had positive effects on my health.

2. _____ a. José works nine hours a day and then goes to school three hours a night.

   _____ b. José is an ambitious man.

3. _____ a. I started college after being away from school for seven years.

   _____ b. Several of my fears about returning to school have proved to be groundless.

4. _____ a. Parts of Walt Disney's *Bambi* make the movie frightening for children.

_____ b. Last summer I visited Disneyland in Anaheim, California.

5. _____ a. My brother was depressed yesterday for several reasons.

_____ b. Yesterday my brother had to pay fifty-two dollars for a motor tune-up.

Activity 3

For each pair of sentences below, write TB beside the statement that is *too broad* to be supported adequately in a short paper. Write OK beside the statement that makes a limited point.

1. ___✓___ a. Professional football is a dangerous sport.

_____ b. Professional sports are violent.

2. _____ a. Married life is the best way of living.

___✓___ b. Teenage marriages often end in divorce for several reasons.

3. ___✓___ a. Aspirin can have several harmful side effects.

_____ b. Drugs are dangerous.

4. _____ a. I've always done poorly in school.

___✓___ b. I flunked math last semester for several reasons.

5. _____ a. Computers are changing our society.

___✓___ b. Using computers to teach schoolchildren is a mistake.

2 Understanding the Two Parts of a Topic Sentence

As stated earlier, the point that opens a paragraph is often called a *topic sentence.* When you look closely at a point, or topic sentence, you can see that it is made up of two parts:

1 The *limited topic*

2 The writer's *attitude* toward the limited topic

The writer's attitude or point of view or idea is usually expressed in one or more *key words.* All the details in a paragraph should support the idea expressed in the key words. In each of the topic sentences below, a single line appears under the topic and a double line under the idea about the topic (expressed in a key word or key words):

My girlfriend is very aggressive.

Highway accidents are often caused by absentmindedness.

The kitchen is the most widely used room in my house.

Voting should be required by law in the United States.

My pick-up truck is the most reliable vehicle I have ever owned.

In the first sentence, the topic is *girlfriend,* and the key word that expresses the writer's idea about his topic is that his girlfriend is *aggressive.* In the second sentence, the topic is *highway accidents,* and the key word that determines the focus of the paragraph is that such accidents are often caused by *absentmindedness.* Notice each topic and key word or key words in the other three sentences as well.

Activity

For each point below, draw a single line under the topic and a double line under the idea about the topic.

1. Billboards should be abolished.

2. My boss is an ambitious man.

3. Politicians are often self-serving.

4. The apartment needed repairs.

5. Television commercials are often insulting.

6. My parents have rigid racial attitudes.

7. The middle child is often a neglected member of the family.

8. The language in many movies today is offensive.

9. Doctors are often insensitive.

10. Homeowners today are more energy-conscious than ever before.

11. My car is a temperamental machine.

12. My friend Debbie, who is only nineteen, is extremely old-fashioned.

13. Looking for a job can be a degrading experience.

14. The daily life of students is filled with conflicts.

15. Regulations in the school cafeteria should be strictly enforced.

16. The national speed limit should be raised.

17. Our vacation turned out to be a disaster.

18. The city's traffic-light system has both values and drawbacks.

19. Insects serve many useful purposes.

20. Serious depression often has several warning signs.

3 Selecting a Topic Sentence

Remember that a paragraph is made up of a topic sentence and a group of related sentences developing the topic sentence. It is also helpful to remember that the topic sentence is a *general* statement. The other sentences provide specific support for the general statement.

Activity

Each group of sentences below could be written as a short paragraph. Circle the letter of the topic sentence in each case. To find the topic sentence, ask yourself, "Which is a general statement supported by the specific details in the other three statements?"

Begin by trying the example item below. First circle the letter of the sentence you think expresses the main idea. Then read the explanation.

Example   a. If you stop carrying matches or a lighter, you can cut down on impulse smoking.

b. If you sit in no-smoking areas, you will smoke less.

c. You can behave in ways that will help you smoke less.

d. By keeping a record of when and where you smoke, you can identify the most tempting situations and then avoid them.

Explanation: Sentence *a* explains one way to smoke less. Sentences *b* and *d* also provide specific ways to smoke less. In sentence *c*, however, no one specific way is explained. The words *ways that will help you smoke less* refer only generally to such methods. Therefore, sentence *c* is the topic sentence; it expresses the author's main idea. The other sentences support that idea by providing examples.

1. a.   "I couldn't study because I forgot to bring my textbook home."

b.   "I couldn't take the final because my grandmother died."

c.   Students give instructors some common excuses.

d.   "I couldn't come to class because I had a migraine headache."

2. a. Its brakes are badly worn.

    b. My old car is ready for the junk pile.

    c. Its floor has rusted through, and water splashes on my feet when the highway is wet.

    d. My mechanic says its engine is too old to be repaired, and the car isn't worth the cost of a new engine.

3. a. Tobacco is one of the most addictive of all drugs.

    b. Selling cigarettes ought to be against the law.

    c. Nonsmokers are put in danger by breathing the smoke from other people's cigarettes.

    d. Cigarette smoking kills many more people than all illegal drugs combined.

4. a. Part-time workers can be easily laid off.

    b. Most part-time workers get no fringe benefits.

    c. The average part-timer earns three dollars less an hour than a full-timer.

    d. Part-time workers have second-class status.

5. a. The last time I ate at the diner, I got food poisoning and was sick for two days.

    b. The city inspector found matches and mice in the diner's kitchen.

    c. Our town diner is a health hazard and ought to be closed down.

    d. The toilets in the diner often back up, and the sinks have only a trickle of water.

4 Writing a Topic Sentence: I

Activity

The following activity will give you practice in writing an accurate point, or topic sentence—one that is neither too broad nor too narrow for the supporting material in a paragraph. Sometimes you will construct your topic sentence after you have decided which details you want to discuss. An added value of this activity is that it shows you how to write a topic sentence that will exactly match the details you have developed.

1. Topic sentence: _The neighbor   untaisocial._

   a. When we brought a "welcome to the neighborhood" present, the family next door didn't even say thank you.

   b. The family never attends the annual block party.

   c. The family's children aren't allowed to play with other neighborhood kids.

   d. Our neighbors keep their curtains closed and never sit out in their yard.

2. Topic sentence: _The dance party was cancel by several reason_

   a. Only about thirty people came to the dance, instead of the expected two hundred.

   b. The band arrived late and spent an hour setting up.

   c. There were at least three males at the dance to every female.

   d. An hour after the dance started, it ended because of a power failure.

3. Topic sentence: _The bed sevice in the Restaurent ._ (trouble)

   a. We had to wait half an hour even though we had reserved a table.

   b. Our appetizer and main course arrived at the same time.

   c. The busboy ignored our requests for more water.

   d. The wrong desserts were served to us.

4. Topic sentence: _Some trouble in the School years of English ._

   a. In early grades we had spelling bees, and I would be among the first to sit down.

   b. In sixth-grade English, my teacher kept me busy diagramming sentences on the board.

   c. In tenth grade we had to recite poems, and I always forgot my lines.

   d. In my senior year, my compositions had more red correction marks than anyone else's.

5. | *Topic sentence:* _____

> a. The crowd scenes were crudely spliced from another film.
>
> b. Mountains and other background scenery were just painted card-board cutouts.
>
> c. The "sync" was off, so that you heard voices even when the actors' lips were not moving.
>
> d. The so-called "monster" was just a spider that had been filmed through a magnifying lens.

5 Writing a Topic Sentence: II

Often you will start with a general topic or a general idea of what you want to write about. You may, for example, want to write a paragraph about some aspect of school life. To come up with a point about school life, begin by limiting your topic. One way to do this is to make a list of all the limited topics you can think of that fit under the general topic.

Activity

Following are five general topics and a series of limited topics that fit under them. Make a point out of *one* of the limited topics in each group.

Hint: To create a topic sentence, ask yourself, "What point do I want to make about _____ (*my limited topic*)?"

Example   Recreation
- Movies
- Dancing
- TV shows
- Reading
- Sports parks

Your point: _Sports parks today have some truly exciting games._

1. Your school
   - Instructor
   - Cafeteria

- Specific course
- Particular room or building
- Particular policy (attendance, grading, etc.)
- Classmate

Your point: _____

_____

2. Job
   - Pay
   - Boss
   - Working conditions
   - Duties
   - Coworkers
   - Customers or clients

   Your point: _I happy with my working place._____

   _____

3. Money
   - Budgets
   - Credit cards
   - Dealing with a bank
   - School expenses
   - Ways to get it
   - Ways to save it

   Your point: _How to diel with you money ._____

   _____

4. Cars
   - First car
   - Driver's test
   - Road conditions
   - Accident
   - Mandatory speed limit
   - Safety problems

   Your point: _____

   _____

5. Sports
   - A team's chances
   - At your school
   - Women's team

- Recreational versus spectator
- Favorite team
- Outstanding athlete

Your point: _____

_____

6 Recognizing Specific Details: I

Specific details are examples, reasons, particulars, and facts. Such details are needed to support and explain a topic sentence effectively. They provide the evidence needed for readers to understand, as well as to feel and experience, a writer's point.

Here is a topic sentence followed by two sets of supporting sentences. Which set provides sharp, specific details?

Topic Sentence

Some poor people must struggle to make meals for themselves.

Set A

They gather up whatever free food they can find in fast-food restaurants and take it home to use however they can. Instead of planning well-balanced meals, they base their diet on anything they can buy that is cheap and filling.

Set B

Some make tomato soup by adding hot water to the free packets of ketchup they get at McDonald's. Others buy cans of cheap dog food and fry it like hamburger.

Set B provides specific details: instead of a general statement about "free food they find in fast-food restaurants and take . . . home to use however they can," we get a vivid detail we can see and picture clearly: "make tomato soup [from] free packets of ketchup." Instead of a general statement about how the poor will "base their diet on anything they can buy that is cheap and filling," we get exact and vivid details: "Others buy cans of cheap dog food and fry it like hamburger."

Specific details are often like the information we might find in a movie script. They provide us with such clear pictures that we could make a film of them if we wanted to. You would know just how to film the information given in set B. You would show a poor person breaking open a packet of ketchup from McDonald's and mixing it with water to make a kind of tomato soup. You would show someone opening a can of dog food and frying its contents like hamburger.

In contrast, the writer of set A fails to provide the specific information needed. If you were asked to make a film based on set A, you would have to figure out for yourself just what particulars you were going to show.

When you are working to provide specific supporting information in a paper, it might help to ask yourself, "Could someone easily film this information?" If the answer is "yes," you probably have good details.

Activity

Each topic sentence below is followed by two sets of supporting details (*a* and *b*). Write S (for *specific*) in the space next to the set that provides specific support for the point. Write G (for *general*) next to the set that offers only vague, general support.

1. *Topic sentence:* My roommate is messy.

   _____ a. He doesn't seem to mind that he can't find any clean clothes or dishes. He never puts anything back in its proper place; he just drops it wherever he happens to be. His side of the room looks as if a hurricane has gone through.

   _____ b. His coffee cup is covered inside with a thick layer of green mold. I can't tell you what color his easy chair is; it has disappeared under a pile of dirty laundry. When he turns over in bed, I can hear the crunch of cracker crumbs beneath his body.

2. *Topic sentence:* Roberta is very aggressive.

   _____ a. Her aggressiveness is apparent in both her personal and her professional life. She is never shy about extending social invitations. And while some people are turned off by her aggressive attitude, others are impressed by it and enjoy doing business with her.

   _____ b. When she meets a man she likes, she is quick to say, "Let's go out sometime. What's your phone number?" In her job as a furniture salesperson, she will follow potential customers out onto the sidewalk as she tries to persuade them to buy.

3. *Topic sentence:* Our new kitten causes us lots of trouble.

   _____ a. He has shredded the curtains in my bedroom with his claws. He nearly drowned when he crawled into the washing machine. And my hands look like raw hamburger from his playful bites and scratches.

   _____ b. He seems to destroy everything he touches. He's always getting into places where he doesn't belong. Sometimes he plays too roughly, and that can be painful.

4. *Topic sentence:* My landlord is softhearted.

_____ a. Even though he wrote them himself, he sometimes ignores the official apartment rules in order to make his tenants happy.

_____ b. Although the lease states "No pets," he brought my daughter a puppy after she told him how much she missed having one.

5. *Topic sentence:* The library is a distracting place to try to study.

_____ a. It's hard to concentrate when a noisy eight-person poker game is going on on the floor beside you. It's also distracting to overhear remarks like, "Hey, Baby, what's your mother's address? I want to send her a thank-you card for having such a beautiful daughter."

_____ b. Many students meet in the library to do group activities and socialize with one another. Others go there to flirt. It's easy to get more interested in all that activity than in paying attention to your studies.

7 Recognizing Specific Details: II

Activity

At several points in the following paragraphs you are given a choice of two sets of supporting details. Write S (for *specific*) in the space next to the set that provides specific support for the point. Write G (for *general*) next to the set that offers only vague, general support.

Paragraph 1

My daughter's boyfriend is a good-for-nothing young man. After knowing him for just three months, everyone in our family is opposed to the relationship. For one thing, Russell is lazy.

_____ a. He is always finding an excuse to avoid putting in an honest day's work. He never pitches in and helps with chores around our house, even when he's asked directly to do so. And his attitude about his job isn't any better. To hear him tell it, he deserves special treatment in the workplace. He thinks he's gone out of his way if he just shows up on time.

_____ b. After starting a new job last week, he announced this Monday that he wasn't going to work because it was his *birthday*—as if he were somebody special. And when my husband asked Russell to help put storm windows on the house next Saturday, Russell answered that he uses his weekends to catch up on sleep.

Another quality of Russell's which no one likes is that he is cheap.

_____ c. When my daughter's birthday came around, Russell said he would take her out to Baldoni's, a fancy Italian restaurant. Then he changed his mind. Instead of spending a lot of money on a meal, he said, he wanted to buy her a really nice pair of earrings. So my daughter cooked dinner for him at her apartment. But there was no present, not even a little one. He claims he's waiting for a jewelry sale at Macy's. I don't think my daughter will ever see that "really nice" gift.

_____ d. He makes big promises about all the nice things he's going to do for my daughter, but he never comes through. His words are cheap, and so is he. He's all talk and no action. My daughter isn't greedy, but it hurts her when Russell says he's going to take her someplace nice or give her something special and then nothing happens.

Worst of all, Russell is mean.

_____ e. Russell seems to get special pleasure from hurting people when he feels they have a weak point. I have heard him make remarks that to him were funny but were really very insensitive. You've got to wonder about someone who needs to be ugly to other people just for the sake of being powerful. Sometimes I want to let him know how I feel.

_____ f. When my husband was out of work, Russell said to him, "Well, you've got it made now, living off your wife." After my husband glared at him, he said, "Why're you getting sore? I'm just kidding." Sometimes he snaps at my daughter, saying things like "Don't make me wait—there are plenty of other babes who would like to take your place." At such times I want to blow off his head with a bazooka.

Everyone in the family is waiting anxiously for the day when my daughter will see Russell the way the rest of us see him.

Paragraph 2

Many adult children move back in with their parents for some period of time. Although living with Mom and Dad again has some advantages, there are certain problems that are likely to arise. One common problem is that children may expect their parents to do all the household chores.

_____ a. They never think that they should take on their share of work around the house. Not only do they not help with their parents' chores; they don't even take responsibility for the extra work that their presence creates. Like babies, they go through the house making a mess that the parents are supposed to clean up. It's as if they think their parents are their servants.

_____ b. They expect meals to appear on the table as if by magic. After they've eaten, they go off to work or play, never thinking about who's going to do the dishes. They drop their dirty laundry beside the washing machine, assuming that Mom will attend to it and return clean, folded clothes to their bedroom door. And speaking of their bedrooms: every day they await the arrival of Mom's Maid Service to make the bed, pick up the floor, and dust the furniture.

Another frequent problem is that parents forget their adult children are no longer adolescents.

_____ c. Parents like this want to know everything about their adult children's lives. They don't think their kids, even though they are adults, should have any privacy. Whenever they see their children doing anything, they want to know all the details. It's as though their children are still teenagers who are expected to report all their activities. Naturally, adult children get irritated when they are treated as if they were little kids.

_____ d. They may insist upon knowing far more about their children's comings and goings than the children want to share. For example, if such parents see their adult son heading out the door, they demand to know: "Where are you going? Who will you be with? What will you be doing? What time will you be back?" In addition, they may not let their adult child have any privacy. If their daughter and a date are sitting in the living room, for instance, they may join them there and start peppering the young man with questions about his family and his job, as if they were interviewing him for the position of son-in-law.

Finally, there may be financial problems when an adult child returns to live at home.

_____ e. Having an extra adult in the household creates extra expenses. But many adult children don't offer to help deal with those extra costs. Adult children often eat at home, causing the grocery bill to climb. They may stay in a formerly unused room, which now needs to be heated and lit. They produce extra laundry to be washed. They use the telephone, adding to the long-distance bill. For all these reasons, adult children should expect to pay a reasonable fee to their parents for room and board.

_____ f. It's expensive to have another adult living in the household. Adult children would be paying a lot of bills on their own if they weren't staying with their parents. It's only fair that they share the expenses at their parents' house. They should consider all the ways that their living at home is increasing their parents' expenses. Then they should insist upon covering their share of the costs.

8 Providing Specific Evidence

Activity

Provide three details that logically support each of the following points, or topic sentences. Your details can be drawn from your own experience, or they can be invented. In each case, the details should show in a specific way what the point expresses in only a general way. You may state your details briefly in phrases, or as complete sentences.

Example   The student had several ways of passing time during the dull lecture.
Shielded his eyes with his hand and dozed awhile.

Read the sports magazine he had brought to class.

Made an elaborate drawing on a page of his notebook.

1. I could tell I was coming down with the flu.

   _____

   _____

   _____

2. The food at the cafeteria was terrible yesterday.

   _____

   _____

   _____

3. I had car problems recently.

   _____

   _____

   _____

4. When your money gets tight, there are several ways to economize.

_____

_____

_____

5. Some people have dangerous driving habits.

_____

_____

_____

9 Identifying Adequate Supporting Evidence

Activity

Two of the following paragraphs provide sufficient details to support their topic sentences convincingly. Write AD, for *adequate development,* beside those paragraphs. There are also three paragraphs that, for the most part, use vague, general, or wordy sentences as a substitute for concrete details. Write U, for *underdeveloped,* beside those paragraphs.

_____ 1.   **My Husband's Stubbornness**

My husband's worst problem is his stubbornness. He simply will not let any kind of weakness show. If he isn't feeling well, he refuses to admit it. He will keep on doing whatever he is doing and will wait until the symptoms get almost unbearable before he will even hint that anything is the matter with him. Then things are so far along that he has to spend more time recovering than he would if he had a different attitude. He also hates to be wrong. If he is wrong, he will be the last to admit it. This happened once when we went shopping, and he spent an endless amount of time going from one place to the next. He insisted that one of them had a fantastic sale on things he wanted. We never found a sale, but the fact that this situation happened will not change his attitude. Finally, he never listens to anyone else's suggestions on a car trip. He always knows he's on the right road, and the results have led to a lot of time wasted getting back in the right direction. Every time one of these incidents happens, it only means that it is going to happen again in the future.

_____ 2.   **Dangerous Games**

Because they feel compelled to show off in front of their friends, some teenagers play dangerous games. In one incident, police found a group of boys performing a dangerous stunt with their cars. The boys would perch on the hoods of cars going thirty-five or forty miles an hour. Then the driver would brake sharply, and the boy who flew the farthest off the car would win. Teenagers also drive their cars with the lights off and pass each other on hills or curves as ways of challenging each other. In addition to cars, water seems to tempt young people to invent dangerous contests. Some students dared each other to swim through a narrow pipe under a four-lane highway. The pipe carried water from a stream to a pond, and the swimmer would have to hold his or her breath for several minutes before coming out on the other side. Another contest involved diving off the rocky sides of a quarry. Because large stones sat under the water in certain places, any dive could result in a broken neck. But the students would egg each other on to go "rock diving." Playing deadly games like these is a horrifying phase of growing up for some teenagers.

_____ 3.   **Attitudes toward Food**

As children, we form attitudes toward food that are not easily changed. In some families, food is love. Not all families are like this, but some children grow up with this attitude. Some families think of food as something precious and not to be wasted. The attitudes children pick up about food are hard to change in adulthood. Some families celebrate with food. If a child learns an attitude, it is hard to break this later. Someone once said: "As the twig is bent, so grows the tree." Children are very impressionable, and they can't really think for themselves when they are small. Children learn from the parent figures in their lives, and later from their peers. Some families have healthy attitudes about food. It is important for adults to teach their children these healthy attitudes. Otherwise, the children may have weight problems when they are adults.

_____ 4.   **Qualities in a Friend**

There are several qualities I look for in a friend. A friend should give support and security. A friend should also be fun to be around. Friends can have faults, like anyone else, and sometimes it is hard to overlook them. But a friend can't be dropped because he or she has faults. A friend should stick to you, even in bad times. There is a saying that "a friend in need is a friend indeed." I believe this means that there are good friends and fair-weather friends. The second type is not a true friend. He or she is the kind of person who runs when there's trouble. Friends don't always last a lifetime. Someone you believed to be your best friend may lose contact with you if you move to a different area or go around with a different group of people. A friend should be generous and understanding. A friend does not have to be exactly like you. Sometimes friends are opposites, but they still like each other and get along. Since I am a very quiet person, I can't say that I have many friends. But these are the qualities I believe a friend should have.

_____ 5.   **A Dangerous Place**

We play touch football on a dangerous field. First of all, the grass on the field is seldom mowed. The result is that we have to run through tangled weeds that wrap around our ankles like trip wires. The tall grass also hides some gaping holes lurking beneath. The best players know the exact positions of all the holes and manage to detour around them like soldiers zigzagging across a minefield. Most of us, though, endure at least one sprained ankle per game. Another danger is the old baseball infield that we use as the last twenty yards of our gridiron. This area is covered with stones and broken glass. No matter how often we clean it up, we can never keep pace with the broken bottles hurled on the field by the teenagers we call the "night shift." These people apparently hold drinking parties every night in the abandoned dugout and enjoy throwing the empties out on the field. During every game, we try to avoid falling on especially big chunks of Budweiser bottles. Finally, encircling the entire field is an old, rusty chain-link fence full of tears and holes. Being slammed into the fence during the play can mean a painful stabbing by the jagged wires. All these dangers have made us less afraid of opposing teams than of the field where we play.

10 Adding Details to Complete a Paragraph

Activity

Each of the following paragraphs needs specific details to back up its supporting points. In the spaces provided, add a sentence or two of realistic details for each supporting point. The more specific you are, the more convincing your details are likely to be.

1.   **A Pushover Instructor**

We knew after the first few classes that the instructor was a pushover. First of all, he didn't seem able to control the class.

_____

_____

_____

In addition, he made some course requirements easier when a few
students complained.

_____

_____

Finally, he gave the easiest quiz we had ever taken.

_____

_____

_____

2.

Helping a Parent in College

There are several ways a family can help a parent who is attending
college. First, family members can take over some of the household
chores that the parent usually does.

_____

_____

Also, family members can make sure that the student has some quiet
study time.

_____

_____

Last, families can take an interest in the student's problems and
accomplishments.

_____

_____

_____

11 Writing a Simple Paragraph

You know now that an effective paragraph does two essential things: (1) it makes
a point, and (2) it provides specific details to support that point. You have considered a number of paragraphs that are effective because they follow these two
basic steps or ineffective because they fail to follow them.

You are ready, then, to write a simple paragraph of your own. Choose one of the three assignments below, and follow carefully the guidelines provided.

Assignment 1

Turn back to the activity on page 72 and select the point for which you have the best supporting details. Develop that point into a paragraph by following these steps:

a If necessary, rewrite the point so that the first sentence is more specific or suits your purpose more exactly. For example, you might want to rewrite the second point so that it includes a specific time and place: "Dinner at the Union Building Cafeteria was terrible yesterday."

b Provide several sentences of information to develop each of your three supporting details fully. Make sure that all the information in your paragraph truly supports your point. As an aid, use the paragraph form on page 635.

c Use the words *First of all, Second,* and *Finally* to introduce your three supporting details.

d Conclude your paragraph with a sentence that refers to your opening point. This last sentence "rounds off" the paragraph and lets the reader know that your discussion is complete. For example, the "Changes in the Family" paragraph on page 48 begins with "Changes in our society in recent years have weakened family life." It closes with a statement that refers to, and echoes, the opening point: "Clearly, modern life is a challenge to family life."

e Supply a title based on your point. For instance, point 4 on page 73 might have the title "Ways to Economize."

Use the following list to check your paragraph for each of the above items:

Yes   No

_____ _____   Do you begin with a point?

_____ _____   Do you provide relevant, specific details that support the point?

_____ _____   Do you use the words *First of all, Second,* and *Finally* to introduce your three supporting details?

_____ _____   Do you have a closing sentence?

_____ _____   Do you have a title based on your point?

_____ _____   Are your sentences clear and free of obvious errors?

Assignment 2

In this chapter you have read two paragraphs (pages 51–52) on reasons for being in college. For this assignment, write a paragraph describing your own reasons for being in college. You might want to look first at the following list of common reasons students give for going to school. Write a check mark next to each reason that applies to you. If you have different reasons for being in college that are not listed here, add them to the list. Then select your three most important reasons for being in school and generate specific supporting details for each reason.

Before starting, reread paragraph B on page 52. *You must provide comparable specific details of your own.* Make your paragraph truly personal; do not fall back on vague generalities like those in paragraph A on page 51. As you work on your paragraph, use the checklist for Assignment 1 as a guide.

Apply in My Case	*Reasons Students Go to College*
_____	To have some fun before getting a job
_____	To prepare for a specific career
_____	To please their families
_____	To educate and enrich themselves
_____	To be with friends who are going to college
_____	To take advantage of an opportunity they didn't have before
_____	To find a husband or wife
_____	To see if college has anything to offer them
_____	To do more with their lives than they've done so far
_____	To take advantage of Veterans Administration benefits or other special funding
_____	To earn the status that they feel comes with a college degree
_____	To get a new start in life
_____	Other: _____

Assignment 3

Write a paragraph about stress in your life. Choose three of the following stressful areas and provide specific examples and details to develop each area.

Stress at school
Stress at work
Stress at home
Stress with a friend or friends

Use the checklist for Assignment 1 as a guide while you are working on the paragraph.

4 The Third Step in Writing

This chapter will show you how to

- organize specific evidence in a paper by using a clear method of organization
- connect the specific evidence by using transitions and other connecting words

You know from Chapter 3 that the first two steps in writing an effective paragraph are making a point and supporting the point with specific evidence. This chapter will deal with the third step. You'll learn the chief ways to organize and connect the supporting information in a paper.

Step 3: Organize and Connect the Specific Evidence

At the same time that you are generating the specific details needed to support a point, you should be thinking about ways to organize and connect those details. All the details in your paper must cohere, or stick together; when they do, your reader is able to move smoothly from one bit of supporting information to the next. This chapter will discuss the following ways to organize and connect supporting details: (1) common methods or organization, (2) transition words, and (3) other connecting words.

Common Methods of Organization: Time Order and Emphatic Order

Time order and emphatic order are common methods used to organize the supporting material in a paper. (You will learn more specialized methods of development in Part Two of the book.)

Time order simply means that details are listed as they occur in time. *First* this is done; *next* this; *then* this; *after* that, this; and so on. Here is a paragraph that organizes its details through time order.

How I Relax

The way I relax when I get home from school on Thursday night is, first of all, to put my three children to bed. Next, I run hot water in the tub and put in lots of perfumed bubble bath. As the bubbles rise, I undress and get into the tub. The water is relaxing to my tired muscles, and the bubbles are tingly on my skin. I lie back and put my feet on the water spigots, with everything but my head under the water. I like to stick my big toe up the spigot and spray water over the tub. After about ten minutes of soaking, I wash myself with scented soap, get out and dry myself off, and put on my nightgown. Then I go downstairs and make myself two ham, lettuce, and tomato sandwiches on white bread and pour myself a tall glass of iced tea with plenty of sugar and ice cubes. I carry these into the living room and turn on the television. To get comfortable, I sit on the couch with a pillow behind me and my legs under me. I enjoy watching The Tonight Show or a late movie. The time is very peaceful after a long, hard day of housecleaning, cooking, washing, and attending night class.

Fill in the missing words: "How I relax" uses the following words to help show time order: _____, _____, _____, _____, and _____.

Emphatic order is sometimes described as "save-the-best-till-last" order. It means that the most interesting or important detail is placed in the last part of a paper. (In cases where all the details seem equal in importance, the writer should impose a personal order that seems logical or appropriate to the details.) The last position in a paper is the most emphatic position because the reader is most likely to remember the last thing read. *Finally, last of all,* and *most important* are typical words showing emphasis. The following paragraph organizes its details through emphatic order.

The National Enquirer

There are several reasons why the National Enquirer is so popular. First of all, the paper is heavily advertised on television. In the ads, attractive-looking people say, with a smile, "I want to know!" as they scan the pages of the Enquirer. The ads reassure people that it's all right to want to read stories such as "Heartbreak for Demi Moore" or "Prince Edward's Fiancée in

New Royal Topless Scandal." In addition, the paper is easily available. In supermarkets, convenience stores, and drugstores, the <u>Enquirer</u> is always displayed in racks close to the cash register. As customers wait in line, they can't help being attracted to the paper's glaring headlines. Then, on impulse, customers will add the paper to their other purchases. Most of all, people read the <u>Enquirer</u> because they love gossip. We find other people's lives fascinating, especially if those people are rich and famous. We want to see and read about their homes; their clothes; their friends, lovers, and families. We also take a kind of mean delight in their unflattering photos and problems and mistakes, perhaps because we're jealous of them. Even though we may be ashamed of our interest, it's hard to resist buying a paper that promises "The Forbidden Love of Julia Roberts" or "Film Star Who Now Looks Like a Cadaver" or even "Hollywood Star Wars: Who Hates Whom and Why." The <u>Enquirer</u> knows how to get us interested and make us buy.

Fill in the missing words: The paragraph lists a total of _____ different reasons people read the *National Enquirer.* The writer of the paragraph feels that the most important reason is _____.

He or she signals this reason by using the emphasis words _____.

Some paragraphs use a *combination of time order and emphatic order.* For example, "Good-Bye, Tony" on page 50 includes time order: it moves from the time Tony arrived to the end of the evening. In addition, the writer uses emphatic order, ending with her most important reason (signaled by the words *most of all*) for not wanting to see Tony anymore.

Transitions

Transitions, or *transition words,* are signal words that help readers follow the direction of the writer's thought. They show the relationship between ideas, connecting one thought to the next. They can be compared to road signs that guide travelers.

To see the value of transitions, look at the following pairs of examples. Write a check mark beside the example in each pair that is clearer to read and easier to understand.

1. _____ a. Our landlord recently repainted our apartment. He replaced our faulty air conditioner.
   __✓__ b. Our landlord recently repainted our apartment. Also, he replaced our faulty air conditioner.

2. _____ a. I turned on the power button. I carefully inserted a disk into the computer.
   _____ b. I turned on the power button. Then I carefully inserted a disk into the computer.

3. _____ a. Moviegoers usually dislike film monsters. Audiences pitied King Kong and even shed tears at his death.
   _____ b. Moviegoers usually dislike film monsters. However, audiences pitied King Kong and even shed tears at his death.

You should have checked the second example in each pair. The transitional words in those sentences—*Also, Then,* and *However*—make the relationship between the sentences clear. Like all effective transitions, they help connect the writer's thoughts.

In the following box are common transitional words and phrases, grouped according to the kind of signal they give readers. Note that certain words provide more than one kind of signal. In the paragraphs you write, you will most often use addition signals: words like *first of all, also, another,* and *finally* will help you move from one supporting reason or detail to the next.

Transitions

Addition signals: first of all, for one thing, second, the third reason, also, next, another, and, in addition, moreover, furthermore, finally, last of all

Time signals: first, then, next, after, as, before, while, meanwhile, now, during, finally

Space signals: next to, across, on the opposite side, to the left, to the right, in front, in back, above, below, behind, nearby

Change-of-direction signals: but, however, yet, in contrast, otherwise, still, on the contrary, on the other hand

Illustration signals: for example, for instance, specifically, as an illustration, once, such as

Conclusion signals: therefore, consequently, thus, then, as a result, in summary, to conclude, last of all, finally

Activity

1. Underline the three *addition* signals in the following paragraph:

    I am opposed to state-supported lotteries for a number of reasons. First of all, by supporting lotteries, states are supporting gambling. I don't see anything morally wrong with gambling, but it is a known cause of suffering for many people who do it to excess. The state should be concerned with relieving suffering, not causing it. Another objection I have to state lotteries is the kind of advertising they do on television. The commercials promote the lotteries as an easy way to get rich. In fact, the odds against getting rich are astronomical. Last, the lotteries take advantage of the people who can least afford them. Studies have shown that people with lower incomes are more likely to play the lottery than people with higher incomes. This is the harshest reality of the lotteries: the state is encouraging people of limited means not to save their money but to throw it away on a state-supported pipe dream.

2. Underline the four *time* signals in the following paragraph:

    It is often easy to spot bad drivers on the road because they usually make more than one mistake: they make their mistakes in series. First, for example, you notice that a man is tailgating you. Then, almost as soon as you notice, he has passed you in a no-passing zone. That's two mistakes already in a matter of seconds. Next, almost invariably, you see him speed down the road and pass someone else. Finally, as you watch in disbelief, glad that he's out of your way, he speeds through a red light or cuts across oncoming traffic in a wild left turn.

3. Underline the three *space* signals in the following paragraph:

    Standing in the burned-out shell of my living room was a shocking experience. Above my head were charred beams, all that remained of our ceiling. In front of me, where our television and stereo had once stood, were twisted pieces of metal and chunks of blackened glass. Strangely, some items seemed little damaged by the fire. For example, I could see the TV tuner knob and a dusty CD under the rubble. I walked through the gritty ashes until I came to what was left of our sofa. Behind the sofa had been a wall of family photographs. Now, the wall and the pictures were gone. I found only a waterlogged scrap of my wedding picture.

4. Underline the four *change-of-direction* signals in the following paragraph:

    In some ways, train travel is superior to air travel. People always marvel at the speed with which airplanes can zip from one end of the country to another. Trains, on the other hand, definitely take longer. But sometimes longer can be better. Traveling across the country by train allows you to experience the trip more completely. You get to see the cities and towns, mountains and prairies that too often pass by unnoticed when you fly. Another advantage of train travel is comfort. Traveling by plane means wedging yourself into a narrow seat with your knees bumping the back of the seat in front of you and being handed a "snack" consisting of a bag of ten roasted peanuts. In contrast, the seats on most trains are spacious and comfortable, permitting even the longest-legged traveler to stretch out and watch the scenery just outside the window. And when train travelers grow hungry, they can get up and stroll to the dining car, where they can order anything from a simple snack to a gourmet meal. There's no question that train travel is definitely slow and old-fashioned compared with air travel. However, in many ways it is much more civilized.

5. Underline the three *illustration* signals in the following selection:

Status symbols are all around us. The cars we drive, for instance, say something about who we are and how successful we have been. The auto makers depend on this perception of automobiles, designing their commercials to show older, well-established people driving Cadillacs and young, fun-loving people driving to the beach in sports cars. Television, too, has become something of a status symbol. Specifically, schoolchildren are often rated by their classmates according to the brand names of their clothing. Another example of a status symbol is the videocassette recorder. This device, not so long ago considered a novelty, is now considered as common as the television set itself. Being without a VCR today is like being without a record player in the seventies.

6. Underline the *conclusion* signal in the following paragraph:

A hundred years ago, miners used to bring caged canaries down into the mines with them to act as warning signals. If the bird died, the miner knew that the oxygen was running out. The smaller animal would be affected much more quickly than the miners. In the same way, animals are acting as warning signals to us today. Baby birds die before they can hatch because pesticides in the environment cause the adults to lay eggs with paper-thin shells. Fish die when lakes are contaminated with acid rain or poisonous mercury. The dangers in our environment will eventually affect all life on earth, including humans. Therefore, we must pay attention to these early warning signals. If we don't, we will be as foolish as a miner who ignored a dead canary—and we will die.

Other Connecting Words

In addition to transitions, there are three other kinds of connecting words that help tie together the specific evidence in a paper: *repeated words, pronouns,* and *synonyms.* Each will be discussed in turn.

Repeated Words

Many of us have been taught by English instructors—correctly so—not to repeat ourselves in our writing. On the other hand, repeating key words can help tie ideas together. In the paragraph that follows, the word *retirement* is repeated to remind readers of the key idea on which the discussion is centered. Underline the word the five times it appears.

> Oddly enough, retirement can pose more problems for the spouse than for the retired person. For a person who has been accustomed to a demanding job, retirement can mean frustration and a feeling of uselessness. This feeling will put pressure on the spouse to provide challenges at home equal to those of the workplace. Often, these tasks will disrupt the spouse's well-established routine. Another problem arising from retirement is filling up all those empty hours. The spouse may find himself or herself in the role of social director or tour guide, expected to come up with a new form of amusement every day. Without sufficient challenges or leisure activities, a person can become irritable and take out the resulting boredom and frustration of retirement on the marriage partner. It is no wonder that many of these partners wish their spouses would come out of retirement and do something—anything—just to get out of the house.

Pronouns

Pronouns (*he, she, it, you, they, this, that,* and others) are another way to connect ideas as you develop a paper. Using pronouns to take the place of other words or ideas can help you avoid needless repetition. (Be sure, though, to use pronouns with care in order to avoid the unclear or inconsistent pronoun references described in Chapters 33 and 34 of this book.) Underline the eight pronouns in the passage below, noting at the same time the words that the pronouns refer to.

> A professor of nutrition at a major university recently advised his students that they could do better on their examinations by eating lots of sweets. He told them that the sugar in cakes and candy would stimulate their brains to work more efficiently, and that if the sugar was eaten for only a month or two, it would not do them any harm.

Synonyms

Using synonyms—words that are alike in meaning—can also help move the reader from one thought to the next. In addition, the use of synonyms increases variety and interest by avoiding needless repetition of the same words. Underline the three words used as synonyms for *false ideas* in the following passage.

There are many false ideas about suicide. One wrong idea is that a person who talks about suicide never follows through. The truth is that about three out of every four people who commit suicide notify one or more other persons ahead of time. Another misconception is that a person who commits suicide is poor or downtrodden. Actually, poverty appears to be a deterrent to suicide rather than a predisposing factor. A third myth about suicide is that people bent on suicide will eventually take their lives one way or another, whether or not the most obvious means of suicide is removed from their reach. In fact, since an attempt at suicide is a kind of cry for help, removing a convenient means of taking one's life, such as a gun, shows people bent on suicide that someone cares enough about them to try to prevent it.

Activity

Read the selection below and then answer the questions about it that follow.

My Worst Experience of the Week

1 The registration process at State College was a nightmare. 2 The night before registration officially began, I went to bed anxious about the whole matter, and nothing that happened the next day served to ease my tension. 3 First, even though I had paid my registration fee early last spring, the people at the bursar's office had no record of my payment. 4 And for some bizarre reason, they wouldn't accept the receipt I had. 5 Consequently, I had to stand in line for two hours, waiting for someone to give me a slip of paper which stated that I had, in fact, paid my registration fee. 6 The need for this new receipt seemed ludicrous to me, since all along I had proof that I had paid. 7 I was next told that I had to see my adviser in the Law and Justice Department and that the department was in Corridor C of the Triad Building. 8 I had no idea what or where the Triad was. 9 But, finally, I found my way to the ugly, gray-white building. 10 Then I began looking for Corridor C. 11 When I found it, everyone there was a member of the Communications Department. 12 No one seemed to know where Law and Justice had gone. 13 Finally, one instructor said she thought Law and Justice was in Corridor A. 14 "And where is Corridor A?" I asked. 15 "I don't know," the teacher

answered. 16 "I'm new here." 17 She saw the bewildered look on my face and said sympathetically, "You're not the only one who's confused." 18 I nodded and walked numbly away. 19 I felt as if I were fated to spend the rest of the semester trying to complete the registration process, and I wondered if I would ever become an official college student.

Questions

1. How many times is the key word *registration* used? _____

2. Write here the pronoun that is used for *people at the bursar's office* (sentence 4): _____; *Corridor C* (sentence 11): _____;

   instructor (sentence 17): _____.

3. Write here the words that are used as a synonym for *receipt* (sentence 5):

   _____

   the words that are used as a synonym for *Triad* (sentence 9):

   _____

   the word that is used as a synonym for *instructor* (sentence 15).

   _____

■ Review Activity

Complete the following statements.

1. *Time order* means _____

   _____

2. *Emphatic order* means _____

   _____

3. _____ are signal words that help readers follow the direction of a writer's thought.

4. In addition to transitions, three other kinds of connecting words that help link sentences and ideas are repeated words, _____, and

   _____.

Practice in Organizing and Connecting Specific Evidence

You now know the third step in effective writing: organizing and connecting the specific evidence used to support the main point of a paper. This closing section will expand and strengthen your understanding of the third step in writing.

You will work through the following series of activities:

1 Organizing through Time Order

2 Organizing through Emphatic Order

3 Organizing through a Combination of Time Order and Emphatic Order

4 Identifying Transitions

5 Providing Transitions

6 Identifying Transitions and Other Connecting Words

1 Organizing through Time Order

Activity

Use time order to organize the scrambled list of sentences below. Write the number 1 beside the point that all the other sentences support. Then number each supporting sentence as it occurs in time.

10 _____ The table is right near the garbage pail.

6 _____ So you reluctantly select a gluelike tuna-fish sandwich, a crushed apple pie, and watery, lukewarm coffee.

12 _____ You sit at the edge of the table, away from the garbage pail, and gulp down your meal.

1 _____ Trying to eat in the cafeteria is an unpleasant experience.

9 _____ Suddenly you spot a free table in the center.

13 _____ With a last swallow of the lukewarm coffee, you get up and leave the cafeteria as rapidly as possible.

11 _____ Flies are flitting into and out of the pail.

4 _____ By the time it is your turn, the few things that are almost good are gone.

6 _____ There does not seem to be a free table anywhere.

3 _____ Unfortunately, there is a line in the cafeteria.

5 _____ The hoagies, coconut-custard pie, and iced tea have all disappeared.

7 _____ You hold your tray and look for a place to sit down.

2 _____ You have a class in a few minutes, and so you run in to grab something to eat quickly.

2 Organizing through Emphatic Order

Activity

Use emphatic order (order of importance) to arrange the following scrambled list of sentences. Write the number 1 beside the point that all the other sentences support. Then number each supporting sentence, starting with what seems to be the least important detail and ending with the most important detail.

_____ The people here are all around my age and seem to be genuinely friendly and interested in me.

_____ The place where I live has several important advantages.

_____ The schools in this neighborhood have a good reputation, so I feel that my daughter is getting a good education.

_____ The best thing of all about this area, though, is the school system.

_____ Therefore, I don't have to put up with public transportation or worry about how much it's going to cost to park each day.

_____ The school also has an extended day-care program, so I know my daughter is in good hands until I come home from work.

_____ First of all, I like the people who live in the other apartments near mine.

_____ Another positive aspect of this area is that it's close to where I work.

_____ That's more than I can say for the last place I lived, where people stayed behind locked doors.

_____ The office where I'm a receptionist is only a six-block walk from my house.

_____ In addition, I save a lot of wear and tear on my car.

3 Organizing through a Combination of Time Order and Emphatic Order

Activity

Use a combination of time and emphatic order to arrange the scrambled list of sentences below. Write the number 1 beside the point that all the other sentences support. Then number each supporting sentence. Paying close attention to transitional words and phrases will help you organize and connect the supporting sentences.

_____ I did not see the spider but visited my friend in the hospital, where he suffered through a week of nausea and dizziness because of the poison.

_____ We were listening to the radio when we discovered that nature was calling.

_____ As I got back into the car, I sensed, rather than felt or saw, a presence on my left hand.

_____ After my two experiences, I suspect that my fear of spiders will be with me until I die.

_____ The first experience was the time when my best friend received a bite from a black widow spider.

_____ I looked down at my hand, but I could not see anything because it was so dark.

_____ I had two experiences when I was sixteen that are the cause of my *arachnophobia,* a terrible and uncontrollable fear of spiders.

_____ We stopped the car at the side of the road, walked into the woods a few feet, and watered the leaves.

_____ My friend then entered the car, putting on the dashboard light, and I almost passed out with horror.

_____ I saw the bandage on his hand and the puffy swelling when the bandage was removed.

_____ Then it flew off my hand and into the dark bushes nearby.

_____ I sat in the car for an hour afterward, shaking and sweating and constantly rubbing the fingers of my hand to reassure myself that the spider was no longer there.

_____ But my more dramatic experience with spiders happened one evening when another friend and I were driving around in his car.

_____ Almost completely covering my fingers was a monstrous brown spider, with white stripes running down each of a seemingly endless number of long, furry legs.

_____ Most of all, I saw the ugly red scab on his hand and the yellow pus that continued oozing from under the scab for several weeks.

_____ I imagined my entire hand soon disappearing as the behemoth relentlessly devoured it.

_____   At the same time I cried out "Arghh!" and flicked my hand violently back and forth to shake off the spider.

_____   For a long, horrible second it clung stickily, as if intertwined for good among the fingers of my hand.

4 Identifying Transitions

Activity

Locate the major transitions used in the following two selections. Then write the transitions in the spaces provided. Mostly, you will find addition words such as *another* and *also*. You will also find several change-of-direction words such as *but* and *however.*

1.   **Watching TV Football**

Watching a football game on television may seem like the easiest thing in the world. However, like the game of football itself, watching a game correctly is far more complicated than it appears. First is the matter of the company. The ideal number of people depends on the size of your living room. Also, at least one of your companions should be rooting for the opposite team. There's nothing like a little rivalry to increase the enjoyment of a football game. Next, you must attend to the refreshments. Make sure to have on hand plenty of everyone's favorite drinks, along with the essential chips, dips, and pretzels. You may even want something more substantial on hand, like sandwiches or pizza. If you do, make everyone wait until the moment of kickoff before eating. Waiting will make everything taste much better. Finally, there is one last piece of equipment you should have on hand: a football. The purpose of this object is not to send lamps hurtling off tables or to smash the television screen, but to toss around—outside—during halftime. If your team happens to be getting trounced, you may decide not to wait until halftime.   —then

a. _____

b. _____

c. _____

d. _____

e. _____

f. _____

2.   **Avoidance Tactics**

　　　Sitting down to study for an exam or write a paper is hard, and so it is tempting for students to use one of the following five avoidance tactics in order to put the work aside. For one thing, students may say to themselves, "I can't do it." They adopt a defeatist attitude at the start and give up without a struggle. They could get help with their work by using such college services as tutoring programs and skills labs. However, they refuse even to try. A second avoidance technique is to say, "I'm too busy." Students may take on an extra job, become heavily involved in social activities, or allow family problems to become so time-consuming that they cannot concentrate on their studies. Yet if college really matters to a student, he or she will make sure that there is enough time to do the required work. Another avoidance technique is expressed by the phrase "I'm too tired." Typically, sleepiness occurs when it is time to study or go to class and then vanishes when the school pressure is off. This sleepiness is a sign of work avoidance. A fourth excuse is to say, "I'll do it later." Putting things off until the last minute is practically a guarantee of poor grades on tests and papers. When everything else seems more urgent than studying—watching TV, calling a friend, or even cleaning the oven—a student may simply be escaping academic work. Last, some students avoid work by saying to themselves, "I'm here and that's what counts." Such students live under the dangerous delusion that, since they possess a college ID, a parking sticker, and textbooks, the course work will somehow take care of itself. But once a student has a college ID in a pocket, he or she has only just begun. Doing the necessary studying, writing, and reading will bring real results: good grades, genuine learning, and a sense of accomplishment.

a. _____

b. _____

c. _____

d. _____

e. _____

f. _____

g. _____

h. _____

5 Providing Transitions

Activity

In the spaces provided, add logical transitions to tie together the sentences and ideas in the following paragraphs. Use the words in the boxes that precede each paragraph.

1.

however	a second	last of all
for one thing	also	on the other hand

Why School May Frighten a Young Child

Schools may be frightening to young children for a number of reasons.

_____, the regimented environment may be a new and disturbing experience. At home, children may have been able to do what

they wanted when they wanted to do it. In school, _____, they are given a set time for talking, working, playing, eating, and even

going to the toilet. _____ source of anxiety may be the public method of discipline that some teachers use. Whereas at home children are scolded in private, in school they may be held up to embarrassment and ridiculed in front of their peers. "Bonnie," the teacher may say, "why are you the only one in the class who didn't do your homework?" Or, "David, why are you the only one who can't work quietly at your seat?" Children

may _____ be frightened by the loss of personal attention. Their little discomforts or mishaps, such as tripping on the stairs, may bring instant sympathy from a parent; in school, there is often no one to notice, or the teacher is frequently too busy to care and just says, "Go do your

work. You'll be all right." _____, a child may be scared by the competitive environment of the school. At home, one hopes, such

competition for attention is minimal. In school, _____, children may vie for the teacher's approving glance or tone of voice, or for stars on a paper, or for favored seats in the front row. For these and other reasons, it is not surprising that children may have difficulty adjusting to school.

2.

as a result	once	finally
second	when	first of all
	but	

Joining a Multicultural Club

One of the best things I've done in college is to join a multicultural club.

_____, the club has helped me become friends with a diverse group of people. At any time in my apartment, I can have someone from Pakistan chatting about music to someone from Sweden, or someone from

Russia talking about politics to someone from Uganda. _____ I watched a Mexican student give tacos to three students from China.

They had never seen such a thing, but they liked it. A _____ benefit of the club is that it's helped me realize how similar people are.

_____ the whole club first assembled, we wound up having a conversation about dating and sex that included the perspectives of fifteen countries and six continents! It was clear we all shared the feeling that sex was fascinating. The talk lasted for hours, with many different persons describing the wildest or funniest experience they had had with the opposite sex. Only a few students, particularly those from the United States

and Japan, seemed bashful. _____, the club has reminded me about the dangers of stereotyping. Before I joined the club, my only direct experience with people from China was when I ordered meals in the local

Chinese restaurant. _____, I believed that most Chinese people

ate lots of rice and worked in restaurants. _____ in the club, I met Chinese people who were soccer players, English majors, and math teachers. I've also seen Jewish and Muslim students—people who I thought would never get along—drop their preconceived notions and become friends. Even more than my classes, the club has been an eye-opener for me.

6 Identifying Transitions and Other Connecting Words

Activity

This activity will give you practice in identifying transitions and other connecting words that are used to help tie ideas together.

Section A: Transitions   Locate the transitional word or words in each sentence and write them in the spaces provided.

1. I decided to pick up a drop-add form from the registrar's office. However, I changed my mind when I saw the long line of students waiting there.

   _____

2. In England, drivers use the left-hand side of the road. Consequently, steering wheels are on the right side.

   _____

3. Crawling babies will often investigate new objects by putting them in their mouths. Therefore, parents should be alert for any pins, tacks, or other dangerous items on floors and carpets.

   _____

4. One technique that advertisers use is to have a celebrity endorse a product. The consumer then associates the star qualities of the celebrity with the product.

   _____

Section B: Repeated Words   In the space provided, write the repeated words.

5. We absorb radiation from many sources in our environment. Our color television sets and microwave ovens, among other things, give off low-level radiation.

   _____

6. Many researchers believe that people have weight set-points their bodies try to maintain. This may explain why many dieters return to their original weight.

   _____

7. At the end of the rock concert, thousands of fans held up Bic lighters in the darkened area. The sea of lighters signaled that the fans wanted an encore.

   _____

8. Establishing credit is important for a woman. A good credit history is often necessary when she is applying for a loan or charge account.

   _____

Section C: Synonyms   In the space provided, write in the synonym for the underlined word.

9. I checked my car's tires, oil, water, and belts before the trip. But the ungrateful machine blew a gasket about fifty miles from home.

_____

10. Women's clothes, in general, use less material than men's clothes. Yet women's garments usually cost more than men's.

_____

11. The temperance movement in this country sought to ban alcohol. Drinking liquor, movement leaders said, led to violence, poverty, prostitution, and insanity.

_____

12. For me, apathy quickly sets in when the weather becomes hot and sticky. This listlessness disappears when the humidity decreases.

_____

Section D: Pronouns   In the space provided, write in the word referred to by the underlined pronoun.

13. At the turn of the century, bananas were still an oddity in the United States. Some people even attempted to eat them with the skins on.

_____

14. Canning vegetables is easy and economical. It can also be very dangerous.

_____

15. There are a number of signs that appear when students are under stress. For example, they start to have trouble studying, eating, and even sleeping.

_____

5 The Fourth Step in Writing

> **This chapter will show you how to**
>
> - revise so that your sentences flow smoothly and clearly
> - edit so that your sentences are error-free

Step 4: Write Clear, Error-Free Sentences

Up to now this book has emphasized the first three steps in writing an effective paragraph: unity, support, and coherence. This chapter will focus on the fourth goal of writing effectively: sentence skills. You'll learn how to revise a paragraph so that your sentences flow smoothly and clearly. Then you'll review how to edit a paragraph for mistakes in grammar, punctuation, and spelling.

Revising Sentences

The following strategies will help you to revise your sentences effectively.

- Use parallelism.
- Use a consistent point of view.
- Use specific words.
- Use concise words.
- Vary your sentences.

Use Parallelism

Words in a pair or a series should have a parallel structure. By balancing the items in a pair or a series so that they have the same kind of structure, you will make a sentence clearer and easier to read. Notice how the parallel sentences that follow read more smoothly than the nonparallel ones.

Nonparallel (Not Balanced)	Parallel (Balanced)
I resolved to lose weight, to study more, and *watching* less TV.	I resolved to lose weight, to study more, and to watch less TV. (A balanced series of *to* verbs: *to lose, to study, to watch*)
A consumer group rates my car as noisy, expensive, and *not having much safety.*	A consumer group rates my car as noisy, expensive, and unsafe. (A balanced series of descriptive words: *noisy, expensive, unsafe*)
Lola likes wearing soft sweaters, eating exotic foods, and *to bathe* in Calgon bath oil.	Lola likes wearing soft sweaters, eating exotic foods, and bathing in Calgon bath oil. (A balanced series of *-ing* words: *wearing, eating, bathing*)
Single life offers more freedom of choice; *more security is offered by marriage.*	Single life offers more freedom of choice; marriage offers more security. (Balanced verbs and word order: *single life offers . . . ; marriage offers . . .*)

You need not worry about balanced sentences when writing first drafts. But when you rewrite, you should try to put matching words and ideas into matching structures. Such parallelism will improve your writing style.

Activity

Cross out and revise the unbalanced part of each of the following sentences.

Example   When Gail doesn't have class, she uses her time to clean house, ~~getting~~ *to get* her laundry done, and to buy groceries.

1. Lola plans to become a model, a lawyer, or to go into nursing.

2. Filling out an income tax form is worse than wrestling a bear or to walk on hot coals.

3. The study-skills course taught me how to take more effective notes, to read a textbook chapter, and preparing for exams.

4. The video store has sections devoted to comedy films, dramatic films, and films made in foreign countries.

5. Martha Grencher likes to water her garden, walking her fox terrier, and arguing with her husband.

6. Filled with talent and ambitious, Eduardo plugged away at his sales job.

7. When I saw my roommate with my girlfriend, I felt worried, angry, and embarrassment as well.

8. Cindy's cat likes sleeping in the dryer, lying in the bathtub, and to chase squirrels.

9. The bacon was fatty, grease was on the potatoes, and the eggs were cold.

10. People in the lobby munched popcorn, sipped sodas, and were shuffling their feet impatiently.

Use a Consistent Point of View

Consistency with Verbs

Do not shift verb tenses unnecessarily. If you begin writing a paper in the present tense, don't shift suddenly to the past. If you begin in the past, don't shift without reason to the present. Notice the inconsistent verb tenses in the following example:

> The shoplifter *walked* quickly toward the front of the store. When a clerk *shouts* at him, he *started* to run.

The verbs must be consistently in the present tense:

> The shoplifter *walks* quickly toward the front of the store. When a clerk *shouts* at him, he *starts* to run.

Or the verbs must be consistently in the past tense:

> The shoplifter *walked* quickly toward the front of the store. When a clerk *shouted* at him, he *started* to run.

Activity

In each item, one verb must be changed so that it agrees in tense with the other verbs. Cross out the incorrect verb and write the correct form above each crossed-out verb.

Example   Kareem wanted to be someplace else when the dentist ~~carries~~ *carried* in a long needle.

1. I played my stereo and watched television before I decided to do some homework.

2. The hitchhiker stopped me as I ~~walks~~ *walked* from the turnpike rest station and said, "Are you on your way to San Jose?"

3. Some students attend all their classes in school and listen carefully during lectures, but they don't take notes. As a result, they often failed tests.

4. His parents stayed together for his sake; only after he graduates from college were they divorced.

5. In the movie, artillery shells exploded on the hide of the reptile monster. It just grinned, tosses off the shells, and kept eating people.

6. Several months a year, monarch butterflies come to live in a spot along the California coast. Thousands and thousands of them hang from the trees and fluttered through the air in large groups.

7. After waking up each morning, Harry stays in bed for a while. First he stretches and yawned loudly, and then he plans his day.

8. The salespeople at Biggs' Department Store are very helpful. When people asked for a product the store doesn't carry or is out of, the salesperson recommends another store.

9. Part-time workers at the company are the first to be laid off. They are also paid less, and they received no union representation.

10. Smashed cars, ambulances, and police cars blocked traffic on one side of the highway. On the other side, traffic slows down as drivers looked to see what happened.

Consistency with Pronouns

Pronouns should not shift point of view unnecessarily. When writing a paper, be consistent in your use of first-, second-, or third-person pronouns.

Type of Pronoun	Singular	Plural
First-person pronouns	I (my, mine, me)	we (our, us)
Second-person pronouns	you (your)	you (your)
Third-person pronouns	he (his, him) she (her) it (its)	they (their, them)

Note: Any person, place, or thing, as well as any indefinite pronoun like *one, anyone, someone,* and so on (page 477), is a third-person word.

For instance, if you start writing in the third person *she*, don't jump suddenly to the second person *you*. Or if you are writing in the first person *I*, don't shift unexpectedly to *one*. Look at the examples.

Inconsistent	*Consistent*
I enjoy movies like *The Return of the Vampire* that frighten *you*. (The most common mistake people make is to let *you* slip into their writing after they start with another pronoun.)	I enjoy movies like *The Return of the Vampire* that frighten me.
As soon as a person walks into Helen's apartment, *you* can tell that Helen owns a cat. (Again, *you* is a shift in point of view.)	As soon as a person walks into Helen's apartment, *he or she* can tell that Helen owns a cat. (See also the note on *his or her* references on pages 477–478.)

Activity

Cross out inconsistent pronouns in the following sentences, and write the correct form of the pronoun above each crossed-out word. You may have to change the form of the verb as well.

Example   My dreams are always the kind that haunt ~~you~~ *me* the next day.

1. Whenever we take our children on a trip, you have to remember to bring snacks, tissues, and toys.

2. In our society, we often need a diploma before you are hired for a job.

3. I discovered that videotapes don't do well if you leave them in a hot car.

4. If a student organizes time carefully, you can accomplish a great deal of work.

5. Although I know you should watch your cholesterol intake, I can never resist an ear of corn dripping with melted butter.

6. A good conversationalist has the ability to make the person he is talking to feel as if they are the only other person in the room.

7. We never go to the Salad Bowl anymore, because you wait so long to be seated and the waiters usually make mistakes with the order.

8. I'm careful about talking to people on the subway because one can get into some really weird situations.

9. We can't afford to move right now, because you need not only the first month's rent but also an extra month's security deposit.

10. In my job as store manager, I'm supposed to be nice to the customer even if they are being totally unreasonable.

Use Specific Words

To be an effective writer, you must use specific words rather than general words. Specific words create pictures in the reader's mind. They help capture interest and make your meaning clear. Compare the following sentences:

General	*Specific*
The boy came down the street.	Theo ran down Woodlawn Avenue.
A bird appeared on the grass.	A blue jay swooped down onto the frost-covered lawn.
She stopped the car.	Jackie slammed on the brakes of her Lincoln.

The specific sentences create clear pictures in our minds. The details *show* us exactly what has happened.

Here are four ways to make your sentences specific.

1   Use exact names.

She loves her *car*.
Renée loves her *Honda*.

2   Use lively verbs.

The garbage truck *went* down Front Street.
The garbage truck *rumbled* down Front Street.

3   Use descriptive words (modifiers) before nouns.

A girl peeked out the window.
A *chubby six-year-old* girl peeked out the *dirty kitchen* window.

4   Use words that relate to the five senses: sight, hearing, taste, smell, and touch.

That woman is a karate expert.
That *tiny, silver-haired* woman is a karate expert. (*Sight*)

When the dryer stopped, a signal sounded.
When the *whooshing* dryer stopped, a *loud buzzer* sounded. (*Hearing*)

Lola offered me an orange slice.
Lola offered me a *sweet, juicy* orange slice. (*Taste*)

The real estate agent opened the door of the closet.
The real estate agent opened the door of the *cedar-scented* closet. (*Smell*)

I pulled the blanket around me to fight off the wind.
I pulled the *scratchy* blanket around me to fight off the *chilling* wind. (*Touch*)

Activity 1

This activity will give you practice in replacing vague, indefinite words with sharp, specific words. Add three or more specific words to replace the general word or words underlined in each sentence. Make changes in the wording of a sentence as necessary.

Example   My bathroom cabinet contains <u>many drugs</u>.
My bathroom cabinet contains aspirin, antibiotics, tranquilizers, and

codeine cough medicine.

1. At the shopping center, we visited <u>several stores</u>.

   _____

   _____

2. Sunday is my day to take care of <u>chores</u>.

   _____

   _____

3. Lola enjoys <u>various activities</u> in her spare time.

   _____

   _____

4. I spent most of my afternoon <u>doing homework</u>.

   _____

   _____

5. We returned home from vacation to discover that <u>several pests</u> had invaded the house.

   _____

   _____

Activity 2

Again, you will practice changing vague, indefinite writing into lively, image-filled writing that helps capture the reader's interest and makes your meaning clear. With the help of the four methods described on page 103, add specific details to the sentences that follow. Note the examples.

Examples   The person got out of the car.
The elderly man painfully lifted himself out of the white Buick

station wagon.

The fans enjoyed the victory.
Many of the fifty thousand fans stood, waved banners, and cheered

wildly when Barnes scored the winning touchdown.

1. The lunch was not very good.

   _____

   _____

2. The animal ran away.

   _____

   _____

3. An accident occurred.

   _____

   _____

4. The instructor came into the room.

   _____

   _____

5. The machine did not work.

   _____

   _____

Use Concise Words

Wordiness—using more words than necessary to express a meaning—is often a sign of lazy or careless writing. Your readers may resent the extra time and energy they must spend when you have not done the work needed to make your writing direct and concise.

Here are examples of wordy sentences:

Anne is of the opinion that the death penalty should be allowed.

I would like to say that my subject in this paper will be the kind of generous person that my father was.

Omitting needless words improves the sentences:

Anne supports the death penalty.

My father was a generous person.

The following box lists some wordy expressions that could be reduced to single words.

Wordy Form	Short Form
a large number of	many
a period of a week	a week
arrive at an agreement	agree
at an earlier point in time	before
at the present time	now
big in size	big
owing to the fact that	because
during the time that	while
five in number	five
for the reason that	because
good benefit	benefit
in every instance	always
in my own opinion	I think
in the event that	if
in the near future	soon
in this day and age	today
is able to	can
large in size	large
plan ahead for the future	plan
postponed until later	postponed
red in color	red
return back	return

Activity

Rewrite the following sentences, omitting needless words.

1. After a lot of careful thinking, I have arrived at the conclusion that drunken drivers should receive jail terms.

   _____

   _____

2. The movie that I went to last night, which was fairly interesting, I must say, was enjoyed by me and my girlfriend.

   _____

   _____

3. Owing to inclement weather conditions of wind and rain, we have decided not to proceed with the athletic competition about to take place on the baseball diamond.

   _____

   _____

4. Without any question, there should be a law making it a requirement for parents of young children to buckle the children into car seats for safety.

   _____

   _____

5. Beyond a doubt, the only two things you can rely or depend on would be the fact that death comes to everyone and also that the government will tax your yearly income.

   _____

   _____

Vary Your Sentences

One aspect of effective writing is to vary the kinds of sentences you write. If every sentence follows the same pattern, writing may become monotonous to read. This chapter explains four ways you can create variety and interest in your writing style. The first two ways involve coordination and subordination—important techniques for achieving different kinds of emphasis in writing.

The following are four methods you can use to make your sentences more varied and more sophisticated:

1 Add a second complete thought (coordination)
2 Add a dependent thought (subordination)
3 Begin with a special opening word or phrase
4 Place adjectives or verbs in a series

Revise by Adding a Second Complete Thought

When you add a second complete thought to a simple sentence, the result is a *compound* (or double) sentence. The two complete statements in a compound sentence are usually connected by a comma plus a joining, or *coordinating,* word (*and, but, for, or, nor, so, yet).*

Use a compound sentence when you want to give equal weight to two closely related ideas. The technique of showing that ideas have equal importance is called *coordination.* Following are some compound sentences. Each contains two ideas that the writer regards as equal in importance.

> Bill has stopped smoking cigarettes, but he is now addicted to chewing gum.
>
> I repeatedly failed the math quizzes, so I decided to drop the course.
>
> Quincy turned all the lights off, and then he locked the office door.

Activity

Combine the following pairs of simple sentences into compound sentences. Use a comma and a logical joining word (*and, but, for, so*) to connect each pair.

Note: If you are not sure what *and, but, for,* and *so* mean, review pages 440–441.

Example   • The cars crept along slowly.
            • Visibility was poor in the heavy fog.
            The cars crept along slowly, for visibility was poor in the heavy fog.

_____

1. • Lee thought she would never master the computer. but
   • In two weeks she was using it comfortably.

_____

_____

2. • Vandals smashed the car's headlights.
   • They slashed the tires as well.

_____

_____

3. • I married at age seventeen.
   • I never got a chance to live on my own.

_____

_____

4. • Mold grew on my leather boots.
   • The closet was warm and humid.

   _____

   _____

5. • My father has a high cholesterol count.
   • He continues to eat red meat almost every day.

   _____

   _____

Revise by Adding a Dependent Thought

When you add a dependent thought to a simple sentence, the result is a complex sentence.* A dependent thought begins with a word or phrase like one of the following:

Dependent Words		
after	if, even if	when, whenever
although, though	in order that	where, wherever
as	since	whether
because	that, so that	which, whichever
before	unless	while
even though	until	who, whoever
how	what, whatever	whose

A *complex* sentence is used to emphasize one idea over another. Look at the following complex sentence:

Although I lowered the thermostat, my heating bill remained high.

---

*The two parts of a complex sentence are sometimes called an *independent clause* and a *dependent clause*. A *clause* is simply a word group that contains a subject and a verb. An independent clause expresses a complete thought and can stand alone. A dependent clause does not express a complete thought in itself and "depends on" the independent clause to complete its meaning. Dependent clauses always begin with a dependent, or subordinating, word.

The idea that the writer wants to emphasize here—*my heating bill remained high*—is expressed as a complete thought. The less important idea—*Although I lowered my thermostat*—is subordinated to this complete thought. The technique of giving one idea less emphasis than another is called *subordination*.

Following are other examples of complex sentences. In each case, the part starting with the dependent word is the less emphasized part of the sentence.

Even though I was tired, I stayed up to watch the horror movie.

Before I take a bath, I check for spiders in the tub.

When Vera feels nervous, she pulls on her earlobe.

Activity

Use logical subordinating words to combine the following pairs of simple sentences into sentences that contain a dependent thought. Place a comma after a dependent statement when it starts the sentence.

Example • Our team lost.
 • We were not invited to the tournament.
  Because our team lost, we were not invited to the tournament.

———————————————————————

1. • I receive my degree in June.
 • I will begin applying for jobs.

———————————————————————

———————————————————————

2. • Lola doesn't enjoy cooking.
 • She often eats at fast-food restaurants.

———————————————————————

———————————————————————

3. • I sent several letters of complaint.
 • The electric company never corrected my bill.

———————————————————————

———————————————————————

4. • Neil felt his car begin to skid.
 • He took his foot off the gas pedal.

———————————————————————

———————————————————————

5. • The final exam covered sixteen chapters.
    • The students complained.

_____

_____

Revise by Beginning with a Special Opening Word or Phrase

Among the special openers that can be used to start sentences are (1) *-ed* words, (2) *-ing* words, (3) *-ly* words, (4) *to* word groups, and (5) prepositional phrases. Here are examples of all five kinds of openers:

-ed *word*
Tired from a long day of work, Sharon fell asleep on the sofa.

-ing *word*
Using a thick towel, Mel dried his hair quickly.

-ly *word*
Reluctantly, I agreed to rewrite the paper.

to *word group*
To get to the church on time, you must leave now.

Prepositional phrase
With Fred's help, Martha planted the evergreen shrubs.

Activity

Combine the simple sentences into one sentence by using the opener shown at the left and omitting repeated words. Use a comma to set off the opener from the rest of the sentence.

Example   -ing word   • The toaster refused to pop up.
                        • It buzzed like an angry hornet.

Buzzing like an angry hornet, the toaster
refused to pop up.

-ed word   1. • Nate dreaded the coming holidays.

    • He was depressed by his recent divorce.

    _____

    _____

-ing word   2. • The star player glided down the court.

    • He dribbled the basketball like a pro.

    _____

    _____

-ly word   3. • I waited in the packed emergency room.

    • I was impatient.

    _____

    _____

to word   4. • The little boy likes to annoy his parents.
group
    • He pretends not to hear them.

    _____

    _____

Prepositional 5. • People must wear rubber-soled shoes.
phrase
    • They must do this in the gym.

    _____

    _____

Revise by Placing Adjectives or Verbs in a Series

Various parts of a sentence may be placed in a series. Among these parts are adjectives (descriptive words) and verbs. Here are examples of both in a series.

Adjectives

The *black, smeary* newsprint rubbed off on my *new butcher-block* table.

Verbs

The quarterback *fumbled* the ball, *recovered* it, and *sighed* with relief.

Activity

Combine the simple sentences in each group into one sentence by using adjectives or verbs in a series and by omitting repeated words. In most cases, use a comma between the adjectives or verbs in a series.

Example
- Before Christmas, I made fruitcakes.
- I decorated the house.
- I wrapped dozens of toys.

Before Christmas, I made fruitcakes, decorated the house, and wrapped dozens of toys.

1.
- My lumpy mattress was giving me a cramp in my neck.
- It was causing pains in my back.
- It was making me lose sleep.

_____

_____

2.
- Lights appeared in the fog.
- The lights were flashing.
- The lights were red.
- The fog was gray.
- The fog was soupy.

_____

_____

3.
- Before going to bed, I locked all the doors.
- I activated the burglar alarm.
- I slipped a kitchen knife under my mattress.

_____

_____

4.
- Lola picked sweater hairs off her coat.
- The hairs were fuzzy.
- The hairs were white.
- The coat was brown.
- The coat was suede.

_____

_____

5. • The contact lens fell onto the floor.
   • The contact lens was thin.
   • The contact lens was slippery.
   • The floor was dirty.
   • The floor was tiled.

_____

_____

Editing Sentences

After revising sentences in a paragraph so that they flow smoothly and clearly, you need to edit the paragraph for mistakes in grammar, punctuation, mechanics, usage, and spelling. Even if a paragraph is otherwise well-written, it will make an unfavorable impression on readers if it contains such mistakes. To edit a paragraph, check it against the agreed-upon rules or conventions of written English—simply called *sentence skills* in this book. Here are the most common of these conventions:

1   Write complete sentences rather than fragments.

2   Do not write run-ons.

3   Use verb forms correctly.

4   Make sure that subject, verbs, and pronouns agree.

5   Eliminate faulty modifiers.

6   Use pronoun forms correctly.

7   Use capital letters where needed.

8   Use the following marks of punctuation correctly: apostrophe, quotation marks, comma, semicolon, colon, hyphen, dash, parentheses.

9   Use correct manuscript form.

10   Eliminate slang, clichés, and pretentious words.

11   Check for possible spelling errors.

12   Eliminate careless errors.

These sentence skills are treated in detail in Part Five of this book, and they can be referred to easily as needed. Both the list of sentence skills on the inside front cover and the correction symbols on the inside back cover include page references so that you can turn quickly to any skill you want to check.

Editing Hints

Here are hints that can help you edit the next-to-final draft of a paper for sentence-skills mistakes:

1 Have at hand two essential tools: a good dictionary (see page 550) and a grammar handbook (you can use the one in this book on pages 411–518).

2 Use a sheet of paper to cover your paragraph so that you will expose only one sentence at a time. Look for errors in grammar, spelling, and typing. It may help to read each sentence out loud. If it does not read clearly and smoothly, chances are something is wrong.

3 Pay special attention to the kinds of errors you tend to make. For example, if you tend to write run-ons or fragments, be especially on the lookout for those errors.

4 Try to work on a typewritten or word-processed draft, where you'll be able to see your writing more objectively than you can on a handwritten page; use a pen with colored ink so that your corrections will stand out.

A Note on Proofreading

Proofreading means checking the final, edited draft of your paragraph closely for typos and other careless errors. A helpful strategy is to read your paper backward, from the last sentence to the first. This helps keep you from getting caught up in the flow of the paper and missing small mistakes. Here are six helpful proofing symbols:

Proofing Symbol	Meaning	Example
^	insert missing letter or word	beleve
ℛ	omit	in the the meantime
‿	reverse order of words or letters	once a upon time
#	add space	alltogether
⌣	close up space	foot ball
cap, lc	Add a capital (or a lowercase) letter	cap My persian Cat lc

If you make too many corrections, retype the page or enter corrections into your word processor file and reprint the page.

Activity

In the spaces at the bottom, write the numbers of the ten word groups that contain fragments or run-ons. Then, in the spaces between the lines, edit by making the necessary corrections. One is done for you as an example.

1 Two groups of researchers have concluded that "getting cold" has little to do with "catching a cold." 2 When the experiment was done for the first time. 3 Researchers exposed more than 400 people to the cold virus. 4 Then divided those people into three groups. 5 One group, wearing winter coats, sat around in 10-degree temperatures the second group was placed in 60 degree temperatures. 6 With the third group staying in a room. 7 Where it was 80 degrees. 8 The number of people who actually caught cold was the same. 9 In each group. 10 Other researchers repeated this experiment ten years later. 11 This time they kept some subjects cozy and warm they submerged others in a tank filled with water. 12 Whose temperature had been lowered to 75 degrees. 13 They made others sit around in their underwear in 40-degree temperatures. 14 The results were the same, the subjects got sick at the same rate. 15 Proving that people who get cold do not always get colds.

1. _____ 2. _____ 3. _____ 4. _____ 5. _____
6. _____ 7. _____ 8. _____ 9. _____ 10. _____

Note: A series of editing tests appears on pages 593–605. You will probably find it most helpful to take these tests after reviewing the sentence skills in Part Five.

Practice in Revising Sentences

You now know the fourth step in effective writing: revising and editing sentences. You also know that practice in *editing* sentences is best undertaken after you have worked through the sentence skills in Part Five. The focus in this closing section, then, will be on *revising* sentences—using a variety of methods to ensure that your sentences flow smoothly and are clear and interesting. You will work through the following series of review tests:

1 Using parallelism.
2 Using a consistent point of view.
3 Using specific words.
4 Using concise words.
5 Varying your sentences.

Using Parallelism

■ **Review Test 1**

Cross out the unbalanced part of each sentence. In the space provided, revise the unbalanced part so that it matches the other item or items in the sentence. The first one is done for you as an example.

1. Our professor warned us that he would give surprise tests, ~~the assignment of term papers~~, and allow no makeup exams.

   assign term papers _____

2. Making a big dinner is a lot more fun than to clean up after it.

   _____

3. The street-corner preacher stopped people walking by, was asking them questions, and handed them a pamphlet.

   _____

4. My teenage daughter enjoys shopping for new clothes, to try different cosmetics, and reading beauty magazines.

   _____

5. Fantastic special effects are part of the "Star Wars" movies, but dialogue that is believable is not.

   _____

6. While you're downtown, please pick up the dry cleaning, return the library books, and the car needs washing too.

   _____

7. I want a job that pays high wages, provides a complete benefits package, and offering opportunities for promotion.

   _____

8. As the elderly woman climbed the long staircase, she breathed hard and was grabbing the railing tightly.

   _____

9. I fell into bed at the end of the hard day, grateful for the sheets that were clean, soft pillow, and cozy blanket.

   _____

10. Ray's wide smile, clear blue eyes, and expressing himself earnestly all make him seem honest, even though he is not.

    _____

■ **Review Test 2**

Cross out the unbalanced part of each sentence. In the space provided, revise the unbalanced part so that it matches the other item or items in the sentence.

1. The neighborhood group asked the town council to repair the potholes and that a traffic light be installed.

   _____

2. Pesky mosquitoes, humidity that is high, and sweltering heat make summer an unpleasant time for me.

   _____

3. The afternoon mail brought advertisements that were unwanted, bills I couldn't pay, and magazines I didn't like.

   _____

4. Our house has a broken garage door, shutters that are peeling, and a crumbling chimney.

   _____

5. My car needed the brakes replaced, the front wheels aligned, and recharging of the battery.

   _____

6. I had to correct my paper for fragments, misplaced modifiers, and there were apostrophe mistakes.

   _____

7. We do not want to stay home during our vacation, but a trip is not something we can afford.

   _____

8. Stumbling out of bed, a cup of coffee that he drinks, and listening to the weather report make up Roy's early-morning routine.

   _____

9. Having a headache, my stomach being upset, and a bad case of sunburn did not put me in a good mood for the evening.

   _____

10. The Gray Panthers is an organization that not only aids older citizens but also providing information for their families.

   _____

Using a Consistent Point of View

■ **Review Test 1**

Change verbs as needed in the following passage so that they are consistently in the past tense. Cross out each incorrect verb and write the correct form above it, as shown in the example. You will need to make nine corrections.

Late one rainy night, Mei Ling woke to the sound of steady dripping. When she got out

splashed

of bed to investigate, a drop of cold water ~~splashes~~ onto her arm. She looks up just in time

to see another drop form on the ceiling, hang suspended for a moment, and fall to the

carpet. Stumbling to the kitchen, Mei Ling reaches deep into one of the cabinets and lifts

out a large roasting pan. As she did so, pot lids and baking tins clattered out and crash onto

the counter. Mei Ling ignored them, stumbled back to the bedroom, and places the pan on

the floor under the drip. But a minute after sliding her icy feet under the covers, Mei Ling

realized she is in trouble. The sound of each drop hitting the metal pan echoed like a

gunshot in the quiet room. Mei Ling feels like crying, but she finally thought of a solution.

She got out of bed and returns a minute later with a thick bath towel. She lined the pan with

the towel and crawls back into bed.

■ **Review Test 2**

Cross out the inconsistent pronouns in the following sentences and revise by writing the correct form of the pronoun above each crossed-out word.

$$I$$

Example   I dislike waitressing, for ~~you~~ can never count on a fair tip.

1. My kitchen is so narrow that one can't open the refrigerator without turning sidewise first.

2. Wanting relief from her headaches, Carla asked her doctor if acupuncture could really do you any good.

3. I love Jell-O because one can eat about five bowls of it and still not feel full.

4. As we entered the house, you could hear someone giggling in the hallway.

5. I hate going to the supermarket because you always have trouble finding a parking space there.

6. In this company, a worker can take a break only after a relief person comes to take your place.

7. Sometimes the Bradleys take the turnpike route, but it costs you five dollars in tolls.

8. As we sat in class waiting for the test results, you could feel the tension.

9. My brother doesn't get enough regular exercise, even though he knows exercise is good for you.

10. My favorite subject is abnormal psychology because the case studies make one seem so normal by comparison.

Using Specific Words

■ **Review Test 1**

Revise the following sentences, changing vague, indefinite words into sharp, specific ones.

1. When I woke up this morning, I had *several signs of a cold.*

   _____

   _____

2. Lin brought *lots of reading materials* to keep her busy in the hospital waiting room.

   _____

   _____

3. To succeed in school, a student must possess *certain qualities.*

   _____

   _____

4. The table at the wedding reception was full of *a variety of appetizers.*

   _____

   _____

5. As I grew older and less stupid, I realized that money cannot buy *certain things.*

   _____

   _____

■ **Review Test 2**

With the help of the methods described on page 103 and summarized below, add specific details to the sentences that follow.

1 Use exact names.

2 Use lively verbs.

3 Use descriptive words (modifiers) before nouns.

4 Use words that relate to the senses—sight, hearing, taste, smell, touch.

1. The crowd grew restless.

   _____

   _____

2. I relaxed.

   _____

   _____

3. The room was cluttered.

   _____

   _____

4. The child threw the object.

   _____

   _____

5. The driver was angry.

   _____

   _____

Using Concise Words

■ **Review Test 1**

Rewrite the following sentences, omitting needless words.

1. There was this one girl in my class who rarely if ever did her homework.

   _____

   _____

2. Judging by the looks of things, it seems to me that it will probably rain very soon.

   _____

   _____

3. Seeing as how the refrigerator is empty of food, I will go to the supermarket in the very near future.

   _____

   _____

4. In this day and age it is almost a certainty that someone you know will be an innocent victim of criminal activity.

   _____

   _____

5. In my personal opinion it is correct to say that the spring season is the most beautiful period of time in the year.

   _____

   _____

■ **Review Test 2**

Rewrite the following sentences, omitting needless words.

1. Workers who are on a part-time basis are attractive to a business because they do not have to be paid as much as full-time workers for a business.

   _____

   _____

2. During the time that I was sick and out of school, I missed a total of three math tests.

   _____

   _____

3. The game, which was scheduled for later today, has been canceled by the officials because of the rainy weather.

   _____

   _____

4. At this point in time, I am quite undecided and unsure about just which classes I will take during this coming semester.

   _____

   _____

5. An inconsiderate person located in the apartment next to mine keeps her radio on too loud a good deal of the time, with the result being that it is disturbing to everyone in the neighboring apartments.

   _____

   _____

Varying Your Sentences

■ **Review Test 1**

Using coordination or subordination or both, combine each of the following groups of simple sentences into one longer sentence. Omit repeated words. Various combinations are possible, so for each group, try to find the combination that flows most smoothly and clearly.

1. • My grandmother is eighty-six.
   • She drives to Florida alone every year.
   • She believes in being self-reliant.

   _____

   _____

2. • They left twenty minutes early for class.
   • They were late anyway.
   • The car overheated.

   _____

   _____

3. • John failed the midterm exam.
   • He studied harder for the final.
   • He passed it.

   _____

   _____

4. • A volcano erupts.
   • It sends tons of ash into the air.
   • This creates flaming orange sunsets.

   _____

   _____

5. • A telephone rings late at night.
   • We answer it fearfully.
   • It could bring tragic news.

   _____

   _____

■ **Review Test 2**

Using coordination or subordination or both, combine each of the following groups of simple sentences into two longer sentences. Omit repeated words. Various combinations are possible, so for each group, try to find the combination that flows most smoothly and clearly.

1. • Wendy pretended not to overhear her coworkers.
   • She couldn't stop listening.
   • She felt deeply embarrassed.
   • They were criticizing her work.

   _____

   _____

   _____

2. • Tony got home from the shopping mall.
   • He discovered that his rented tuxedo did not fit.
   • The jacket sleeves covered his hands.
   • The pants cuffs hung over his shoes.

   _____

   _____

   _____

3. • The boys waited for the bus.
   • The wind shook the flimsy shelter.
   • They shivered with cold.
   • They were wearing thin jackets.

   _____

   _____

   _____

4. • The engine almost started.
   • Then it died.
   • I realized no help would come.
   • I was on a lonely road.
   • It was very late.

   _____

   _____

   _____

5. • Gary was leaving the store.
   • The shoplifting alarm went off.
   • He had not stolen anything.
   • The clerk had forgotten to remove the magnetic tag.
   • The tag was on a shirt Gary had bought.

   _____

   _____

   _____

■ **Review Test 3**

Part A: Combine the simple sentences into one sentence by using the opener shown in the margin and omitting repeated words. Use a comma to set off the opener from the rest of the sentence.

-ed word

1. • We were exhausted from four hours of hiking.
   • We decided to stop for the day.

   _____

   _____

-ing word

2. • Gus was staring out the window.
   • He didn't hear the instructor call on him.

   _____

   _____

-ly word

3. • Nobody saw the thieves steal our bikes.
   • This was unfortunate.

   _____

   _____

to word
group

4. • Wayne rented a limousine for the night.
   • He wanted to make a good impression.

   _____

   _____

Prepositional
phrase

5. • Joanne goes online to visit her friends.
   • She does this during her lunch breaks.

   _____

   _____

Part B: Combine the simple sentences in each group into one sentence by using adjectives or verbs in a series and by omitting repeated words. In most cases, use a comma between the adjectives or verbs in a series.

6. The photographer waved a teddy bear at the baby.
   He made a funny face.
   He quacked like a duck.

   _____

   _____

7. The bucket held a bunch of daisies.
   The bucket was shiny.
   The bucket was aluminum.
   The daisies were fresh.
   The daisies were white.

   _____

   _____

8. Amy poured herself a cup of coffee.
   She pulled her hair back into a ponytail.
   She opened her textbook.
   She sat down at her desk.
   She fell asleep.

   _____

   _____

9. The box in the dresser drawer was stuffed with letters.
   The box was cardboard.
   The dresser drawer was locked.
   The letters were faded.
   The letters were about love.

   _____

   _____

10. The boy asked the girl to dance.
    The boy was short.
    The boy was self-confident.
    The girl was tall.
    The girl was shy.

    _____

    _____

6 Four Bases for Revising Writing

In the preceding chapters, you learned four essential steps in writing an effective paragraph. The box below shows how these steps lead to four standards, or bases, you can use in revising a paper.

Four Steps ⟶	*Four Bases*
1 If you make one point and stick to that point,	your writing will have *unity*.
2 If you back up the point with specific evidence,	your writing will have *support*.
3 If you organize and connect the specific evidence,	your writing will have *coherence*.
4 If you write clear, error-free sentences,	your writing will demonstrate effective *sentence skills*.

This chapter will discuss the four bases—unity, support, coherence, and sentence skills—and will show how these four bases can be used to evaluate and revise a paragraph.

Base 1: Unity

Understanding Unity

The following two paragraphs were written by students on the topic "Why Students Drop Out of College." Read them and decide which one makes its point more clearly and effectively, and why.

Paragraph A

Why Students Drop Out

Students drop out of college for many reasons. First of all, some students are bored in school. These students may enter college expecting nonstop fun or a series of fascinating courses. When they find out that college is often routine, they quickly lose interest. They do not want to take dull required courses or spend their nights studying, and so they drop out. Students also drop out of college because the work is harder than they thought it would be. These students may have made decent grades in high school simply by showing up for class. In college, however, they may have to prepare for two-hour exams, write fifteen-page term papers, or make detailed presentations to a class. The hard work comes as a shock, and students give up. Perhaps the most common reason students drop out is that they are having personal or emotional problems. Younger students, especially, may be attending college at an age when they are also feeling confused, lonely, or depressed. These students may have problems with roommates, family, boyfriends, or girlfriends. They become too unhappy to deal with both hard academic work and emotional troubles. For many types of students, dropping out seems to be the only solution they can imagine.

Paragraph B

Student Dropouts

There are three main reasons students drop out of college. Some students, for one thing, are not really sure they want to be in school and lack the desire to do the work. When exams come up, or when a course requires a difficult project or term paper, these students will not do the required studying or research. Eventually, they may drop out because their grades are so poor they are about to flunk out anyway. Such students sometimes come back to school later with a completely different attitude about school. Other students drop out for financial reasons. The pressures of paying tuition, buying textbooks, and possibly having to support themselves can be overwhelming. These students can often be helped by the school because financial aid is available, and some schools offer work-study programs. Finally, students drop out because they have personal problems. They cannot concentrate on their courses because they are unhappy at home, they are lonely, or they are having trouble with boyfriends or girlfriends. Instructors should suggest that such troubled students see counselors or join support groups. If instructors would take a more personal interest in their students, more students would make it through troubled times.

Activity

Fill in the blanks: Paragraph _____ makes its point more clearly and effectively

because _____

_____

_____

Comment: Paragraph A is more effective because it is *unified.* All the details in paragraph A are *on target;* they support and develop the single point expressed in the first sentence—that there are many reasons students drop out of college.

On the other hand, paragraph B contains some details irrelevant to the opening point—that there are three main reasons students drop out. These details should be omitted in the interest of paragraph unity. Go back to paragraph B and cross out the sections that are off target—the sections that do not support the opening idea.

You should have crossed out the following sections: "Such students sometimes . . . attitude about school"; "These students can often . . . work-study programs"; and "Instructors should suggest . . . through troubled times."

The difference between these two paragraphs leads us to the first base, or standard, of effective writing: *unity.* To achieve unity is to have all the details in your paper related to the single point expressed in the topic sentence, the first sentence. Each time you think of something to put in, ask yourself whether it relates to your main point. If if does not, leave it out. For example, if you were writing about a certain job as the worst job you ever had and then spent a couple of sentences talking about the interesting people that you met there, you would be missing the first and most essential base of good writing.

Checking for Unity

To check a paper for unity, ask yourself these questions:

1 Is there a clear opening statement of the point of the paper?

2 Is all the material on target in support of the opening point?

Base 2: Support

Understanding Support

The following student paragraphs were written on the topic "A Quality of Some Person You Know." Both are unified, but one communicates more clearly and effectively. Which one, and why?

Paragraph A

My Quick-Tempered Father

My father is easily angered by normal everyday mistakes. One day my father told me to wash the car and cut the grass. I did not hear exactly what he said, and so I asked him to repeat it. Then he went into a hysterical mood and shouted, "Can't you hear?" Another time he asked my mother to go to the store and buy groceries with a fifty-dollar bill, and he told her to spend no more than twenty dollars. She spent twenty-two dollars. As soon as he found out, he immediately took the change from her and told her not to go anywhere else for him; he did not speak to her the rest of the day. My father even gives my older brothers a hard time with his irritable moods. One day he told them to be home from their dates by midnight; they came home at 12:15. He informed them that they were grounded for three weeks. To my father, making a simple mistake is like committing a crime.

Paragraph B

My Generous Grandfather

My grandfather is the most generous person I know. He gave up a life of his own in order to give his children everything they wanted. Not only did he give up many years of his life to raise his children properly, but he is now sacrificing many more years to his grandchildren. His generosity is also evident in his relationship with his neighbors, his friends, and the members of his church. He has been responsible for many good deeds and has always been there to help all the people around him in times of trouble. Everyone knows that he will gladly lend a helping hand. He is so generous that you almost have to feel sorry for him. If one day he suddenly became selfish, it would be earthshaking. That's my grandfather.

Activity

Fill in the blanks: Paragraph _____ makes its point more clearly and effectively because _____

_____

_____

Comment: Paragraph A is more effective, for it offers specific examples that show us the father in action. We see for ourselves why the writer describes the father as quick-tempered.

Paragraph B, on the other hand, gives us no specific evidence. The writer of paragraph B tells us repeatedly that the grandfather is generous but never shows us examples of that generosity. Just how, for instance, did the grandfather sacrifice his life for his children and grandchildren? Did he hold two jobs so that his son could go to college, or so that his daughter could have her own car? Does he give up time with his wife and friends to travel every day to his daughter's house to baby-sit, go to the store, and help with the dishes? Does he wear threadbare suits and coats and eat Hamburger Helper and other inexpensive meals (with no desserts) so that he can give money to his children and toys to his grandchildren? We want to see and judge for ourselves whether the writer is making a valid point about the grandfather, but without specific details we cannot do so. In fact, we have almost no picture of him at all.

Consideration of these two paragraphs leads us to the second base of effective writing: *support.* After realizing the importance of specific supporting details, one student writer revised a paper she had done on a restaurant job as the worst job she ever had. In the revised paper, instead of talking about "unsanitary conditions in the kitchen," she referred to such specifics as "green mold on the bacon" and "ants in the potato salad." All your papers should include many vivid details!

Checking for Support

To check a paper for support, ask yourself these questions:

1 Is there *specific* evidence to support the opening point?

2 Is there *enough* specific evidence?

Base 3: Coherence

Understanding Coherence

The following two paragraphs were written on the topic "The Best or Worst Job You Ever Had." Both are unified and both are supported. However, one communicates more clearly and effectively. Which one, and why?

Paragraph A

Pantry Helper

My worst job was as a pantry helper in one of San Diego's well-known restaurants. I had an assistant from three to six in the afternoon who did little but stand around and eat the whole time she was there. She would listen for the sound of the back door opening, which was a sure sign the boss was coming in. The boss would testily say to me, "You've got a lot of things to do here, Alice. Try to get a move on." I would come in at two o'clock to relieve the woman on the morning shift. If her day was busy, that meant I would have to prepare salads, slice meat and cheese, and so on. Orders for sandwiches and cold platters would come in and have to be prepared. The worst thing about the job was that the heat in the kitchen, combined with my nerves, would give me an upset stomach by seven o'clock almost every night. I might be going to the storeroom to get some supplies, and one of the waitresses would tell me she wanted a bacon, lettuce, and tomato sandwich on white toast. I would put the toast in and head for the supply room, and a waitress would holler out that her customer was in a hurry. Green flies would come in through the torn screen in the kitchen window and sting me. I was getting paid only $3.60 an hour. At five o'clock, when the dinner rush began, I would be dead tired. Roaches scurried in all directions whenever I moved a box or picked up a head of lettuce to cut.

Paragraph B

My Worst Job

The worst job I ever had was as a waiter at the Westside Inn. First of all, many of the people I waited on were rude. When a baked potato was hard inside or a salad was flat or their steak wasn't just the way they wanted it, they blamed me, rather than the kitchen. Or they would ask me to light their cigarettes, or chase flies from their tables, or even take their children to the bathroom. Also, I had to contend not only with the customers but with the kitchen staff as well. The cooks and busboys were often undependable and surly. If I didn't treat them just right, I would wind up having to apologize to customers because their meals came late or their water glasses weren't filled. Another reason I didn't like the job was that I was always moving. Because of the constant line at the door, as soon as one group left, another would take its place. I usually had only a twenty-minute lunch break and a ten-minute break in almost nine hours of work. I think I could have put up with the job if I had been able to pause and rest more often. The last and most important reason I hated the job was my boss. She played favorites, giving some of the waiters and waitresses the best-tipping repeat customers and preferences on holidays. She would hover around during my break to make sure I didn't take a second more than the allotted time. And even when I helped out by working through a break, she never had an appreciative word but would just tell me not to be late for work the next day.

Activity

Fill in the blanks: Paragraph _____ makes its point more clearly and effectively because _____

_____

_____

Comment: Paragraph B is more effective because the material is organized clearly and logically. Using emphatic order, the writer gives us a list of four reasons why the job was so bad: rude customers, unreliable kitchen staff, constant motion, and—most of all—an unfair boss. Further, the writer includes transitional words that act as signposts, making movement from one idea to the next easy to follow. The major transitions are *First of all, Also, Another reason,* and *The last and most important reason.*

While paragraph A is unified and supported, the writer does not have any clear and consistent way of organizing the material. Partly, emphatic order is used, but this is not made clear by transitions or by saving the most important reason for last. Partly, time order is used, but it moves inconsistently from two to seven to five o'clock.

These two paragraphs lead us to the third base of effective writing: *coherence.* The supporting ideas and sentences in a composition must be organized so that they cohere, or "stick together." As has already been mentioned, key techniques for tying material together are a clear method of organization (such as time order or emphatic order), transitions, and other connecting words.

Checking for Coherence

To check a paper for coherence, ask yourself these questions:

1 Does the paper have a clear method of organization?

2 Are transitions and other connecting words used to tie the material together?

Base 4: Sentence Skills

Understanding Sentence Skills

Two versions of a paragraph are given below. Both are unified, supported, and organized, but one version communicates more clearly and effectively. Which one, and why?

Paragraph A

Falling Asleep Anywhere

1There are times when people are so tired that they fall asleep almost anywhere. 2For example, there is a lot of sleeping on the bus or train on the way home from work in the evenings. 3A man will be reading the newspaper, and seconds later it appears as if he is trying to eat it. 4Or he will fall asleep on the shoulder of the stranger sitting next to him. 5Another place where unplanned naps go on is the lecture hall. 6In some classes, a student will start snoring so loudly that the professor has to ask another student to shake the sleeper awake. 7A more embarrassing situation occurs when a student leans on one elbow and starts drifting off to sleep. 8The weight of the head pushes the elbow off the desk, and this momentum carries the rest of the body along. 9The student wakes up on the floor with no memory of getting there. 10The worst place to fall asleep is at the wheel of a car. 11Police reports are full of accidents that occur when people lose consciousness and go off the road. 12If the drivers are lucky, they are not seriously hurt. 13One woman's car, for instance, went into a river. 14She woke up in four feet of water and thought it was raining. 15When people are really tired, nothing will stop them from falling asleep—no matter where they are.

Paragraph B

"Falling Asleep Anywhere"

1There are times when people are so tired that they fall asleep almost anywhere. 2For example, on the bus or train on the way home from work. 3A man will be reading the newspaper, seconds later it appears as if he is trying to eat it. 4Or he will fall asleep on the shoulder of the stranger sitting next to him. 5Another place where unplanned naps go on are in the lecture hall. 6In some classes, a student will start snoring so loudly that the professor has to ask another student to shake the sleeper awake. 7A more embarrassing situation occurs when a student leans on one elbow and starting to drift off to sleep. 8The weight of the head push the elbow off the desk, and this momentum carries the rest of the body along. ⁹The student wakes up on the floor with no memory of getting there. ¹⁰The worst time to fall asleep is when driving a car. ¹¹Police reports are full of accidents that occur when people conk out and go off the road. ¹²If the drivers are lucky they are not seriously hurt. ¹³One womans car, for instance, went into a river. ¹⁴She woke up in four feet of water. ¹⁵And thought it was raining. ¹⁶When people are really tired, nothing will stop them from falling asleep— no matter where they are.

Activity 1

Fill in the blanks: Paragraph _____ makes its point more clearly and effectively because _____

_____

_____

Comment: Paragraph A is more effective because it incorporates *sentence skills,* the fourth base of competent writing.

Activity 2

See if you can identify the ten sentence-skills mistakes in paragraph B. Do this, first of all, by going back and underlining the ten spots in paragraph B that differ in wording or punctuation from paragraph A. Then try to identify the ten sentence-skills mistakes by circling what you feel is the correct answer in each of the ten statements below.

Note: Comparing paragraph B with the correct version may help you guess correct answers even if you are not familiar with the names of certain skills.

1. The title should not be set off with
   a. capital letters.
   b. quotation marks.

2. In word group 2, there is a
   a. missing comma.
   b. missing apostrophe.
   c. sentence fragment.
   d. dangling modifier.

3. In word group 3, there is a
   a. run-on.
   b. sentence fragment.
   c. mistake in subject-verb agreement.
   d. mistake involving an irregular verb.

4. In word group 5, there is a
   a. sentence fragment.
   b. spelling error.
   c. run-on.
   d. mistake in subject-verb
      agreement.

5. In word group 7, there is a
   a. misplaced modifier.
   b. dangling modifier.
   c. mistake in parallelism.
   d. run-on.

6. In word group 8, there is a
   a. nonstandard English verb.
   b. run-on.
   c. comma mistake.
   d. missing capital letter.

7. In word group 11, there is a
   a. mistake involving an
      irregular verb.
   b. sentence fragment.
   c. slang phrase.
   d. mistake in subject-verb
      agreement.

8. In word group 12, there is a
   a. missing apostrophe.
   b. missing comma.
   c. mistake involving an
      irregular verb.
   d. sentence fragment.

9. In word group 13, there is a
   a. mistake in parallelism.
   b. mistake involving an
      irregular verb.
   c. missing apostrophe.
   d. missing capital letter.

10. In word group 15, there is a
    a. missing quotation mark.
    b. mistake involving an
       irregular verb.
    c. sentence fragment.
    d. mistake in pronoun
       point of view.

Comment: You should have chosen the following answers:

1. b   2. c   3. a   4. d   5. c
6. a   7. c   8. b   9. c   10. c

Part Five of this book explains these and other sentence skills. You should review all the skills carefully. Doing so will ensure that you know the most important rules of grammar, punctuation, and usage—rules needed to write clear, error-free sentences.

Checking for Sentence Skills

Sentence skills and the other bases of effective writing are summarized in the following chart and on the inside front cover of the book.

A Summary of the Four Bases of Effective Writing

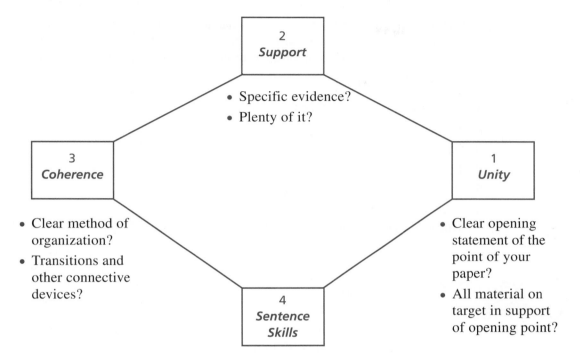

- Fragments eliminated? (page 419)
- Run-ons eliminated? (435)
- Correct verb forms? (450)
- Subject and verb agreement? (468)
- Faulty parallelism and faulty modifiers eliminated? (97, 493, 497)
- Faulty pronouns eliminated? (475, 482)
- Capital letters used correctly? (507)
- Punctuation marks where needed?
  - (a) Apostrophe (519)
  - (b) Quotation marks (528)
  - (c) Comma (535)
  - (d) Semicolon; colon (546–547)
  - (e) Hyphen; dash (547–548)
  - (f) Parentheses (549)
- Correct paper format? (502)
- Needless words eliminated? (105)
- Effective word choices? (579)
- Possible spelling errors checked? (559)
- Careless errors eliminated through proofreading? (114–116, 166, 593)
- Sentences varied? (107)

Practice in Using the Four Bases

You are now familiar with four bases, or standards, of effective writing: unity, support, coherence, and sentence skills. In this closing section, you will expand and strengthen your understanding of the four bases as you work through the following activities:

1 Evaluating Scratch Outlines for Unity

2 Evaluating Paragraphs for Unity

3 Evaluating Paragraphs for Support

4 Evaluating Paragraphs for Coherence

5 Revising Paragraphs for Coherence

6 Evaluating Paragraphs for All Four Bases:
Unity, Support, Coherence, and Sentence Skills

1 Evaluating Scratch Outlines for Unity

The best time to check a paper for unity is at the outline stage. A scratch outline, as explained on page 23, is one of the best techniques for getting started with a paper.

Look at the following scratch outline that one student prepared and then corrected for unity:

I had a depressing weekend.

1. Hay fever bothered me
2. Had to pay seventy-seven-dollar car bill
3. ~~Felt bad~~
4. Boyfriend and I had a fight
5. ~~Did poorly in my math test today as a result~~
6. My mother yelled at me unfairly

Four reasons support the opening statement that the writer was depressed over the weekend. The writer crossed out "Felt bad" because it was not a reason for her depression. (Saying that she felt bad is only another way of saying that she was depressed.) She also crossed out the item about the math test because the point she is supporting is that she was depressed over the weekend.

Activity

In each outline, cross out the items that do not support the opening point. These items must be omitted in order to achieve paragraph unity.

1. The cost of raising a child keeps increasing.
   a. School taxes get higher every year.
   b. A pair of children's sneakers now costs over $100.
   c. Overpopulation is a worldwide problem.
   d. Providing nutritious food is more costly because of inflated prices.
   e. Children should work at age sixteen.

2. My father's compulsive gambling hurt our family life.
   a. We were always short of money for bills.
   b. Luckily, my father didn't drink.
   c. My father ignored his children to spend time at the racetrack.
   d. Gamblers' Anonymous can help compulsive gamblers.
   e. My mother and father argued constantly.

3. There are several ways to get better mileage in your car.
   a. Check air pressure in tires regularly.
   b. Drive at no more than fifty-five miles per hour.
   c. Orange and yellow cars are the most visible.
   d. Avoid jackrabbit starts at stop signs and traffic lights.
   e. Always have duplicate ignition and trunk keys.

4. My swimming instructor helped me overcome my terror of the water.
   a. He talked with me about my fears.
   b. I was never good at sports.
   c. He showed me how to hold my head under water and not panic.
   d. I held on to a floating board until I was confident enough to give it up.
   e. My instructor was on the swimming team at his college.

5. Fred Wilkes is the best candidate for state governor.
   a. He has fifteen years' experience in the state senate.
   b. His son is a professional football player.
   c. He has helped stop air and water pollution in the state.
   d. His opponent has been divorced.
   e. He has brought new industries and jobs to the state.

2 Evaluating Paragraphs for Unity

Activity

Each of the following five paragraphs contains sentences that are off target—sentences that do not support the opening point—and so the paragraphs are not unified. In the interest of paragraph unity, such sentences must be omitted.

Cross out the irrelevant sentences and write the numbers of those sentences in the spaces provided. The number of spaces will tell you the number of irrelevant sentences in each paragraph.

1.
A Kindergarten Failure

¹In kindergarten I experienced the fear of failure that haunts many schoolchildren. ²My moment of panic occurred on my last day in kindergarten at Charles Foos Public School in Riverside, California. ³My family lived in California for three years before we moved to Omaha, Nebraska, where my father was a personnel manager for Mutual of Omaha. ⁴Our teacher began reading a list of names of all those students who were to line up at the door in order to visit the first-grade classroom. ⁵Our teacher was a pleasant-faced woman who had resumed her career after raising her own children. ⁶She called off every name but mine, and I was left sitting alone in the class while everyone else left, the teacher included. ⁷I sat there in absolute horror. ⁸I imagined that I was the first kid in human history who had flunked things like crayons, sandbox, and sliding board. ⁹Without getting the teacher's permission, I got up and walked to the bathroom and threw up into a sink. ¹⁰Only when I ran home in tears to my mother did I get an explanation of what had happened. ¹¹Since I was to go to a parochial school in the fall, I had not been taken with the other children to meet the first-grade teacher at the public school. ¹²My moment of terror and shame had been only a misunderstanding.

The numbers of the irrelevant sentences: _____   _____

2.
How to Prevent Cheating

¹Instructors should take steps to prevent students from cheating on exams. ²To begin with, instructors should stop reusing old tests. ³A test that has been used even once is soon known on the student grapevine. ⁴Students will check with their friends to find out, for example, what was on Dr. Thompson's biology final last term. ⁵They may even manage to find

a copy of the test itself, "accidentally" not turned in by a former student of Dr. Thompson's. 6 Instructors should also take some commonsense precautions at test time. 7 They should make students separate themselves— by at least one seat—during an exam, and they should watch the class closely. 8 The best place for the instructor to sit is in the rear of the room, so that a student is never sure if the instructor is looking at him or her. 9 Last of all, instructors must make it clear to students that there will be stiff penalties for cheating. 10 One of the problems with our school systems is a lack of discipline. 11 Instructors never used to give in to students' demands or put up with bad behavior, as they do today. 12 Anyone caught cheating should immediately receive a zero for the exam. 13 A person even suspected of cheating should be forced to take an alternative exam in the instructor's office. 14 Because cheating is unfair to honest students, it should not be tolerated.

The numbers of the irrelevant sentences: _____ _____

3.   **Other Uses for Cars**

1 Many people who own a car manage to turn the vehicle into a trash can, a clothes closet, or a storage room. 2 People who use their cars as trash cans are easily recognized. 3 Empty snack bags, hamburger wrappers, pizza cartons, soda cans, and doughnut boxes litter the floor. 4 On the seats are old cassette tapes with their innards hanging out, blackened fruit skins, crumpled receipts, crushed cigarette packs, and used tissues. 5 At least the trash stays in the car, instead of adding to the litter on our highways. 6 Other people use a car as a clothes closet. 7 The car contains several pairs of shoes, pants, or shorts, along with a suit or dress that's been hanging on the car's clothes hanger for over a year. 8 Sweaty, smelly gym clothes will also find a place in the car, a fact passengers quickly discover. 9 The world would be better off if people showed more consideration of others. 10 Finally, some people use a car as a spare garage or basement. 11 In the backseats or trunks of these cars are bags of fertilizer, beach chairs, old textbooks, chainsaws, or window screens that have been there for months. 12 The trunk may also contain an extra spare tire, a dented hubcap, a gallon container of window washer fluid, and old stereo equipment. 13 If apartments offered more storage space, probably fewer people would resort to using their cars for such storage purposes. 14 All in all, people get a lot more use out of their cars than simply the miles they travel on the road.

The numbers of the irrelevant sentences: _____ _____ _____

4.   **Why Adults Visit Amusement Parks**

¹Adults visit amusement parks for several reasons. ²For one thing, an amusement park is a place where it is acceptable to "pig out" on junk food. ³At the park, everyone is drinking soda and eating popcorn, ice cream, or hot dogs. ⁴No one seems to be on a diet, and so buying all the junk food you can eat is a guilt-free experience. ⁵Parks should provide stands where healthier food, such as salads or cold chicken, would be sold. ⁶Another reason people visit amusement parks is to prove themselves. ⁷They want to visit the park that has the newest, scariest ride in order to say that they went on the Parachute Drop, the seven-story Elevator, the Water Chute, or the Death Slide. ⁸Going on a scary ride is a way to feel courageous and adventurous without taking much of a risk. ⁹Some rides, however, can be dangerous. ¹⁰Rides that are not properly inspected or maintained have killed people all over the country. ¹¹A final reason people visit amusement parks is to escape from everyday pressures. ¹² When people are poised at the top of a gigantic roller coaster, they are not thinking of bills, work, or personal problems. ¹³A scary ride empties the mind of all worries—except making it to the bottom alive. ¹⁴Adults at an amusement park may claim they have come for their children, but they are there for themselves as well.

The numbers of the irrelevant sentences: _____   _____   _____

5.   **A Dangerous Cook**

¹When my friend Tom sets to work in the kitchen, disaster often results. ²Once he tried to make toasted cheese sandwiches for us by putting slices of cheese in the toaster along with the bread; he ruined the toaster. ³Unfortunately, the toaster was a fairly new one that I had just bought for him three weeks before, on his birthday. ⁴On another occasion, he had cut up some fresh beans and put them in a pot to steam. ⁵I was really looking forward to the beans, for I eat nothing but canned vegetables in my dormitory. ⁶I, frankly, am not much of a cook either. ⁷The water in the Teflon pan steamed away while Tom was on the telephone, and both the beans and the Teflon coating in the pan were ruined. ⁸Finally, another time Tom made spaghetti for us, and the noodles stuck so tightly together that we had to cut off slices with a knife and fork. ⁹In addition, the meatballs were burned on the outside but almost raw inside. ¹⁰The tomato sauce, on the other hand, turned out well. ¹¹For some reason, Tom is very good at making meat and vegetable sauces. ¹²Because of Tom's kitchen mishaps, I never eat at his place without an Alka-Seltzer in my pocket, or without money in case we have to go out to eat.

The numbers of the irrelevant sentences: _____   _____   _____

_____   _____

3 Evaluating Paragraphs for Support

Activity

The five paragraphs that follow lack sufficient supporting details. In each paragraph, identify the spot or spots where more specific details are needed.

1.
Chicken: Our Best Friend

¹Chicken is the best-selling meat today for a number of good reasons. ²First of all, its reasonable cost puts it within everyone's reach. ³Chicken is popular, too, because it can be prepared in so many different ways. ⁴It can, for example, be cooked by itself, in spaghetti sauce, or with noodles and gravy. ⁵It can be baked, boiled, broiled, or fried. ⁶Chicken is also convenient. ⁷Last and most important, chicken has a high nutritional value. ⁸Four ounces of chicken contain twenty-eight grams of protein, which is almost half the recommended daily dietary allowance.

Fill in the blanks: The first spot where supporting details are needed occurs after sentence number _____. The second spot occurs after sentence number _____

2.
A Car Accident

¹I was on my way home from work when my terrible car accident took place. ²As I drove my car around the curve of the expressway exit, I saw a number of cars ahead of me, backed up because of a red light at the main road. ³I slowly came to a stop behind a dozen or more cars. ⁴In my rearview mirror, I then noticed a car coming up behind me that did not slow down or stop. ⁵I had a horrible, helpless feeling as I realized the car would hit me. ⁶I knew there was nothing I could do to signal the driver in time, nor was there any way I could get away from the car. ⁷Minutes after the collision, I picked up my glasses, which were on the seat beside me. ⁸My lip was bleeding, and I got out a tissue to wipe it. ⁹The police arrived quickly, along with an ambulance for the driver of the car that hit me. ¹⁰My car was so damaged that it had to be towed away. ¹¹Today, eight years after the accident, I still relive the details of the experience whenever a car gets too close behind me.

Fill in the blank: The point where details are needed occurs after sentence number _____.

3.   **Tips on Bringing Up Children**

¹In some ways, children should be treated as mature people. ²For one thing, adults should not use baby talk with children. ³Using real words with children helps them develop language skills more quickly. ⁴Baby talk makes children feel patronized, frustrated, and confused, for they want to understand and communicate with adults by learning their speech. ⁵So animals should be called cows and dogs, not "moo-moos" and "bow-wows." ⁶Second, parents should be consistent when disciplining children. ⁷For example, if a parent tells a child, "You cannot have dessert unless you put away your toys," it is important that the parent follow through on the warning. ⁸By being consistent, parents will teach children responsibility and give them a stable center around which to grow. ⁹Finally, and most important, children should be allowed and encouraged to make simple decisions. ¹⁰Parents will thus be helping their children prepare for the complex decisions that they will have to deal with in later life.

Fill in the blank: The spot where supporting details are needed occurs after sentence number _____.

4.   **Being on TV**

¹People act a little strangely when a television camera comes their way. ²Some people behave as if a crazy puppeteer were pulling their strings. ³Their arms jerk wildly about, and they begin jumping up and down for no apparent reason. ⁴Often they accompany their body movements with loud screams, squeals, and yelps. ⁵Another group of people engage in an activity known as the cover-up. ⁶They will be calmly watching a sports game or other televised event when they realize the camera is focused on them. ⁷The camera operator can't resist zooming in for a close-up of these people. ⁸Then there are those who practice their funny faces on the unsuspecting public. ⁹They take advantage of the television time to show off their talents, hoping to get that big break that will carry them to stardom. ¹⁰Finally, there are those who pretend they are above reacting for the camera. ¹¹They wipe an expression from their faces and appear to be interested in something else. ¹²Yet if the camera stays on them long enough, they will slyly check to see if they are still being watched. ¹³Everybody's behavior seems to be slightly strange in front of a TV camera.

Fill in the blanks: The first spot where supporting details are needed occurs after sentence number _____. The second spot occurs after sentence number _____.

5. **Culture Conflict**

¹I am in a constant tug-of-war with my parents over conflicts between their Vietnamese culture and American culture. ²To begin with, my parents do not like me to have American friends. ³They think that I should spend all my time with other Vietnamese people and speak English only when necessary. ⁴I get into an argument whenever I want to go to a fast-food restaurant or a movie at night with my American friends. ⁵The conflict with my parents is even worse when it comes to plans for a career. ⁶My parents want me to get a degree in science and then go on to medical school. ⁷On the other hand, I think I want to become a teacher. ⁸So far I have been taking both science and education courses, but soon I will have to concentrate on one or the other. ⁹The other night my father made his attitude about what I should do very clear. ¹⁰The most difficult aspect of our cultural differences is the way our family is structured. ¹¹My father is the center of our family, and he expects that I will always listen to him. ¹²Although I am twenty-one years old, I still have a nightly curfew at an hour which I consider insulting. ¹³Also, I am expected to help my mother perform certain household chores that I've really come to hate. ¹⁴My father expects me to live at home until I am married to a Vietnamese man. ¹⁵When that happens, he assumes I will obey my husband just as I obey him. ¹⁶I do not want to be a bad daughter, but I want to live like my American female friends.

Fill in the blanks: The first spot where supporting details are needed occurs after sentence number _____. The second spot occurs after sentence number _____. The third spot occurs after sentence number _____.

4 Evaluating Paragraphs for Coherence

Activity

Answer the questions about coherence that follow each of the two paragraphs below.

1. **Why I Bought a Handgun**

¹I bought a handgun to keep in my house for several reasons. ²Most important, I have had a frightening experience with an obscene phone caller. ³For several weeks, a man has called me once or twice a day, sometimes as late as three in the morning. ⁴As soon as I pick up the phone, he whispers something obscene or threatens me by saying, "I'll get you." ⁵I decided to buy a gun because crime is increasing in my neighborhood.

⁶One neighbor's house was burglarized while she was at work; the thieves not only stole her appliances but also threw paint around her living room and slashed her furniture. ⁷Not long after this incident, an elderly woman from the apartment house on the corner was mugged on her way to the supermarket. ⁸The man grabbed her purse and threw her to the ground, breaking her hip. ⁹Buying a gun was my response to listening to the nightly news. ¹⁰It seemed that every news story involved violence of some kind— rapes, murders, muggings, and robberies. ¹¹I wondered if some of the victims in the stories would still be alive if they had been able to frighten off the criminal with a gun. ¹²As time passed, I became more convinced that I should keep a gun in the house.

a. The paragraph should use emphatic order. Write 1 before the reason that seems slightly less important than the other two, 2 before the second-most-important reason, and 3 before the most important reason.

_____ Obscene phone caller

_____ Crime increase in neighborhood

_____ News stories about crime

b. Before which of the three reasons should the transitional words *First of all* be added? _____

c. Before which of the three reasons could the transition *In addition* be added?

_____

d. Which words show emphasis in sentence 2? _____

e. In sentence 8, to whom does the pronoun *her* refer? _____

f. How often does the key word *gun* appear in the paragraph? _____

g. What is a synonym for *burglarized* in sentence 6? _____

2.   **Apartment Hunting**

¹Apartment hunting is a several-step process. ²Visit and carefully inspect the most promising apartments. ³Check each place for signs of unwanted guests such as roaches or mice. ⁴Make sure that light switches and appliances work and that there are enough electrical outlets. ⁵Turn faucets and flush the toilet to be sure that the plumbing works smoothly. ⁶Talk to the landlord for a bit to get a sense of him or her as a person. ⁷If a problem develops after you move in, you want to know that a decent and capable person will be there to handle the matter. ⁸Find out what's available that matches your interests. ⁹Your town newspaper and local real estate offices can provide you with a list of apartments for rent. ¹⁰Family and friends may be able to give you leads. ¹¹And your school may have a housing office that keeps a list of

approved apartments for rent. [12]Decide just what you need. [13]If you can afford no more than $400 a month, you need to find a place that will cost no more than that. [14]If you want a location that's close to work or school, you must take that factor into account. [15]If you plan to cook, you want a place with a workable kitchen. [16]By taking these steps, you should be ready to select the apartment that is best for you.

a. The paragraph should use time order. Write 1 before the step that should come first, 2 before the intermediate step, and 3 before the final step.

_____ Visit and carefully inspect the most promising apartments.

_____ Decide just what you need.

_____ Find out what's available that matches your interests.

b. Before which of three steps could the transitional words *The first step is to* be added? _____

c. Before which step could the transitional words *After you have decided what you are looking for, the next step is to* be added? _____

d. Before which step could the transitional words *The final step* be added? _____

e. To whom does the pronoun *him or her* in sentence 6 refer to? _____

f. What is a synonym for *landlord* in sentence 7? _____

g. What is a synonym for *apartment* in sentence 13? _____

5 Revising Paragraphs for Coherence

The two paragraphs in this section begin with a clear point, but in each case the supporting material that follows the point is not coherent. Read each paragraph and the comments that follow it on how to organize and connect the supporting material. Then do the activity for the paragraph.

Paragraph 1

A Difficult Period

Since I arrived in the Bay Area in midsummer, I have had the most difficult period of my life. I had to look for an apartment. I found only one place that I could afford, but the landlord said I could not move in until it was painted. When I first arrived in San Francisco, my thoughts were to stay with my father and stepmother. I had to set out looking for a job so that I could afford my own place, for I soon realized that my stepmother was not at all happy having me live with them. A three-week search led to a job shampooing rugs for a housecleaning company. I painted the apartment myself, and at least that problem was ended. I was in a hurry to get settled because I was starting school at the University of San Francisco in September. A transportation problem developed because my stepmother insisted that I return my father's bike, which I was using at first to get to school. I had to rely on a bus that often arrived late, with the result that I missed some classes and was late for others. I had already had a problem with registration in early September. My counselor had made a mistake with my classes, and I had to register all over again. This meant that I was one week late for class. Now I'm riding to school with a classmate and no longer have to depend on the bus. My life is starting to order itself, but I must admit that at first I thought it was hopeless to stay here.

Comments on Paragraph 1:   The writer of this paragraph has provided a good deal of specific evidence to support the opening point. The evidence, however, needs to be organized. Before starting the paragraph, the writer should have decided to arrange the details by using time order. He or she could then have listed in a scratch outline the exact sequence of events that made for such a difficult period.

Activity 1

Here is a list of the various events described by the writer of paragraph 1. Number the events in the correct time sequence by writing 1 in front of the first event that occurred, 2 in front of the second event, and so on.

Since I arrived in the Bay Area in midsummer, I have had the most difficult period of my life.

_____ I had to search for an apartment I could afford.

_____ I had to find a job so that I could afford my own place.

_____ My stepmother objected to my living with her and my father.

_____ I had to paint the apartment before I could move in.

_____ I had to find an alternative to unreliable bus transportation.

_____ I had to register again for my college courses because of a counselor's mistake.

Your instructor may now have you rewrite the paragraph on separate paper. If so, be sure to use time signals such as *first, next, then, during, when, after,* and *now* to help guide your reader from one event to the next.

Paragraph 2

Childhood Cruelty

When I was in grade school, my classmates and I found a number of excuses for being cruel to a boy named Andy Poppovian. Sometimes Andy gave off a strong body odor, and we knew that several days had passed since he had taken a bath. Andy was very slow in speaking, as well as very careless in personal hygiene. The teacher would call on him during a math or grammar drill. He would sit there silently for so long before answering that she sometimes said, "Are you awake, Andy?" Andy had long fingernails that he never seemed to cut, with black dirt caked under them. We called him "Poppy," or we accented the first syllable in his name and mispronounced the rest of it and said to him, "How are you today, POP-o-van?" His name was funny. Other times we called him "Popeye," and we would shout at him. "Where's your spinach today, Popeye?" Andy always had sand in the corners of his eyes. When we played tag at recess, Andy was always "it" or the first one who was caught. He was so physically slow that five guys could dance around him and he wouldn't be able to touch any of them. Even when we tried to hold a regular conversation with him about sports or a teacher, he was so slow in responding to a question that we got bored talking with him. Andy's hair was always uncombed, and it was often full of white flakes of dandruff. Only when Andy died suddenly of spinal meningitis in seventh grade did some of us begin to realize and regret our cruelty toward him.

Comments on Paragraph 2:   The writer of this paragraph provides a number of specifics that support the opening point. However, the supporting material has not been organized clearly. Before writing this paragraph, the author should have (1) decided to arrange the supporting evidence by using emphatic order and (2) listed in a scratch outline the reasons for the cruelty to Andy Poppovian and the supporting details for each reason. The writer could also have determined which reason to use in the emphatic final position of the paper.

Activity 2

Create a clear outline for paragraph 2 by filling in the scheme below. The outline is partially completed.

When I was in grade school, my classmates and I found a number of excuses for being cruel to a boy named Andy Poppovian.

Reason   1. *Funny name* _____

Details   a. _____

                     b. _____

                     c. _____

Reason	2.	*Physically slow*
Details		a. _____
		b. *Five guys could dance around him*
Reason	3.	_____
Details		a. _____
		b. *In regular conversation*
Reason	4.	_____
Details		a. _____
		b. *Sand in eyes*
		c. _____
		d. _____

Your instructor may have you rewrite the paragraph on separate paper. If so, be sure to introduce each of the four reasons with transitions such as *First, Second, Another reason,* and *Finally.* You may also want to use repeated words, pronouns, and synonyms to help tie your sentences together.

6 Evaluating Paragraphs for All Four Bases: Unity, Support, Coherence, and Sentence Skills

Activity

In this activity, you will evaluate paragraphs in terms of all four bases: unity, support, coherence, and sentence skills. Evaluative comments follow each paragraph below. Circle the letter of the statement that best applies in each case.

1.
Drunk Drivers

   People caught driving while drunk—even first offenders—should be jailed. Drunk driving, first of all, is more dangerous than carrying around a loaded gun. In addition, a jail term would show drivers that society will no longer tolerate such careless and dangerous behavior. Finally, severe penalties might encourage solutions to the problem of drinking and driving. People who go out for a good time and intend to have several drinks would always designate one person, who would stay completely sober, as the driver.

a.   The paragraph is not unified.

b.   The paragraph is not adequately supported.

c.   The paragraph is not well organized.

d.   The paragraph does not show a command of sentence skills.

e.   The paragraph is well written in terms of the four bases.

2.
A Frustrating Moment

A frustrating moment happened to me several days ago. When I was shopping. I had picked up a tube of crest toothpaste and a jar of noxema skin cream. After the cashier rang up the purchases, which came to $4.15. I handed her $10. Then got back my change, which was only $0.85. I told the cashier that she had made a mistake. Giving me change for $5 instead of $10. But she insist that I had only gave her $5, I became very upset and demand that she return the rest of my change. She refused to do so instead she asked me to step aside so she could wait on the next customer. I stood very rigid, trying not to lose my temper. I simply said to her, I'm not going to leave here, Miss, without my change for $10. Giving in at this point a bell was rung and the manager was summoned. After the situation was explain to him, he ask the cashier to ring off her register to check for the change. After doing so, the cashier was $5 over her sale receipts. Only then did the manager return my change and apologize for the cashier mistake.

a.   The paragraph is not unified.

b.   The paragraph is not adequately supported.

c.   The paragraph is not well organized.

d.   The paragraph does not show a command of sentence skills.

e.   The paragraph is well written in terms of the four bases.

3.
Asking Girls Out

There are several reasons I have trouble asking girls to go out with me. I have asked some girls out and have been turned down. This is one reason that I can't talk to them. At one time I was very shy and quiet, and people sometimes didn't even know I was present. I can talk to girls now as friends, but as soon as I want to ask them out, I usually start to become quiet, and a little bit of shyness comes out. When I finally get the nerve up, the girl will turn me down, and I swear that I will never ask another one out again. I feel sure I will get a refusal, and I have no confidence in myself. Also, my friends mock me, though they aren't any better than I am. It can become discouraging when your friends get on you. Sometimes I just stand there and wait to hear what line the girl will use. The one they use a lot is "We like you as a friend, Ted, and it's better that way." Sometimes I want to have the line put on a tape recorder, so they won't have to waste their breath on me. All my past experiences with girls have been just as bad. One girl used me to make her old boyfriend jealous. Then when she succeeded, she started going out with him again. I had a bad experience when I took a girl to the prom. I spent a lot of money on her. Two days later, she told me that she was going steady with another guy. I feel that when I meet a girl I have to be sure I can trust her. I don't want her to turn on me.

a.   The paragraph is not unified.

b.   The paragraph is not adequately supported.

c.   The paragraph is not well organized.

d.   The paragraph does not show a command of sentence skills.

e.   The paragraph is well written in terms of the four bases.

4.   **A Change in My Writing**

A technique in my present English class has corrected a writing problem that I've always had. In past English courses, I had major problems with commas in the wrong places, bad spelling, capitalizing the wrong words, sentence fragments, and run-on sentences. I never had any big problems with unity, support, or coherence, but the sentence skills were another matter. They were like little bugs that always appeared to infest my writing. My present instructor asked me to rewrite papers, just concentrating on sentence skills. I thought that the instructor was crazy because I didn't feel that rewriting would do any good. I soon became certain that my instructor was out of his mind, for he made me rewrite my first paper four times. It was very frustrating, for I became tired of doing the same paper over and over. I wanted to belt my instructor against the wall when I'd show him each new draft and he'd find skills mistakes and say, "Rewrite." Finally, my papers began to improve and the sentence skills began to fall into place. I was able to see them and correct them before turning in a paper, whereas I couldn't before. Why or how this happened I don't know, but I think that rewriting helped a lot. It took me most of the semester, but I stuck it out and the work paid off.

a.   The paragraph is not unified.

b.   The paragraph is not adequately supported.

c.   The paragraph is not well organized.

d.   The paragraph does not show a command of sentence skills.

e.   The paragraph is well written in terms of the four bases.

5.   **Luck and Me**

I am a very lucky man, though the rest of my family has not always been lucky. Sometimes when I get depressed, which is too frequently, it's hard to see just how lucky I am. I'm lucky that I'm living in a country that is free. I'm allowed to worship the way I want to, and that is very important to me. Without a belief in God a person cannot live with any real certainty in life. My relationship with my wife is a source of good fortune for me. She gives me security, and that's something I need a lot. Even with these positive realities in my life, I still seem to find time for insecurity, worry, and, worst of all, depression. At times in my life I have had bouts of terrible luck. But overall, I'm a very lucky guy. I plan to further develop the positive aspects of my life and try to eliminate the negative ones.

a.   The paragraph is not unified.

b.   The paragraph is not adequately supported.

c.   The paragraph is not well organized.

d.   The paragraph does not show a command of sentence skills.

e.   The paragraph is well written in terms of the four bases.

Part Two

Paragraph Development

Preview

Part Two introduces you to paragraph development and gives you practice in the following common types of paragraph development:

Providing Examples

Explaining a Process

Examining Cause and Effect

Comparing or Contrasting

Defining a Term

Dividing and Classifying

Describing a Scene or Person

Narrating an Event

Arguing a Position

After a brief explanation of each type of paragraph development, student paragraphs illustrating each type are presented, followed by questions about those paragraphs. The questions relate to the standards of effective writing described in Part One. You are then asked to write your own paragraph. In each case, writing assignments progress from personal-experience topics to more formal and objective topics; some topics require simple research, and the last assignment in each section asks you to write with a specific purpose and audience in mind. At times, points or topic sentences for development are suggested, so that you can concentrate on (1) making sure your evidence is on target in support of your opening idea, (2) providing plenty of specific supporting details to back up your point, and (3) organizing your supporting material clearly. The last chapter in Part Two provides some additional assignments.

7 Introduction to Paragraph Development

Nine Patterns of Paragraph Development

Traditionally, writing has been divided into the following patterns of development:

- Exposition

Examples	Comparison and contrast
Process	Definition
Cause and effect	Division and classification

- Description
- Narration
- Argumentation

In *exposition*, the writer provides information about and explains a particular subject. Patterns of development within exposition include giving *examples*, detailing a *process* of doing or making something, analyzing *causes and effects*, *comparing* and *contrasting*, *defining* a term or concept, and *dividing* something into parts or *classifying* it into categories.

In addition to exposition, three other patterns of development are common: description, narration, and argumentation. A *description* is a verbal picture of a person, place, or thing. In *narration*, a writer tells the story of something that happened. Finally, in *argumentation*, a writer attempts to support a controversial point or defend a position on which there is a difference of opinion.

The pages ahead present individual chapters on each pattern. You will have a chance, then, to learn nine different patterns or methods for organizing material in your papers. Each pattern has its own internal logic and provides its own special strategies for imposing order on your ideas. As you practice each pattern, you should remember two points:

- *Point 1:* While each paragraph that you write will involve one predominant pattern, very often one or more additional patterns may be involved as well. For instance, the "Good-Bye, Tony" paragraph that you have already read presents a series of causes leading to an effect—that the writer will not go out with Tony again. But the writer also presents examples to explain each of the causes (Tony was late, he was bossy, he was abrupt). And there is an element of narration, as the writer presents examples that occur from the beginning to the end of the date.

- *Point 2:* No matter which pattern or patterns you use, each paragraph will probably involve some form of argumentation. You will advance a point and then go on to support your point. To convince the reader that your point is valid, you may use a series of examples, or narration, or description, or some other pattern of organization. Among the paragraphs you will read in Part Two, one writer supports the point that a certain pet shop is depressing by providing a number of descriptive details. Another writer labels a certain experience in his life as heartbreaking and then uses a narrative to demonstrate the truth of his statement. A third writer advances the opinion that good horror movies can be easily distinguished from bad horror movies and then supplies comparative information about both to support her claim. Much of your writing, in short, will have the purpose of persuading your reader that the idea you have advanced is valid.

The Progression in Each Chapter

After each type of paragraph development is explained, student papers illustrating that type are presented, followed by questions about the paragraphs. The questions relate to unity, support, and coherence—principles of effective writing explained earlier in this book. You are then asked to write your own paragraph. In most cases, the first assignment is fairly structured and provides a good deal of guidance for the writing process. The other assignments offer a wide choice of writing topics. The fourth assignment always requires some simple research, and the fifth assignment requires writing with a specific purpose and for a specific audience.

Important Considerations in Paragraph Development

Before you begin work on particular types of paragraphs, there are several general considerations about writing to keep in mind. They will be discussed in turn.

Knowing Your Subject

Whenever possible, try to write on a subject that interests you. You will then find it easier to put more time into your work. Even more important, try to write on a subject that you already know something about. If you do not have direct experience with the subject, you should at least have indirect experience—knowledge gained through thinking, prewriting, reading, or talking about the subject.

If you are asked to write on a topic about which you have no experience or knowledge, you should do whatever research is required to gain the information you need. Chapter 24, "Using the Library and the Internet," will show you how to look up relevant information. Without direct or indirect experience, or the information you gain through research, you may not be able to provide the specific evidence needed to develop whatever point you are trying to make. Your writing will be starved for specifics.

Knowing Your Purpose and Audience

The three most common purposes of writing are to inform, to persuade, and to entertain. As already noted, much of the writing you do in this book will involve some form of argumentation or persuasion. You will advance a point or thesis and then support it in a variety of ways. To some extent, also, you will write papers to inform—to provide readers with information about a particular subject. And since, in practice, writing often combines purposes, you might find yourself at times providing vivid or humorous details in order to entertain your readers as well.

Your audience will be primarily your instructor and sometimes other students. Your instructor is really a symbol of the larger audience you should see yourself writing for—an educated adult audience that expects you to present your ideas in a clear, direct, organized way. If you can learn to write to persuade or inform such a general audience, you will have accomplished a great deal.

It will also be helpful for you to write some papers for a more specific audience. By so doing, you will develop an ability to choose words and adopt a tone of voice that is just right for a given purpose and a given group of people. In this part of the book, then, there is an assignment at or near the end of each chapter that asks you to write with a very specific purpose in mind and for a very specific audience.

You will be asked, for example, to imagine yourself as an employee writing a description of a new job opening at your workplace, as a graduate of a local high school advising a counselor there about a drug problem, as an aide at a day-care center preparing instructions for children, as an apartment tenant complaining to a landlord about neighbors, or as a travel agent providing suggestions for different kinds of family vacations. Through these and other assignments, you will learn how to adjust your style and tone of voice to a given writing situation.

Using a Computer

If you don't yet write on a computer, it's time to start. In today's world, word processing is an essential mechanical skill, just as effective writing is a vital communication skill.

The computer can be a real aid in the writing process. You can quickly add or delete anything, from a word to an entire section. You can "cut" material and "paste" it elsewhere in seconds. A word-processing program makes it easy to set margins, space lines, and number pages. It can also help you check your spelling, your grammar, and to some extent your style. And at any point during your work, you can print out one or more copies of your text.

Word processing is not hard to learn. Just as you don't need to know how a car works to drive one, you don't need to understand how a computer functions to use it. With a few simple keystrokes under your belt, you can begin. You do not even need to own your own computer. Nearly every college has at least one computer center, complete with rows of computers and staff members to provide assistance. Free classes in word processing may be available as well.

Tips on Using a Computer

- If you are using your school's computer center, allow yourself enough time. You may have to wait for a computer or printer to be free. In addition, you may need several sessions at the computer and printer to complete your paper.

- Every word-processing program allows you to "save" your writing by hitting one or more keys. Save your work frequently as you work on a draft. Work that is saved is preserved by the computer. Work that is not saved is lost when the file you are working on is closed, when the computer is turned off—or if there's a power or system failure.

- Keep your work in two places—the hard drive or disk you are working on and a backup disk. At the end of each session with the computer, copy your work onto the backup disk. Then if the hard drive or working disk becomes damaged, you'll have the backup copy.

- Print out your work at least at the end of every session. Then you'll not only have your most recent draft to work on away from the computer; you'll also have a copy in case something should happen to your disks.

- Work in single spacing so you can see as much of your writing on the screen at one time as possible. Just before you print out your work, change to double-spacing.

- Before making major changes in a paper, create a copy of your file. For example, if your file is titled "Worst Job," create a file called "Worst Job 2." Then make all your changes in that file. If the changes don't work out, you can always go back to the original file.

Ways to Use a Computer at Each Stage of the Writing Process

Following are some ways to make word processing a part of your writing. Note that the sections that follow correspond to the stages of the writing process described in Chapter 2, pages 17–45.

Prewriting

If you're a fast typist, many kinds of prewriting will go well on the computer. With freewriting in particular, you can get ideas onto the screen almost as quickly as they occur to you. A passing thought that could be productive is not likely to get lost. You may even find it helpful, when freewriting, to dim the screen of your monitor so that you can't see what you're typing. If you temporarily can't see the screen, you won't have to worry about grammar or spelling or typing errors (all of which do not matter in prewriting); instead, you can concentrate on getting down as many ideas and details as possible about your subject.

After any initial freewriting, questioning, and list-making on a computer, it's often very helpful to print out a hard copy of what you've done. With a clean printout in front of you, you'll be able to see everything at once and revise and expand your work with handwritten comments in the margins of the paper.

If you have prepared a list of items, you may be able to turn that list into an outline right on the screen. Delete the ideas you feel should not be in your paper (saving them at the end of the file in case you change your mind), and add any new ideas that occur to you. Then use the cut and paste functions to shuffle the supporting ideas around until you find the best order for your paper.

Word processing also makes it easy for you to experiment with the wording of the point of your paper. You can try a number of versions in a short time. After you have decided upon the version that works best, you can easily delete the other versions—or simply move them to a temporary "leftover" section at the end of the paper.

Writing Your First Draft

Like many writers, you may want to write out your first draft by hand and then type it into the computer for revision. Even as you type your handwritten draft, you may find yourself making some changes and improvements. And once you have a draft on the screen, or printed out, you will find it much easier to revise than a handwritten draft.

If you feel comfortable composing directly on the screen, you can benefit from the computer's special features. For example, if you have written an anecdote in your freewriting that you plan to use in your paper, simply copy the story from your freewriting file and insert it where it fits in your paper. You can refine it then or later. Or if you discover while typing that a sentence is out of place, cut it out from where it is and paste it wherever you wish. And if while writing you realize that an earlier sentence can be expanded, just move your cursor back to that point and type in the added material.

Revising

It is during revision that the virtues of word processing really shine. All substituting, adding, deleting, and rearranging can be done easily within an existing file. All changes instantly take their proper places within the paper, not scribbled above the line or squeezed into the margin. You can concentrate on each change you want to make, because you never have to type from scratch or work on a messy draft. You can carefully go through your paper to check that all your supporting evidence is relevant and to add new support here and there where needed. Anything you decide to eliminate can be deleted in a keystroke. Anything you add can be inserted precisely where you choose. If you change your mind, all you have to do is delete or cut and paste. Then you can sweep through the paper focusing on other changes, such as improving word choice, increasing sentence variety, eliminating wordiness, and so on.

If you are like many students, you will find it convenient to print out a hard copy of your file at various points throughout the revision. You can then revise in longhand—adding, crossing out, and indicating changes—and later quickly make those changes in the document.

Editing and Proofreading

Editing and proofreading also benefit richly from word processing. Instead of crossing out or whiting out mistakes, or rewriting an entire paper to correct numerous errors, you can make all necessary changes within the most recent draft. If you find editing or proofreading on the screen hard on your eyes, print out a copy. Mark any corrections on that copy, and then transfer them to the final draft.

If the word-processing package you're using includes spelling and grammar checks, by all means use them. The spell-check function tells you when a word is not in the computer's dictionary. Keep in mind, however, that the spell-check cannot tell you how to spell a name correctly or when you have mistakenly used, for example, *their* instead of *there*. To a spell-check, *Thank ewe four the complement* is as correct as *Thank you for the compliment*. Also use the grammar check with caution. Any errors it doesn't uncover are still your responsibility.

A word-processed paper, with its clean appearance and attractive formatting, looks so good that you may think it is in better shape than it really is. Do not be fooled by your paper's appearance. Take sufficient time to carefully review your grammar, punctuation, and spelling.

Even after you hand in your paper, save the computer file. Your teacher may ask you to do some revising, and then the file will save you from having to type the paper from scratch.

Using Peer Review

In addition to having your instructor as an audience for your writing, you will benefit by having another student in your class as an audience. On the day a paper is due, or on a day when you are writing papers in class, your instructor may ask you to pair up with another student. That student will read your paper, and you will read his or her paper.

Ideally, read the other paper aloud while your partner listens. If that is not practical, read it in a whisper while he or she looks on. As you read, both you and your partner should look and listen for spots where the paper does not read smoothly and clearly. Check or circle the trouble spots where your reading snags.

Your partner should then read your paper, marking possible trouble spots while doing so. Then each of you should do three things:

1 Identification

On a separate sheet of paper, write at the top the title and author of the paper you have read. Under it, put your name as the reader of the paper.

2 Scratch Outline

"X-ray" the paper for its inner logic by making up a scratch outline. The scratch outline need be no more than twenty words or so, but it should show clearly the logical foundation on which the essay is built. It should identify and summarize the overall point of the paper and the three areas of support for the point.

Your outline can look as follows.

Point: _____

Support:

   1. _____

   2. _____

   3. _____

For example, here is a scratch outline of the paper on page 195 about a new puppy in the house:

Point: <u>A new puppy can have drastic effects in a house.</u>

Support:

   1. <u>Keeps family awake at night</u>

   2. <u>Destroys possessions</u>

   3. <u>Causes arguments</u>

3 Comments

Under the outline, write the heading "Comments." Here is what you should comment on:

- Look at the spots where your reading of the paper snagged: Are words missing or misspelled? Is there a lack of parallel structure? Are there mistakes with punctuation? Is the meaning of a sentence confused? Try to figure out what the problems are and suggest ways of fixing them.

- Are there spots in the paper where you see problems with *unity*, *support*, or *organization*? (You'll find it helpful to refer to the checklist on the inside front cover of this book.) If so, offer comments. For example, you might say, "More details are needed in the first supporting paragraph," or "Some of the details in the last supporting paragraph don't really back up your point."
- Finally, make note of something you really liked about the paper, such as good use of transitions or an especially realistic or vivid specific detail.

After you have completed your evaluation of the paper, give it to your partner. Your instructor may provide you with the option of rewriting a paper in light of this feedback. Whether or not you rewrite, be sure to hand in the peer evaluation form with your paper.

Doing a Personal Review

1 While you're writing and revising an essay, you should be constantly evaluating it in terms of *unity, support,* and *organization.* Use as a guide the detailed checklist on the inside front cover of this book.

2 After you've finished the next-to-final draft of an essay, check it for the *sentence skills* listed on the inside front cover. It may also help to read the paper out loud. If a given sentence does not sound right—that is, if it does not read clearly and smoothly—chances are something is wrong. Then revise or edit as needed until your paper is complete.

8 Providing Examples

In our daily conversations, we often provide *examples*—that is, details, particulars, specific instances—to explain statements that we make. Consider the several statements and supporting examples in the box below:

Statement	Examples
The A&P was crowded today.	There were at least four carts waiting at each of the checkout counters, and it took me forty-five minutes to get through a line.
The corduroy shirt I bought is poorly made.	When I washed it, the colors began to fade, one button cracked and another fell off, a shoulder seam opened, and the sleeves shrank almost two inches.
My son Peter is unreliable.	If I depend on him to turn off a pot of beans in ten minutes, the family is likely to eat burned beans. If I ask him to turn down the thermostat before he goes to bed, the heat is likely to stay on all night.

In each case, the examples help us *see for ourselves* the truth of the statement that has been made. In paragraphs, too, explanatory examples help the audience fully understand a point. Lively, specific examples also add interest to a paper.

In this chapter, you will be asked to provide a series of examples to support a topic sentence. Providing examples to support a point is one of the most common and simplest methods of paragraph development. First read the paragraphs ahead; they all use examples to develop their points. Then answer the questions that follow.

Paragraphs to Consider

Inconsiderate Drivers

1Some people are inconsiderate drivers. 2In the city, they will at times stop right in the middle of the street while looking for a certain home or landmark. 3If they had any consideration for the cars behind them, they would pull over to the curb first. 4Other drivers will be chatting on their cell phones and then slow down unexpectedly at a city intersection to make a right or left turn. 5The least they could do is use their turn signals to let those behind them know in advance of their intention. 6On the highway, a common example of inconsiderateness is night drivers who fail to turn off their high beams, creating glare for cars approaching in the other direction. 7Other rude highway drivers move to the second or passing lane and then stay there, making it impossible for cars behind to go around them. 8Yet other drivers who act as if they have special privileges are those who do not wait their turn in bottleneck situations where the cars in two lanes must merge alternately into one lane. 9Perhaps the most inconsiderate drivers are those who throw trash out their windows, creating litter that takes away some of the pleasure of driving and that must be paid for with everyone's tax dollars.

Office Politics

1Office politics is a destructive game played by several types of people. 2For instance, two supervisors may get into a conflict over how to do a certain job. 3Instead of working out an agreement like adults, they carry on a power struggle that turns the poor employees under them into human Ping-Pong balls being swatted between two angry players. 4Another common example of office politics is the ambitious worker who takes credit for other people's ideas. 5He or she will chat in a "friendly" fashion with inexperienced employees, getting their ideas about how to run the office more smoothly. 6Next thing you know, Mr. or Ms. Idea-Stealer is having a closed-door session with the boss and getting promotion points for his or her "wonderful creativity." 7Yet another illustration of office politics is the spy. 8This employee acts very buddy-buddy with other workers, often dropping little comments about things he or she doesn't like in the workplace. 9The spy encourages people to talk about their problems at work, how they don't like their boss, the pay, and the working conditions. 10Then the spy goes straight back and repeats all he or she has heard to the boss, and the employees get blamed for their "poor attitude." 11A final example of office politics is people who gossip. 12Too often, office politics can turn a perfectly fine work situation into a stressful one.

An Egotistical Neighbor

1 I have an egotistical neighbor named Alice. 2 If I tell Alice how beautiful her dress is, she will take the time to tell me the name of the store where she bought it, the type of material that was used in making it, and the price. 3 Alice is also egotistical when it comes to her children. 4 Because they are hers, she thinks they just have to be the best children on the block. 5 I am wasting my time by trying to tell her I have seen her kids expose themselves on the street or take things from parked cars. 6 I do not think parents should praise their children too much. 7 Kids have learned how to be good at home and simply awful when they are not at home. 8 Finally, Alice is quick to describe the furnishings of her home for someone who is meeting her for the first time. 9 She tells how much she paid for the paneling in her dining room. 10 She mentions that she has three color television sets and that they were bought at an expensive furniture store. 11 She lets the person know that the stereo set in her living room cost more than a thousand dollars, and that she has such a large collection of CDs that she would not be able to play them all in one week. 12 Poor Alice is so self-centered that she never realizes how boring she can be.

■ Questions

About Unity

1. Which two sentences in "An Egotistical Neighbor" are irrelevant to the point that Alice is egotistical? (*Write the sentence numbers here.*)

   _____   _____

About Support

2. In "Inconsiderate Drivers," how many examples are given of inconsiderate drivers?

   _____ two   _____ four   _____ six   _____ seven

3. After which sentence in "Office Politics" are specific details needed?

   _____

About Coherence

4. What are the four transition words or phrases that are used to introduce each new example in "Office Politics"?

   _____   _____   _____   _____

5. What two transition words are used to introduce examples in "An Egotistical Neighbor"?

   _____   _____

6. Which paragraph clearly uses emphatic order to organize its details, saving for last what the writer regards as the most important example?

Developing an Examples Paragraph

Development through Prewriting

Backing up your statements with clear, specific illustrations is the key to a successful examples paragraph. When Charlene, the writer of "Office Politics," was assigned an examples paragraph, she at first did not know what to write about.

Then her teacher made a suggestion. "Imagine yourself having lunch with some friends," the teacher said. "You're telling them *how* you feel about something and *why*. Maybe you're saying, 'I am so mad at my boyfriend!' or 'My new apartment is really great.' You wouldn't stop there—you'd continue by saying what your boyfriend does that is annoying, or in what way your apartment is nice. In other words, you'd be making a general point and backing it up with examples. That's what you need to do in this paper."

That night, Charlene was on the telephone with her brother. She was complaining about the office where she worked. "Suddenly I realized what I was doing," Charlene said. "I was making a statement—I hate the politics in my office—and giving examples of those politics. I knew what I could write about!"

Charlene began preparing to write her paragraph by freewriting. She gave herself ten minutes to write down everything she could think of on the subject of politics in her office. This is what she wrote:

> Of all the places I've ever worked this one is the worst that way. Can't trust anybody there—everybody's playing some sort of game. Worst one of all is Bradley and the way he pretends to be friendly with people. Gets them to complain about Ms. Bennett and Mr. Hankins and then runs back to them and reports everything. He should realize that people are catching on to his game and figuring out what a jerk he is. Melissa steals people's ideas and then takes credit for them. Anything to get brownie points. She's always out for herself first, you can tell. Then there's all the gossip that goes on. You think you're in a soap opera or something, and it's kind of fun in a way but it also is very distracting people always talking about each other and worrying about what they say about you. And people talk about our bosses a lot. Nobody knows why Ms. Bennett and Mr. Hankins hate each other so much but they each want the workers on their side. You do something one boss's way, but then the other boss appears and is angry that you're not doing it another way. You don't know what to do at times to keep people happy.

Charlene read over her freewriting and then spent some time asking questions about her paragraph. "Exactly what do I want my point to be?" she asked. "And exactly how am I going to support that point?" Keeping those points in mind, she worked on several scratch outlines and wound up with the following:

Office politics are ruining the office.
1.   Bradley reports people's complaints.
2.   Melissa steals ideas.
3.   People gossip.
4.   Ms. Bennett and Mr. Hankins make workers choose sides.

Working from this outline, she then wrote the following first draft:

My office is being ruined by office politics. It seems like everybody is trying to play some sort of game to get ahead and don't care what it does to anybody else. One example is Bradley. Although he pretends to be friendly with people he isn't sincere. What he is trying to do is get them to complain about their bosses. Once they do, he goes back to the bosses and tells them what's been said and gets the worker in trouble. I've seen the same kind of thing happen at two other offices where I've worked. Melissa is another example of someone who plays office politics games. She steals other people's ideas and takes the credit for them. I had a good idea once to save paper. I told her we ought to use E-mail to send office memos instead of typing them on paper. She went to Ms. Bennett and pretended the idea was hers. I guess I was partly to blame for not acting on the idea myself. And Ms. Bennett and Mr. Hankins hate each other and try to get us to take sides in their conflict. Then there is all the gossip that goes on. People do a lot of backbiting, and you have to be very careful about your behavior or people will start talking about you. All in all, office politics is really a problem where I work.

Development through Revising

After completing her first draft, Charlene put it aside until the next day. When she reread it, this was her response:

"I think the paragraph would be stronger if I made it about office politics in general instead of just politics in my office. The things I was writing about happen in many offices, not just in mine. And our instructor wants us to try some third-person writing. Also, I need to make better use of transitions to help the reader follow as I move from one example to another."

With these thoughts in mind, Charlene began revising her paper, and after several drafts she produced the paragraph that appears on page 172.

Writing an Examples Paragraph

■ Writing Assignment 1

The assignment here is to complete an unfinished paragraph (in the box), which has as its topic sentence, "My husband Roger is a selfish person." Provide the supporting details needed to develop the examples of Roger's selfishness. The first example has been done for you.

A Selfish Person

My husband Roger is a selfish person. For one thing, he refuses to move out of the city, even though it is a bad place to raise the children. *We inherited some money when my parents died, and it might be enough for a down payment on a small house in a nearby town. But Roger says he would miss his buddies in the neighborhood.*

_____

Also, when we go on vacation, we always go where Roger wants to go. _____

_____

_____

Another example of Roger's selfishness is that he always spends any budget money that is left over. _____

_____

_____

_____

Finally, Roger leaves all the work of caring for the children to me.

_____

_____

_____

Prewriting

a On a separate piece of paper, jot down a couple of answers for each of the following questions:

- What specific vacations did the family go on because Roger wanted to go? Write down particular places, length of stay, time of year. What vacations has the family never gone on (for example, to visit the wife's relatives), even though the wife wanted to?
- What specific items has Roger bought for himself (rather than for the whole family's use) with leftover budget money?
- What chores and duties involved in the everyday caring for the children has Roger never done?

Note: Your instructor may ask you to work with one or two other students in generating the details needed to develop the three examples in the paragraph. The groups may then be asked to read their details aloud, with the class deciding which details are the most effective for each example.

Here and in general in your writing, try to generate *more* supporting material than you need. You are then in a position to choose the most convincing details for your paper.

b Read over the details you have generated and decide which sound most effective. Jot down additional details as they occur to you.

c Take your best details, reshape them as needed, and use them to complete the paragraph about Roger.

Revising

Read over the paragraph you have written. Ask yourself these questions:

- Do the examples I have provided really support the idea that Roger is selfish?
- Are there enough examples to make my point about Roger and have people agree with me?
- Have I checked my paper for spelling and other sentence skills, as listed on the inside front cover of the book?

Continue revising your work until you can answer "yes" to all these questions.

■ Writing Assignment 2

Write an examples paragraph about one quality of a person you know well. The person might be a member of your family, a friend, a roommate, a boss or supervisor, a neighbor, an instructor, or someone else. Here is a list of descriptive qualities that you might consider choosing from. Feel free to choose another quality that does not appear here.

Honest	Hardworking	Jealous
Bad-tempered	Supportive	Materialistic
Ambitious	Suspicious	Sarcastic
Prejudiced	Open-minded	Self-centered
Considerate	Lazy	Spineless
Argumentative	Independent	Good-humored
Softhearted	Stubborn	Cooperative
Energetic	Flirtatious	Self-disciplined
Patient	Irresponsible	Sentimental
Reliable	Stingy	Defensive
Generous	Trustworthy	Dishonest
Persistent	Aggressive	Insensitive
Shy	Courageous	Unpretentious
Sloppy	Compulsive	Tidy

Prewriting

a Select the individual you will write about and the quality of this person that you will focus on. For example, you might choose your cousin and her quality of self-discipline. This will be the point of your paper.

b Make a list of examples that will support your point. Such a list about the self-disciplined cousin might look like this:

Exercises every day for forty-five minutes

Never lets herself watch TV until homework is done

Keeps herself on a strict budget

Organizes her school papers in color-coordinated notebooks

Eats no more than one dessert every week

Balances her checkbook the day her statement arrives

c Read over your list and see how you might group the items into categories. The list above, for example, could be broken into three categories: schoolwork, fitness, and money.

Exercises every day for forty-five minutes (fitness)

Never lets herself watch TV until homework is done (schoolwork)

Keeps herself on a strict budget (money)

Organizes her school papers in color-coordinated notebooks (schoolwork)

Eats no more than one dessert every week (fitness)

Balances her checkbook the day her bank statement arrives (money)

d Prepare a scratch outline made up of the details you've generated, with those details grouped into appropriate categories.

    1. <u>Self-disciplined about fitness</u>
       A. Exercises every day for forty-five minutes
       B. Eats no more than one dessert every week

    2. <u>Self-disciplined about schoolwork</u>
       A. Never lets herself watch TV until homework is done
       B. Organizes her school papers in color-coordinated notebooks

    3. <u>Self-disciplined about money</u>
       A. Keeps herself on a strict budget
       B. Balances her checkbook the day her bank statement arrives

e Write the topic sentence of your paragraph. You should include the name of the person you're writing about, your relationship to that person, and the specific quality you are focusing on. For example, you might write, "Keisha, a schoolmate of mine, is very flirtatious," or "Stubbornness is Uncle Carl's outstanding characteristic." And a topic sentence for the paragraph about the self-disciplined cousin might be: "My cousin Mari is extremely self-disciplined."

Remember to focus on only *one* characteristic. Also remember to focus on a *specific* quality, not a vague, general quality. For instance, "My English instructor is a nice person" is too general.

f Now you have a topic sentence and an outline and are ready to write the first draft of your paragraph. Remember, as you flesh out the examples, that your goal is not just to *tell* us about the person but to *show* us the person by detailing his or her words, actions, or both. In preparation for this writing assignment, you might want to go back and reread the examples provided in "An Egotistical Neighbor."

Revising

It's hard to criticize your own work honestly, especially right after you've done it. If at all possible, put your paragraph away for a day or so and then return to it. Better yet, wait a day and then read it aloud to a friend whose judgment you trust.
Read the paragraph with these questions in mind:

- Does my topic sentence clearly state whom I am writing about, what that person's relationship is to me, and what quality of that person I am going to focus on?
- Do the examples I provide truly show that my subject has the quality I'm writing about?
- Have I provided enough specific details to solidly support my point that my subject has a certain quality?
- Have I organized the details in my paragraph into several clearly defined categories?
- Have I used transitional words such as *also, in addition, for example,* and *for instance* to help the reader follow my train of thought?
- Have I checked my paper for sentence skills, as listed on the inside front cover of the book?

Continue revising your work until you and your reader can answer "yes" to all these questions.

■ Writing Assignment 3

Write a paragraph that uses examples to develop one of the following statements or a related statement of your own.

1. _____ is a distracting place to try to study.
2. The daily life of a student is filled with conflicts.
3. Abundant evidence exists that the United States has become a health-conscious nation.
4. Despite modern appliances, many household chores are still drudgery.
5. One of my instructors, _____, has some good (*or* unusual) teaching techniques.
6. Wasted electricity is all around us.
7. Life in the United States is faster-paced than ever before.

8. Violence on television is widespread.

9. Today, some people are wearing ridiculous fashions.

10. Some students here at _____ do not care about learning (*or* are overly concerned about grades).

Be sure to choose examples that truly support your topic sentence. They should be relevant facts, statistics, personal experiences, or incidents you have heard or read about. Organize your paragraph by listing several examples that support your point. Save the most vivid, most convincing, or most important example for last.

■ Writing Assignment 4

Write a paragraph with this topic sentence: "The diet of the average American is unhealthy." Using strategies described in the chapter on the library and the Internet (pages 361–378), research the topic. Your reading will help you think about just how to proceed with the paper.

■ Writing Assignment 5

Imagine that you are a television critic for a daily newspaper. Your job is to recommend to viewers, every day, the programs most worth watching. You've decided that there is nothing particularly good on TV today. Therefore, your plan is to write a one-paragraph article about TV commercials, supporting this point: "Television advertisements are more entertaining than the programs they interrupt." To prepare for this article, spend some time watching television, taking detailed notes on several ads. Decide on two or three ways in which the ads are entertaining; these ways will be the main supporting points in your outline. Then choose at least one ad to use as a specific example to illustrate each of those points. Here are some entertaining qualities that may be seen in ads:

Humor

Cleverness

Music

Drama

Emotion

Suspense

Beauty

9 Explaining a Process

Every day we perform many activities that are *processes*—that is, series of steps carried out in a definite order. Many of these processes are familiar and automatic: for example, tying shoelaces, changing bed linen, using a vending machine, and starting a car. We are thus seldom aware of the sequence of steps making up each activity. In other cases, such as when we are asked for directions to a particular place, or when we try to read and follow the directions for a new table game, we may be painfully conscious of the whole series of steps involved in the process.

In this section, you will be asked to write a process paragraph—one that explains clearly how to do or make something. To prepare for this assignment, you should first read the student process papers below and then respond to the questions that follow.

Note: In process writing, where you are often giving instruction to the reader, the pronoun *you* can appropriately be used. Two of the model paragraphs here use *you*—as indeed does much of this book, which gives instruction on how to write effectively. As a general rule, though, do not use *you* in your writing.

Paragraphs to Consider

Sneaking into the House at Night

¹The first step I take is bringing my key along with me. ²Obviously, I don't want to have to knock on the door at 1:30 in the morning and rouse my parents out of bed. ³Second, I make it a point to stay out past midnight. ⁴If I come in before then, my father is still up, and I'll have to face his disapproving look. ⁵All I need in my life is for him to make me feel guilty. ⁶Trying to make it as a college student is as much as I'm ready to handle. ⁷Next, I am careful to be very quiet upon entering the house. ⁸This involves lifting the front door up slightly as I open it, so that it does not creak. ⁹It also means treating the floor and steps to the second floor like a minefield, stepping carefully over the spots that squeak. ¹⁰When I'm upstairs, I stop briefly in the bathroom without turning on the light. ¹¹Finally, I tiptoe to my room, put my clothes in a pile on a chair, and slip quietly into bed. ¹²With my careful method of sneaking into the house at night, I have avoided some major hassles with my parents.

How to Harass an Instructor

1There are several steps you can take to harass an instructor during a class. 2First of all, show up late, so that you can interrupt the beginning of the instructor's presentation. 3Saunter in nonchalantly and try to find a seat next to a friend. 4In a normal tone of voice, speak some words of greeting to your friends as you sit down, and scrape your chair as loudly as possible while you make yourself comfortable in it. 5Then just sit there and do anything but pay attention. 6When the instructor sees that you are not involved in the class, he or she may pop a quick question, probably hoping to embarrass you. 7You should then say, in a loud voice, "I DON'T KNOW THE ANSWER." 8This declaration of ignorance will throw the instructor off guard. 9If the instructor then asks you why you don't know the answer, say, "I don't even know what page we're on" or "I thought the assignment was boring, so I didn't do it." 10After the instructor calls on someone else, get up loudly from your seat, walk to the front of the classroom, and demand to be excused for an emergency visit to the washroom. 11Stay there at least fifteen minutes and take your time coming back. 12If the instructor asks you where you've been when you reenter the room, simply ignore the question and go to your seat. 13Flop into your chair, slouching back and extending your legs as far out as possible. 14When the instructor informs you of the assignment that the class is working on, heave an exaggerated sigh and very slowly open up your book and start turning the pages. 15About a half hour before class is over, begin to look at the clock every few minutes. 16Ten minutes before dismissal time, start noisily packing up your books and papers. 17Then get up and begin walking to the door a couple of minutes before the class is supposed to end. 18The instructor will look at you and wonder whether it wouldn't have been better to go into business instead of education.

Dealing with Verbal Abuse

1If you are living with a man who abuses you verbally with criticism, complaints, and insults, you should take steps to change your situation. 2First, realize that you are not to blame for his abusive behavior. 3This may be difficult for you to believe. 4Years of verbal abuse have probably convinced you that you're responsible for everything that's wrong with your relationship. 5But that is a lie. 6If your partner is verbally abusive, it is his responsibility to learn why he chooses to deal with his problems by saying nasty things. 7Perhaps he observed his father treating his mother that same way. 8Maybe he never learned any more positive ways to deal with negative emotions, like anger, fear, or disappointment. 9Steps two and three need to be done one right after the other. 10Step two is for you to announce that you will no longer tolerate being verbally abused. 11State that you are a person who deserves respect and civil behavior, and that you will accept no less. 12 Next, offer to go with him to talk to a counselor who will help both of you learn new ways to communicate. 13 While he learns to express his feelings without attacking you, you can learn to stand up for yourself and express your feelings clearly. 14 If he refuses to take responsibility for changing his abusive behavior, then you must consider step four: to leave him. 15 You were not put here on earth to have your self-concept demolished by serving as someone else's verbal punching-bag.

■ Questions

About Unity

1. Which paragraph lacks an opening topic sentence?

   _____

2. Which two sentences in "Sneaking into the House at Night" should be eliminated in the interest of paragraph unity? *(Write the sentence numbers here.)*

   _____   _____

About Support

3. After which sentence in "How to Harass an Instructor" are supporting details (examples) needed?

   _____

4. Summarize the four steps in the process of dealing with verbal abuse.

   a. _____

   b. _____

   c. _____

   d. _____

About Coherence

5. Do these paragraphs use time order or emphatic order?

   _____

6. Which transition words introduce the first, second, and third steps in "Sneaking into the House at Night"?

   _____   _____   _____

Developing a Process Paragraph

Development through Prewriting

To be successful, a process essay must explain clearly each step of an activity. The key to preparing to write such an essay is thinking through the activity as though you're doing it for the first time. Selma is the author of "Dealing with Verbal Abuse." As she considered possible topics for her paper, she soon focused on a situation in her own life: living with an abusive man. Selma had not known how to change her situation. But with the help of a counselor, she realized there were steps she could take—a process she could follow. She carried out that process and finally left her abusive partner. Remembering this, Selma decided to write about how to deal with abuse.

She began by making a list of the steps she followed in coping with her own abusive relationship. This is what she wrote:

> Tell him you won't accept any more abuse.
>
> Open your own checking account.
>
> Apply for credit cards in your own name.
>
> Offer to go with him to counseling.
>
> Realize you're not to blame.
>
> Learn to stand up for yourself.
>
> Go into counseling yourself if he won't do it.
>
> Call the police if he ever becomes violent.
>
> Leave him if he refuses to change.

Next, she numbered the steps in the order in which she had performed them. She crossed out some items she realized weren't really part of the process of dealing with verbal abuse.

> 2 Tell him you won't accept any more abuse.
>
> ~~Open your own checking account.~~
>
> ~~Apply for credit cards in your own name.~~
>
> 3 Offer to go with him to counseling.
>
> 1 Realize you're not to blame.
>
> 5 Learn to stand up for yourself.
>
> 4 Go into counseling yourself if he won't do it.
>
> ~~Call the police if he ever becomes violent.~~
>
> 6 Leave him if he refuses to change.

Then Selma grouped her items into four steps. Those steps were (1) realize you're not to blame; (2) tell the abuser you won't accept more abuse; (3) get into counseling, preferably with him; and (4) if necessary, leave him.

Selma was ready to write her first draft. Here it is:

> Some people think that "abuse" has to mean getting punched and kicked, but that's not so. Verbal abuse can be as painful inside as physical abuse is on the outside. It can make you feel worthless and sad. I know because I lived with a verbally abusive man for years. Finally I found the courage to deal with the situation. Here is what I did. With the help of friends, I finally figured out that I wasn't to blame. I thought it was my fault because that's what he always told me—that if I wasn't so stupid, he wouldn't criticize and insult me. When I told him I wanted him to stop insulting and criticizing me, he just laughed at me and told me I was a crybaby. One of my friends suggested a counselor, and I asked Harry to go talk to him with me. We went together once but Harry wouldn't go back. He said he didn't need anyone to tell him how to treat his woman. I wasn't that surprised because Harry grew up with a father who treated his mother like dirt and his mom just accepts it to this day. Even after Harry refused to go see the counselor, though, I kept going. The counselor helped me see that I couldn't make Harry change, but I was still free to make my own choices. If I didn't want to live my life being Harry's verbal punching bag, and if he didn't want to change, then I would have to. I told Harry that I wasn't going to live that way anymore. I told him if he wanted to work together on better ways to communicate, I'd work with him. But otherwise, I would leave. He gave me his usual talk about "Oh, you know I don't really mean half the stuff I say when I'm mad." I said that wasn't a good enough excuse, and that I did mean what I was saying. He got mad all over again and called me every name in the book. I stuck around for a little while after that but then realized "This is it. I can stay here and take this or I can do what I know is right for me." So I left. It was a really hard decision but it was the right one. Harry may be angry at me forever but I know now that his anger and his verbal abuse is his problem, not mine.

Development through Revising

After Selma had written her first draft, she showed it to a classmate for her comments. Here is what the classmate wrote in response:

> In order for this to be a good process essay, I think you need to do a couple of things.
>
> First, although the essay is based on what you went through, I think it's too much about your own experience. I'd suggest you take yourself out of it and just write about how any person could deal with any verbally abusive situation. Otherwise this paper is about you and Harry, not the process.

Second, you need a clear topic sentence that tells the reader what process you're going to explain.

Third, I'd use transitions like 'first' and 'next' to make the steps in the process clearer. I think the steps are all there, but they get lost in all the details about you and Harry.

When Selma reread her first draft, she agreed with her classmate's suggestions. She then wrote the version of "Dealing with Verbal Abuse" that appears on page 184.

Writing a Process Paragraph

■ Writing Assignment 1

Choose one of the topics below to write about in a process paper.

How to feed a family on a budget

How to break up with a boyfriend or girlfriend

How to balance a checkbook

How to change a car or bike tire

How to get rid of house or garden pests, such as mice, roaches, or wasps

How to play a simple game like checkers, tick tack toe, or an easy card game

How to shorten a skirt or pants

How to meet new people, for either dating or friendship

How to plant a garden

How to deal with a nosy person

How to fix a leaky faucet, a clogged drain, or the like

How to build a campfire or start a fire in a fireplace

How to study for an important exam

How to conduct a yard or garage sale

How to wash dishes efficiently, clean a bathroom, do laundry, or the like

Prewriting

a Begin by freewriting on your topic for ten minutes. Do not worry about spelling, grammar, organization, or other matters of form. Just write whatever comes into your head regarding the topic. Keep writing for more than ten minutes if ideas keep coming to you. This freewriting will give you a base of raw material to draw from during the next phase of your work on the paragraph. After freewriting, you should have a sense of whether there is enough material available for you to write a process paragraph about the topic. If so, continue as explained below. If there is not enough material, choose another topic and freewrite about *it* for ten minutes.

b Write a clear, direct topic sentence stating the process you are going to describe. For instance, if you are going to describe a way to study for major exams, your topic sentence might be "My study-skills instructor has suggested a good way to study for major exams." Or you can state in your topic sentence the process and the number of steps involved: "My technique for building a campfire involves four main steps."

c List all the steps you can think of that may be included in the process. Don't worry, at this point, about how each step fits or whether two steps overlap. Here, for example, is the list prepared by the author of "Sneaking into the House at Night":

Quiet on stairs
Come in after Dad's asleep
House is freezing at night
Bring key
Know which steps to avoid
Lift up front door
Late dances on Saturday night
Don't turn on bathroom light
Avoid squeaky spots on floor
Get into bed quietly

d Number your items in the order in which they occur; strike out items that do not fit in the list; add others that come to mind. The author of "Sneaking into the House at Night" did this step as follows:

~~Quiet on stairs~~
2 Come in after Dad's asleep
~~House is freezing at night~~
1 Bring key
5 Know which steps to avoid
3 Lift up front door
~~Late dances on Saturday night~~
6 Don't turn on bathroom light

4 Avoid squeaky spots on floor

8 Get into bed quietly

7 Undress quietly

e Use your list as a guide to write the first draft of your paper. As you write, try to think of additional details that will support your opening sentence. Do not expect to finish your paper in one draft. After you complete your first rough draft, in fact, you should be ready to write a series of drafts as you work toward the goals of unity, support, and coherence.

Revising

After you have written the first draft of your paragraph, set it aside for a while if you can. Then read it out loud, either to yourself or (better yet) to a friend or class-mate who will be honest with you about how it sounds. You (or you and your friend) should keep these points in mind:

- An effective process paper describes a series of activities in a way that is clear and easy to follow. Are the steps in this paper described in a clear, logical way? Have you used transitions such as *first, next, also, then, after, now, during,* and *finally* to make the paper move smoothly from one step to another?
- Does the paragraph explain every necessary step so that a reader could perform the task described?
- Can you answer "yes" to other questions about unity, support, and coherence on the inside front cover of this book?
- Is the point of view consistent? For example, if you begin by writing "This is how I got rid of mice" (first person), do not switch to "You must buy the right traps" (second person). Write your paragraph either from the first-person point of view (using *I* and *we*) or from the second-person point of view (*you*)—do not jump back and forth between the two.
- Have you corrected any sentence-skills mistakes that you noticed while read-ing the paper out loud? Have you checked the paper carefully for sentence skills, including spelling, as listed on the inside front cover of the book?

Continue revising your work until you and your reader can answer "yes" to all these questions.

■ Writing Assignment 2

Write a paragraph about one of the following processes. For this assignment, you will be working with more general topics than those in Writing Assignment 1. In fact, many of the topics are so broad that entire books have been written about them. A big part of your task, then, will be to narrow the topic down enough so that it can be covered in one paragraph. Then you'll have to invent your own steps for the process. In addition, you'll need to make decisions about how many steps to include and the order in which to present them.

How to break a bad habit such as smoking, overeating, or excess drinking

How to improve a course you have taken

How to make someone you know happy

How to discipline a child

How to improve the place where you work

How to show appreciation to others

How to make someone forgive you

How to make yourself depressed

How to get over a broken relationship

How to procrastinate

How to flirt

Prewriting

a   Choose a topic that appeals to you. Then ask yourself, "How can I make this broad, general topic narrow enough to be covered in a paragraph?" A logical way to proceed would be to think of a particular time you have gone through this process. For instance, if the general topic is "How to decorate economically," you might think about a time you decorated your own apartment.

b   Write a topic sentence about the process you are going to describe. Your topic sentence should clearly reflect the narrowed-down topic you have chosen. If you chose the topic described in step *a*, for example, your topic sentence could be "I made my first apartment look nice without spending a fortune."

c   Make a list of as many different items as you can think of that concern your topic. Don't worry about repeating yourself, about putting them in order, about whether details are major or minor, or about spelling. Simply make a list of everything about your topic that occurs to you. Here, for instance, is a list of items generated by the student writing about decorating her apartment on a budget:

Bought pretty towels and used them as wall hangings

Trimmed overgrown shrubs in front yard

Used old mayonnaise jars for vases to hold flowers picked in the yard

Found an old oriental rug at a yard sale

Painted mismatched kitchen chairs in bright colors

Kept dishes washed and put away

Bought a slipcover for a battered couch

Used pink lightbulbs

Hung pretty colored sheets over the windows

d   Next, decide what order you will present your items in and number them. (As in the example of "decorating an apartment," there may not be an order that the steps *must* be done in. If that is the case, you'll need to make a decision about a sequence that makes sense, or that you followed yourself.) As you number your items, strike out items that do not fit in the list and add others that you think of, like this:

6   Bought pretty towels and used them as wall hangings

~~Trimmed overgrown shrubs in front yard~~

7   Used old mayonnaise jars for vases to hold flowers picked in the yard

4   Found an old oriental rug at a yard sale

2   Painted mismatched kitchen chairs in bright colors

~~Kept dishes washed and put away~~

1   Bought a slipcover for a battered couch

8   Used pink lightbulbs

5   Hung pretty colored sheets over the windows

3   Built bookshelves out of cinder blocks and boards

e   Referring to your list of steps, write the first draft of your paper. Add additional steps as they occur to you.

Revising

If you can, put your first draft away for a day or so and then return to it. Read it out loud to yourself or, better yet, to a friend who will give you honest feedback.

Here are questions to ask yourself as you read over your first draft and the drafts to follow:

- Have I included a clear topic sentence that tells what process I will be describing?
- Have I included all the essential information so that anyone reading my paper could follow the same process?
- Have I made the sequence of steps easy to follow by using transitions like *first, second, then, next, during*, and *finally*?

- Can I answer "yes" to other questions about unity, support, and coherence found on the inside front cover of the book?
- Have I corrected sentence-skills mistakes, including spelling?

Continue revising your work until you can answer "yes" to all these questions.

■ Writing Assignment 3

Everyone is an expert at something. Write a process paragraph on some skill that you can perform very well. The skill might be, for example, refereeing a game, fishing for perch, painting a room, putting up a tent, making an ice-cream soda, becoming a long-distance runner, or fine-tuning a car engine. Your topic sentence should be a general statement that summarizes in some way the process described, such as the following:

> Building a good deck requires time and care.
>
> Getting my four-year-old to bed at night is a lengthy process.
>
> You can create a beautiful centerpiece for your Thanksgiving table using a pumpkin and dried flowers.

■ Writing Assignment 4

Write a process paragraph on how to succeed at a job interview. Using strategies described in the chapter on the library and the Internet (pages 361–378), research the topic. Your reading will help you think about how to proceed with the paper.

Condense the material you have found into three, four, or five basic steps. Choose the steps, tips, and pointers that seem most important to you or that recur most often in the material. Remember that you are reading only to obtain background information for your paper. Do not copy material or repeat someone else's words or phrases in your own work.

■ Writing Assignment 5

Option 1: Imagine that you have a part-time job helping out in a day-care center. The director, who is pleased with your work and wants to give you more responsibility, has put you in charge of a group activity (for example, an exercise session, an alphabet lesson, or a valentine-making project). But before you actually begin the activity, the director wants to see a summary of how you would go about it. What advance preparation would be needed, and what exactly would you be doing throughout the time of the project? Write a paragraph explaining the steps you would follow in conducting the activity.

Option 2:   Alternatively, write an explanation you might give to one of the children of how to do a simple classroom task—serving juice and cookies, getting ready for nap time, watering a plant, putting toys or other classroom materials away, or any other task you choose. Explain each step of the task in a way that a child would understand.

10 Examining Cause and Effect

What caused Pat to drop out of school? Why are soap operas so popular? Why does our football team do so poorly each year? How has retirement affected Dad? What effects does divorce have on children? Every day we ask such questions and look for answers. We realize that situations have causes and also effects—good or bad. By examining causes and effects, we seek to understand and explain things.

In this section, you will be asked to do some detective work by examining the causes of something or the effects of something. First read the three paragraphs that follow and answer the questions about them. All three paragraphs support their opening points by explaining a series of causes or a series of effects.

Paragraphs to Consider

New Puppy in the House

[1] Buying a new puppy can have significant effects on a household. [2] For one thing, the puppy keeps the entire family awake for at least two solid weeks. [3] Every night when the puppy is placed in its box, it begins to howl, yip, and whine. [4] Even after the lights go out and the house quiets down, the puppy continues to moan. [5] A second effect is that the puppy tortures the family by destroying material possessions. [6] Every day something different is damaged. [7] Family members find chewed belts and shoes, gnawed table legs, and ripped sofa cushions leaking stuffing. [8] In addition, the puppy often misses the paper during the paper-training stage of life, thus making the house smell like the public restroom at a city bus station. [9] Maybe the most serious problem, though, is that the puppy causes family arguments. [10] Parents argue with children about who is supposed to feed and walk the dog. [11] Children argue about who gets to play with the puppy first. [12] Everyone argues about who left socks and shoes around for the puppy to find. [13] These continual arguments, along with the effects of sleeplessness and the loss of valued possessions, can really disrupt a household. [14] Only when the puppy gets a bit older does the household settle back to normal.

My Car Accident

[1]Several factors caused my recent car accident. [2]First of all, because a heavy snow and freezing rain had fallen the day before, the road that I was driving on was hazardous. [3]The road had been plowed but was dangerously icy in spots where dense clusters of trees kept the early-morning sun from hitting the road and melting the ice. [4]Second, despite the slick patches, I was stupidly going along at about fifty miles an hour instead of driving more cautiously. [5]I have a daredevil streak in my nature and sometimes feel I want to become a stock-car racer after I finish school, rather than an accountant as my parents want me to be. [6]A third factor contributing to my accident was a dirty green Chevy van that suddenly pulled onto the road from a small intersecting street about fifty yards ahead of me. [7]The road was a sheet of ice at that point, but I was forced to apply my brake and also swing my car into the next lane. [8]Unfortunately, the fourth and final cause of my accident now came into play. [9]The rear of my Honda Civic was heavy because I had a set of barbells in the backseat. [10]I was selling this fairly new weight-lifting set to someone at school, since the weights had failed to build up my muscles immediately and I had gotten tired of practicing with them. [11]The result of all the weight in the rear was that after I passed the van, my car spun completely around on the slick road. [12]For a few horrifying, helpless moments, I was sliding down the highway backward at fifty miles an hour, with no control whatsoever over the car. [13]Then, abruptly, I slid off the road, thumping into a huge snowbank. [14]I felt stunned for a moment but then also relieved. [15]I saw a telephone pole about six feet to the right of me and realized that my accident could have been disastrous.

Why I Stopped Smoking

[1]For one thing, I realized that my cigarette smoke bothered others, irritating people's eyes and causing them to cough and sneeze. [2]They also had to put up with my stinking smoker's breath. [3]Also, cigarettes are a messy habit. [4]Our house was littered with ashtrays piled high with butts, matchsticks, and ashes, and the children were always knocking them over. [5]Cigarettes are expensive, and I estimated that the carton a week that I was smoking cost me about $1,060 a year. [6]Another reason I stopped was that the message about cigarettes being harmful to health finally got through to me. [7]I'd known they could hurt the smoker—in fact, a heavy smoker I know from work is in Eagleville Hospital now with lung cancer. [8]But when I realized what secondhand smoke could do to my wife and children, causing them bronchial problems and even increasing their risk of cancer, it really bothered me. [9]Cigarettes were also inconvenient. [10]Whenever I smoked, I would have to drink something to wet my dry throat, and that meant I had to keep going to the bathroom all the time. [11]I sometimes seemed to spend whole weekends doing nothing but smoking, drinking, and going to the

bathroom. [12]Most of all, I resolved to stop smoking because I felt exploited. [13]I hated the thought of wealthy, greedy corporations making money off my sweat and blood. [14]The rich may keep getting richer, but—at least as regards cigarettes—with no thanks to me.

■ Questions

About Unity

1. Which two sentences in "My Car Accident" do not support the opening idea and so should be omitted? (*Write the sentence numbers here.*)

   _____   _____

2. Which of the above paragraphs lacks a topic sentence?

   _____

About Support

3. How many separate causes are given in "Why I Stopped Smoking"?

   _____ four   _____ six   _____ seven   _____ eight

4. How many effects of bringing a new puppy into the house are given in "New Puppy in the House"?

   _____ one   _____ two   _____ three   _____ four

About Coherence

5. What transition words or phrases are used to introduce the four reasons listed in "My Car Accident"?

   _____   _____   _____   _____

6. In "New Puppy in the House," what words signal the effect that the author feels may be the most important?

   _____

Developing a Cause-and-Effect Paragraph

Development through Prewriting

In order to write a good cause-and-effect paragraph, you must clearly define an effect (*what* happened) and the contributing causes (*why* it happened). In addition, you will need to provide details that support the causes and effects you're writing about.

Jerome is the student author of "Why I Stopped Smoking." As soon as the topic occurred to him, he knew he had his *effect* (he had stopped smoking). His next task was to come up with a list of *causes* (reasons he had stopped). He decided to make a list of all the reasons for his quitting smoking that he could think of. This is what he came up with:

Annoyed others
Messy
Bad for health
Expensive

Taking his list, Jerome then jotted down details that supported each of those reasons:

Annoyed others
Bad breath
Irritates eyes
Makes other people cough
People hate the smell

Messy
Ashtrays, ashes, butts everywhere
Messes up my car interior

Bad for health
Marco in hospital with lung cancer
Secondhand smoke dangerous to family
My morning cough

Expensive
Carton a week costs more than $1,000 a year
Tobacco companies getting rich off me

Jerome then had an effect and four causes with details to support them. On the basis of this list, he wrote a first draft:

My smoking annoyed other people, making them cough and burning their eyes. I bothered them with my smoker's breath. Nonsmokers usually hate the smell of cigarettes and I got embarrassed when nonsmokers visited my house. I saw them wrinkle their noses in disgust at the smell. It is a messy habit. My house was full of loaded ashtrays that the kids were always knocking over. My car was messy too. A guy from work, Marco, who has smoked for years, is in the hospital now with lung cancer. It doesn't look like he's going to make it. Secondhand smoke is bad for people too and

I worried it would hurt my wife and kids. Also I realized I was coughing once in a while. The price of cigarettes keeps going up and I was spending too much on smokes. When I see things in the paper about tobacco companies and their huge profits it made me mad.

Development through Revising

The next day, Jerome traded first drafts with his classmate Roger. This is what Roger had to say about Jerome's work:

> The biggest criticism I have is that you haven't used many transitions to tie your sentences together. Without them, the paragraph sounds like a list, not a unified piece of writing.
>
> Is one of your reasons more important than the others? If so, it would be good if you indicated that.
>
> You could add a little more detail in several places. For instance, how could secondhand smoke hurt your family? And how much were you spending on cigarettes?

As Jerome read his own paper, he realized he wanted to add one more reason to his paragraph: the inconvenience to himself. "Maybe it sounds silly to write about always getting drinks and going to the bathroom, but that's one of the ways that smoking takes over your life that you never think about when you start," he said. Using Roger's comments and his own new idea, he produced the paragraph that appears on page 196.

Writing a Cause-and-Effect Paragraph

■ Writing Assignment 1

Choose one of the three topic sentences and brief outlines below. Each is made up of three supporting points (causes or effects). Your task is to turn the topic sentence and outline into a cause or effect paragraph.

Option 1

Topic sentence: There are several reasons why some high school graduates are unable to read.

(1) Failure of parents (*cause*)

(2) Failure of schools (*cause*)

(3) Failure of students themselves (*cause*)

Option 2

Topic sentence: Attending college has changed my personality in positive ways.

(1) More confident (*effect*)

(2) More knowledgeable (*effect*)

(3) More adventurous (*effect*)

Option 3

Topic sentence: Living with roommates (or family) makes attending college difficult.

(1) Late-night hours (*cause*)

(2) More temptations to cut class (*cause*)

(3) More distractions from studying (*cause*)

Prewriting

a   After you've chosen the option that appeals to you most, jot down all the details you can think of that might go under each of the supporting points. Use separate paper for your lists. Don't worry yet about whether you can use all the items—your goal is to generate more material than you need. Here, for example, are some of the details generated by the author of "New Puppy in the House" to back up her supporting points:

Topic sentence: Having a new puppy disrupts a household.

1. Keeps family awake
    a. Whines at night
    b. Howls
    c. Loss of sleep
2. Destroys possessions
    a. Chews belts and shoes
    b. Chews furniture
    c. Tears up toys it's supposed to fetch
3. Has accidents in house
    a. Misses paper
    b. Disgusting clean-up
    c. Makes house smell bad
4. Causes arguments
    a. Arguments about walking dog
    b. Arguments about feeding dog
    c. Arguments about who gets to play with dog
    d. Arguments about vet bills

b Now go through the details you have generated and decide which are most effective. Strike out the ones you decide are not worth using. Do other details occur to you? If so, jot them down as well.

c Now you are ready to write your paragraph. Begin the paragraph with the topic sentence you chose. Make sure to develop each of the supporting points from the outline into a complete sentence, and then back it up with the best of the details you have generated.

Revising

Review your paragraph with these questions in mind:

- Have I begun the paragraph with the topic sentence provided?
- Is each supporting point stated in a complete sentence?
- Have I provided effective details to back up each supporting point?
- Have I used transitions such as *in addition, another thing,* and *also* to make the relationships between the sentences clear?
- Have I proofread the paragraph for sentence skills errors, including spelling?

Revise your paragraph until you are sure the answer to each question is "yes."

■ Writing Assignment 2

Most of us find it easy to criticize other people, but we may find it harder to give compliments. In this assignment, you will be asked to write a one-paragraph letter praising someone. The letter may be to a person you know (for instance, a parent, relative, or friend); to a public figure (an actor, politician, religious leader, sports star, and so on); or to a company or organization (for example, the people who manufactured a product you own, a newspaper, a government agency, or a store where you shop).

Prewriting

a The fact that you are writing this letter indicates that its recipient has had an *effect* on you: you like, admire, or appreciate the person or organization. Your job will be to put into words the *causes*, or reasons, for this good feeling. Begin by making a list of reasons for your admiration. Here, for example, are a few reasons a person might praise an automobile manufacturer:

My car is dependable.

The price was reasonable.

I received prompt action on a complaint.

The car is well-designed.

The car dealer was honest and friendly.

The car has needed little maintenance.

Reasons for admiring a parent might include these:

You are patient with me.

You are fair.

You have a great sense of humor.

You encourage me in several ways.

I know you have made sacrifices for me.

Develop your own list of reasons for admiring the person or organization you've chosen.

b   Now that you have a list of reasons, you need details to back up each reason. Jot down as many supporting details as you can for each reason. Here is what the writer of a letter to the car manufacturer might do:

My car is dependable.
Started during last winter's coldest days when neighbors' cars wouldn't start
Has never stranded me anywhere

The price was reasonable.
Compared with other cars in its class, it cost less
Came standard with more options than other cars of the same price

I received prompt action on a complaint.
When I complained about rattle in door, manufacturer arranged for a part to be replaced at no charge

The car is well-designed.
Controls are easy to reach
Dashboard gauges are easy to read

The car dealer was honest and friendly.
No pressure, no fake "special deal only today" prices

The car has needed little maintenance.
Haven't done anything but regular tune-ups and oil changes

c   Next, select from your list the three or four reasons that you can best support with effective details. These will make up the body of your letter.

d   For your topic sentence, make the positive statement you wish to support. For example, the writer of the letter to the car manufacturer might begin like this: "I am a very satisfied owner of a 1998 Meteor."

e Now combine your topic sentence, reasons, and supporting details, and write a draft of your letter.

Revising

If possible, put your letter aside for a day. Then read it aloud to a friend. As you and he or she listen to your words, you should both keep these questions in mind:

- Is my topic sentence a positive statement that is supported by the details?
- Do I clearly state several different reasons why I like or admire the person or organization I'm writing to?
- Do I support each of those reasons with specific evidence?
- Have I linked my sentences together with transitional words and phrases?
- Is my letter free of sentence-skills mistakes, including spelling errors?

Continue revising your work until you and your reader can answer "yes" to all these questions.

■ Writing Assignment 3

What do you do to keep yourself well and fit? Do you eat or avoid certain foods? Do you exercise? Write a paragraph explaining in detail one or more healthy habits you've adopted and the results each has had. For instance, if you jog several times a week, tell where and when you jog and for how long, and then explain what you think are the effects. Give specific examples and descriptive details from your experience to illustrate each effect. Below are a couple of sample topic sentences for this assignment.

> Adding a few hours of jogging to my weekly schedule has had several very positive effects.
>
> The discipline I have used over the past year to stick to a healthy diet has had some good results.

Feel free to use a tongue-in-cheek approach. For example, you might want to use a topic sentence like the following:

> I have managed to avoid becoming overly thin and muscular by giving up all exercise and including plenty of chocolate in my diet.

Even with humor, however, you must support your topic sentence with specific details. For instance, one supporting detail for the above topic sentence might be the point that giving up exercise leaves you plenty of time for homework in your health sciences class.

■ Writing Assignment 4

Investigate the reasons behind a current news event. For example, you may want to discover the causes of one of the following:

A labor strike or some other protest

A military action by our or some other government

A murder or some other act of violence

A tax increase

A traffic accident, a fire, a plane crash, or some other disastrous event

Research the reasons for the event by reading current newspapers (especially big-city dailies that are covering the story in detail), reading weekly newsmagazines (such as *Time* and *Newsweek*), watching television shows and specials, or consulting an Internet news source.

Decide on the major cause or causes of the event and their specific effects. Then write a paragraph explaining in detail the causes and effects. Below is a sample topic sentence for this assignment.

The rape and murder that occurred recently on X Street have caused much fear and caution throughout the neighborhood.

Note how this topic sentence uses general words (*fear, caution*) that can summarize specific supporting details. Support for the word *caution,* for example, might include specific ways in which people in the neighborhood are doing a better job of protecting themselves.

■ Writing Assignment 5

Option 1:   Assume that there has been an alarming increase in drug abuse among the students at the high school you attended. What might be the causes of this increase? Spend some time thinking and freewriting about several possible causes. Then, as a concerned member of the community, write a letter to the high school guidance counselor explaining the reasons for the increased drug abuse. Your purpose is to provide information the counselor may be able to use in dealing with the problem.

Option 2:   Your roommate has been complaining that it's impossible to succeed in Mr. X's class because the class is too stressful. You volunteer to attend the class and see for yourself. Afterward, you decide to write a letter to the instructor calling attention to the stressful conditions and suggesting concrete ways to deal with them. Write this letter, explaining in detail the causes and effects of stress in the class.

11 Comparing or Contrasting

Comparison and contrast are two everyday thought processes. When we *compare* two things, we show how they are similar; when we *contrast* two things, we show how they are different. We might compare or contrast two brand-name products (for example, Nike versus Adidas running shoes), two television shows, two instructors, two jobs, two friends, or two courses of action we could take in a given situation. The purpose of comparing or contrasting is to understand each of the two things more clearly and, at times, to make judgments about them.

In this section, you will be asked to write a paper of comparison or contrast. First, however, you must learn the two common methods of developing a comparison or contrast paragraph. Read the two paragraphs that follow and try to explain the difference in the two methods of development.

Paragraphs to Consider

My Senior Prom

₁My senior prom was nothing like what I expected it to be. ₂From the start of my senior year, I had pictured getting dressed in a sleek silvery slip dress that my aunt would make and that would cost $200 in any store. ₃No one else would have a gown as attractive as mine. ₄I imagined my boyfriend coming to the door with a lovely deep-red corsage, and I pictured myself happily inhaling its perfume all evening long. ₅I saw us setting off for the evening in his brother's 2000 BMW convertible. ₆We would make a flourish as we swept in and out of a series of parties before the prom. ₇Our evening would be capped by a delicious shrimp dinner at the prom and by dancing close together into the early morning hours. ₈The prom was held on May 15, 2000, at the Pony Club on Black Horse Pike. ₉However, because of sickness in her family, my aunt had no time to finish my gown and I had to buy an ugly pink one off the discount rack at the last minute. ₁₀My corsage of red roses looked terrible on my pink gown, and I do not remember its having any scent. ₁₁My boyfriend's brother was out of town, and I stepped outside and saw the stripped-down Chevy that he used at the races on weekends. ₁₂We went to one party where I drank a lot of wine that made me sleepy and upset my stomach. ₁₃After we arrived at the prom, I did not have much more to eat than a roll and some celery sticks. ₁₄Worst of all, we left early without dancing because my boyfriend and I had had a fight several days before, and at the time we did not really want to be with each other.

Day versus Evening Students

¹As a part-time college student who has taken both day and evening courses, I have observed notable differences between day and evening students. ²First of all, day and evening students differ greatly in age, styles, and interests. ³The students in my daytime classes are all about the same age, with similar clothing styles and similar interests. ⁴Most are in their late teens to early twenties, and whether male or female, they pretty much dress alike. ⁵Their uniform consists of jeans, a T-shirt, running shoes, a baseball cap, and maybe a gold earring or two. ⁶They use the same popular slang, talk about the same movies and TV shows, and know the same musical artists. ⁷But students in my evening courses are much more diverse. ⁸Some are in their late teens, but most range from young married people in their twenties and thirties to people my grandparents' age. ⁹Generally, their clothing is more formal than the day students'. ¹⁰They are dressed for the workplace, not for a typical college classroom. ¹¹Many of the women wear skirts or dresses; the men often wear dress shirts or sweaters. ¹²And they are more comfortable talking about their mortgages or work schedules or child care than about what was on TV last night. ¹³Day and evening students also have very different responsibilities. ¹⁴For day students, college and a part-time job are generally the only major responsibilities. ¹⁵They have plenty of time to study and get assignments done. ¹⁶However, evening students lead much more complicated lives than most day students. ¹⁷They may come to campus after putting in a nine-to-five day at work. ¹⁸Most have children to raise or grandchildren to baby-sit for. ¹⁹When they miss a class or hand in an assignment late, it's usually because of a real problem, such as a sick child or an important deadline at work. ²⁰Finally, day and evening students definitely have different attitudes toward school. ²¹Day students often seem more interested in the view out the window or the cute classmate in the next row than in what the instructor is saying. ²²They doze, draw cartoons, whisper, and write notes instead of paying attention. ²³Evening students sit up straight, listen hard, and ask the instructor lots of questions. ²⁴They obviously are there to learn, and they don't want their time wasted. ²⁵In short, day students and night students are as different as . . . day and night.

Complete this comment: The difference in the methods of contrast in the two paragraphs is that

_____

_____

_____

Compare your answer with the following explanation of the two methods of development used in comparison or contrast paragraphs.

Methods of Development

There are two common methods, or formats, of development in a comparison or contrast paper. One format presents the details *one side at a time*. The other presents the details *point by point*. Each format is explained below.

One Side at a Time

Look at the outline of "My Senior Prom":

Topic sentence: My senior prom was nothing like what I had expected it to be.

A. Expectations (<u>first half of paper</u>)
    1. Dress (expensive, silver)
    2. Corsage (deep red, fragrant)
    3. Car (BMW convertible)
    4. Parties (many)
    5. Dinner (shrimp)
    6. Dancing (all night)
B. Reality (<u>second half of paper</u>)
    1. Dress (cheap, pink)
    2. Corsage (wrong color, no scent)
    3. Car (stripped-down Chevy)
    4. Parties (only one)
    5. Dinner (roll and celery)
    6. Dancing (none because of quarrel)

When you use the one-side-at-a-time method, follow the same order of points of contrast or comparison for each side, as in the outline above. For example, both the first half of the paper and the second half begin with the topic of what dress would be worn. Then both sides go on to the corsage, the car, and so on.

Point by Point

Now look at the outline of "Day versus Evening Students":

Topic sentence: There are notable differences between day and night students.

A. Age and related interests and tastes in clothing
    1. Youthful nature of day students
    2. Older nature of evening students
B. Amount of responsibilities
    1. Lighter responsibilities of day students
    2. Heavier responsibilities of evening students

    C.   Attitude toward school
        1.   Casual attitude of day students
        2.   Serious attitude of evening students

The outline shows how the two kinds of students are contrasted point by point. First, the writer contrasts the ages, clothing styles, and interests of the young daytime students and the older evening students. Next, the writer contrasts the limited responsibilities of the daytime students with the heavier responsibilities of the evening students. Finally, the writer contrasts the casual attitude toward school of the daytime student and the serious attitude of the evening student.

    When you begin a comparison or contrast paper, you should decide right away which format you are going to use: one side at a time or point by point. An outline is an essential step in helping you decide which format will be more workable for your topic. Keep in mind, however, that an outline is just a guide, not a permanent commitment. If you later feel that you've chosen the wrong format, you can reshape your outline to the other format.

Activity

Complete the partial outlines provided for the two paragraphs that follow.

1.
How My Parents' Divorce Changed Me

    In the three years since my parents' divorce, I have changed from a spoiled brat to a reasonably normal college student. Before the divorce, I expected my mother to wait on me. She did my laundry, cooked and cleaned up after meals, and even straightened up my room. My only response was to complain if the meat was too well done or if the sweater I wanted to wear was not clean. In addition, I expected money for anything I wanted. Whether it was a portable CD player or my own pager, I expected Mom to hand over the money. If she refused, I would get it from Dad. However, he left when I was fifteen, and things changed. When Mom got a full-time job to support us, I was the one with the free time to do housework. Now, I did the laundry, started the dinner, and cleaned not only my own room but also the rest of the house. Also, I no longer asked her for money, since I knew there was none to spare. Instead, I got a part-time job on weekends to earn my own spending money. Today, I have my own car that I am paying for, and I am putting myself through college. Things have been hard sometimes, but I am glad not to be that spoiled kid any more.

Topic sentence: In the three years since my parents' divorce, I have changed from a spoiled brat to a reasonably normal college student.

a.   Before the divorce

(1) _____

(2) _____

b.   After the divorce

(1) _____

(2) _____

Complete the following statement: Paragraph 1 uses the _____
method of development.

2.   **Good and Bad Horror Movies**

A good horror movie is easily distinguishable from a bad one. A good
horror movie, first of all, has both male and female victims. Both sexes suffer
terrible fates at the hands of monsters and maniacs. Therefore, everyone in
the audience has a chance to identify with the victim. Bad horror movies, on
the other hand, tend to concentrate on women, especially half-dressed ones.
These movies are obviously prejudiced against half the human race. Second,
a good horror movie inspires compassion for its characters. For example,
the audience will feel sympathy for the victims in the horror classics about
the Wolfman, played by Lon Chaney, Jr., and also for the Wolfman himself,
who is shown to be a sad victim of fate. In contrast, a bad horror movie
encourages feelings of aggression and violence in viewers. For instance,
in the Halloween films, the murders are seen from the murderer's point of
view. The effect is that the audience stalks the victims along with the killer
and feels the same thrill he does. Finally, every good horror movie has a
sense of humor. In <u>Alien</u>, as a crew member is coughing and choking just
before the horrible thing bursts out of his chest, a colleague chides him,
"The food ain't <u>that</u> bad, man." Humor provides relief from the horror and
makes the characters more human. A bad horror movie, though, is
humorless and boring. One murder is piled on top of another, and the
characters are just cardboard figures. Bad horror movies may provide cheap
thrills, but the good ones touch our emotions and live forever.

Topic sentence: A good horror movie is easily distinguished from a bad one.

a.   Kinds of victims

(1) _____

(2) _____

b. Effect on audience

(1) _____

(2) _____

c. Tone

(1) _____

(2) _____

Complete the following statement: Paragraph 1 uses the _____
method of development.

Additional Paragraphs to Consider

Read these additional paragraphs of comparison or contrast and then answer the questions that follow.

My Broken Dream

¹When I became a police officer in my town, the job was not as I had dreamed it would be. ²I began to dream about being a police officer at about age ten. ³I could picture myself wearing a handsome blue uniform with an impressive-looking badge on my chest. ⁴I could also picture myself driving a powerful patrol car through town and seeing everyone stare at me with envy. ⁵But most of all, I dreamed of wearing a gun and using all the equipment that "TV cops" use. ⁶I just knew everyone would be proud of me. ⁷I could almost hear the guys on the block saying, "Boy, Steve made it big. ⁸Did you hear he's a cop?" ⁹I dreamed of leading an exciting life, solving big crimes, and meeting lots of people. ¹⁰I just knew that if I became a cop, everyone in town would look up to me. ¹¹However, when I actually did become a police officer, I soon found out that the reality was different. ¹²My first disappointment came when I was sworn in and handed a well-used, baggy uniform. ¹³My disappointment continued when I was given a badge that looked like something pulled out of a Cracker Jack box. ¹⁴I was assigned a beat-up old junker and told that it would be my patrol car. ¹⁵It had a striking resemblance to a car that had lost in a demolition derby at a stock-car raceway. ¹⁶Disappointment seemed to continue. ¹⁷I soon found out that I was not the envy of all my friends. ¹⁸When I drove through town, they acted as if they had not seen me, despite the gun and nightstick at my side. ¹⁹I was told I was crazy doing this kind of job by people I thought would look up to me. ²⁰My job was not as exciting as

I had dreamed it would be, either. [21]Instead of solving robberies and murders every day, I found that I spent a great deal of time comforting a local resident because a neighborhood dog had watered his favorite bush.

Two Views on Toys

[1]Children and adults have very different preferences. [2]First, there is the matter of taste. [3]Adults pride themselves on taste, while children ignore the matter of taste in favor of things that are fun. [4]Adults, especially grandparents, pick out tasteful toys that go unused, while children love the cheap playthings advertised on television. [5]Second, of course, there is the matter of money. [6]The new games on the market today are a case in point. [7]Have you ever tried to lure a child away from some expensive game in order to get him or her to play with an old-fashioned game or toy? [8]Finally, there is a difference between an adult's and a child's idea of what is educational. [9]Adults, filled with memories of their own childhood, tend to be fond of the written word. [10]Today's children, on the other hand, concentrate on anything electronic. [11]These things mean much more to them than to adults. [12]Next holiday season, examine the toys that adults choose for children. [13]Then look at the toys the children prefer. [14]You will see the difference.

Mike and Helen

[1]Like his wife, Helen, Mike has a good sense of humor. [2]Also, they are both short, dark-haired, and slightly pudgy. [3]Unlike Helen, Mike tends to hold a grudge. [4]He is slow to forget a cruel remark, a careless joke, or an unfriendly slight. [5]Mike enjoys swimming, camping, and tennis, but Helen is an indoor type. [6]Both Mike and Helen can be charming when they want to be, and they seem to handle small crises in a calm, cool way. [7]A problem such as an overflowing washer, a stalled car, or a sick child is not a cause for panic; they seem to take such events in stride. [8]In contrast to Helen, though, Mike tends to be disorganized. [9]He is late for appointments and unable to keep important documents—bank records, receipts, and insurance papers—where he can find them.

■ Questions

About Unity

1. Which paragraph lacks a topic sentence?

_____

2. Which paragraph has a topic sentence that is too broad?

_____

About Support

3. Which paragraph contains almost no specific details?

_____

4. Which paragraph provides the most complete support?

_____

About Coherence

5. What method of development (one side at a time or point by point) is used in "My Broken Dream"?

_____

In "Two Views in Toys"?

_____

6. Which paragraph offers specific details, but lacks a clear, consistent method of development?

_____

Developing a Comparison or Contrast Paragraph

Development through Prewriting

Gayle, the author of "My Senior Prom," had little trouble thinking of a topic for her comparison or contrast paragraph.

"My instructor said, 'You might compare or contrast two individuals, jobs you've had, or places you've lived,'" Gayle said. "Then he added, 'Or you might compare or contrast your expectations of a situation with the reality.' I immediately thought of my prom—boy, were my expectations different from the reality! I had thought it would be the high point of my senior year, but instead it was a total disaster."

Because she is a person who likes to think visually, Gayle started her preparations for her paragraph by clustering. She found this a helpful way to "see" the relationships between the points she was developing. Her diagram looked like this:

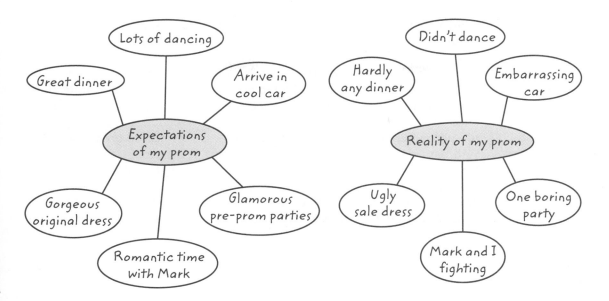

Taking a detail first from the "Expectations" part of the diagram, then one from the "Reality" portion, then another from "Expectations," and so on, Gayle began to write her paragraph using a point-by-point format:

> My senior prom was nothing like what I expected. First of all, I expected to be wearing a beautiful dress that my aunt would make for me. But because she couldn't finish it in time, I had to buy an ugly one at the last minute. Second, I thought I'd have a wonderful romantic evening with my boyfriend. But we'd been fighting that week and by the time the prom came around we were barely speaking. I thought we'd have a great time stopping in at lots of parties before the prom, but we went to only one and I left with an upset stomach.

Gayle stopped here, because she wasn't satisfied with the way the paragraph was developing. "I wanted the reader to picture the way I had imagined my prom, and I didn't like interrupting that picture with the reality of the evening. So I decided to try the one-side-at-a-time approach instead." Here is Gayle's first draft:

> My senior prom was nothing like what I expected. I imagined myself wearing a beautiful, expensive-looking dress that my aunt would make. I thought my boyfriend and I would have a wonderful romantic evening together. We'd dance all through the night and we would cruise around

in my boyfriend's brother's hot car. We would stop in at a lot of fun pre-prom parties, I thought, and we'd have a delicious shrimp dinner at the prom itself. But instead my uncle had a gall-bladder attack that they thought might be a heart attack and my aunt went to the hospital with him instead of finishing my dress. I had to go to the mall at the last minute and buy an ugly dress that nobody else had wanted off the sale rack. Mark and I had been fighting all week. Because he's in track and has a part-time job too we don't have much time together and still he wants to go out on Saturdays with his guy friends. So by the night of the prom we were hardly speaking to each other. We went to only one party before the prom and I left it feeling sick. And the restaurant was so crowded and noisy that I hardly got anything to eat. Because we were angry at each other, we didn't dance at all. And instead of his brother's luxury car, we had to use a stripped-down racing car.

Development through Revising

Gayle's instructor reviewed the first drafts of students who wanted his feedback. Here are his comments on Gayle's work:

> All this is very promising, but some of your details are out of order—for example, you mention the pre-prom parties after the dance itself. Be sure to follow the evening's sequence of events.
>
> More descriptive details are needed! For instance, what was your "beautiful" dress supposed to look like, and what did the "ugly" one you ended up with look like?
>
> You include some unnecessary information: for example, the details of your uncle's illness. Everything in your paragraph should support your topic sentence.

Taking her instructor's suggestions (and remembering a few more details she wanted to include), Gayle wrote the version of her paragraph that appears on page 205.

Writing a Comparison or Contrast Paragraph

■ Writing Assignment 1

Write a comparison or contrast paragraph on one of the topics below:

Two holidays	Two jobs
Two instructors	Two characters in the same movie or TV show
Two children	Two homes
Two kinds of eaters	Two neighborhoods
Two drivers	Two cartoon strips
Two co-workers	
Two members of a team (or two teams)	Two cars
	Two friends
Two singers or groups	Two crises
Two pets	Two bosses or supervisors
Two parties	Two magazines

Prewriting

a Choose your topic, the two subjects you will write about.

b Decide whether your paragraph will *compare* the two subjects (discuss their similarities) or *contrast* them (discuss their differences). Students most often choose to write about differences. For example, you might write about how a musical group you enjoy differs from a musical group you dislike. You might discuss important differences between two employers you have had or between two neighborhoods you've lived in. You might contrast a job you've had in a car factory with a white-collar job you've had as a receptionist.

c Write a direct topic sentence for your paragraph. Here's an example: "My job in a car-parts factory was very different from my job as a receptionist."

d Come up with at least three strong points to support your topic sentence. If you are contrasting two jobs, for example, your points might be that they differed greatly (1) in their physical setting, (2) in the skills they required, and (3) in the people they brought you into contact with.

e Use your topic sentence and supporting points to create a scratch outline for your paragraph. For the jobs paragraph, the outline would look like this:

Topic sentence: My job in a car-parts factory was very different from my job as a receptionist.

1. The jobs differed in physical setting.
2. The jobs differed in the skills they required.
3. The jobs differed in the people they brought me into contact with.

f Under each of your supporting points, jot down as many details as occur to you. Don't worry yet about whether the details all fit perfectly or whether you will be able to use them all. Your goal is to generate a wealth of material to draw on. An example:

Topic sentence: My job in a car-parts factory was very different from my job as a receptionist.

1. The jobs differed in physical setting.
    Factory loud and dirty
    Office clean and quiet
    Factory full of machines, hunks of metal, tools
    Office full of desks, files, computers
    Factory smelled of motor oil
    Office smelled of new carpet
    Windows in factory too high and grimy to look out of
    Office had clean windows onto street

2. The jobs differed in the skills and behavior they required.
    Factory required physical strength
    Office required mental activity
    Didn't need to be polite in factory
    Had to be polite in office
    Didn't need to think much for self in factory
    Constantly had to make decisions in office

3. The jobs differed in the people they brought me into contact with.
    In factory, worked with same crew every day
    In office, saw constant stream of new customers
    Most co-workers in factory had high-school education or less
    Many co-workers and clients in office well educated
    Co-workers in factory spoke variety of languages
    Rarely heard anything but English in office

g Decide which format you will use to develop your paragraph: one side at a time or point by point. Either is acceptable; it is up to you to decide which you prefer. The important thing is to be consistent: whichever format you choose, be sure to use it throughout the entire paragraph.

h Write the first draft of your paragraph.

Revising

Put your writing away for a day or so. You will return to it with a fresh perspective and a better ability to critique what you have done.

Reread your work with these questions in mind:

- Does my topic sentence make it clear what two things I am comparing or contrasting?

- Have I compared or contrasted the subjects in at least three important ways?

- Have I provided specific details that effectively back up my supporting points?

- If I have chosen the point-by-point format, have I consistently discussed a point about one subject, then immediately discussed the same point about the other subject before moving on to the next point?

- If I have chosen the one-side-at-a-time format, have I discussed every point about one of my subjects, then discussed the same points *in the same order* about the second subject?

- Have I used appropriate transitions, such as *first*, *in addition*, *also*, and *another way*, to help the reader follow my train of thought?

- Have I carefully proofread my paragraph, using the list on the inside front cover of the book, and corrected all sentence-skills mistakes, including spelling?

Continue revising your work until you can answer "yes" to all these questions.

■ Writing Assignment 2

Write a paragraph in which you compare or contrast your life in the real world with your life in an imagined "perfect world." Your paragraph may be humorous or serious.

Prewriting

a   As your "real life" and "ideal life" are too broad for a paragraph, decide on three specific areas to focus on. You might select from any of the areas below, or others you think of yourself.

Work
Money
Romance
Physical location
Personal appearance
Friends
Possessions
Housing
Talents

b   Write the name of one of your three areas (for example, "Work"), across the top of a page. Divide the page into two columns. Label one column "real world" and the other "perfect world." Under "real world," write down as many details as you can think of describing your real-life work situation. Under "perfect world," write down details describing what your perfect work life would be like. Repeat the process on separate pages for your other two major areas.

c   Write a topic sentence for your paragraph. Here's an example: "In my perfect world, my life would be quite different in the areas of work, money, and housing."

d   Decide which approach you will take: one side at a time or point by point.

e   Write a scratch outline that reflects the format you have selected. The outline for a point-by-point format would look like this:

<u>Topic sentence:</u> In my perfect world, my life would be quite different in the areas of work, money, and housing.

1.   Work
 a.   Real-life work
 b.   Perfect-world work
2.   Money
 a.   Real-life money
 b.   Perfect-world money
3.   Housing
 a.   Real-life housing
 b.   Perfect-world housing

The outline for a one-side-at-a-time format would look like this:

<u>Topic sentence:</u> In my perfect world, my life would be quite different in the areas of work, money, and housing.

1.   Real life
 a.   Work
 b.   Money
 c.   Housing
2.   Perfect world
 a.   Work
 b.   Money
 c.   Housing

f   Drawing from the three pages of details you generated in step *b*, complete your outline by jotting down your strongest supporting details for each point.

g   Write the first draft of your paragraph.

Revising

Reread your paragraph, and then show it to a friend who will give you honest feedback. You should both review it with these questions in mind:

- Does the topic sentence make it clear what three areas of life are being compared or contrasted?
- Does the paragraph follow a consistent format: point by point or one side at a time?
- Does the paragraph provide specific details that describe both the "real life" situation and the "perfect world" situation?
- Does the paragraph include transitional words and phrases that make it easy to follow?
- Have all sentence-skills mistakes, including spelling, been corrected?

Continue revising your work until you and your reader can answer "yes" to all these questions.

■ ## Writing Assignment 3

Write a contrast paragraph on one of the fifteen topics below.

Neighborhood stores versus a shopping mall
Driving on an expressway versus driving on country roads
People versus *Us* (or any other two popular magazines)
Camping in a tent versus camping in a recreational vehicle
Working parents versus stay-at-home parents
Shopping at a department store versus shopping on the Internet
A used car versus a new one
Recorded music versus live music
PG-rated movies versus R-rated movies
News in a newspaper versus news on television or on the Internet
Yesterday's toys versus today's toys
Fresh food versus canned or frozen food
The locker room of a winning team after a game versus the locker room of a losing team
An ad on television versus an ad for the same product in a magazine
Amateur sports teams versus professional teams

Follow the directions for prewriting and rewriting given in Writing Assignment 2.

■ Writing Assignment 4

Television talk shows share certain features, but they also differ in significant ways. Write a paragraph contrasting two talk shows. In preparation, watch two different talk shows, taking notes on various aspects of the shows. Then arrange the details of your notes into a few categories, such as the performance of the hosts, the types of guests, and the behavior of their audiences. Use your notes to help you decide on a point of view to take in your topic sentence, which might be similar to this one:

> While the *(fill in the name of show 1)* _____ aims to help its viewers, the *(fill in the name of show 2)* _____ is more interested in satisfying viewers' desire for dramatic conflict.

Once you decide on your topic sentence, use only those details that support it. Then decide which method of organization you will use, and prepare a brief outline. Be sure to use transition words and to edit the next-to-final draft carefully.

■ Writing Assignment 5

Imagine that you are living in an apartment building in which new tenants are making life unpleasant for you. Write a letter of complaint to your landlord comparing and contrasting life before and after the tenants arrived. You might want to focus on one or more of the following:

Noise
Trash
Safety hazards
Parking situation

12 Defining a Term

In talking with other people, we sometimes offer informal definitions to explain just what we mean by a particular term. Suppose, for example, we say to a friend, "Karen can be so clingy." We might then expand on our idea of "clingy" by saying, "You know, a clingy person needs to be with someone every single minute. If Karen's best friend makes plans that don't include her, she becomes hurt. And when she dates someone, she calls him several times a day and gets upset if he even goes to the grocery store without her. She hangs on to people way too tightly." In a written definition, we make clear in a more complete and formal way our own personal understanding of a term. Such a definition typically starts with one meaning of a term. The meaning is then illustrated with a series of examples or a story.

In this section, you will be asked to write a paragraph that begins with a one-sentence definition; that sentence will be the topic sentence. The three student papers below are all examples of definition paragraphs. Read them and then answer the questions that follow.

Paragraphs to Consider

Luck

1Luck is putting $1.75 into a vending machine and getting the money back with your snack. 2It is an instructor's decision to give a retest on a test on which you first scored thirty. 3Luck refers to moments of good fortune that happen in everyday life. 4It is not going to the dentist for two years and then going and finding out that you do not have any cavities. 5It is calling up a plumber to fix a leak on a day when the plumber has no other work to do. 6Luck is finding a used car for sale at a good price at exactly the time when your car rolls its last mile. 7It is driving into a traffic bottleneck and choosing the lane that winds up moving most rapidly. 8Luck is being late for work on a day when your boss arrives later than you do. 9It is having a new checkout aisle at the supermarket open up just as your cart arrives. 10The best kind of luck is winning a new wide-screen TV on a chance for which you paid only a quarter.

Disillusionment

¹Disillusionment is the feeling we have when one of our most cherished beliefs is stolen from us. ²I learned about disillusionment firsthand the day Mr. Keller, our eighth-grade teacher, handed out the grades for our class biology projects. ³I had worked hard to assemble what I thought was the best insect collection any school had ever seen. ⁴For weeks, I had set up homemade traps around our house, in the woods, and in vacant lots. ⁵At night, I would stretch a white sheet between two trees, shine a lantern on it, and collect the night-flying insects that gathered there. ⁶With my own money, I had bought killing jars, insect pins, gummed labels, and display boxes. ⁷I carefully arranged related insects together, with labels listing each scientific name and the place and date of capture. ⁸Slowly and painfully, I wrote and typed the report that accompanied my project at the school science fair. ⁹In contrast, my friend Eddie did almost nothing for his project. ¹⁰He had his father, a doctor, build an impressive maze complete with live rats and a sign that read, "You are the trainer." ¹¹A person could lift a little plastic door, send a rat running through the maze, and then hit a button to release a pellet of rat food as a reward. ¹²This exhibit turned out to be the most popular one at the fair. ¹³I felt sure that our teacher would know that Eddie could not have built it, and I was certain that my hard work would be recognized and rewarded. ¹⁴Then the grades were finally handed out, and I was crushed. ¹⁵Eddie had gotten an A-plus, but my grade was a B. ¹⁶I suddenly realized that honesty and hard work don't always pay off in the end. ¹⁷The idea that life is not fair, that sometimes it pays to cheat, hit me with such force that I felt sick. ¹⁸I will never forget that moment.

A Mickey Mouse Course

¹A Mickey Mouse course is any college course that is so easy that even Mickey Mouse could achieve an A. ²A student who is taking a heavy schedule, or who does not want four or five especially difficult courses, will try to sandwich in a Mickey Mouse course. ³A student can find out about such a course by consulting other students, since word of a genuine Mickey Mouse course spreads like wildfire. ⁴Or a student can study the college master schedule for telltale course titles like The Art of Pressing Wildflowers, History of the Comic Book, or Watching Television Creatively. ⁵In an advanced course such as microbiology, though, a student had better be prepared to spend a good deal of time during the semester on the course. ⁶Students in a Mickey Mouse course can attend classes while half-asleep, hung-over, or wearing Walkman earphones or a blindfold; they will still pass. ⁷The course exams (if there are any) would not challenge a five-year-old. ⁸The course lectures usually consist of information that anyone with common sense knows anyway. ⁹Attendance may be required, but

participation or involvement in the class is not. [10]The main requirement for passing is that a student's body is there, warming a seat in the classroom. [11]There are no difficult labs or special projects, and term papers are never mentioned. [12]Once safely registered for such a course, all the students have to do is sit back and watch the credits accumulate on their transcripts.

■ Questions

About Unity

1. Which paragraph places its topic sentence within the paragraph rather than, more appropriately, at the beginning?

   _____

2. Which sentence in "A Mickey Mouse Course" should be omitted in the interest of paragraph unity? *(Write the sentence number here.)* _____

About Support

3. Which two paragraphs develop their definitions through a series of short examples?

   _____

   _____

4. Which paragraph develops its definition through a single extended example?

   _____

About Coherence

5. Which paragraph uses emphatic order, saving its best detail for last?

   _____

6. Which paragraph uses time order to organize its details?

   _____

Developing a Definition Paragraph

Development through Prewriting

When Harry, the author of "Disillusionment," started working on his assignment, he did not know what he wanted to write about. He looked around the house for inspiration. His two-year-old twins racing around the room made him think about defining "energy." The fat cat asleep on a sunny windowsill suggested that he might write about "laziness" or "relaxation." Still not sure of a topic, he looked over his notes from that day's class. His instructor had jotted a list of terms on the blackboard, saying, "Maybe you could focus on what one of these words has meant in your own life." Harry looked over the words he had copied down: *honesty, willpower, faith, betrayal, disillusionment*—"When I got to the word 'disillusionment,' the eighth-grade science fair flashed into my mind," Harry said. "That was a bitter experience that definitely taught me what disillusionment was all about."

Because the science fair had occurred many years before, Harry had to work to remember it well. He decided to try the technique of questioning himself to come up with the details of what had happened. Here are the questions Harry asked himself and the answers he wrote:

<u>When did I learn about disillusionment?</u>
When I was in eighth grade

<u>Where did it happen?</u>
At the school science fair

<u>Who was involved?</u>
Me, Eddie Loomis and his father, and Mr. Keller

<u>What happened?</u>
I had worked very hard on my insect collection. Eddie had done almost nothing but he had a rat maze that his father had built. I got a B on my project while Eddie got an A+.

<u>Why was the experience so disillusioning?</u>
I thought my hard work would be rewarded. I was sure Mr. Keller would recognize that I had put far more effort into my project than Eddie had. When Eddie won, I learned that cheating can pay off and that honest work isn't always rewarded.

<u>How did I react?</u>
I felt sick to my stomach. I wanted to confront Mr. Keller and Eddie and make them see how unfair the grades were. But I knew I'd just look like a poor loser, so I didn't do anything.

<u>On the basis of this experience, how would I define disillusionment?</u>
It's finding out that something you really believed in isn't true.

Drawing from the ideas generated by his self-questioning, Harry wrote the following draft of his paragraph:

Disillusionment is finding out that one of your most important beliefs isn't true. I learned about disillusionment at my eighth-grade science fair. I had worked very hard on my project, an insect collection. I was sure it would get an A. I had worked so hard on it, even spending nights outside making sure it was very good. My friend Eddie also did a project, but he barely worked on his at all. Instead, he had his father build a maze for a rat to run through. The trainer lifted a little plastic door to let the rat into the maze, and if he completed the maze, the trainer could release a pellet of food for it to eat. It was a nice project, but the point is that Eddie hadn't made it. He just made things like the banner that hung over it. Mr. Keller was our science teacher. He gave Eddie an A+ and me just a B. So that really taught me about disillusionment.

Development through Revising

The next day, Harry's teacher divided the class up into groups of three. The groups reviewed each member's paragraph. Harry was grouped with Curtis and Jocelyn. After reading through Harry's paper several times, the group had the following discussion:

"My first reaction is that I want to know more about your project," said Jocelyn. "You give details about Eddie's, but not many about your own. What was so good about it? You need to show us, not just tell us. Also, you said that you worked very hard, but you didn't show us how hard."

"Yeah," said Harry. "I remember my project clearly, but I guess the reader has to know what it was like and how much effort went into it."

Curtis said, "I like your topic sentence, but when I finished the paragraph I wasn't sure what 'important belief' you'd learned wasn't true. What would you say that belief was?"

Harry thought a minute. "I'd believed that honest hard work would always be rewarded. I found out that it doesn't always happen that way, and that cheating can actually win."

Curtis nodded. "I think you need to include that in your paper."

Jocelyn added, "I'd like to read how you felt or reacted after you saw your grade, too. If you don't explain that, the paragraph ends sort of abruptly."

Harry agreed with his classmates' suggestions. After he had gone through several revisions, he produced the version that appears on page 222.

Writing a Definition Paragraph

■ **Writing Assignment 1**

Write a paragraph that defines the term *TV addict*. Base your paragraph on the topic sentence and three supporting points provided below.

> *Topic sentence*: Television addicts are people who will watch all the programs they can, for as long as they can, without doing anything else.
>
> (1) TV addicts, first of all, will watch anything on the tube, no matter how bad it is. . . .
>
> (2) In addition, addicts watch more hours of TV than normal people do. . . .
>
> (3) Finally, addicts feel that TV is more important than other people or any other activities that might be going on. . . .

Prewriting

a   Generate as many examples as you can for each of the three qualities of a TV addict. You can do this by asking yourself the following questions:

- What are some truly awful shows that I (or TV addicts I know) watch just because the television is turned on?
- What are some examples of the large amounts of time that I (or TV addicts I know) watch television?
- What are some examples of ways that I (or TV addicts I know) neglect people or give up activities in order to watch TV?

Write down every answer you can think of for each question. At this point, don't worry about writing full sentences or even about grammar or spelling. Just get your thoughts down on paper.

b   Look over the list of examples you have generated. Select the strongest examples you have thought of. You should have at least two or three for each quality. If not, ask yourself the questions in step *a* again.

c   Write out the examples you will use, this time expressing them in full, grammatically correct sentences.

d   Start with the topic sentence and three points provided in the assignment. Fill in the examples you've generated to support each point and write a first draft of your paragraph.

Revising

Put your first draft away for a day or so. When you come back to it, reread it critically, asking yourself these questions:

- Have I used the topic sentence and the three supporting points that were provided?
- Have I backed up each supporting point with at least two examples?
- Does each of my examples truly illustrate the point that it backs up, or should I substitute another one?
- Have I used appropriate transitional language (*another, in addition, for example*) to tie my thoughts together?
- Have I proofread my paragraph and corrected any sentence-skills mistakes, including spelling?

Keep revising your paragraph until you can answer "yes" to each question.

■ Writing Assignment 2

Write a paragraph that defines one of the following terms. Each term refers to a certain kind of person.

Know-it-all	Clown	Workaholic
Charmer	Jellyfish	Showoff
Loser	Leader	Control freak
Lazybones	Nerd	Mother hen
Snob	Good neighbor	Toady
Con artist	Optimist	Fusspot
Fair-weather friend	Pessimist	
Good sport	Pack rat	

Prewriting

a   Write a topic sentence for your definition paragraph. This is a two-part process:

- *First,* place the term in a class, or category. For example, if you are writing about a certain kind of person, the general category is *person*. If you are describing a type of friend, the general category is *friend*.
- *Second,* describe what you consider the special feature or features that set your term apart from other members of its class. For instance, say what *kind* of person you are writing about or what *type* of friend.

In the following topic sentence, try to identify three things: the term being defined, the class it belongs to, and the special feature that sets the term apart from other members of the class.

A chocoholic is a person who craves chocolate.

The term being defined is *chocoholic*. The category it belongs to is *person*. The words that set *chocoholic* apart from any other person are *craves chocolate*.

Below is another example of a topic sentence for this assignment. It is a definition of *whiner*. The class, or category, is underlined: A whiner is a type of person. The words that set the term *whiner* apart from other members of the class are double-underlined.

A whiner is a <u>person</u> who <u>feels wronged by life</u>.

In the following sample topic sentences, underline the class and double-underline the special features.

A clotheshorse is a person who needs new clothes to be happy.
The class clown is a student who gets attention through silly behavior.
A worrywart is a person who sees danger everywhere.

b Develop your definition by using one of the following methods:
Examples. Give several examples that support your topic sentence.
Extended example. Use one longer example to support your topic sentence.
Contrast. Support your topic sentence by contrasting what your term *is* with what it is *not*. For instance, you may want to define a *fair-weather friend* by contrasting his or her actions with those of a true friend.

c Once you have created a topic sentence and decided how to develop your paragraph, make a scratch outline. If you are using a contrast method of development, remember to present the details one side at a time or point by point (see page 207).

d Write a first draft of your paragraph.

Revising

As you revise your paragraph, keep these questions in mind:

- Does my topic sentence (1) place my term in a class and (2) name some special features that set it apart from its class?

- Have I made a clear choice to develop my topic sentence through either several examples, one extended example, or contrast?
- If I have chosen to illustrate my topic through contrast, have I consistently followed either a point-by-point or a one-side-at-a-time format?
- Have I used appropriate transitions (*another, in addition, in contrast, for example*) to tie my thoughts together?
- Is my paragraph free of sentence-skills and spelling errors?

Continue revising your work until you can answer "yes" to all these questions.

■ Writing Assignment 3

Write a paragraph that defines one of the abstract terms below.

Arrogance	Family	Persistence
Assertiveness	Fear	Practicality
Class	Freedom	Rebellion
Common sense	Gentleness	Responsibility
Conscience	Innocence	Self-control
Curiosity	Insecurity	Sense of humor
Danger	Jealousy	Shyness
Depression	Nostalgia	Violence
Escape	Obsession	

As a guide in writing your paper, use the suggestions for prewriting and rewriting in Writing Assignment 2. Remember to place your term in a class or category and to describe what *you* feel are the distinguishing features of that term.

After writing your topic sentence, check that it is complete and correct by doing the following:

- Single-underline the category of the term you're defining.
- Double-underline the term's distinguishing characteristic or characteristics.

Here are three sample topic sentences:

Laziness is the trait of resisting all worthwhile work as much as possible.
Jealousy is the feeling of wanting a possession or quality that someone else has.
A family is a group whose members are related to one another in some way.

■ Writing Assignment 4

Since it affects all of us to some degree, *stress* is a useful word to explore. Write a paragraph defining that word. Organize your paragraph in one of the ways listed below:

- Use a series of examples (see page 171) of stress.

- Use narration (see page 257) to provide one longer example of stress: Create a hypothetical person (or use a real person) and show how this person's typical morning or day illustrates your definition of *stress*.

Using strategies described in the chapter on the library and the Internet (pages 361–378), research the topic of stress. Your reading will help you think about how to proceed with the paper.

Hints: Do not simply write a series of general, abstract sentences that repeat and reword your definition. If you concentrate on providing specific support, you will avoid the common trap of getting lost in a maze of generalities.

   Make sure your paper is set firmly on the four bases: unity, support, coherence, and sentence skills. Edit the next-to-final draft of the paragraph carefully for sentence-skills errors, including spelling.

■ Writing Assignment 5

Option 1:   Imagine that at the place where you work, one employee has just quit, creating a new job opening. Since you have been working there for a while, your boss has asked you to write a description of the position. That description, a detailed definition of the job, will be sent to employment agencies. These agencies will be responsible for interviewing candidates. Choose any position you know about, and write a paragraph defining it. First state the purpose of the job, and then list its duties and responsibilities. Finally, describe the qualifications for the position. Below is a sample topic sentence for this assignment.

> Purchasing-department secretary is a <u>position</u> in which someone <u>provides a variety of services to the purchasing-department managers</u>.

   In a paragraph with the topic sentence above, the writer would go on to list and explain the various services the secretary must provide.

Option 2:   Alternatively, imagine that a new worker has been hired, and your boss has asked you to explain "team spirit" to him or her. The purpose of your explanation will be to give the newcomer an idea of the kind of teamwork that is expected in this workplace. Write a paragraph that defines in detail what your boss means by *team spirit*. Use examples or one extended example to illustrate each of your general points about team spirit.

13 Dividing and Classifying

If you were doing the laundry, you might begin by separating the clothing into piles. You would then put all the whites in one pile and all the colors in another. Or you might classify the laundry, not according to color, but according to fabric—putting all cottons in one pile, polyesters in another, and so on. *Classifying* is the process of taking many things and separating them into categories. We generally classify to better manage or understand many things. Librarians classify books into groups (novels, travel, health, etc.) to make it easier to find books. A scientist sheds light on the world by classifying all living things into two main groups, animals and plants.

Dividing, in contrast, is taking one thing and breaking it down into parts. We often divide, or analyze, to better understand, teach, or evaluate something. For instance, a tinkerer might take apart a clock to see how it works; a science text might divide a tree into its parts to explain their functions. A music reviewer may analyze the elements of a band's performance—for example, the skill of the various players, rapport with the audience, selections, and so on.

In short, if you are classifying, you are sorting *numbers of things* into categories. If you are dividing, you are breaking *one thing* into parts. It all depends on your purpose—you might classify flowers into various types or divide a single flower into its parts.

In this section, you will be asked to write a paragraph in which you classify a group of things into categories according to a single principle. To prepare for this assignment, first read the paragraphs below, and then work through the questions and the activity that follow.

Paragraphs to Consider

Types of E-Mail

¹As more and more people take advantage of e-mailing, three categories of e-mail have emerged. ²One category of e-mail is junk mail. ³When most people sign on to their computers, they are greeted with a flood of get-rich-quick schemes, invitations to pornographic websites, and ads for a variety of unwanted products. ⁴E-mail users quickly become good at hitting the "delete" button to get rid of this garbage. ⁵The second category that clogs most people's electronic mailbox is forwarded mail, most

of which also gets deleted without being read. 6The third and best category of e-mail is genuine personal e-mail from genuine personal friends. 7Getting such real, thoughtful e-mail can almost make up for the irritation of the other two categories.

Studying for a Test

1Phase 1 of studying for a test, often called the "no problem" phase, runs from the day the test is announced to approximately forty-eight hours before the dreaded exam is passed out. 2During phase 1, the student is carefree, smiling, and kind to helpless animals and small children. 3When asked by classmates if he or she has studied for the test yet, the reply will be an assured "No problem." 4During phase 1, no actual studying takes place. 5Phase 2 is entered two days before the test. 6For example, if the test is scheduled for 9 A.M. Friday, phase 2 begins at 9 A.M. Wednesday. 7During phase 2, again, no actual studying takes place. 8Phase 3, the final phase, is entered twelve hours before "zero hour." 9This is the cram phase, characterized by sweaty palms, nervous twitches, and confused mental patterns. 10For a test at nine o'clock on Friday morning, a student begins exhibiting these symptoms at approximately nine o'clock on Thursday night. 11Phase 3 is also termed the "shock" phase, since the student is shocked to discover the imminence of the exam and the amount of material to be studied. 12During this phase, the student will probably be unable to sleep and will mumble meaningless phrases like "$a^2 + c^2$." 13This phase will not end until the exam is over. 14If the cram session has worked, the student will fall gratefully asleep that night. 15On waking up, he or she will be ready to go through the whole cycle again with the next test.

Three Kinds of Dogs

1A city walker will notice that most dogs fall into one of three categories. 2First there are the big dogs, which are generally harmless and often downright friendly. 3They walk along peacefully with their masters, their tongues hanging out and big goofy grins on their faces. 4Apparently they know they're too big to have anything to worry about, so why not be nice? 5Second are the spunky medium-sized dogs. 6When they see a stranger approaching, they go on alert. 7They prick up their ears, they raise their hackles, and they may growl a little deep in their throats. 8"I could tear you up," they seem to be saying, "but I won't if you behave yourself." 9Unless the walker leaps for their master's throat, these dogs usually won't do anything more than threaten. 10The third category is made up of the shivering neurotic little yappers whose shrill barks could shatter glass and whose needle-like little teeth are eager to sink into a friendly outstretched hand. 11Walkers always wonder about these dogs—don't they know that anyone who really wanted to could squash them under their feet like bugs?

12Apparently not, because of all the dogs a walker meets, these provide the most irritation. 13Such dogs are only one of the potential hazards that the city walker encounters.

■ Questions

About Unity

1. Which paragraph lacks a topic sentence?

   _____

2. Which sentence in "Three Kinds of Dogs" should be eliminated in the interest of paragraph unity? *(Write the sentence number here.)* _____

About Support

3. Which of the three phases in "Studying for a Test" lacks specific details?

   _____

4. After which sentence in "Types of E-Mail" are supporting details needed? *(Write the sentence number here.)* _____

About Coherence

5. Which paragraph uses emphatic order to organize its details?

   _____

6. Which words in the emphatic-order paragraph signal the most important detail?

   _____

Activity

This activity will sharpen your sense of the classifying process. In each of the ten groups, cross out the one item that has not been classified on the same basis as the other three. Also, indicate in the space provided the single principle of classification used for the remaining three items. Note the examples.

Examples   Water
           a. Cold
           b. ~~Lake~~
           c. Hot
           d. Lukewarm
           Unifying principle:
           Temperature _____

Household pests
a. ~~Mice~~
b. Ants
c. Roaches
d. Flies
Unifying principle:
Insects _____

1. Eyes
   a. Blue
   b. Nearsighted
   c. Brown
   d. Hazel
   Unifying principle:

   _____

2. Mattresses
   a. Double
   b. Twin
   c. Queen
   d. Firm
   Unifying principle:

   _____

3. Zoo animals
   a. Flamingo
   b. Peacock
   c. Polar bear
   d. Ostrich
   Unifying principle:

   _____

4. Vacation
   a. Summer
   b. Holiday
   c. Seashore
   d. Weekend
   Unifying principle:

   _____

5. Books
   a. Novels
   b. Biographies
   c. Boring
   d. Short stories
   Unifying principle:

   _____

6. Wallets
   a. Leather
   b. Plastic
   c. Stolen
   d. Fabric
   Unifying principle:

   _____

7. Newspaper
   a. Wrapping garbage
   b. Editorials
   c. Making paper planes
   d. Covering floor while painting
   Unifying principle:

   _____

8. Students
   a. First-year
   b. Transfer
   c. Junior
   d. Sophomore
   Unifying principle:

   _____

9. Exercise
   a. Running
   b. Swimming
   c. Gymnastics
   d. Fatigue
   Unifying principle:

   _____

10. Leftovers
    a. Cold chicken
    b. Feed to dog
    c. Reheat
    d. Use in a stew
    Unifying principle:

    _____

Developing a Division-Classification Paragraph

Development through Prewriting

Marcus walked home from campus to his apartment, thinking about the assignment to write a division-classification paragraph. As he strolled along his familiar route, his observations made him think of several possibilities. "First I thought of writing about the businesses in my neighborhood, dividing them into the ones run by Hispanics, Asians, and African-Americans," he said. "When I stopped in at my favorite coffee shop, I thought about dividing the people who hang out there. There is a group of old men who meet to drink coffee and play cards, and there are students like me, but there didn't seem to be a third category and I wasn't sure two was enough. As I continued walking home, though, I saw Mr. Enriquez and his big golden retriever, and some lady with two nervous little dogs that acted as if they wanted to eat me, and the newsstand guy with his mutt that's always guarding the place, and I thought 'Dogs! I can classify different types of dogs.'"

But how would he classify them? Thinking further, Marcus realized that he thought of dogs as having certain personalities depending on their size. "I know there are exceptions, of course, but since this was going to be a lighthearted, even comical paragraph, I thought it would be OK if I exaggerated a bit." He wrote down his three categories:

Big dogs
Medium-sized dogs
Small dogs

Under each division, then, he wrote down as many characteristics as he could think of:

<u>Big dogs</u>
    calm
    friendly
    good-natured
    dumb
    lazy

<u>Medium-sized dogs</u>
>   spunky
>   energetic
>   ready to fight
>   protective
>   friendly if they know you

<u>Small dogs</u>
>   nervous
>   trembling
>   noisy
>   yappy
>   snappy
>   annoying

Marcus then wrote a topic sentence: "Dogs seem to fall into three categories." Using that topic sentence and the scratch outline he'd just produced, he wrote the following paragraph:

> Most dogs seem to fall into one of three categories. First there are the big dumb friendly dogs. They give the impression of being sweet but not real bright. One example of this kind of dog is Lucy. She's a golden retriever belonging to a man in my neighborhood. Lucy goes everywhere with Mr. Enriquez. She doesn't even need a leash but just follows him. Dogs like Lucy never bother anybody. She just lies at Mr. Enriquez's feet when he stops to talk to anyone. The guy who runs the corner newsstand I pass every day has a spunky medium-sized dog. Once the dog knows you he's friendly and even playful. But he's always on the lookout for a stranger who might mean trouble. For a dog who's not very big he can make himself look pretty fierce if he wants to. Then there are my least favorite kind of dogs. Little nervous yappy ones. My aunt used to have a Chihuahua like that. It knew me for nine years and still went crazy shaking and yipping at me every time we met. She loved that dog but I can't imagine why. If I had a dog it would definitely come from category 1 or 2.

Development through Revising

Marcus traded his first draft with a fellow student, Rachel, and asked her to give him feedback. Here are the comments Rachel wrote on his paper:

Most dogs seem to fall into three categories. First there are the big dumb friendly dogs. They give the impression of being sweet but not real bright. One example of this kind of dog is Lucy, a golden retriever belonging to a man in my neighborhood. Lucy goes everywhere with Mr. Enriquez. She doesn't even need a leash but just follows him everywhere. Lucy never bothers you. She just lies at Mr. Enriquez's feet when he stops to talk to anyone. The guy who runs the corner newsstand I pass every day has a spunky medium-sized dog. Once the dog knows you he's friendly and even playful. But he's always on the lookout for a stranger who might mean trouble. For a dog who's not very big he can make himself look pretty fierce if he wants to scare you. Then there are my least favorite kind of dogs. Little nervous yappy ones. My aunt used to have a Chihuahua like that. It knew me for nine years and still went crazy shaking and yipping at me every time we met. She loved that dog but I can't imagine why. If I had a dog it would definitely come from category 1 or 2.

This is a change in point of view— you haven't been using "you" before.

Is this the beginning of a second category? That's not clear.

Not a complete sentence.

Another point of view change— you've gone from writing in the third person to "you" to "me."

Marcus—I think you need to make your three categories clearer. Your first one is OK—"big dogs," which you say are friendly—but categories 2 and 3 aren't stated as clearly.

It's distracting to have your point of view change from third person to "you" to "me."

Since you're trying to divide and classify all dogs, I'm not sure it's a good idea to talk only about three individual dogs. This way it sounds as if you're just describing those three dogs instead of putting them into three groups.

When Marcus considered Rachel's comments and reread his own paragraph, he agreed with what she had written. "I realized it was too much about three particular dogs and not enough about the categories of dogs," he said. "I decided to revise it and focus on the three classes of dogs."

Marcus then wrote the version that appears on page 232.

Writing a Division-Classification Paragraph

■ **Writing Assignment 1**

Below are four options to develop into a classification paragraph. Each one presents a topic to classify into three categories. Choose one option to develop into a paragraph.

Option 1

Supermarket shoppers

(1)   Slow, careful shoppers

(2)   Average shoppers

(3)   Hurried shoppers

Option 2

Eaters

(1)   Very conservative eaters

(2)   Typical eaters

(3)   Adventurous eaters

Option 3

Types of housekeepers

(1)   Never clean

(2)   Clean on a regular basis

(3)   Clean constantly

Option 4

Attitudes toward money

(1)   Tightfisted

(2)   Reasonable

(3)   Extravagant

Prewriting

a   Begin by doing some freewriting on the topic you have chosen. For five or ten minutes, simply write down everything that comes into your head when you think about "types of housekeepers, "attitudes toward money," or whichever option you choose. Don't worry about grammar, spelling, or organization—just write.

b Now that you've "loosened up your brain" a little, try asking yourself questions about the topic and writing down your answers. If you are writing about supermarket shoppers, for instance, you might ask questions like these:

How do the three kinds of shoppers prepare for their shopping trip?

How many aisles will each kind of shopper visit?

What do the different kinds of shoppers bring along with them—lists, calculators, coupons, etc.?

How long does each type of shopper spend in the store?

Write down whatever answers occur to you for these and other questions. Again, do not worry at this stage about writing correctly. Instead, concentrate on getting down all the information you can think of that supports your three points.

c Reread the material you have accumulated. If some of the details you have written make you think of even better ones, add them. Select the details that best support your three points. Number them in the order you will present them.

d Restate your topic as a grammatically complete topic sentence. For example, if you're writing about eaters, your topic sentence might be "Eaters can be divided into three categories." Turn each of your three supporting points into a full sentence as well.

e Using your topic sentence and three supporting sentences and adding the details you have generated, write the first draft of your paragraph.

Revising

Put away your work for a day or so. Reread it with a critical eye, asking yourself these questions:

- Does my paragraph include a complete topic sentence and three supporting points?
- Have I backed up each supporting point with strong, specific details?
- Does my paragraph hang together in terms of unity, support, and coherence?
- Have I edited my paragraph and corrected sentence-skills mistakes, including spelling errors?

Continue revising your work until you can answer "yes" to all these questions.

■ Writing Assignment 2

Write a classification paragraph on one of the following topics:

Instructors	Drivers
Sports fans	Mothers or fathers
Restaurants	Women's or men's magazines
Attitudes toward life	Presents
Commercials	Neighbors
Employers	Rock, pop, rap, or country singers
Jobs	Houseguests
Bars	Baseball, basketball, football, or hockey players
Family get-togethers	Cars
First dates	

Prewriting

a Classify members of the group you are considering writing about into three categories. Remember: *You must use a single principle of division when you create your three categories.* For example, if your topic is "School courses" and you classify them into easy, moderate, and challenging, your basis for classification is "degree of difficulty." It would not make sense to have as a fourth type "foreign language" (the basis of such a categorization would be "subject matter") or "early morning" (the basis of that classification would be "time of day the classes meet"). You *could* categorize school courses on the basis of subject matter or time of day they meet, for almost any subject can be classified in more than one way. In a single paper, however, you must choose *one* basis for classification and stick to it.

b Once you have a satisfactory three-part division, spend at least five minutes freewriting about each of your three points. Don't be concerned yet with grammar, spelling, or organization. Just write whatever comes into your mind about each of the three points.

c Expand your topic into a fully stated topic sentence.

d At this point, you have all three elements of your paragraph: the topic sentence, the three main points, and the details needed to support each point. Now weave them all together in one paragraph.

Revising

Do not attempt to revise your paragraph right away. Put it away for a while, if possible until the next day. When you reread it, try to be as critical of it as you would be if someone else had written it. As you go over the work, ask yourself these questions:

- Have I divided my topic into three distinct parts?
- Is each of those three parts based on the same principle of division?
- Have I given each of the three parts approximately equal weight? In other words, have I spent about the same amount of time discussing each part?
- Have I provided effective details to back up each of my three points?
- Does my paragraph satisfy the requirements of unity, coherence, and support?
- Have I edited my paragraph for sentence-skills mistakes, including spelling?

Continue revising until you are sure the answer to each question is "yes."

■ Writing Assignment 3

There are many ways you could classify your fellow students. Pick out one of your courses and write a paragraph in which you classify the students in that class according to one underlying principle. You may wish to choose one of the classification principles below.

Attitude toward the class	Punctuality
Participation in the class	Attendance
Method of taking notes in class	Level of confidence
Performance during oral reports, speeches, presentations, lab sessions	

If you decide, for instance, to classify students according to their attitude toward class, you might come up with these three categories:

Students actually interested in learning the material
Students who know they need to learn the material, but don't want to overdo it
Students who find the class a good opportunity to catch up with lost sleep

Of course, you may use any other principle of classification that seems appropriate. Follow the steps listed under "Prewriting" and "Rewriting" for Writing Assignment 2.

■ Writing Assignment 4

Write a review of a restaurant by analyzing its (1) food, (2) service, and (3) atmosphere. For this assignment, you should visit a restaurant, take a notebook with you, and write down observations about such elements as:

Quantity of food you receive	Attitude of the servers
Taste of the food	Efficiency of the servers
Temperature of the food	Decor
Freshness of the ingredients	Level of cleanliness
How the food is presented (garnishes, dishes, and so on)	Noise level and music, if any

Feel free to write about details other than those listed above. Just be sure each detail fits into one of your three categories: food, service, or atmosphere.

For your topic sentence, rate the restaurant by giving it from one to five stars, on the basis of your overall impression. Include the restaurant's name and location in your topic sentence. Here are some examples:

Guido's, an Italian restaurant downtown, deserves three stars.

The McDonald's on Route 70 merits a four-star rating.

The Circle Diner in Westfield barely earns a one-star rating.

■ Writing Assignment 5

Imagine that you are a travel agent and someone has asked you for suggestions for family vacations. Write a paragraph classifying vacations for families into three or more types, for example, vacations in theme parks, in national parks, or in cities. For each type, include an explanation with one or more examples (see page 179).

14 Describing a Scene or Person

When you describe something or someone, you give your readers a picture in words. To make this "word picture" as vivid and real as possible, you must observe and record specific details that appeal to your readers' senses (sight, hearing, taste, smell and touch). More than any other type of writing, a descriptive paragraph needs sharp, colorful details.

Here is a description in which only the sense of sight is used:

A rug covers the living-room floor.

In contrast, here is a description rich in sense impressions:

A thick, reddish-brown shag rug is laid wall to wall across the living-room floor. The long, curled fibers of the shag seem to whisper as you walk through them in your bare feet, and when you squeeze your toes into the deep covering, the soft fibers push back at you with a spongy resilience.

Sense impressions include sight (*thick, reddish-brown shag rug; laid wall to wall; walk through them in your bare feet; squeeze your toes into the deep covering; push back*), hearing (*whisper*), and touch (*bare feet, soft fibers, spongy resilience*). The sharp, vivid images provided by the sensory details give us a clear picture of the rug and enable us to share in the writer's experience.

In this section, you will be asked to describe a person, place, or thing for your readers by using words rich in sensory details. To prepare for the assignment, first read the three paragraphs ahead and then answer the questions that follow.

Paragraphs to Consider

My Teenage Son's Room

¹I push open the door with difficulty. ²The doorknob is loose and has to be jiggled just right before the catch releases from the doorjamb. ³Furthermore, as I push at the door, it runs into a basketball shoe lying on the floor. ⁴I manage to squeeze in through the narrow opening. ⁵I am

immediately aware of a pungent odor in the room, most of which is coming from the closet, to my right. 6That's the location of a white wicker clothes hamper, heaped with grass-stained jeans, sweat-stained T-shirts, and smelly socks. 7But the half-eaten burrito, lying dried and unappetizing on the bedside table across the room, contributes a bit of aroma, as does the glass of curdled sour milk sitting on the sunny windowsill. 8To my left, the small wire cage on Greg's desk is also fragrant, but pleasantly. 9From its nest of sweet-smelling cedar chips, the gerbil peers out at me with its bright eyes, its tiny claws scratching against the cage wall. 10The floor around the wastebasket that is next to the desk is surrounded by what appears to be a sprinkling of snowballs. 11They're actually old wadded-up school papers, and I can picture Greg sitting on his bed, crushing them into balls and aiming them at the "basket" of the trash can. 12I glance at the bed across from the desk and chuckle because pillows stuffed under the tangled nest of blankets make it look as if someone is still sleeping there, though I know Greg is in history class right now. 13I step carefully through the room, trying to walk through the obstacle course of science-fiction paperbacks, a wristwatch, assorted CD cases, and the radio with a wire coat hanger for an antenna. 14I leave everything as I find it, but tape a note to Greg's door saying, "Isn't it about time to clean up?"

A Depressing Place

1The pet shop in the mall is a depressing place. 2A display window attracts passersby who stare at the prisoners penned inside. 3In the right-hand side of the window, two puppies press their forepaws against the glass and attempt to lick the human hands that press from the outside. 4A cardboard barrier separates the dogs from several black-and-white kittens piled together in the opposite end of the window. 5Inside the shop, rows of wire cages line one wall from top to bottom. 6At first, it is hard to tell whether a bird, hamster, gerbil, cat, or dog is locked inside each cage. 7Only an occasional movement or a clawing, shuffling sound tells visitors that living creatures are inside. 8Running down the center of the store is a line of large wooden perches that look like coatracks. 9When customers pass by, the parrots and mynas chained to these perches flutter their clipped wings in a useless attempt to escape. 10At the end of this center aisle is a large plastic tub of dirty, stagnant-looking water containing a few motionless turtles. 11The shelves against the left-hand wall are packed with all kinds of pet-related items. 12The smell inside the entire shop is an unpleasant mixture of strong chemical deodorizers, urine-soaked newspapers, and musty sawdust. 13Because so many animals are crammed together, the normally pleasant, slightly milky smell of the puppies and kittens is sour and strong. 14The droppings inside the uncleaned birdcages give off a dry, stinging odor. 15Visitors hurry out of the shop, anxious to feel fresh air and sunlight. 16The animals stay on.

Karla

[1]Karla, my brother's new girlfriend, is a catlike creature. [2]Framing her face is a layer of sleek black hair that always looks just-combed. [3]Her face, with its wide forehead, sharp cheekbones, and narrow, pointed chin, resembles a triangle. [4]Karla's skin is a soft, velvety brown. [5]Her large brown eyes slant upward at the corners, and she emphasizes their angle with a sweep of maroon eye shadow. [6]Karla's habit of looking sidelong out of the tail of her eye makes her look cautious, as if she were expecting something to sneak up on her. [7]Her nose is small and flat. [8]The sharply outlined depression under it leads the observer's eye to a pair of red-tinted lips. [9]With their slight upward tilt at the corners, Karla's lips make her seem self-satisfied and secretly pleased. [10]One reason Karla may be happy is that she recently was asked to be in a local beauty contest. [11]Her long neck and slim body are perfectly in proportion with her face. [12]Karla manages to look elegant and sleek no matter how she is standing or sitting, for her body seems to be made up of graceful angles. [13]Her slender hands are tipped with long, polished nails. [14]Her narrow feet are long, too, but they appear delicate even in flat-soled running shoes. [15]Somehow, Karla would look perfect in a cat's jeweled collar.

■ Questions

About Unity

1. Which paragraph lacks a topic sentence?

   _____

2. Which sentence in the paragraph about Karla should be omitted in the interest of paragraph unity? (*Write the sentence number here.*) ___10___

About Support

3. Label as *sight*, *touch*, *hearing*, or *smell* all the sensory details in the following sentences taken from the three paragraphs. The first one is done for you as an example.

   a. From its nest of *smell* sweet-smelling cedar chips, the gerbil peers out at me with its *sight* bright eyes, its tiny *sight* claws scratching *hearing* against the cage wall.

   b. Because so many animals are crammed together, the normally pleasant, slightly milky smell of the puppies and kittens is sour and strong.

   c. Her slender hands are tipped with long, polished nails.

d.   That's the location of a white wicker clothes hamper, heaped with grass-stained jeans, sweat-stained T-shirts, and smelly socks.

4. After which sentence in "A Depressing Place" are specific details needed?
_____

About Coherence

5. Spatial signals (*above, next to, to the right*, and so on) are often used to help organize details in a descriptive paragraph. List four space signals that appear in "My Teenage Son's Room":

_____ _____ _____ _____

6. The writer of "Karla" organizes the details by observing Karla in an orderly way. Which of Karla's features is described first? _____ Which is described last? _____ Check the method of spatial organization that best describes the paragraph:

_____ Interior to exterior

_____ Near to far

_____ Top to bottom

Developing a Descriptive Paragraph

Development through Prewriting

When Victor was assigned a descriptive paragraph, he thought at first of describing his own office at work. He began by making a list of details he noticed while looking around the office:

adjustable black chair

beige desk

piles of papers

computer

pictures of Marie and kids on desk

desk calendar

But Victor quickly became bored. Here is how he describes what happened next:

"As I wrote down what I saw in my office, I was thinking, 'What a drag.' I gave up and worked on something else. Later that evening I told my wife that I was going to write a boring paragraph about my boring office. She started laughing at me. I said 'What's so funny?' and she said, 'You're so certain that a writing assignment has to be boring that you deliberately chose a subject that bores you. How about writing about something you care about?' At first I was annoyed, but then I realized she was right. When I hear 'assignment' I automatically think 'pain in the neck' and just want to get it over with."

Victor's attitude is not uncommon. Many students who are not experienced writers don't take the time to find a topic that interests them. They grab the one closest at hand and force themselves to write about it just for the sake of completing the assignment. Like Victor, they ensure that they (and probably their instructors as well) will be bored with the task.

In Victor's case, he decided that this assignment would be different. That evening as he talked with his son, Mikey, he remembered a visit the two had made to a mall a few days earlier. Mikey had asked Victor to take him to the pet store. Victor had found the store a very unpleasant place. "As I remembered the store, I recalled a lot of descriptive details—sounds, smells, sights," Victor said. "I realized not only that would it be easier to describe a place like that than my bland, boring office, but that I would actually find it an interesting challenge to make a reader see it through my words. For me to realize writing could be enjoyable was a real shock!"

Now that Victor had his subject, he began making a list of details about the pet shop. Here is what he wrote:

Sawdust, animal droppings on floor

Unhappy-looking puppies and kittens

Dead fish floating in tanks

Screech of birds

Chained parrots

Tanks full of dirty water

Strong urine smell

No place for animals to play

Bored-looking clerks

Animals scratching cages for attention

As he looked over his list of details, the word that came to mind was "depressing." He decided his topic sentence would be "The pet store in the mall is depressing." He then wrote this first draft:

The pet store in the mall is depressing. There are sawdust and animal droppings all over the floor. Sad-looking puppies and kittens scratch on their cages for attention. Dead fish and motionless turtles float in tanks of stagnant water. The loud screeching of birds is everywhere, and parrots with clipped wings try to escape when customers walk too near. Everywhere there is the smell of animal urine that has soaked the sawdust and newspapers. The clerks, who should be cleaning the cages, stand around talking to each other and ignoring the animals.

Development through Revising

The next day Victor's instructor asked to see the students' first drafts. This is what she wrote in response to Victor's:

This is a very good beginning. You have provided some strong details that appeal to the reader's senses of smell, hearing, and sight.

In your next draft, organize your paragraph by using spatial order. In other words, describe the room in some logical physical order—maybe from left to right, or from the front of the store to its back. Such an organization mirrors the way a visitor might move through the store.

I encourage you to become even more specific in your details. For instance, in what way did the puppies and kittens seem sad? As you work on each sentence, ask yourself if you can add more descriptive details to paint a more vivid picture in words.

In response to his teacher's suggestion about a spatial order method of organization, Victor rewrote the paragraph, beginning with the display window that attracts visitors, then going on to the store's right-hand wall, the center aisle, and the left-hand wall. He ended the paragraph with a sentence that brought the reader back outside the shop. Thinking about the shop in this way enabled Victor to remember and add a number of new specific details as well. He then wrote the version of "A Depressing Place" that appears on page 244.

Writing a Descriptive Paragraph

■ Writing Assignment 1

Write a paragraph describing a certain person's room. Use as your topic sentence "I could tell by looking at the room that a _____ lived there." There are many kinds of people who could be the focus for such a paragraph. You can select any one of the following, or think of another type of person.

Photographer	Music lover	Carpenter
Cook	TV addict	Baby
Student	Camper	Cat or dog lover
Musician	Computer expert	World traveler
Hunter	Cheerleader	Drug addict
Slob	Football player	Little boy or girl
Outdoors person	Actor	Alcoholic
Doctor	Prostitute	Inline skater

Prewriting

a After choosing a topic, spend a few minutes making sure it will work. Prepare a list of all the details you can think of that support the topic. For example, a student who planned to describe a soccer player's room made this list:

soccer balls

shin guards

posters of professional soccer teams

soccer trophies

shirt printed with team name and number

autographed soccer ball

medals and ribbons

photos of player's own team

sports clippings

radio that looks like soccer ball

soccer socks

soccer shorts

If you don't have enough details, then choose another type of person. Check your new choice with a list of details before committing yourself to the topic.

b You may want to use other prewriting techniques, such as freewriting or questioning, to develop more details for your topic. As you continue prewriting, keep the following in mind:

- Everything in the paragraph should support your point. For example, if you are writing about a soccer player's room, every detail should serve to show that the person who lives in that room plays and loves soccer. Other details—for example, the person's computer, tropical fish tank, or daily "to-do" list—should be omitted.

- Description depends on the use of specific rather than general descriptive words. For example:

General	Specific
Mess on the floor	The obstacle course of science-fiction paperbacks, a wristwatch, assorted CD cases, and the radio with a wire coat hanger for an antenna
Ugly turtle tub	Large plastic tub of dirty, stagnant-looking water containing a few motionless turtles
Bad smell	Unpleasant mixture of strong chemical deodorizers, urine-soaked newspapers, and musty sawdust
Nice skin	Soft, velvety brown skin

Remember that you want your readers to experience the room vividly. Your words should be as detailed as a clear photograph, giving readers a real feel for the room. Appeal to as many senses as possible. Most of your description will involve the sense of sight, but you may be able to include details about touch, hearing, and smell as well.

- Spatial order is a good way to organize a descriptive paragraph. Move as a visitor's eye might move around the room, from right to left or from larger items to smaller ones. Here are a few transition words of the sort that show spatial relationships.

to the left	across from	on the opposite side
to the right	above	nearby
next to	below	

Such transitions will help prevent you—and your reader—from getting lost as the description proceeds.

c   Before you write, see if you can make a scratch outline based on your list. Here is one possible outline of the paragraph about the soccer player's room. Note that the details are organized according to spatial order—from the edges of the room in toward the center.

<u>Topic sentence:</u> I could tell by looking at the room that a soccer player lived there.

1. Walls
2. Bookcase
3. Desk
4. Chair
5. Floor

d Then proceed to write a first draft of your paragraph.

Revising

Read your descriptive paragraph slowly out loud to a friend. Ask the friend to close his or her eyes and try to picture the room as you read. Read it aloud a second time. Ask your friend to answer these questions:

- Does every detail in the paragraph support the topic sentence? Here's one way to find out: Ask your friend to imagine omitting the key word or words (in the case of our example, "soccer player") in your topic sentence. Would readers know what word should fit in that empty space?
- Are the details specific and vivid rather than general?
- Has the writer included details that appeal to as many senses as possible?
- Does the paragraph follow a logical spatial order?
- Has the writer used transitions (such as *on top of, beside, to the left of*) to help the reader follow that order?

Continue revising your work until you and your reader can answer "yes" to all these questions.

In the later drafts of your paragraph, edit carefully for sentence-skills mistakes, including spelling. Refer to the checklist of these skills on the inside front cover of this book.

■ Writing Assignment 2

Write a paragraph describing a specific person. Select a dominant impression of the person, and use only details that will convey that impression. You might want to write about someone who falls into one of these categories.

TV or movie personality	Co-worker
Instructor	Clergyman or clergywoman
Employer	Police officer
Child	Store owner or manager

Older person   Bartender

Close friend   Joker

Enemy   Neighbor

Prewriting

a Reread the paragraph about Karla that appears earlier in this chapter. Note the dominant impression that the writer wanted to convey: that Karla is a catlike person. Having decided to focus on that impression, the writer included only details that contributed to her point. Similarly, you should focus on one dominant aspect of your subject's appearance, personality, or behavior.

Once you have chosen the person you will write about and the impression you plan to portray, put that information into a topic sentence. Here are some examples of topic sentences that mention a particular person and the dominant impression of that person:

Kate gives the impression of being permanently nervous.

The old man was as faded and brittle as a dying leaf.

The child was an angelic little figure.

Our high school principal resembled a cartoon drawing.

The TV newscaster seems as synthetic as a piece of Styrofoam.

Our neighbor is a fussy person.

The rock singer seemed to be plugged into some special kind of energy source.

The drug addict looked as lifeless as a corpse.

My friend Jeffrey is a slow, deliberate person.

The owner of that grocery store seems burdened with troubles.

b Make a list of the person's qualities that support your topic sentence. Write quickly; don't worry if you find yourself writing down something that doesn't quite fit. You can always edit the list later. For now, just write down all the details that occur to you that support the dominant impression you want to convey. Include details that involve as many senses as possible (sight, sound, hearing, touch, smell). For instance, here's a list one writer jotted down to support the sentence "The child was an angelic little figure":

soft brown ringlets of hair

pink cheeks

wide shining eyes

shrieking laugh

joyful smile

starched white dress

white flowers in hair

c   Edit your list, striking out details that don't support your topic sentence and adding others that do. The author of the paragraph on an angelic figure crossed out one detail from the original list and added a new one:

soft brown ringlets of hair

pink cheeks

wide shining eyes

~~shrieking laugh~~

joyful smile

starched white dress

white flowers in hair

sweet singing voice

d   Decide on a spatial order of organization. In the example above, the writer ultimately decided to describe the child from head to toe.

e   Make a scratch outline for your paragraph, based on the organization you have chosen.

f   Then proceed to write a first draft of your paragraph.

Revising

Put your paragraph away for a day or so if at all possible. When you read it and your later drafts, ask yourself these questions:

- Does my topic sentence clearly state my dominant impression of my subject?
- If I left out the key words in my topic sentence (the words that state my dominant impression), would a reader know what idea fits there?
- Does every detail support my topic sentence?
- Are the details I have included specific rather than vague and general?
- Have I used a logical spatial organization that helps my reader follow my description?
- Have I checked my paper for sentence skills, as listed on the inside front cover of the book?

Continue revising your work until you can answer "yes" to all these questions.

■ Writing Assignment 3

Write a paragraph describing an animal you have spent some time with—a pet, a friend's pet, an animal you've seen in a park or zoo or even on television. Write a paragraph about how the animal looks and behaves. Select details that support a dominant impression of your subject. Once you decide on the impression you wish to convey, compose a topic sentence, such as either of those below, that summarizes the details you will use.

> The appearance of a gorilla named Koko gives no hint of the animal's intelligence and gentleness.
>
> A cute squirrel who has taken up residence in my backyard exhibits surprising agility and energy.

Remember to provide colorful, detailed descriptions to help your readers picture the features and behavior you are writing about. Note the contrast in the two items below.

> *Lacks rich descriptive details:* The squirrel was gray and enjoyed our deck.
>
> *Includes rich descriptive details:* On our deck, the young gray squirrel dug a hole in the dirt in a planter full of marigolds and then deposited an acorn in the hole, his fluffy tail bobbing enthusiastically all the while.

■ Writing Assignment 4

Visit a place you have never gone to before and write a paragraph describing it. You may want to visit:

> A restaurant
>
> A classroom, a laboratory, an office, a workroom, or some other room in your school
>
> A kind of store you ordinarily don't visit: for example, a hardware store, toy store, record shop, gun shop, or sports shop, or a particular men's or women's clothing store
>
> A bus terminal, train station, or airport
>
> A place of worship
>
> A park, vacant lot, or street corner

You may want to jot down details about the place while you are there or very soon after you leave. Again, decide on a dominant impression you want to convey of the place, and use only those details which will support that impression. Follow the notes on prewriting, writing, and revising for Writing Assignment 2.

■ Writing Assignment 5

Option 1:   Imagine that you are an interior designer. A new dormitory is going to be built on campus, and you have been asked to create a sample dormitory room for two students. Write a paragraph describing your design of the room, telling what it would include and how it would be arranged. In your prewriting for this assignment, you might list all the relevant student needs you can think of, such as a good study space, storage space, and appropriate lighting and colors. Then put all of the parts together so that they work well as a whole. Use a spatial order in your paragraph to help readers "see" your room. Begin with the following topic sentence or something like it:

> My design for a dormitory room offers both efficiency and comfort for two students.

Feel free to use a less-than-serious tone.

Option 2:   Alternatively, write a paragraph describing your design of another type of room, including any of the following:

a child's bedroom	a kitchen
a schoolroom	a porch
a restaurant	a bakery

15 Narrating an Event

At times we make a statement clear by relating in detail something that has happened. In the story we tell, we present the details in the order in which they happened. A person might say, for example, "I was embarrassed yesterday," and then go on to illustrate the statement with the following narrative:

> I was hurrying across campus to get to a class. It had rained heavily all morning, so I was hopscotching my way around puddles in the pathway. I called to two friends ahead to wait for me, and right before I caught up to them, I came to a large puddle that covered the entire path. I had to make a quick choice of either stepping into the puddle or trying to jump over it. I jumped, wanting to seem cool, since my friends were watching, but didn't clear the puddle. Water splashed everywhere, drenching my shoe, sock, and pants cuff, and spraying the pants of my friends as well. "Well done, Dave!" they said. My embarrassment was all the greater because I had tried to look so casual.

The speaker's details have made his moment of embarrassment vivid and real for us, and we can see and understand just why he felt as he did.

In this section, you will be asked to tell a story that illustrates or explains some point. The paragraphs below all present narrative experiences that support a point. Read them and then answer the questions that follow.

Paragraphs to Consider

Heartbreak

¹Bonnie and I had gotten engaged in August, just before she left for college at Penn State. ²A week before Thanksgiving, I drove up to see her as a surprise. ³When I knocked on the door of her dorm room, she was indeed surprised, but not in a pleasant way. ⁴She introduced me to her roommate, who looked uncomfortable and quickly left. ⁵I asked Bonnie how classes were going, and at the same time I tugged on the sleeve of my heavy sweater in order to pull it off. ⁶As I was slipping it over my head, I noticed a large photo on the wall—of Bonnie and a tall guy laughing together. ⁷It was decorated with paper flowers and a yellow ribbon, and on the ribbon was written "Bonnie and Blake." ⁸"What's going on?" I said.

[9]I stood there stunned and then felt an anger that grew rapidly. [10]"Who is Blake?" I asked. [11]Bonnie laughed nervously and said, "What do you want to hear about—my classes or Blake?" [12]I don't really remember what she then told me, except that Blake was a sophomore math major. [13]I felt a terrible pain in the pit of my stomach, and I wanted to rest my head on someone's shoulder and cry. [14]I wanted to tear down the sign and run out, but I did nothing. [15]Clumsily I pulled on my sweater again. [16]My knees felt weak, and I barely had control of my body. [17]I opened the room door, and suddenly more than anything I wanted to slam the door shut so hard that the dorm walls would collapse. [18]Instead, I managed to close the door quietly. [19]I walked away understanding what was meant by a broken heart.

Losing My Father

[1]Although my father died ten years ago, I felt that he'd been lost to me four years earlier. [2]Dad had been diagnosed with Alzheimer's disease, an illness that destroys the memory. [3]He couldn't work any longer, but in his own home he got along pretty well. [4]I lived hundreds of miles away and wasn't able to see my parents often. [5]So when my first child was a few weeks old, I flew home with the baby to visit them. [6]After Mom met us at the airport, we picked up Dad and went to their favorite local restaurant. [7]Dad was quiet, but kind and gentle as always, and he seemed glad to see me and his new little grandson. [8]Everyone went to bed early. [9]In the morning, Mom left for work. [10]I puttered happily around in my old bedroom. [11]I heard Dad shuffling around in the kitchen, making coffee. [12]Eventually I realized that he was pacing back and forth at the foot of the stairs as if he were uneasy. [13]I called down to him, "Everything all right there? [14]I'll be down in a minute." [15]"Fine!" he called back, with a forced-sounding cheerfulness. [16]Then he stopped pacing and called up to me, "I must be getting old and forgetful. [17]When did you get here?" [18]I was surprised, but made myself answer calmly. [19]"Yesterday afternoon. [20]Remember, Mom met us at the airport, and then we went to The Skillet for dinner." [21]"Oh, yes," he said. [22]"I had roast beef." [23]I began to relax. [24]But then he continued, hesitantly, "And . . . who are you?" [25]My breath stopped as if I'd been punched in the stomach. [26]When I could steady my voice, I answered, "I'm Laura; I'm your daughter. [27]I'm here with my baby son, Max." [28]"Oh," is all he said. [29]"Oh." [30]And he wandered into the living room and sat down. [31]In a few minutes I joined him and found him staring blankly out the window. [32]He was a polite host, asking if I wanted anything to eat, and if the room was too cold. [33]I answered with an aching heart, mourning for his loss and for mine.

A Frustrating Job

[1]Working as a baby-sitter was the most frustrating job I ever had. [2]I discovered this fact when my sister asked me to stay with her two sons for the evening. [3]I figured I would get them dinner, let them watch a little TV, and then put them to bed early. [4]The rest of the night I planned to watch TV and collect an easy twenty dollars. [5]It turned out to be anything but easy. [6]First, right before we were about to sit down for a pizza dinner, Rickie let the parakeet out of its cage. [7]This bird is really intelligent and can repeat almost any phrase. [8]The dog started chasing it around the house, so I decided to catch it before the dog did. [9]Rickie and Jeff volunteered to help, following at my heels. [10]We had the bird cornered by the fireplace when Rickie jumped for it and knocked over the hamster cage. [11]Then the bird escaped again, and the hamsters began scurrying around their cage like crazy creatures. [12]The dog had disappeared by this point, so I decided to clean up the hamsters' cage and try to calm them down. [13]While I was doing this, Rickie and Jeff caught the parakeet and put it back in its cage. [14]It was time to return to the kitchen and eat cold pizza. [15]But upon entering the kitchen, I discovered why the dog had lost interest in the bird chase. [16]What was left of the pizza was lying on the floor, and tomato sauce was dripping from the dog's chin. [17]I cleaned up the mess and then served chicken noodle soup and ice cream to the boys. [18]Only at nine o'clock did I get the kids to bed. [19]I then returned downstairs to find that the dog had thrown up pizza on the living-room rug. [20]When I finished cleaning the rug, my sister returned. [21]I took the twenty dollars and told her that she should get someone else next time.

■ Questions

About Unity

1. Which paragraph lacks a topic sentence?

   _____

   Write a topic sentence for the paragraph.

   _____

   _____

2. Which sentence in "A Frustrating Job" should be omitted in the interest of paragraph unity? (Write the sentence number here.) _____

About Support

3. What is for you the best (most real and vivid) detail or image in the paragraph "Heartbreak"?

    _____

    _____

    What is the best detail or image in "Losing My Father"?

    _____

    _____

    What is the best detail or image in "A Frustrating Job"?

    _____

    _____

4. Which two paragraphs include the actual words spoken by the participants?

    _____

    _____

About Coherence

5. Do the three paragraphs use time order or emphatic order to organize details?

    _____

6. What are four transition words used in "A Frustrating Job"?

    _____   _____   _____   _____

Developing a Narrative Paragraph

Development through Prewriting

Gary's instructor was helping her students think of topics for their narrative paragraphs. "A narrative is simply a story that illustrates a point," she said. "That point is often about an emotion you felt. Looking at a list of emotions may help you think of a topic. Ask yourself what incident in your life has made you feel any of these emotions."

The instructor then jotted these feelings on the board:

Anger

Embarrassment

Jealousy

Amusement

Confusion

Thankfulness

Loneliness

Sadness

Terror

Relief

As Gary looked over the list, he thought of several experiences in his life. "The word 'angry' made me think about a time when I was a kid. My brother took my skateboard without permission and left it in the park, where it got stolen. 'Amused' made me think of when I watched my roommate, who claimed he spoke Spanish, try to bargain with a street vendor in Mexico. He got so flustered that he ended up paying even more than the vendor had originally asked for. When I got to 'sad,' though, I thought about when I visited Bonnie and found out she was dating someone else. 'Sad' wasn't a strong enough word, though—I was heartbroken. So I decided to write about heartbreak."

Gary's first step was to do some freewriting. Without worrying about spelling or grammar, he simply wrote down everything that came into his mind concerning his visit to Bonnie. Here is what he came up with:

> I hadn't expected to see Bonnie until Christmas. We'd got engaged just before she went off to college. The drive to Penn State took ten hours each way and that seemed like to much driving for just a weekend visit. But I realized I had a long weekend over thanksgiving I decided to surprise her. I think down deep I knew something was wrong. She had sounded sort of cool on the phone and she hadn't been writing as often. I guess I wanted to convince myself that everything was OK. We'd been dating since we were 16 and I couldn't imagine not being with her. When I knocked at her dorm door I remember how she was smiling when she opened the door. Her expression changed to one of surprise. Not happy surprise. I hugged her and she sort of hugged me back but like you'd hug your brother. Another girl was in the room. Bonnie said, "This is Pam," and Pam shot out of the room like I had a disease. Everything seemed wrong and confused. I started taking off my sweater and then I saw it. On a bulletin board was this photo of Bonnie with Blake, the guy she had been messing around with. They broke up about a year later, but by then I never wanted to see Bonnie again. I couldn't believe Bonnie would start seeing somebody else when we were planning to get married. It had even been her idea to get engaged. Before she left for college. Later on I realized that wasn't the first dishonest thing she'd done. I got out of there as quick as I could.

Development through Revising

Gary knew that the first, freewritten version of his paragraph needed work. Here are the comments he made after he reread it the following day:

> "Although my point is supposed to be that my visit to Bonnie was heartbreaking, I didn't really get that across. I need to say more about how the experience felt.
>
> "I've included some information that doesn't really support my point. For instance, what happened to Bonnie and Blake later isn't important here. Also, I think I spend too much time explaining the circumstances of the visit. I need to get more quickly to the point where I arrived at Bonnie's dorm.
>
> "I think I should include more dialogue, too. That would make the reader feel more like a witness to what really happened."

With this self-critique in mind, Gary revised his paragraph until he had produced the version that appears on page 257.

Writing a Narrative Paragraph

Writing Assignment 1

Write a paragraph about an experience in which a certain emotion was predominant. The emotion might be fear, pride, satisfaction, embarrassment, or any of these:

Frustration	Sympathy	Shyness
Love	Bitterness	Disappointment
Sadness	Violence	Happiness
Terror	Surprise	Jealousy
Shock	Nostalgia	Anger
Relief	Loss	Hate
Envy	Silliness	Nervousness

The experience you write about should be limited in time. Note that the three paragraphs presented in this chapter all detail experiences that occurred within relatively short periods. One writer describes a heartbreaking surprise he received the day he visited his girlfriend; another describes the loss of her father; the third describes a frustrating night of baby-sitting.

A good way to bring an event to life for your readers is to include some dialogue, as the writers of two of the three paragraphs in this chapter have done.

Words that you said, or that someone else said, help make a situation come alive. First, though, be sure to check the section on quotation marks on pages 528–534.

Prewriting

a Begin by freewriting. Think of an experience or event that caused you to feel a certain emotion strongly. Then spend ten minutes writing freely about the experience. Do not worry at this point about such matters as spelling or grammar or putting things in the right order. Instead, just try to get down all the details you can think of that seem related to the experience.

b This preliminary writing will help you decide whether your topic is promising enough to develop further. If it is not, choose another emotion and repeat step *a*. If it does seem promising, do two things:

- First, write your topic sentence, underlining the emotion you will focus on. For example, "My first day in kindergarten was one of the <u>scariest</u> days of my life."
- Second, make up a list of all the details involved in the experience. Then number these details according to the order in which they occurred.

c Referring to your list of details, write a rough draft of your paragraph. Use time signals such as *first, then, after, next, while, during,* and *finally* to help connect details as you move from the beginning to the middle to the end of your narrative. Be sure to include not only what happened but also how you felt about what was going on.

Revising

Put your first draft away for a day or so. When you return to it, read it over, asking yourself these questions:

- Does my topic sentence clearly state what emotion the experience made me feel?
- Have I included some dialogue to make the experience come alive?
- Have I explained how I felt as the experience occurred?
- Have I used time order to narrate the experience from beginning to end?
- Have I used time signals to connect one detail to the next?
- Have I checked my paper for sentence skills, including spelling, as listed on the inside front cover of the book?

Continue revising your work until you can answer "yes" to all these questions.

■ Writing Assignment 2

Narrate a real-life event you have witnessed. Listed below are some places where interesting personal interactions often happen. Think of an event that you saw happen at one of these places, or visit one of them and take notes on an incident to write about.

> The traffic court or small-claims court in your area
>
> The dinner table at your or someone else's home
>
> A waiting line at a supermarket, unemployment office, ticket counter, movie theater, or cafeteria
>
> A doctor's office
>
> An audience at a movie, concert, or sports event
>
> A classroom
>
> A restaurant
>
> A student lounge

Prewriting

a Decide what point you will make about the incident. What one word or phrase characterizes the scene you witnessed? Your narration of the incident will emphasize that characteristic.

b Write your topic sentence. The topic sentence should state where the incident happened as well as your point about it. Here are some possibilities:

> I witnessed a *heartwarming* incident at Burger King yesterday.
>
> Two fans at last week's baseball game got into a *hilarious* argument.
>
> The scene at our family dinner table Monday was one of complete *confusion*.
>
> A *painful* dispute went on in Atlantic County small-claims court yesterday.

c Use the questioning technique to remind yourself of details that will make your narrative come alive. Ask yourself questions like these and write down your answers:

> Whom was I observing?
>
> How were they dressed?
>
> What were their facial expressions like?
>
> What tones of voice did they use?
>
> What did I hear them say?

d Drawing details from the notes you have written, write the first draft of your paragraph. Remember to use time signals such as *then, after that, during, meanwhile,* and *finally* to connect one sentence to another.

Revising

After you have put your paragraph away for a day, read it to a friend who will give you honest feedback. You and your friend should consider these questions:

- Does the topic sentence make a general point about the incident?
- Do descriptions of the appearance, tone of voice, and expressions of the people involved paint a clear picture of the incident?
- Is the sequence of events made clear by transitional words such as *at first, later,* and *then*?

Continue revising your work until you and your reader can answer "yes" to all these questions. Then check to make sure your paragraph is free of sentence-skills mistakes, including spelling errors. Use the list on the inside front cover of this book.

■ Writing Assignment 3

Write an account of a memorable personal experience. Make sure that your story has a point, expressed in the first sentence of the paragraph. If necessary, tailor your narrative to fit your purpose. Use time order to organize your details (*first* this happened; *then* this; *after that*, this; *next*, this; and so on). Concentrate on providing as many specific details as possible so that the reader can really share your experience. Try to make it as vivid for the reader as it was for you when you first experienced it.

Use one of the topics below or a topic of your own choosing. Regardless, remember that your story must illustrate or support a point stated in the first sentence of your paper.

The first time you felt grown-up

A major decision you made

A moment you knew you were happy

Your best or worst date

A time you took a foolish risk

An argument you will never forget

An incident that changed your life

A time when you did or did not do the right thing

Your best or worst holiday or birthday, or some other special occasion

A time you learned a lesson or taught a lesson to someone else

An occasion of triumph in sports or some other area

You may want to refer to the suggestions for prewriting and rewriting in Writing Assignment 1.

■ Writing Assignment 4

Write a paragraph that shows, through some experience you have had, the truth or falsity of a popular belief. You might write about any one of the following statements or some other popular saying.

Every person has a price.

Haste makes waste.

Don't count your chickens before they're hatched.

A bird in the hand is worth two in the bush.

It isn't what you know, it's who you know.

Borrowing can get you into trouble.

What you don't know won't hurt you.

A promise is easier made than kept.

You never really know people until you see them in an emergency.

If you don't help yourself, nobody will.

An ounce of prevention is worth a pound of cure.

Hope for the best but expect the worst.

Never give advice to a friend.

You get what you pay for.

A stitch in time saves nine.

A fool and his money are soon parted.

There is an exception to every rule.

Nice guys finish last.

Begin your narrative paragraph with a topic sentence that expresses your agreement or disagreement with a popular saying or belief, for example:

"Never give advice to a friend" is not always good advice, as I learned after helping a friend reunite with her boyfriend.

My sister learned recently that it is easier to make a promise than to keep one.

Refer to the suggestions for prewriting and revising on pages 262–263. Remember that the purpose of your story is to support your topic sentence. Omit details from the experience you're writing about that don't support your topic sentence. Also, feel free to use made-up details that will strengthen your support.

■ Writing Assignment 5

Imagine that a younger brother or sister, or a young friend, has to make a difficult decision of some kind. Perhaps he or she must decide how to prepare for a job interview, whether or not to get help with a difficult class, or what to do about a co-worker who is taking money from the cash register. Narrate a story from your own experience (or that of someone you know) that will teach a younger person something about the decision he or she must make. In your paragraph, include a comment or two about the lesson your story teaches. Write about any decision young people often face, including any of those already mentioned or those listed below.

Should he or she save a little from a weekly paycheck?

Should he or she live at home or move to an apartment with some friends?

How should he or she deal with a group of friends who are involved with drugs, stealing, or both?

16 Arguing a Position

Most of us know someone who enjoys a good argument. Such a person usually challenges any sweeping statement we might make. "Why do you say that?" he or she will ask. "Give your reasons." Our questioner then listens carefully as we cite our reasons, waiting to see if we really do have solid evidence to support our point of view. Such a questioner may make us feel a bit nervous, but we may also appreciate the way he or she makes us think through our opinions.

The ability to advance sound and compelling arguments is an important skill in everyday life. We can use argument to get an extension on a term paper, obtain a favor from a friend, or convince an employer that we are the right person for a job. Understanding persuasion based on clear, logical reasoning can also help us see through the sometimes faulty arguments advanced by advertisers, editors, politicians, and others who try to bring us over to their side.

In this section, you will be asked to argue a position and defend it with a series of solid reasons. In a general way, you are doing the same thing with all the paragraph assignments in the book: making a point and then supporting it. The difference here is that, in a more direct and formal manner, you will advance a point about which you feel strongly and seek to persuade others to agree with you.

Paragraphs to Consider

Let's Ban Proms

1While many students regard proms as peak events in high school life, I believe that high school proms should be banned. 2One reason is that even before the prom takes place, it causes problems. 3Teenagers are separated into "the ones who were asked" and "the ones who weren't." 4Being one of those who weren't asked can be heartbreaking to a sensitive young person. 5Another pre-prom problem is money. 6The price of the various items needed can add up quickly to a lot of money. 7The prom itself can be unpleasant and frustrating, too. 8At the beginning of the evening, the girls enviously compare dresses while the boys sweat nervously inside their rented suits. 9During the dance, the couples who have gotten together only to go to the prom have split up into miserable singles. 10When the prom draws to a close, the popular teenagers drive off happily to other parties while the less popular ones head home, as usual. 11Perhaps the main reason proms should be banned, however, is the drinking and driving that go on after the prom is over. [12]Teenagers pile into their cars on their way to "after-proms" and pull out the bottles and cans stashed under the seat. [13]By the time the big night is finally over, at 4 or 5 A.M., students are trying to weave home without encountering the police or a roadside tree. [14]Some of them do not make it, and prom night turns into tragedy. [15]For all these reasons, proms have no place in our schools.

Bashing Men

[1]Our culture now puts down men in ways that would be considered very offensive if the targets were women. [2]For instance, men are frequently portrayed in popular culture as bumbling fools. [3]The popular TV show The Simpsons, for instance, shows the father, Homer, as a total idiot, dishonest and childish. [4]His son, Bart, is equally foolish; but the mother, Marge, and the sister, Lisa, are levelheaded and responsible. [5]Little children love the "Berenstain Bears" books, which are supposed to teach lessons about subjects including honesty, bad habits, and going to the doctor. [6]In every book, while the mother bear gives her cubs good advice, the father bear acts stupidly and has to be taught a lesson along with the kids. [7]In addition, society teaches us to think of men as having no value in a family other than to contribute money. [8]Popular stars like Madonna go on national TV and proclaim that their babies don't need a father because they are financially independent women. [9]Families on welfare are denied benefits if the children's father stays in the home—apparently if he isn't bringing in money, the family is better off without him. [10]The welfare system is deeply flawed in other ways as well. [11]And women tell each other men-bashing jokes that would be considered sexist and offensive if they were directed at women. [12]Here's one: "Question: A woman has a flat tire. [13]Santa Claus, Oprah Winfrey, and a decent man all stop to help her. [14]Who actually changes the tire?" [15]The answer: "Oprah, of course. [16]The other two are fictional characters." [17]Women deserve to be treated with respect, but that doesn't mean men should be put down.

Living Alone

[1]Living alone is quite an experience. [2]People who live alone, for one thing, have to learn to do all kinds of tasks by themselves. [3]They must learn—even if they have had no experience—to change fuses, put up curtains and shades, temporarily dam an overflowing toilet, cook a meal, and defrost a refrigerator. [4]When there is no father, husband, mother, or wife to depend on, a person can't fall back on the excuse, "I don't know how to do that." [5]Those who live alone also need the strength to deal with people. [6]Alone, singles must face noisy neighbors, unresponsive landlords,

dishonest repair people, and aggressive bill collectors. [7]Because there are no buffers between themselves and the outside world, people living alone have to handle every visitor—friendly or unfriendly—alone. [8]Finally, singles need a large dose of courage to cope with occasional panic and unavoidable loneliness. [9]That weird thump in the night is even more terrifying when there is no one in the next bed or the next room. [10]Frightening weather or unexpected bad news is doubly bad when the worry can't be shared. [11]Even when life is going well, little moments of sudden loneliness can send shivers through the heart. [12]Struggling through such bad times taps into reserves of courage that people may not have known they possessed. [13]Facing everyday tasks, confronting all types of people, and handling panic and loneliness can shape singles into brave, resourceful, and more independent people.

■ Questions

About Unity

1. The topic sentence in "Living Alone" is too broad. Circle the topic sentence below that states accurately what the paragraph is about.

    a. Living alone can make one a better person.

    b. Living alone can create feelings of loneliness.

    c. Living alone should be avoided.

2. Which sentence in "Bashing Men" should be eliminated in the interest of paragraph unity? (*Write the sentence number here.*) _____

3. How many reasons are given to support the topic sentence in each paragraph?

    a. In "Let's Ban Proms" ____ one   ____ two   ____ three   ____ four

    b. In "Bashing Men"   ____ one   ____ two   ____ three   ____ four

    c. In "Living Alone"   ____ one   ____ two   ____ three   ____ four

4. After which sentence in "Let's Ban Proms" are more specific details needed?

    _____

About Coherence

5. Which paragraph uses a combination of time and emphatic order to organize its details? _____

6. What are the three main transition words in "Living Alone"?

    _____   _____   _____

Activity

Complete the outline below of "Bashing Men." Summarize in a few words the supporting material that fits under the topic sentence: After *1, 2,* and *3,* write in the three main points of support for the topic sentence. In the spaces after the numbers, write in the examples used to support those three main points. Two items have been done for you as examples.

Topic sentence: It's become more and more acceptable to bash men, acting as though they are less deserving of respect than women.

1. _____

    a. _____

    b.   Berenstain Bears

2. _____

    a. _____

    b.   Welfare benefits cut off if father in home

3. _____

    a. _____

Developing an Argument Paragraph

Development through Prewriting

Yolanda is the student author of "Let's Ban Proms." She decided on her topic after visiting her parents' home one weekend and observing her younger brother's concern about his upcoming prom.

"I really felt bad for Martin as I saw what he was going through," Yolanda said. "He's usually a happy kid who enjoys school. But this weekend he wasn't talking about his track meets or term papers or any of the things he's usually chatting about. Instead he was all tied up in knots about his prom. The girl he'd really wanted to go with had already been asked, and so friends had fixed him up with a girl he barely knew who didn't have a date either. Neither of them was excited about being together, but they felt that they just 'had' to go. And now he's worried about how to afford renting a tux, and how will he get a cool car to go in, and all that stuff. It's shaping up to be a really stressful, expensive evening. When I was in high school, I saw a lot of bad things associated with the prom, too. I hate to see young kids feeling pressured to attend an event that is fun for only a few."

Yolanda began prewriting by making a list of all the negative aspects of proms. This is what she came up with:

Drinking after prom

Car accidents (most important!)

Competition for dates

Preparation for prom cuts into school hours

Rejection of not being asked

Waste of school money

Going with someone you don't like

Separates popular from unpopular

Expensive

Bad-tempered chaperones

Next, Yolanda numbered the details in the order she was going to present them. She also struck out details she decided not to use:

6   Drinking after prom

7   Car accidents (most important!)

3   Competition for dates

~~Preparation for prom cuts into school hours~~

1   Rejection of not being asked

~~Waste of school money~~

4   Going with someone you don't like

5   Separates popular from unpopular

2   Expensive

~~Bad-tempered chaperones~~

Drawing from these notes, Yolanda wrote the following first draft of her paragraph:

In my opinion, high school proms should be banned. First, they cause unhappiness by separating students into "the ones who were asked" and "the ones who weren't." Proms are also expensive, as anyone who has attended one knows. The competition for dates can damage previously strong friendships. Many couples get together only in order to have a date for the prom and do not enjoy each other's company. After the prom, too, the kids are separated into "more popular" and "less popular" groups, with the popular ones going to after-prom parties. The biggest reason to ban proms, though, is the prom-night drinking that commonly occurs. Teenagers hide liquor in their cars and then try to drive home drunk. Some of them do not make it. For all these reasons, proms should be banned.

Development through Revising

Yolanda's instructor reviewed her first draft and made these comments:

> The order of your paragraph could be made stronger. Although you make good use of emphatic order (by ending with "the biggest reason to ban proms"), it's less clear that the paragraph is also organized according to time—in other words, you move from before the prom starts to during the prom to after it. Better use of transitional language will make the organization more clear.
>
> Also, you could make the paragraph more alive by including concrete details and illustrations. Your main points would be stronger with such support.

With these comments in mind, Yolanda revised her paragraph until she produced the version that appears on page 269.

Writing an Argument Paragraph

■ Writing Assignment 1

Develop an argument paragraph based on one of the following statements:

1. Condoms should (*or* should not) be made available in schools.
2. _____ (*name a specific athlete*) is the athlete most worthy of admiration in his *or* her sport.
3. Television is one of the best (*or* worst) inventions of this century.
4. _____ make the best (*or* worst) pets.
5. Cigarette and alcohol advertising should (*or* should not) be banned.
6. Teenagers make poor parents.
7. _____ is one public figure today who can be considered a hero.
8. This college needs a better _____ (cafeteria *or* library *or* student center *or* grading policy *or* attendance policy).

Prewriting

a Make up brief outlines for any three of the eight statements above. Make sure you have three separate and distinct reasons for each statement. Below is an example of a brief outline for a paragraph making another point.

> Large cities should outlaw passenger cars.
> 1. Cut down on smog and pollution
> 2. Cut down on noise
> 3. Make more room for pedestrians

b Decide, perhaps through discussion with your instructor or classmates, which of your outlines is the most promising for development into a paragraph. Make sure your supporting points are logical by asking yourself in each case, "Does this item truly support my topic sentence?"

c Do some prewriting. Prepare a list of all the details you can think of that might actually support your point. Don't limit yourself; include more details than you can actually use. Here, for example, are details generated by the writer of "Living Alone":

Deal with power failures	Noisy neighbors
Nasty landlords	Develop courage
Scary noises at night	Do all the cooking
Spiders	Home repairs
Bill collectors	Obscene phone calls
Frightening storms	Loneliness

d Decide which details you will use to develop your paragraph. Number the details in the order in which you will present them. Because presenting the strongest reason last (emphatic order) is the most effective way to organize an argument paragraph, be sure to save your most powerful reason for last. Here is how the author of "Living Alone" made decisions about details:

> 1 Deal with power failures
>
> 4 Nasty landlords
>
> 7 Scary noises at night
>
> ~~Spiders~~
>
> 6 Bill collectors

      8   Frightening storms

      5   Noisy neighbors

   10   Develop courage

      2   Do all the cooking

      3   Home repairs

          ~~Obscene phone calls~~

      9   Loneliness

e Write the first draft of your paragraph. As you write, develop each reason with specific details. For example, in "Living Alone," notice how the writer makes the experience of living alone come alive with phrases like "That weird thump in the night" or "little moments of sudden loneliness can send shivers through the heart."

Revising

- Put your paragraph away for a day or so. When you reread it, imagine that your audience is a jury that will ultimately render a verdict on your argument. Have you presented a convincing case? If you were on the jury, would you be favorably impressed with this argument?

- As you work on subsequent drafts of your paragraph, keep in mind unity, support, and coherence.

- Edit the next-to-final draft of your paper for sentence-skills mistakes, including spelling. Use the list on the inside front cover of this book.

■ Writing Assignment 2

Write a paragraph in which you take a stand on one of the controversial points below. Support the point with three reasons.

1. Students should not be required to attend high school.
2. All handguns should be banned.
3. Homosexuals should not be allowed in the armed forces.
4. The death penalty should exist for certain crimes.
5. Abortion should be legal.
6. Federal prisons should be coed, and prisoners should be allowed to marry.
7. Parents of girls under eighteen should be informed if their daughters receive birth-control aids.

8. The government should set up centers where sick or aged persons can go voluntarily to commit suicide.

9. Any woman on welfare who has more than two illegitimate children should be sterilized.

10. Parents should never hit their children.

Prewriting

a As a useful exercise to help you begin developing your argument, your instructor might give class members a chance to "stand up" for what they believe in. One side of the front of the room should be designated *strong agreement* and the other side *strong disagreement,* with an imaginary line representing varying degrees of agreement or disagreement in between. As the class stands in front of the room, the instructor will read one value statement at a time from the list above, and students will move to the appropriate spot, depending on their degree of agreement or disagreement. Some time will be allowed for students, first, to discuss with those near them the reasons they are standing where they are, and second, to state to those at the other end of the scale the reasons for their position.

b Begin your paragraph by writing a sentence that expresses your attitude toward one of the value statements above, for example, "I feel that prostitution should be legalized."

c Outline the reason or reasons you hold the opinion that you do. Your support may be based on your own experience, the experience of someone you know, or logic. For example, an outline of a paragraph based on one student's logic looked like this:

I feel that prostitution should be legalized for the following reasons:
1. Prostitutes would then have to pay their fair share of income tax.
2. Government health centers would administer regular checkups. This would help prevent the spread of AIDS and venereal disease.
3. Prostitutes would be able to work openly and independently and would not be controlled by pimps and gangsters.
4. Most of all, prostitutes would be less looked down upon—an attitude that is psychologically damaging to those who may already have emotional problems.

Another outline, based on experience, proceeded as follows:

The experiences of a former prostitute I know show that prostitution should not be legalized.

1. The attention Linda received as a prostitute prevented her from seeing and working on her personal problems.
2. She became bitter toward all men, suspecting them all of wanting to exploit her.
3. She developed a negative self-image and felt that no one could love her.

d Write a first draft of your paragraph, providing specific details to back up each point in your outline.

Revising

Put your paragraph away for a while, ideally at least a day. Ask a friend whose judgment you trust to read and critique it. Your friend should consider each of these questions as he or she reads:

- Does the topic sentence clearly state the author's opinion on a controversial subject?
- Does the paragraph include at least three separate and distinct reasons that support the author's argument?
- Is each of the three reasons backed up by specific, relevant evidence?
- Has the author saved the most powerful reason for last?
- Is the paragraph free of spelling errors and the other sentence-skills mistakes listed on the inside front cover of the book?

Continue revising your work until you and your reader can answer "yes" to all these questions.

■ Writing Assignment 3

Where do you think it is best to bring up children—in the country, the suburbs, or the city? Write a paragraph in which you argue that one of those three environments is best for families with young children. Your argument should cover two types of reasons: (1) the advantages of living in the environment you've chosen and (2) the disadvantages of living in the other places. Use the following, or something much like it, for your topic sentence:

For families with young children, (*the country, a suburb,* or *the city*) _____ is the best place to live.

For each reason you advance, include at least one persuasive example. For instance, if you argue that the cultural life in the city is one important reason to live there, you should explain in detail just how going to a science museum is interesting and helpful to children. After deciding on your points of support, arrange them in a brief outline, saving your strongest point for last. In your paragraph, introduce each of your reasons with an addition transition, such as *first of all, another, also,* and *finally.*

■ Writing Assignment 4

Write a paper in which you use research findings to help support one of the following statements.

> Wearing seat belts in automobiles should be mandatory.
>
> Many people do not need vitamin pills.
>
> Disposable cans and bottles should be banned.
>
> Everyone should own a pet.
>
> Mandatory retirement ages should be abolished.
>
> Cigarettes should be illegal.
>
> Penalties against drunken drivers should be sharply increased.
>
> Advertising should not be permitted on Saturday morning cartoon shows.

Using strategies described in the chapter on the library and the Internet (pages 361–378), research the topic you have chosen. Reading material on your topic will help you think about that topic. See if you can then organize your paper in the form of three reasons that support the topic. Put these reasons into a scratch outline, and use it as a guide in writing your paragraph. Here is an example:

> Wearing seat belts should be mandatory.
> 1. Seat belts are now comfortable and easy to use . . .
> 2. A seat-belt law would be easy to enforce . . .
> 3. Seat belts would save lives . . .

Note that statistics (on how many lives could be saved) would support the last reason. Do not hesitate to cite studies and other data in a limited way; they make your argument more objective and compelling.

■ Writing Assignment 5

Imagine that you have finally met Mr. or Ms. Right—but your parents don't approve of him or her. Specifically, they are against your doing one of the the following:

Continuing to see this person

Going steady

Moving in together

Getting married at the end of the school year

Write a letter to your parents explaining in detail why you have made your choice. Do your best to convince them that it is a good choice.

17 Additional Paragraph Assignments

This section contains a variety of paragraph writing assignments. The earlier assignments are especially suited for writing practice at the beginning of a course; the later ones can be used to measure progress at the end of the course. In general, more detailed instructions are provided with the earlier assignments; fewer guidelines appear for the later ones, so that writers must make more individual decisions about exactly how to proceed. In short, the section provides a wide range of writing assignments. Many choices are possible, depending on the needs and interests of students and the purposes of the instructor.

■ 1   Best or Worst Experience

Your instructor may pass out slips of paper and ask you to write, in the middle of the slip, your name; in the top left-hand corner, the best or worst job (or chore) you have ever had; in the top right-hand corner, the best or worst instructor you have ever had; in the lower left-hand corner, the best or worst place you have ever eaten in; in the lower right-hand corner, the best or worst thing that has happened to you in the past week. The instructor may also participate by writing on the board. Here is one student's paper.

Baby-sitting for my sister	B. O. Sullivan (tenth-grade history teacher)
	Gail Battaglia	
Fourth Street Diner	Trying to register

You should then get together with any person in the room whom you do not know, exchange papers, and talk for a bit about what you wrote. Then the two of you should join another pair, with members of the resulting group of four doing two things:

- Mastering the first names of all the members of the group, so that, if asked, they could introduce the instructor to everyone in the group.
- Giving a "mini" speech to the group in which they talk with *as much specific detail as possible* about any one of the four responses on their slips of paper. During or after this speech, other members of the group should ask questions to get as full a sense as possible of why the experience described was "best" or "worst."

Finally, you should write a paper about any one of the best or worst experiences. The main purpose in writing this paper is to provide plenty of specific details that *show clearly* why your choice was "best" or worst." The papers on pages 136–137 are examples of students' responses to this assignment.

■ 2   Writing Up an Interview

Interview someone in the class. Take notes as you ask the person a series of questions.

How to Proceed

a Begin by asking a series of factual questions about the person. You might ask such questions as:

Where is the person from? Where does he or she live now?

Does the person have brothers or sisters? Does the person live with other people, or alone?

What kinds of jobs (if any) has the person had? Where does he or she work now?

What are the person's school or career plans? What courses is he or she taking?

What are the person's favorite leisure activities?

Work at getting specific details rather than general ones. You do not want your introduction to include lines such as "Regina graduated from high school and worked for a year." You want to state specific places and dates: "Regina graduated from DeWitt Clinton High School in the Bronx in 2000. Within a week of graduation, she had gotten a job as a typist for a branch of the Allstate Insurance Company located in Queens." Or if you are writing about a person's favorite activities, you do not want to simply say, "Regina enjoys watching TV in her few spare hours." Instead, go on and add details such as "Her favorite shows are *60 Minutes, Friends,* and *NYPD Blue.*"

b Then ask a series of questions about the person's attitudes and thoughts on various matters. You might ask the person's feeling about his or her

> Writing ability
>
> Parents
>
> Boss (if any)
>
> Courses
>
> Past schooling
>
> Strengths and talents
>
> Areas for self-improvement

> You might also ask what things make the person angry or sad or happy, and why.

c After collecting all this information, use it in two paragraphs. Begin your introduction to the person with a line like "This is a short introduction to _____. Here is some factual information about him (her)." Then begin your second paragraph with the line, "New let's take a brief look at some of _____'s attitudes and beliefs."

■ 3   Keeping a Journal

Keep a journal for one week, or for whatever time period your instructor indicates. At some point during each day—perhaps right before going to bed—write for fifteen minutes or more about some of the specific happenings, thoughts, and feelings of your day. You do not have to prepare what to write or be in the mood or worry about making mistakes; just write down whatever words come out. As a minimum, you should complete at least one page in each writing session.

Keeping a journal will help you develop the habits of thinking on paper and writing in terms of specific details. Also, the journal can serve as a sourcebook of ideas for possible papers.

A sample journal entry was given on page 14. It includes general ideas that the writer might develop into paragraphs; for example:

> Working at a department store means that you have to deal with some irritating customers.
>
> Certain preparations are advisable before you quit a job.

See if you can construct another general point from this journal entry that might be the basis for a detailed and interesting paragraph. Write the point in the space below.

_____

■ 4   Writing a Dialogue

Make up and write a *realistic* dialogue between two or more people. Don't have your characters talk like cardboard figures; have them talk the way people would in real life. Also, make sure their voices are consistent. (Do not have them suddenly talk out of character.)

The dialogue should deal with a lifelike situation. It may, for example, be a discussion or argument of some kind between two friends or acquaintances, a husband and wife, a parent and child, a brother and sister, a boyfriend and girlfriend, a clerk and customer, or other people. The conversation may or may not lead to a decision or action of some kind.

When writing dialogue, enclose your characters' exact words within quotation marks. (You should first review the material on quotation marks on pages 528–534.) Begin a new paragraph to mark each change in speaker. Also, include brief descriptions of whether your characters smile, sit down or stand up, or make other facial gestures or movements during the conversation. And be sure to include a title for your dialogue. The example that follows can serve as a guide.

A Supermarket Conversation

The supermarket checker rang up the total and said to the young woman in line, "That'll be $43.61."

The young woman fumbled with her pocketbook and then said in an embarrassed voice, "I don't think I have more than $40. How much did you say it was again?"

"It's $43.61," the checker said in a sharp, impatient tone.

As the young woman searched her pocketbook for the dollars she needed, the checker said loudly, "If you don't have enough money, you'll have to put something back."

A middle-aged man behind the young woman spoke up. "Look, Ma'am, I'll lend you a couple of dollars."

"No, I couldn't do that," said the young woman, "If . . . I don't think I need those sodas," she said hesitantly.

"Look lady, make up your mind. You're holding up the line," the checker snapped.

The man turned to the checker and said coldly, "Why don't you try being a little more courteous to people? If we weren't here buying things, you'd be out of a job."

■ 5   Annoyances in Everyday Life

Make up a list of things that bother you in everyday life. One student's list of "pet peeves" included the following items:

Drivers who suddenly slow down to turn without having signaled

The cold floor in my bathroom on a winter morning

Not having cable television to watch football and basketball games

The small napkin holder in my parents' home that is always running out of napkins

Not being able to fall asleep at night when I know I have to get up at 6:30 the next morning

Suggestions on How to Proceed

a Brainstorm a list of everyday annoyances by asking yourself questions: "What annoys me at home (or about my kitchen, bathroom, closets, and so on)?" "What annoys me about getting to school?" "What annoys me at school or work?" "What annoys me while I am driving or shopping?" You will probably be able to think of other questions.

b Decide which annoyances seem most promising to develop. Which are the most interesting or important? Which can be developed with specific, vivid details? Cross out the items you will not use. Next, number the annoyances you have listed in the order in which you will present them. You may want to group related items together (all those that are connected with shopping, for instance). Be sure to end with the item that annoys you the most.

c Now write a rough draft of the paragraph. Begin with a topic sentence that makes clear what your paragraph is about. Concentrate on providing plenty of details about each of the annoyances you are describing.

d In a second or third draft, add signal words (such as *one, also, another,* and *last*) to set off each annoyance.

e Use the checklist on the inside back cover to edit your paper for sentence-skills mistakes, including spelling.

■ 6 Getting Comfortable

Getting comfortable is a quiet pleasure in life that we all share. Write a paper about the special way you make yourself comfortable, providing plenty of specific details so that the reader can really see and understand your method. Use transition words such as *first, next, then, in addition, also, finally,* and so on to guide readers through your paper. Transitions act like signposts on an unfamiliar route—they prevent your readers from getting lost.

A student paragraph on getting comfortable ("How I Relax") is on page 80.

■ 7 A Special Person

Write in detail about a person who provided help at an important time in your life. State in the first sentence who the person is and the person's relationship to you (friend, father, cousin, etc.). For example, "My grandmother gave me a lot of direction during the difficult time when my parents were getting divorced." Then show through specific examples (the person's words and actions) why he or she was so special for you.

■ 8 A Favorite Childhood Place

Describe a favorite childhood place that made you feel secure, safe, private, or in a world of your own. Here are some possibilities:

A closet

Under a piece of furniture

A grandparent's room

A basement or attic

The woods

A shed or barn

A tree

A bunk bed

Begin with a topic sentence something like this: "_____ was a place that made me feel _____ when I was a child." Keep the point of your topic sentence in mind as you describe this place. Include only details that will support the idea that your place was one of security, safety, privacy, or the like.

■ 9 Expressing Uniqueness

Write a paragraph providing examples of one quality or habit that helps make you unique. One student's response to this assignment appears below.

Floor-Cleaning Freak

The one habit that makes me unique is that I am a floor-cleaning freak. I use my Dustbuster to snap up crumbs seconds after they fall. When a rubber heel mark appears on my vinyl floor, I run for the steel wool. As I work in my kitchen preparing meals, I constantly scan the tiles, looking for spots where some liquid has been spilled or for a crumb that has somehow miraculously escaped my vision. After I scrub and wax my floors, I stand to one side of the room and try to catch the light in such a way as to reveal spots that have gone unwaxed. As I travel from one room to the other, my experienced eye is faithfully searching for lint that may have invaded my domain since my last passing. If I discover an offender, I discreetly tuck it into my pocket. The amount of lint I have gathered in the course of the day is the ultimate test of how diligently I am performing my task. I give my vacuum cleaner quite a workout, and I spend an excessive amount on replacement bags. My expenses for floor-cleaners and wax are alarmingly high, but somehow this does not stop me. Where my floors are concerned, money is not a consideration!

■ 10   Making It through the Day

Write about techniques you use to make it through a day of school or work. These may include:

Caffeine

A system of rewards

Humor

Food

Fantasizing

You might organize the paragraph by using time order. Show how you turn to your supports at various times during the day in order to cope with fatigue or boredom. For example, in the morning you might use coffee (with its dose of caffeine) to get started. Later in the day, you would go on to use other supports.

■ 11   Life without TV

Imagine that all the televisions in the United States go blank, starting tonight. What would you and your family do on a typical night without television? You may want to write about

What each individual would be doing

What the family could do together

Problems the lack of TV would cause

Benefits of family life without TV

Choose any of these approaches, or some other single approach, in writing about your family life without TV.

■ 12   Ten Topics

Write a paper on one of the following topics. Begin with a clear, direct sentence that states exactly what your paper will be about. For example, if you choose the first topic, your opening sentence might be, "There were several delightful childhood games I played that occupied many of my summer days." An opening sentence for the second topic might be, "The work I had to do to secure my high school diploma is one of the special accomplishments of my life." Be sure to follow your opening sentence with plenty of specific supporting details that develop your topic.

A way you had fun as a child

A special accomplishment

A favorite holiday and why it is your favorite

Some problems a family member or friend is having

A superstition or fear

A disagreement you have had with someone

A debt you have repaid or have yet to repay

The sickest you've ever been

How your parents (or you and a special person in your life) met

Your father's or mother's attitude toward you

■ 13   Ten More Topics

Write a paper on one of the topics below. Follow the instructions given for Assignment 12.

A wish or dream you have or had

Everyday pleasures

Ways you were punished by your parents as a child

Ways you were rewarded by your parents as a child

A difficult moment in your life

An experience you or someone you know has had with drugs

Your weaknesses as a student

Your strengths as a student

A time a prayer was answered

Something you would like to change

■ **14   Fifteen Topics**

Write a paper on one of the following topics:

Crime	Music	Books
Lies	Exercise	Transportation
Television	Debt	Exhaustion
Plants	Parking meters	Telephone
Comic books	Hunger	Drugs

Suggestions on How to Proceed

a You might begin by writing several statements about your general topic. For example, suppose that you choose to do a paper on the subject "Neighborhood." Here are some statements you might write:

My neighborhood is fairly rural.

The neighborhood where I grew up was unique.

Many city neighborhoods have problems with crime.

My new neighborhood has no playgrounds for children.

Everyone in my neighborhood seems to mow the lawn almost daily.

My neighborhood became a community when it was faced with a hurricane last summer.

My neighborhood is a noisy place.

b Choose (or revise) one of the statements that you could go on to develop in a paragraph. You should not select a narrow statement like "My new neighborhood has no playgrounds for children," for it is a simple factual sentence needing no support. Nor should you begin with a point such as "Many city neighborhoods have problems with crime," which is too broad for you to develop adequately in a single paragraph. (See also the information on topic sentences on pages 57–60.)

c After you have chosen a promising sentence, make a scratch outline of supporting details that will develop the point of that sentence. For example, one student provided the following outline:

My neighborhood is a noisy place.
1. Businesses
    a. Tavern with loud music
    b. Twenty-four-hour drive-in burger restaurant

    2. Children
        a. Skating and biking while carrying loud radios
        b. Street games
    3. Traffic
        a. Truck route nearby
        b. Horn-blowing during frequent delays at intersection

d While writing your paper, use the checklist on the inside front cover to make sure you can answer "yes" to the questions about unity, support, and coherence. Also, refer to the checklist when you edit the next-to-final draft of your paper for sentence-skills mistakes, including spelling.

■ 15   Fifteen More Topics

Write a paper on one of the topics below. Follow the instructions given for Assignment 14.

Comics	Tryouts
Babies	Pens
Vacation	Hospital
Red tape	Parties
Dependability	Criticism
Illness	Success
Failure	Wisdom teeth
Home	

Part Three

Essay Development

Preview

Part Three moves from the single-paragraph paper to the several-paragraph essay. The differences between a paragraph and an essay are explained and then illustrated with a paragraph that has been expanded into an essay. You are shown how to begin an essay, how to tie its supporting paragraphs together, and how to conclude it. Three student essays are presented, along with questions to increase your understanding of the essay form. Finally, directions on how to plan an essay are followed by a series of essay writing assignments.

18 Writing the Essay

What Is an Essay?

Differences between an Essay and a Paragraph

An essay is simply a paper of several paragraphs, rather than one paragraph, that supports a single point. In an essay, subjects can and should be treated more fully than they would be in a single-paragraph paper.

The main idea or point developed in an essay is called the *thesis statement* or *thesis sentence* (rather than, as in a paragraph, the *topic sentence*). The thesis statement appears in the introductory paragraph, and it is then developed in the supporting paragraphs that follow. A short concluding paragraph closes the essay.

The Form of an Essay

The diagram on the next page shows the form of an essay.

Introductory Paragraph

> Introduction
> Thesis statement
> Plan of development:
> Points 1, 2, 3

The *introduction* attracts the reader's interest.

The *thesis statement* (or *thesis sentence*) states the main idea advanced in the paper.

The *plan of development* is a list of points that support the thesis. The points are presented in the order in which they will be developed in the paper.

First Supporting Paragraph

> Topic sentence (point 1)
> Specific evidence

The *topic sentence* advances the first supporting point for the thesis, and the *specific evidence* in the rest of the paragraph develops that first point.

Second Supporting Paragraph

> Topic sentence (point 2)
> Specific evidence

The *topic sentence* advances the second supporting point for the thesis, and the *specific evidence* in the rest of the paragraph develops that second point.

Third Supporting Paragraph

> Topic sentence (point 3)
> Specific evidence

The *topic sentence* advances the third supporting point for the thesis, and the *specific evidence* in the rest of the paragraph develops that third point.

Concluding Paragraph

> Summary, conclusion,
> or both

A *summary* is a brief restatement of the thesis and its main points. A *conclusion* is a final thought or two stemming from the subject of the paper.

A Model Essay

Gene, the writer of the paragraph on working in an apple plant (page 5), later decided to develop his subject more fully. Here is the essay that resulted.

My Job in an Apple Plant

Introductory paragraph

1In the course of working my way through school, I have taken many jobs I would rather forget. 2I have spent nine hours a day lifting heavy automobile and truck batteries off the end of an assembly belt. 3I have risked the loss of eyes and fingers working a punch press in a textile factory. 4I have served as a ward aide in a mental hospital, helping care for brain-damaged men who would break into violent fits at unexpected moments. 5But none of these jobs was as dreadful as my job in an apple plant. 6The work was physically hard; the pay was poor; and, most of all, the working conditions were dismal.

First supporting paragraph

7First of all, the job made enormous demands on my strength and energy. 8For ten hours a night, I took cartons that rolled down a metal track and stacked them onto wooden skids in a tractor trailer. 9Each carton contained twelve heavy bottles of apple juice. 10A carton shot down the track about every fifteen seconds. 11I once figured out that I was lifting an average of twelve tons of apple juice every night. 12When a truck was almost filled, I or my partner had to drag fourteen bulky wooden skids into the empty trailer nearby and then set up added sections of the heavy metal track so that we could start routing cartons to the back of the empty van. 13While one of us did that, the other performed the stacking work of two men.

Second supporting paragraph

14I would not have minded the difficulty of the work so much if the pay had not been so poor. 15I was paid the minimum wage at that time, $3.65 an hour, plus just a quarter extra for working the night shift. 16Because of the low salary, I felt compelled to get as much overtime pay as possible. 17Everything over eight hours a night was time-and-a-half, so I typically worked twelve hours a night. 18On Friday I would sometimes work straight through until Saturday at noon—eighteen hours. 19I averaged over sixty hours a week but did not take home much more than $180.

Third supporting paragraph

20But even more than the low pay, what upset me about my apple plant job was the working conditions. 21Our humorless supervisor cared only about his production record for each night and tried to keep the assembly line moving at breakneck pace. 22During work I was limited to two ten-minute breaks and an unpaid half hour for lunch. 23Most of my time was spent outside on the truck loading dock in near-zero-degree temperatures. 24The steel floors of the trucks were like ice; the quickly penetrating cold made my feet feel like stone. 25I had no shared interests with the man I loaded cartons with, and so I had to work without companionship on the job. ²⁶And after the production line shut down and most people left, I had to spend two hours alone scrubbing clean the apple vats, which were coated with a sticky residue.

Concluding
paragraph

²⁷I stayed on the job for five months, all the while hating the difficulty of the work, the poor money, and the conditions under which I worked. ²⁸By the time I quit, I was determined never to do such degrading work again.

Important Points about the Essay

Introductory Paragraph

An introductory paragraph has certain purposes or functions and can be constructed using various methods.

Purposes of the Introduction

An introductory paragraph should do three things:

1 Attract the reader's *interest*. Using one of the suggested methods of introduction described below can help draw the reader into your paper.

2 Present a *thesis sentence*—a clear, direct statement of the central idea that you will develop in your paper. The thesis statement, like a topic sentence, should have a keyword or -words reflecting your attitude about the subject. For example, in the essay on the apple plant job, the keyword is *dreadful*.

3 Indicate a *plan of development*—a preview of the major points that will support your thesis statement, listed in the order in which they will be presented. In some cases, the thesis statement and plan of development may appear in the same sentence. In some cases, also, the plan of development may be omitted.

Activity

1. In "My Job in an Apple Plant," which sentences are used to attract the reader's interest?

    _____ sentences 1 to 3   _____ 1 to 4   _____ 1 to 5

2. The thesis in "My Job in an Apple Plant" is presented in

    _____ sentence 4   _____ sentence 5   _____ sentence 6

3. Is the thesis followed by a plan of development?

    _____ Yes   _____ No

4. Which words in the plan of development announce the three major supporting points in the essay? Write them below.

a. _____

b. _____

c. _____

Common Methods of Introduction

Here are some common methods of introduction. Use any one method, or a combination of methods, to introduce your subject in an interesting way.

1 *Broad statement.* Begin with a broad, general statement of your topic and narrow it down to your thesis statement. Broad, general statements ease the reader into your thesis statement by providing a background for it. In "My Job in an Apple Plant," Gene writes generally on the topic of his worst jobs and then narrows down to a specific worst job.

2 *Contrast.* Start with an idea or situation that is the opposite of the one you will develop. This approach works because your readers will be surprised, and then intrigued, by the contrast between the opening idea and the thesis that follows it. Here is an example of a "contrast" introduction:

> When I was a girl, I never argued with my parents about differences between their attitudes and mine. My father would deliver his judgment on an issue, and that was usually the end of the matter. Discussion seldom changed his mind, and disagreement was not tolerated. But the situation is different with today's parents and children. My husband and I have to contend with radical differences between what our children think about a given situation and what we think about it. We have had disagreements with all three of our daughters, Stephanie, Diana, and Giselle.

3 *"Relevance."* Explain the importance of your topic. If you can convince your readers that the subject applies to them in some way, or is something they should know more about, they will want to continue reading. The introductory paragraph of "Sports-Crazy America" (page 301) provides an example of a "relevance" introduction.

4 *Anecdote.* Use an incident or brief story. Stories are naturally interesting. They appeal to a reader's curiosity. In your introduction, an anecdote will grab the reader's attention right away. The story should be brief and should be related to your central idea. The incident in the story can be something that happened to you, something that you may have heard about, or something that you have read about in a newspaper or magazine. Here is an example of a paragraph that begins with a story:

> The husky man pushes open the door of the bedroom and grins as he pulls out a .38 revolver. An elderly man wearing thin pajamas looks at him and whimpers. In a feeble effort at escape, the old man slides out of his bed and moves to the door of the room. The husky man, still grinning, blocks his way. With the face of a small, frightened animal, the old man looks up and whispers, "Oh God, please don't hurt me." The grinning man then fires four times. The television movie cuts now to a soap commercial, but the little boy who has been watching the set has begun to cry. Such scenes of direct violence on television must surely be harmful to children for a number of psychological reasons.

5 *Questions.* Ask your readers one or more questions. These questions catch the readers' interest and make them want to read on. Here is an example of a paragraph that begins with questions:

> What would happen if we were totally honest with ourselves? Would we be able to stand the pain of giving up self-deception? Would the complete truth be too much for us to bear? Such questions will probably never be answered, for in everyday life we protect ourselves from the onslaught of too much reality. All of us cultivate defense mechanisms that prevent us from seeing, hearing, or feeling too much. Included among such defense mechanisms are rationalization, reaction formation, and substitution.

Note, however, that the thesis itself must not be a question.

6 *Quotation.* A quotation can be something you have read in a book or an article. It can also be something that you have heard: a popular saying or proverb ("Never give advice to a friend"); a current or recent advertising slogan ("Just do it"); a favorite expression used by your friends or family ("My father always says . . ."). Using a quotation in your introductory paragraph lets you add someone else's voice to your own. Here is an example of a paragraph that begins with a quotation:

> "Evil," wrote Martin Buber, "is lack of direction." In my school days as a fatherless boy, with a mother too confused by her own life to really care for me, I strayed down a number of dangerous paths. Before my eighteenth birthday, I had been a car thief, a burglar, and a drug seller.

Supporting Paragraphs

Most essays have three supporting points, developed in three separate paragraphs. (Some essays will have two supporting points; others, four or more.) Each of the supporting paragraphs should begin with a topic sentence that states the point to be detailed in that paragraph. Just as the thesis provides a focus for the entire essay, the topic sentence provides a focus for each supporting paragraph.

Activity

1. What is the topic sentence for the first supporting paragraph of "My Job in an Apple Plant"? (*Write the sentence number here.*) _____

2. What is the topic sentence for the second supporting paragraph? _____

3. What is the topic sentence for the third supporting paragraph? _____

Transitional Sentences

In paragraphs, transitions and other connective devices (pages 81–87) are used to help link sentences. Similarly, in an essay *transitional sentences* are used to help tie the supporting paragraphs together. Such transitional sentences usually occur near the end of one paragraph or the beginning of the next.

In "My Job in an Apple Plant," the first transitional sentence is:

> I would not have minded the difficulty of the work so much if the pay had not been so poor.

In this sentence, the keyword *difficulty* reminds us of the point of the first supporting paragraph, while *pay* tells us the point to be developed in the second supporting paragraph.

Activity

Here is the other transitional sentence in "My Job in an Apple Plant":

> But even more than the low pay, what upset me about my apple plant job was the working conditions.

Complete the following statement: In the sentence above, the keywords _____ echo the point of the second supporting paragraph, and the keywords _____ announce the topic of the third supporting paragraph.

Concluding Paragraph

The concluding paragraph often summarizes the essay by briefly restating the thesis and, at times, the main supporting points. Also, the conclusion brings the paper to a natural and graceful end, sometimes leaving the reader with a final thought on the subject.

Activity

1. Which sentence in the concluding paragraph of "My Job in an Apple Plant" restates the thesis and supporting points of the essay? _____

2. Which sentence contains the concluding thought of the essay? _____

Essays to Consider

Read the three student essays below and then answer the questions that follow.

Giving Up a Baby

[1]As I awoke, I overheard a nurse say, "It's a lovely baby boy. [2]How could a mother give him up?" [3]"Be quiet," another voice said. [4]"She's going to wake up soon." [5]Then I heard the baby cry, but I never heard him again. [6]Three years ago, I gave up my child to two strangers, people who wanted a baby but could not have one. [7]I was in pain over my decision, and I can still hear the voices of people who said I was selfish or crazy. [8]But the reasons I gave up my child were important ones, at least to me.

[9]I gave up my baby, first of all, because I was very young. [10]I was only seventeen, and I was unmarried. [11]Because I was so young, I did not yet feel the desire to have and raise a baby. [12]I knew that I would be a child raising a child and that, when I had to stay home to care for the baby, I would resent the loss of my freedom. [13]I might also blame the baby for that loss. [14]In addition, I had not had the experiences in life that would make me a responsible, giving parent. [15]What could I teach my child, when I barely knew what life was all about myself?

[16]Besides my age, another factor in my decision was the problems my parents would have. [17]I had dropped out of high school before graduation, and I did not have a job or even the chance of a job, at least for a while. [18]My parents would have to support my child and me, possibly for years. [19]My mom and dad had already struggled to raise their family and were not well off financially. [20]I knew I could not burden them with an unemployed teenager and her baby. [21]Even if I eventually got a job, my parents would have to help raise my child. [22]They would have to be full-time baby-sitters

while I tried to make a life of my own. 23Because my parents are good people, they would have done all this for me. 24But I felt I could not ask for such a big sacrifice from them.

25The most important factor in my decision was, I suppose, a selfish one. 26I was worried about my own future. 27I didn't want to marry the baby's father. 28I realized during the time I was pregnant that we didn't love each other. 29My future as an unmarried mother with no education or skills would certainly have been limited. 30I would be struggling to survive, and I would have to give up for years my dreams of getting a job and my own car and apartment. 31It is hard to admit, but I also considered the fact that, with a baby, I would not have the social life most young people have. 32I would not be able to stay out late, go to parties, or feel carefree and irresponsible, for I would always have an enormous responsibility waiting for me at home. 33With a baby, the future looked limited and insecure.

34In summary, thinking about my age, my responsibility to my parents, and my own future made me decide to give up my baby. 35As I look back today at my decision, I know that it was the right one for me at the time.

Sports-Crazy America

1Almost all Americans are involved with sports in some way. 2They may play basketball or volleyball or go swimming or skiing. 3They may watch football or basketball games on the high school, college, or professional level. 4Sports may seem like an innocent pleasure, but it is important to look under the surface. 5In reality, sports have reached a point where they play too large a part in daily life. 6They take up too much media time, play too large a role in the raising of children, and give too much power and prestige to athletes.

7The overemphasis on sports can be seen most obviously in the vast media coverage of athletic events. 8It seems as if every bowl game play-off, tournament, trial, bout, race, meet, or match is shown on one television channel or another. 9On Saturday and Sunday, a check of <u>TV Guide</u> will show almost forty sports programs on network television alone, and many more on cable stations. 10In addition, sports make up about 30 percent of local news at six and eleven, and network world news shows often devote several minutes to major American sports events. 11Radio offers a full roster of games and a wide assortment of sports talk shows. 12Furthermore, many daily papers such as <u>USA Today</u> are devoting more and more space to sports coverage, often in an attempt to improve circulation. 13The paper with the biggest sports section is the one people will buy.

14The way we raise and educate our children also illustrates our sports mania. 15As early as age six or seven, kids are placed in little leagues, often to play under screaming coaches and pressuring parents. 16Later, in high school, students who are singled out by the school and by the community are not those who are best academically but those who are best athletically.

¹⁷And college sometimes seems to be more about sports than about learning. ¹⁸The United States may be the only country in the world where people often think of their colleges as teams first and schools second. ¹⁹The names Penn State, Notre Dame, and Southern Cal mean "sports" to the public.

²⁰Our sports craziness is especially evident in the prestige given to athletes in the United States. ²¹For one thing, we reward them with enormous salaries. ²²In 1995, for example, baseball players averaged over $1,000,000 a year; the average annual salary in the United States is $20,000. ²³Besides their huge salaries, athletes receive the awe, the admiration, and sometimes the votes of the public. ²⁴Kids look up to a Kobe Bryant or a Roger Clemens as a true hero, while adults wear the jerseys and jackets of their favorite teams. ²⁵Ex-players become senators and congressmen. ²⁶And an athlete like Mia Hamm or Tiger Woods needs to make only one commercial for advertisers to see the sales of a product boom.

²⁷Americans are truly mad about sports. ²⁸Perhaps we like to see the competitiveness we experience in our daily lives acted out on playing fields. ²⁹Perhaps we need heroes who can achieve clear-cut victories in the space of only an hour or two. ³⁰Whatever the reason, the sports scene in this country is more popular than ever.

An Interpretation of <u>Lord of the Flies</u>

¹Modern history has shown us the evil that exists in human beings. ²Assassinations are common, governments use torture to discourage dissent, and six million Jews were exterminated during World War II. ³In <u>Lord of the Flies</u>, William Golding describes a group of schoolboys shipwrecked on an island with no authority figures to control their behavior. ⁴One of the boys soon yields to dark forces within himself, and his corruption symbolizes the evil in all of us. ⁵First, Jack Merridew kills a living creature; then, he rebels against the group leader; and finally, he seizes power and sets up his own murderous society.

⁶The first stage in Jack's downfall is his killing of a living creature. ⁷In Chapter 1, Jack aims at a pig but is unable to kill. ⁸His upraised arm pauses "because of the enormity of the knife descending and cutting into living flesh, because of the unbearable blood," and the pig escapes. ⁹Three chapters later, however, Jack leads some boys on a successful hunt. ¹⁰He returns triumphantly with a freshly killed pig and reports excitedly to the others, "I cut the pig's throat." ¹¹Yet Jack twitches as he says this, and he wipes his bloody hands on his shorts as if eager to remove the stains. ¹²There is still some civilization left in him.

¹³After the initial act of killing the pig, Jack's refusal to cooperate with Ralph shows us that this civilized part is rapidly disappearing. ¹⁴With no adults around, Ralph has made some rules. ¹⁵One is that a signal fire must be kept burning. ¹⁶But Jack tempts the boys watching the fire to go hunting, and the

fire goes out. [17]Another rule is that at a meeting, only the person holding a special seashell has the right to speak. [18]In Chapter 5, another boy is speaking when Jack rudely tells him to shut up. [19]Ralph accuses Jack of breaking the rules. [20]Jack shouts: "Bollocks to the rules! We're strong—we hunt! If there's a beast, we'll hunt it down! We'll close in and beat and beat and beat—!" [21]He gives a "wild whoop" and leaps off the platform, throwing the meeting into chaos. [22]Jack is now much more savage than civilized.

[23]The most obvious proof of Jack's corruption comes in Chapter 8, when he establishes his own murderous society. [24]Insisting that Ralph is not a "proper chief" because he does not hunt, Jack asks for a new election. [25]After he again loses, Jack announces, "I'm going off by myself. . . . Anyone who wants to hunt when I do can come too." [26]Eventually, nearly all the boys join Jack's "tribe." [27]Following his example, they paint their faces like savages, sacrifice to "the beast," brutally murder two of their schoolmates, and nearly succeed in killing Ralph as well. [28]Jack has now become completely savage—and so have the others.

[29]Through Jack Merridew, then, Golding shows how easily moral laws can be forgotten. [30]Freed from grown-ups and their rules, Jack learns to kill living things, defy authority, and lead a tribe of murdering savages. [31]Jack's example is a frightening reminder of humanity's potential for evil. [32]The "beast" the boys try to hunt and kill is actually within every human being.

■ Questions

1. In which essay does the thesis statement appear in the last sentence of the introductory paragraph?

_____

2. In the essay on *Lord of the Flies,* which sentence of the introductory paragraph contains the plan of development? _____

3. Which method of introduction is used in "Giving Up a Baby"?
   a. General to narrow   c. Incident or story
   b. Stating importance of topic   d. Questions

4. Complete the following brief outline of "Giving Up a Baby":
   I gave up my baby for three reasons:

   a. _____

   b. _____

   c. _____

5. Which *two* essays use a transitional sentence between the first and second supporting paragraphs?

_____

6. *Complete the following statement:* Emphatic order is shown in the last supporting paragraph of "Giving Up a Baby" with the words *most important factor;* in the last supporting paragraph of "Sports-Crazy America" with the words _____; and in the last supporting paragraph of "An Interpretation of *Lord of the Flies*" with the words _____.

7. Which essay uses time order as well as emphatic order to organize its three supporting paragraphs? _____

8. List four major transitions used in the supporting paragraphs of "An Interpretation of *Lord of the Flies.*"

   a. _____   c. _____

   b. _____   d. _____

9. Which *two* essays include a sentence in the concluding paragraph that summarizes the three supporting points?

   _____

   _____

10. Which essay includes two final thoughts in its concluding paragraph?

   _____

Planning the Essay

Outlining the Essay

When you write an essay, planning is crucial for success. You should plan your essay by outlining in two ways:

1 Prepare a scratch outline. This should consist of a short statement of the thesis followed by the main supporting points for the thesis. Here is Gene's scratch outline for his essay on the apple plant:

Working at an apple plant was my worst job.
1. Hard work
2. Poor pay
3. Bad working conditions

Do not underestimate the value of this initial outline—or the work involved in achieving it. Be prepared to do a good deal of plain hard thinking at this first and most important stage of your paper.

2 Prepare a more detailed outline. The outline form that follows will serve as a guide. Your instructor may ask you to submit a copy of this form either before you actually write an essay or along with your finished essay.

Form for Planning an Essay

To write an effective essay, use a form like the one that follows.

Introduction	Opening remarks
	Thesis statement _____
	_____
	Plan of development

Body	***Topic sentence 1*** _____
	_____
	Specific supporting evidence
	Topic sentence 2 _____
	_____
	Specific supporting evidence
	Topic sentence 3 _____
	_____
	Specific supporting evidence

Conclusion	Summary, closing remarks, or both

Essay Writing Assignments

Hints: Keep the following points in mind when writing an essay on any of the topics below.

1 Your first step must be to plan your essay. Prepare both a scratch outline and a more detailed outline, as explained on the preceding pages.

2 While writing your essay, use the checklist below to make sure your essay touches all four bases of effective writing.

Base 1: Unity

_____ Clearly stated thesis in the introductory paragraph of your paper

_____ All the supporting paragraphs on target in backing up your thesis

Base 2: Support

_____ Three separate supporting points for your thesis

_____ *Specific* evidence for each of the three supporting points

_____ *Plenty* of specific evidence for each supporting point

Base 3: Coherence

_____ Clear method of organization

_____ Transitions and other connecting words

_____ Effective introduction and conclusion

Base 4: Sentence Skills

_____ Clear, error-free sentences (use the checklist on the inside front cover of this book)

■ 1 Your House or Apartment

Write an essay on the advantages *or* disadvantages (not both) of the house or apartment where you live. In your introductory paragraph, describe briefly the place you plan to write about. End the paragraph with your thesis statement and a plan of development. Here are some suggestions for thesis statements:

The best features of my apartment are its large windows, roomy closets, and great location.

The drawbacks of my house are its unreliable oil burner, tiny kitchen, and old-fashioned bathroom.

An inquisitive landlord, sloppy neighbors, and platoons of cockroaches came along with our rented house.

My apartment has several advantages, including friendly neighbors, lots of storage space, and a good security system.

■ 2 A Big Mistake

Write an essay about the biggest mistake you made within the past year. Describe the mistake and show how its effects have convinced you that it was the wrong thing to do. For instance, if you write about "taking a full-time job while going to school" as your biggest mistake, show the problems it caused. (You might discuss such matters as low grades, constant exhaustion, and poor performance at work, for example.)

To get started, make a list of all the things you did last year that, with hindsight, now seem to be mistakes. Then pick out the action that has had the most serious consequences for you. Make a brief outline to guide you as you write, as in the examples below.

Thesis: Separating from my husband was the worst mistake I made last year.
1.   Children have suffered
2.   Financial troubles
3.   Loneliness

Thesis: Buying a used car to commute to school was the worst mistake of last year.
1.   Unreliable—late for class or missed class
2.   Expenses for insurance, repairs
3.   Led to an accident

■ 3 A Valued Possession

Write an essay about a valued material possession. Here are some suggestions:

Car	Appliance
Portable radio	Cassette deck
TV set	Photograph album
Piece of furniture	Piece of clothing
Piece of jewelry	Stereo system (car or home)
Camera	Piece of hobby equipment

In your introductory paragraph, describe the possession: tell what it is, when and where you got it, and how long you have owned it. Your thesis statement should center on the idea that there are several reasons this possession is so important to you. In each of your supporting paragraphs, provide details to back up one of the reasons.

For example, here is a brief outline of an essay written about a leather jacket:

1.   It is comfortable.
2.   It wears well.
3.   It makes me look and feel good.

■ 4 Summarizing a Selection

Write an essay in which you summarize three of the study skills described on pages 321–333. Summarizing involves condensing material by highlighting main points and key supporting details. You can eliminate minor details and most examples given in the original material. You should avoid using the exact language in the original material; put the ideas into your own words.

The introductory paragraph of the essay and suggested topic sentences for the supporting paragraphs are provided below. In addition to developing the supporting paragraphs, you should write a brief conclusion for the essay.

Introductory Paragraph

Using Study Skills

Why do some students in a college class receive A's, while others get D's and F's? Are some people just naturally smarter? Are other students doomed to failure? Motivation—willingness to do the work—is a factor in good grades. But the main difference between successful and unsuccessful students is that the students who do well have mastered the specific skills needed to handle college work. Fortunately, these skills can be learned by anyone. Doing well in college depends on knowing how to . . . *(Complete this sentence with the three study skills you decide to write about.)*

Suggested Topic Sentences for the Supporting Paragraphs (Choose Any Three)

Time control is one aid to success as a student. . . .

Another aid is the use of memory techniques. . . .

Knowing how to concentrate is another essential skill. . . .

Studying a textbook effectively is another key to success. . . .

Perhaps the most crucial step of all is effective classroom note-taking. . . .

5 How Study Skills Help

You may already be practicing some of the study skills described on pages 321–333. If so, write an essay on how study skills are helping you to succeed in school. Your thesis might be, "Study skills are helping me to succeed in college." You could organize the essay by describing, in separate paragraphs, how three different study skills have improved your work. Your topic sentences might be similar to these:

> First of all, time control has helped me to make the best use of my time.
>
> In addition, taking good notes in class has enabled me to do well in discussions and on tests.
>
> Finally, I can study a textbook effectively now.

Alternatively, begin applying some of the techniques and be prepared to write an essay at a later time on how these study skills helped you become a better student. Or you might want to write about three successful study techniques of your own.

6 Single Life

Write an essay on the advantages or drawbacks of single life. To get started, make a list of all the advantages and drawbacks you can think of. Advantages might include:

> Fewer expenses
>
> Fewer responsibilities
>
> More personal freedom
>
> More opportunities to move or travel

Drawbacks might include:

> Parental disapproval
>
> Being alone at social events
>
> No companion for shopping, movies, and so on
>
> Sadness at holiday time

After you make up two lists, select the thesis for which you feel you have more supporting material. Then organize your material into a scratch outline. Be sure to include an introduction, a clear topic sentence for each supporting paragraph, and a conclusion.

Alternatively, write an essay on the advantages or drawbacks of married life. Follow the directions given above.

■ 7 Influences on Your Writing

Are you as good a writer as you want to be? Write an essay analyzing the reasons you have become a good writer or explaining why you are not as good as you'd like to be. Begin by considering some factors that may have influenced your writing ability.

> *Your family background:* Did you see people writing at home? Did your parents respect and value the ability to write?
>
> *Your school experience:* Did you have good writing teachers? Did you have a history of failure or success with writing? Was writing fun, or was it a chore? Did your school emphasize writing?
>
> *Social influences:* How did your school friends do at writing? What were your friends' attitudes toward writing? What feelings about writing did you pick up from TV or the movies?

You might want to organize your essay by describing the three greatest influences on your writing skill (or lack of writing skill). Show how each of these has contributed to the present state of your writing.

■ 8 A Major Decision

All of us come to various crossroads in our lives—times when we must make an important decision about which course of action to follow. Think about a major decision you had to make (or one you are planning to make). Then write an essay on the reasons for your decision. In your introduction, describe the decision you have reached. Each of the body paragraphs that follow should fully explain one of the reasons for your decision. Here are some examples of major decisions that often confront people:

> Enrolling in or dropping out of college
>
> Accepting or quitting a job
>
> Getting married or divorced
>
> Breaking up with a boyfriend or girlfriend
>
> Having a baby
>
> Moving away from home

Student papers on this topic include the essay on page 300 and the paragraphs on pages 51–52.

■ 9 Reviewing a TV Show or Movie

Write an essay about a television show or movie you have seen very recently. The thesis of your essay will be that the show (or movie) has both good and bad features. (If you are writing about a TV series, be sure that you evaluate only one episode.)

In your first supporting paragraph, briefly summarize the show or movie. Don't get bogged down in small details here; just describe briefly the major characters and give the highlights of the action.

In your second supporting paragraph, explain what you feel are the best features of the show or movie. Listed below are some examples of good features you might write about:

Suspenseful, ingenious, or realistic plot

Good acting

Good scenery or special effects

Surprise ending

Good music

Believable characters

In your third supporting paragraph, explain what you feel are the worst features of the show or movie. Here are some possibilities:

Farfetched, confusing, or dull plot

Poor special effects

Bad acting

Cardboard characters

Unrealistic dialogue

Remember to cover only a few features in each paragraph; do not try to include everything.

■ 10 Good Qualities

We are often quick to point out a person's flaws, saying, for example, "That instructor is conceited," "My boss has no patience," or "My sister is lazy." We are usually equally hard on ourselves; we constantly analyze our own faults. We rarely, though, spend as much time thinking about another person's, or our own, good qualities. Write an essay on the good qualities of a particular person. The person might be an instructor, a job supervisor, a friend, a relative, some other person you know well, or even yourself.

■ 11 Your High School

Imagine that you are an outside consultant called in as a neutral observer to examine the high school you attended. After your visit, you must send the school board a five-paragraph letter in which you describe the most striking features (good, bad, or a combination of both) of the school and the evidence for each of these features.

In order to write the letter, you may want to think about the following features of your high school:

Attitude of the teachers, student body, or administration

Condition of the buildings, classrooms, recreational areas, and so on

Curriculum

How classes are conducted

Extracurricular activities

Crowded or uncrowded conditions

Be sure to include an introduction, a clear topic sentence for each supporting paragraph, and a conclusion.

■ 12 Reacting to a Reading Selection

Read the following article by a man whose sexual attitudes undergo a significant change. Then do the activities that follow the article.

Full Circle
Grant Berry

While searching for salad croutons at a convenience store the other day, I passed a magazine rack and spotted a sultry young woman on the cover of 'Teen magazine. She looked about twenty-three and was blessed with improbably clear skin (not a zit in sight)—and improbably ample cleavage. Her belly button was exposed in a firm stretch of provocative flesh between the bottom of her skimpy red T shirt and the top of her unfastened blue jeans. Head tilted seductively, she flung back tousled "I-just-got-out-of-bed" blond curls, revealing come-hither eyes rimmed heavily with mascara.

The young woman had an uncanny resemblance to a girl I knew twelve years ago, when I was between my junior and senior years in high school. The girl's name was Denise. But how odd, I thought, for a *woman* to grace a magazine intended for *young teens*. Curiosity getting the best of me, I looked both ways to make sure no one saw me, then plucked the magazine off the shelf. Imagine my surprise when a biographical profile inside revealed that the cover girl was a mere thirteen years old.

• • •

Seeing the 'Teen cover set me to thinking about the first time I met Denise. We were at a party and quickly started a conversation. During our chitchat, I asked her age. Talkative and outgoing until that point, Denise grinned coyly and murmured, "Guess."

"Eighteen!" I answered, not missing a beat. She shook her head "no" proudly. "Seventeen," I tried. She shook her head again. I began counting backward, each time receiving the same reaction until I reached fourteen; then Denise giggled and I realized, with disbelief, that she was barely more than a child.

Although young, Denise was far from innocent. Later that evening, as the party was winding down, she looked up at me with teasing eyes and asked if I'd like to have some fun, explaining that because her parents were out of town, I could go home with her. Believing I was doing what any "red-blooded American male" would do, I accepted her offer—all of it.

It was only when I took Denise out the second time that I discovered an insecure little girl rather than the sultry seductress of our first date. Pain filling her eyes, Denise told me that her success-driven parents bestowed praise on her older sister for garnering straight A's in school, while they belittled her harshly for receiving grades that lagged behind their expectations. Desperately in need of approval and affection, she used sex to build her self-esteem. Having sex, she confessed, was a surefire way to get guys to pay attention to her.

At seventeen, I wasn't prepared to deal with Denise's emotional troubles. Confused about whether to treat her as a sex object or a person, I soon stopped seeing her.

For three months, Denise called me almost every day. I was seldom home and never returned her calls or responded to the messages she left. My mother was as relieved as I was when the phone stopped ringing.

A few weeks later in school a boy asked if I knew Denise. Aware that Denise had a reputation for being easy, I sat back in my seat, folded my arms across my chest, and smugly said, "Yeah, I know her."

"Well, then," he replied, "you probably know she killed herself."

I was stunned and for a moment speechless. I looked hard at the boy and knew that he was not kidding. Everything seemed very unreal. Hanging my head, I said, "No, I didn't know." Then I felt tears press against my eyes, and I had to fight to hold them in. I listened while he told how Denise had swallowed a bottle of pills when she was home alone over the weekend. Later that afternoon when I told my mother what had happened, we both wept bitterly. It took my mother a long time to convince me that I was not personally responsible for the death of a troubled young girl. To this day, I have not stopped feeling shame and regret when I remember Denise.

• • •

Flooded by these memories, I placed *'Teen* magazine back in the rack and halfheartedly resumed my search for salad croutons, thinking how ironic it was that the two girls I'd mistaken for adults looked so much alike. Distracted, I wandered aimlessly through the store and continued to ponder my past.

• • •

There had been a time—before Denise—that I wouldn't have accepted a proposition like the one she had advanced. My parents had raised me to be a gentleman and to respect the opposite sex. I remember that a girl called Joan repeatedly invited me to go back to her apartment after a date, telling me we'd be alone because her single mother worked nights. Eager to uphold the morals and standards my parents had taught me, I never took her up on her offer. I did not realize that my refusal to have sex would eventually undermine my sense of self-worth, which was all too dependent on the values of my peers.

One night while I was driving Joan home from a date, she bluntly asked, "Are you gay?" Face redder than the pimples speckling my skin, I gulped nervously and answered, "No; why would you ask such a thing?"

"We've been dating for months," she retorted, "and we've had our chances, but . . ."

Tongue-tied, I couldn't tell her how I really felt—that she had smashed my fragile sense of myself as a male. I wanted to say, "I respect you and plan to marry you, and I though you were a nice girl." Instead, anxious to restore my worth in my own eyes as well as in hers, I called her bluff. "Do you want me to *prove* I'm not gay?" I asked, with mock assurance. To my dismay, she leaned back and said, "Yes." Not prepared to meet her challenge, I dropped Joan off early that night. The next day she dumped me.

Once I had recovered from losing the girl I had hoped to marry simply because I wouldn't have sex with her, I started dating a young lady I met in my church youth group. I fell hard for her, but within a month, she also jilted me because I was "too nice."

Perhaps I was simply a poor judge of character, but having my male ego leveled twice was more than I could stand. I decided to abandon my good-boy behavior and to seek to gain the respect of the sexually active boys at school. Instead of eavesdropping from the sidelines, instead of shyly waiting until the coast was clear to take a shower, I wanted—like them—to banter in the locker room about sexual conquests, to engage in towel-snapping fights while walking around naked and unashamed. Longing for the self-confidence they seemed to possess and with my own self-respect at an all-time low, I concluded that the solution to my problem would be to have sex. I figured it would make me a man and would wipe away the squeaky-clean image that was causing me such grief.

I asked out a girl I barely knew—a girl with a reputation. The day of our date, I tried to back out, but her persistence persuaded me otherwise. Although we were both underage, she knew a liquor store that would sell us alcohol. With two bottles of Boone's Farm Tickle Pink Wine on the front seat of my car, we drove to a well-known spot where we could park, drink, and neck. When we got back to her home, she invited me in, reassuring me that her parents were away and that the house would be ours. We watched the last half hour of *Saturday Night Live.* Then, on a scratchy couch, I gave my virginity to a girl I neither loved nor respected. Neither of us ever called the other again; we both understood that we were simply using each other to "have sex." We were, really, just blindly doing what our sex-saturated culture expected us to do.

While my baptism into sex was less than memorable, that didn't matter. I'd had sex, and I now could consider myself one of the guys. The stupid young man that I was at the time felt very self-satisfied and that he had earned bragging rights. Picking up the phone, I called my best friend, eager to gloat over my sexual conquest. "Are you gonna see her again?" he asked. "No," I replied arrogantly. "Did you *use* anything?" he questioned. "Whaddya mean?" I asked. "Protection. Did you use any protection?" "No, that's her problem," I said.

Following this, my first sexual encounter, all the values my parents taught me seemed to fall by the wayside. I adopted instead the values of my peers—values that they in turn picked up from an MTV society that celebrates sex over human care, kindness, and love. Girls were not human beings but merely toys for my amusement. I'd literally "charm the pants off them" and then move on to the next. To my delight, my sexual activity gained me quite a reputation. Guys admired my love bites as much as if a gold medal were draped around my neck, and girls fought for the right to sit by me on the bus and at football games. I ate up the attention like a hog wallowing in slop.

Some time went by and one night at a party, I unexpectedly ran into Kathy, a girl I worked with at an after-school job. Swaying to the suggestive beat of the music on the stereo, we danced together seductively. Even though I knew she had a boyfriend at college, I coldheartedly calculated what my chances were of having sex with her. At work the next day, I asked her out for the following weekend, and she accepted. But she indicated that she wanted to double-date with her sister. Although her proposal thwarted my game plan, I gave in, and the four of us had a surprisingly enjoyable evening together. As I dropped Kathy home following the double date, I asked her out for the next weekend. It had been a long time since I'd taken anyone out more than once, but I liked her energy and spirit. By our third date, I was hooked.

It was with Kathy that I had my first long-term sexual relationship. At the time, Kathy was twenty and I was still in high school. The intensity of my sexual drive and the continuing need to prove my masculinity kept me out late—often until 3:00 A.M. on school nights. Dragging myself to school, I skipped classes to catch up on sleep and almost forfeited the chance to graduate.

One cold February morning, what Kathy and I had been fearing for weeks was confirmed. She was pregnant. Terrified at the prospect of becoming parents, we decided not to have the baby. I'll never forget how leaden my heart felt and how Kathy's voice shook as she made the appointment at the abortion clinic. Wanting nothing more than to slip back into my boyhood, I longed for a time when things were less complicated. Sexual activity, which I had relied upon to make me feel like a man and to make my life easier, had ended up presenting me with an overwhelming problem.

After much soul-searching, I decided to ask Kathy if she would consider marrying me. She said yes. Yet once we made our decision and canceled the appointment at the clinic, I was overcome by panic and even confessed to my best friend that I didn't know if I loved Kathy.

Against the odds, we made it through the toughest part—the first year of marriage. Besides getting to know one another, we had to take care of our tiny, red-faced, screeching baby girl, whose paraphernalia took up every inch of our minuscule apartment. Nevertheless, both of us were determined to hold tightly to our commitment to remain a couple and to raise our daughter together.

Although Kathy and I stayed together, our sex life was far from a loving bond that strengthened our marriage. The passionate intensity we had felt earlier was gone. Instead, sex deteriorated into a caveman ritual with me grunting, rolling over, and falling asleep. Not surprisingly, we began to have sex less frequently, and when I asked Kathy why, she admitted that she didn't enjoy it. Once again, I was guilty of modeling lessons of macho sexual behavior in our culture, instead of seeing sexual experience as a human exchange.

Stung by Kathy's comment, I went on a quest to find ways to improve our sexual relationship. I scoured bookstores for helpful books and read countless magazine articles about "lovemaking." For the first time, I began to view sex as something the two of us could *share together* instead of something we *had separately*. Abandoning the caveman approach, I actively sought my wife's sexual fulfillment. In the process, my enjoyment of sex increased along with Kathy's. Indeed, our sexual closeness and sharing began to have a positive effect on all aspects of our marriage—and on the self-esteem of both of us. Feeling safe and loved in my marriage, I finally obtained the inner self-worth I had been seeking for so long.

• • •

My sexual attitudes have, then, come full circle. My parents' morals and values, which I rejected as a teenager, fit me perfectly at this point in my life. My daughter, who's now only a year younger than the girl-woman on the cover of 'Teen, is beginning to show a tentative interest in boys. Unsure of themselves and not knowing how to respond appropriately, the boys claim they "hate her cootie-infested guts." "Give them a year of two," I tell my daughter, who is understandably hurt and confused by the boys' taunts. "They'll change." But when the boys do begin to be as interested in my daughter as she is in them, I only hope that her all-too-natural need to gain acceptance won't override all I've tried to teach her—that being different is OK; that only losers go along with the crowd for the sake of being liked; that sex alone is not an adequate basis for a human relationship. I want her to know that she's special and important because of who she is. I want her to know that giving in to sexual pressure isn't the way to self-respect.

I realize that my daughter's transition won't be easy, because pressure from her peers and the media will be relentless. I wonder how she'll react when she eventually picks up a copy of 'Teen magazine and sees kids her age made up to the hilt, wearing attire suited for streetwalkers. Will such images and the messages they convey confuse her and shake her sense of self-worth? Will she forget that people must be valued above all for being kind and decent persons, and not for their sexuality? Will the distorted sexual messages in our culture damage her in the same way they affected poor Denise? I hope not.

• • •

After seeing 'Teen magazine at the convenience store, I sat at the dinner table, munching salad without croutons, my earlier musings having caused me to forget why I had gone to the store in the first place. I looked across the table at my wide-eyed, fresh-faced little girl and said, "Honey, I love you." Aglow with pleasure, my daughter shook her head and playfully replied, "Oh, Daddy, you're silly, but I love when you say that." Seeing how strong and secure she's been made to feel by the love in our family, I tried to relax. She's going to be fine, I tried to convince myself. She's going to be fine.

Questions on Assignment 12

1. a. How does Berry describe the girl on the cover of 'Teen?
   b. In what ways does she remind him of Denise?

2. a. Berry writes that he wasn't sure about whether to treat Denise "as a sex object or a person." How do you think he feels a sex object is treated?
   b. How do you think he feels a "person" is treated?

3. a. Why do you suppose Denise committed suicide?
   b. Who do you think was responsible? Denise? Her parents? Berry? Our society?

4. a. What forces do you think pressured Berry into having sex?
   b. Why do you think he was initially able to resist these forces?
   c. Why did he finally give in?

5. a. How do Berry's ideas on sex and manhood change throughout the piece? In answering, cite specific points of the essay.
   b. What does Berry mean when he says, "My sexual attitudes have, then, come full circle"?

6. How has Berry's relationship with Kathy changed from the time he first met her until today?

7. What can you deduce from the essay about the kind of father Berry is?

8. Do you think Berry's daughter will avoid the pitfalls he's concerned about? What does Berry say that supports your answer?

9. What might Berry feel are some good ways for young people to handle their "all-too-natural need to gain acceptance"?

10. Berry refers to the "MTV society that celebrates sex over human care, kindness, and love." He calls the pressure from the media "relentless." Cite some specific examples from the media in which sexuality is promoted as something apart from fully developed human relationships.

Writing Activity for Assignment 12

Option 1:   In mentioning the cover of *'Teen* magazine, Grant Berry addresses the practice of using young people in sexually suggestive ways, a practice common not only in magazines but also in popular music, television, and advertising. How do you feel about this practice? In developing your opinion, think about how you feel this portrayal of sexuality influences young people and society at large.

Then write a letter to *'Teen* magazine defending or attacking the editor's decision to use the picture Berry describes at the beginning of his essay. Begin your letter with a brief introductory paragraph stating your view *(thesis)* and summarizing briefly your reasons for that view *(plan of development)*. Then write a supporting paragraph for each of your reasons. Develop your reasons using specific details from Berry's essay and from other sources.

Option 2:   Write a several-paragraph essay in which you provide evidence from the text to support one of the following thesis statements:

Grant Berry's sexual attitudes and behavior have truly come full circle.

Grant Berry's sexual attitudes and behavior have not really come full circle.

Option 3:   Imagine that you are an attorney defending or accusing someone in a trial about Denise's death. Whom would you charge—would it be Denise? Her family? Grant Berry? Society? Likewise, who is innocent? Write a several-paragraph presentation explaining either of the following:

1. Your arguments supporting your case against the guilty party or parties. Your argument should be based strongly on the details presented in Berry's essay.

2. Your arguments supporting the innocence of the accused party or parties. Your argument should be specific, explaining why—despite any evidence to the contrary—the defendant is not guilty.

Part Four

Special Skills

Preview

Part Four presents skills that will help you in a variety of study and writing situations. "Developing Key Study Skills" explains five skills that will make you a better student in all your courses. In "Writing an Exam Essay," you will learn how to prepare for and take essay exams, which are among the most common types of writing students do in college. Similarly, "Writing a Summary," "Writing a Report," and "Writing a Résumé and Job Application Letter" provide explanations and models for three practical kinds of writing that you may need to know. Finally, "Using the Library and the Internet" and "Writing a Research Paper" will prepare you for writing projects that require research.

19 Developing Key Study Skills

Following are brief guides to several important reading and study skills needed for success in school. A short comprehension test follows each guide. The skills include class note-taking, time control, concentrating, studying a textbook, and memory training.

Taking Effective Classroom Notes

One of the most important single things you can do to perform well in a college course is to take effective class notes. The following hints should help you become a better note-taker.

Attend Class

First, attend class faithfully. Your alternatives—reading the text, reading someone else's notes, or both—cannot substitute for the class experience of hearing ideas in person as someone presents them to you. Also, in class lectures and discussions, your instructor typically presents and develops the main ideas and facts of the course—the ones you will be expected to know on exams.

Use Abbreviations

Another valuable hint is to make use of abbreviations when you take notes. Using abbreviations saves time when you are trying to get down a great deal of information. Abbreviate terms that recur frequently in a lecture, and put a key to your abbreviations at the top of your notes. For example, in sociology class, *eth* could stand for *ethnocentrism;* in a psychology class, *STM* could stand for *short-term memory.* (When a lecture is over, you may want to go back and write out the terms you have abbreviated.) Also, use *e* or *ex* or *X* for *example; def* for *definition; info* for *information; +* for *and,* and so on. If you use the same abbreviations all the time, you will soon develop a kind of personal shorthand that makes taking notes much easier.

Be Alert for Signals

A third hint about taking notes is to be on the lookout for signals of importance. For one thing, write down *whatever your instructor puts on the board.* If he or she takes the time to put material on the board, it is probably important, and the chances are good that it will come up later on exams.

Always write down *definitions* and *enumerations.* Enumerations are lists of items. They are signaled in such ways as: "The four steps in the process are . . ."; "There were three reasons for . . ."; "The two effects were . . ."; "Five characteristics of . . ."; and so on. In your notes, always number such enumerations (1, 2, 3, etc.). They will help you understand relationships among ideas and organize the material of the lecture.

Watch for *emphasis words*—words your instructor may use to indicate that something is important. Examples of such words are "This is an important reason . . ."; "A point that will keep coming up later . . ."; "The chief cause was . . ."; "The basic idea here is . . ."; and so on. Always write down the important statements announced by these and other emphasis words.

If your instructor *repeats* a point, you can assume that it is important. You might put an *R* for *repeated* in the margin, so that later you will know that your instructor stressed it.

Be sure to write down the instructor's *examples* and mark them *e, ex,* or *X.* The examples help you understand abstract points. If you do not write them down, you are likely to forget them later, when they are needed to help make sense of an idea.

Also, be sure to write down the *connections between ideas.* Too many students merely copy terms the instructor puts on the board. They forget that, as time passes, the details that serve as connecting bridges between ideas quickly fade. You should, then, write down the relationships and connections in class. That way you'll have them to help tie together your notes later on.

Review Your Notes

Review your notes as soon as possible after class. You must make them as clear as possible while they are fresh in your mind. A day later may be too late, because forgetting sets in very quickly. Make sure that punctuation is clear, that all words are readable and correctly spelled, and that unfinished sentences are completed (or at least marked off so that you can check your notes with another student's). Add clarifying or connecting comments wherever necessary. Make sure that important ideas are clearly marked. Improve the organization if necessary, so that you can see at a glance main points and relationships among them.

Keep a Written Record

Finally, try in general to get down a written record of each class. You must do this because forgetting begins almost immediately. Studies have shown that within two weeks you are likely to have forgotten 80 percent or more of what you have heard. And in four weeks you are lucky if 5 percent remains! This is so crucial that it bears repeating: To guard against the relentlessness of forgetting, it is absolutely essential that you write down what you hear in class. Later you can concentrate on working to understand fully and to remember the ideas that have been presented in class. And the more complete your notes are at this time of study, the more you are likely to learn.

Activity

Check your understanding by answering the following questions.

1. *True or false?* _____ Forgetting will begin several days after you have attended a class.

2. How would you abbreviate the term *traditional authority* during a fast-moving sociology lecture?

   _____

3. Often the most important single step you can take to perform well in a course is to
   a. sit where the instructor can see you and listen carefully.
   b. write down definitions and examples.
   c. be there and take effective notes.
   d. continue taking notes during discussion periods or at the end of a class.

4. Which of the following should be taken down in your notes?
   a. Enumerations
   b. Definitions
   c. Material written on the board
   d. All of the above

5. When you review your notes after a class, you should
   a. memorize them.
   b. clarify them.
   c. type them.
   d. reduce them.

Controlling Your Time

Success in college depends on time control. *Time control* means that you deliberately organize and plan your time, instead of letting it drift by. *Planning* means that you should never be faced with a night-before-the-test "cram" session or an overdue term paper. There are three steps involved in time control: (1) a monthly calendar, (2) a weekly study schedule, and (3) a weekly or daily "to do" list.

Prepare a Monthly Calendar

First, you should prepare a large monthly calendar. Buy or make a calendar with a large white block around each date. At the beginning of the semester, circle important dates on this calendar. Circle the days on which tests are scheduled; circle the days when papers are due. This calendar can also be used to schedule study plans. At the beginning of the week, you can jot down your plans for each day. An alternative method would be to make plans for each day the night before. On Tuesday night, for example, you might write down "Read Chapter 5 in psychology" in the Wednesday block. Hang this calendar where you will see it every day—your kitchen, bedroom, even your bathroom!

Prepare a Weekly Study Schedule

The *second step* in time control is to have a weekly study schedule for the semester—a chart that covers all the days of the week and all the waking hours in each day. Below is part of one student's schedule.

Sample Weekly Study Schedule

Time	Mon.	Tues.	Wed.	Thurs.	Fri.	Sat.	Sun.
6:00 A.M.							
7:00	Breakfast	Breakfast	Breakfast	Breakfast	Breakfast		
8:00	Math	STUDY	Math	STUDY	Math		
9:00	STUDY	Biology	STUDY	Biology	STUDY	Job	
10:00	Psychology	↓	Psychology	↓	Psychology		
11:00	STUDY	English	English	English		↓	
12:00	Lunch		Lunch	↓	Lunch		

On your own schedule, mark in all the fixed hours in each day—hours for meals, classes, job (if any), and travel time. Next, mark in the time blocks that you can *realistically* plan to use for study each day. Depending on the number of courses you are taking and the demands of the courses, you may want to block off five, ten, or even twenty or more hours of study time a week. Keep in mind that you should not block off time for study that you do not truly intend to use for study. Otherwise, your schedule will be a meaningless gimmick. Also, remember that you should allow time in your schedule for "rest and relaxation." You will be happiest, and you will be able to accomplish the most, when you have time for both work and play.

Make Up a "To Do" List

The *third step* in time control is to make a daily or weekly "to do" list. This may be the most valuable time control method you ever use. On this list, you write down the things you need to do for the following day or the following week. If you choose to write a weekly list, do it on Sunday night. If you choose to write a daily list, do it the night before.

You may use a three- by five-inch note pad or a small spiral-bound notebook for this list. Carry the list around with you during the day. To make the best use of your time, mark high-priority items with an asterisk and give them precedence over low-priority items. Always concentrate on doing the most important items first. For instance, you may find yourself wondering what to do after dinner on Thursday evening. Among the items on your list are "Clean inside of car" and "Review chapter for math quiz." It is obviously more important for you to review your notes at this point; you can clean out the car some other time. As you complete items on your "to do" list, cross them out. Do not worry about unfinished items. They can be rescheduled. You will still be accomplishing a great deal and making more effective use of your time.

Here is part of one student's daily list:

To Do	Tuesday
*1.	Review biology notes before class
*2.	Proofread English paper due today
3.	See Dick about game on Friday
*4.	Gas for car
5.	Read next chapter of psychology text

Activity

Check your understanding by answering the following questions.

1. *True or false?* _____ Do not list personal chores on your "to do" list.

2. *True or false?* _____ On a large monthly calendar, you should circle the dates when tests are scheduled and papers are due.

3. When you make up a "to do" list, you should
   a. schedule one-hour blocks of study time.
   b. mark down deadlines.
   c. decide on priorities.
   d. hang it on the wall.

4. On your weekly schedule, you should block out time periods for
   a. commuting.
   b. study.
   c. rest and relaxation.
   d. all of the above.

5. Circle the highest-priority item on the following "to do" list:
   a. Buy new shirt
   b. Study notes for tomorrow's lab quiz
   c. Wax car
   d. Preview next chapter for Friday's sociology class

Developing Concentration

Loss of concentration happens to everyone. But if you are a student, you cannot afford to let it happen too often. Nor can you merely say, "This time, I'm going to keep my mind on my work," and have it magically happen. A much better method is to figure out what in particular is interfering with your concentration— and then to do something about it.

Causes of Loss of Concentration

What causes loss of concentration? It can happen, first of all, because of physical factors. If you are sick, hungry, thirsty, or sleepy, you will not be able to concentrate. Or the factors could be mental, not physical. You could be suffering from indecision: other things keep popping into your head, and you do not know what to do first. You could be distracted by daydreaming or worrying about a personal problem. Finally, the cause of your failure to concentrate could be external. Your study environment could be the problem if it is too warm or too cold, too noisy, or not properly lighted. If your study spot lacks the right equipment—writing pads, pens and pencils, or a dictionary, for instance—distraction may result. Any of these factors can take your mind off the assignment.

How to Concentrate

Concentration allows you to focus on just one thought or bit of information at a time, eliminating everything else. The first step in achieving a high level of concentration is having the right attitude. If you want to absorb something, you'll do so, no matter what else is going on—as anyone glued to a television set in the middle of a family argument proves. Take a positive attitude—here's a chance to learn something new. Or take a realistic attitude—the job simply has to be done today. And forget about how you felt or performed in the past. You are making a fresh start.

Next, if you want to concentrate, create a good atmosphere. Choose a room or area where you can work without being disturbed. Find a desk or table and clear it off. Sit in a straight chair. On your desk or table, place a good light source, such as a gooseneck fluorescent lamp. Then, add the study equipment you'll need: textbooks and notebooks, dictionary, pens, pencils, paper, a clock, calendar, calculator, and so on. Keep this special area only for studying; when you sit down there, the atmosphere will say "Work!"

The third step toward concentration is planning study time. Make up a weekly schedule and block out regular study periods that you plan to stick to. Schedule at least one hour of study time for each hour of class time. Organized, planned study time can aid concentration—you know exactly when you will study, and you're sure that there won't be any conflicts then with other activities.

Finally, study with a goal in mind. Do not just read the history chapter; read it to discover the specific causes of World War II. Work quickly. Have a clock in sight or put your watch next to your book, and try to cover each page in a designated period of time. Plan to take a break after a certain number of pages; keep the break brief, however. Remember, you want to get the job done so that you can go to the next item on your schedule. If you do feel your concentration slipping as you study, make a pencil mark in the margin each time you are distracted. The mark will remind you to concentrate.

What to Avoid: A Few Warnings

When you are trying to concentrate, watch out for several pitfalls. For one thing, do not try to study when you are physically uncomfortable. If you are too warm, open a window. If you are hungry, eat. Make sure you get enough sleep. And make a real effort to exercise regularly. Your mind will concentrate better when your body is in shape.

In addition, do not allow distractions to disturb you. Some people claim that noise does not bother them when they are trying to study. In general, though, it helps to avoid noisy places such as a college cafeteria or a lounge, and to keep the radio and television turned off. Do not waste brain power blocking out sounds that intrude on your concentration. Should a distracting thought get in your way, write it down and go back to your studying. You can always deal with the idea later; once it's written down, it can't be lost.

Last of all, don't be a passive learner. When you read, do not just sit quietly and let your eyes roam across the page. Get involved with the assignment. Have a pen or pencil in hand and use it to underline, check, and star material. Write key-words and questions in the margins. Turn the chapter headings and subheadings into questions and look for the answers as you read. You might want to close your eyes after you have read several paragraphs and see if you can restate what you have learned. If you cannot, go back, reread, and try again. If nothing else works, read aloud. You'll hear the words as well as see them—and the more senses you involve in studying, the easier the process will be.

Activity

Check your understanding by answering the following questions.

1. *True or false?* _____ Loss of concentration could be caused by hunger.

2. The first step in achieving a high level of concentration is
   a. buying a fluorescent light.
   b. solving a personal problem.
   c. studying with a goal in mind.
   d. having the right attitude.

3. *True or false?* _____ Concentrating means reading a textbook selection as slowly as you can.

4. Being an active learner means
   a. underlining material.
   b. turning headings into questions.
   c. trying to recall what you read.
   d. all of the above.

5. A good study area should have
   a. soothing music.
   b. a straight chair.
   c. a telephone.
   d. exercise equipment.

Studying Textbooks Systematically

In many college courses, success means being able to read and study a textbook skillfully. For many students, unfortunately, textbooks are heavy going. After an hour or two of study, the textbook material is as formless and as hard to understand as ever. But there is a way to attack even the most difficult textbook and make sense of it. Use a sequence in which you (1) preview a chapter, (2) mark it, (3) take notes on it, and then (4) study the notes.

Previewing

Previewing a selection is an important first step to understanding. Taking the time to preview a section or chapter can give you a bird's-eye view of the way the material is organized. You will have a sense of where you are beginning, what you will cover, and where you will end.

There are several steps in previewing a selection. First, study the title. The title is the shortest possible summary of a selection and will often tell you the limits of the material you will cover. For example, the title "FDR and the Supreme Court" tells you to expect a discussion of President Roosevelt's dealings with the Court. You know that you will probably not encounter any material dealing with FDR's foreign policy or personal life. Next, quickly read over the first and last paragraphs of the selection; these may contain important introductions to, and summaries of, the main ideas. Then briefly examine the headings and subheadings in the selection. Together, the headings and subheadings are a mini-outline of what you are reading. Headings are often main ideas or important concepts in capsule form; subheadings are breakdowns of ideas within main areas. Finally, read the first sentence of some paragraphs, look for words set off in **boldface** or *italics,* and look at pictures or diagrams. After you have previewed a selection in this way, you should have a good general sense of the material to be read.

Textbook Marking

You should mark a textbook selection at the same time that you read it through carefully. Use a felt-tip highlighter to shade material that seems important, or use a ballpoint pen and put symbols in the margin next to the material: stars, checks, or *NB* (for *nota bene,* a Latin phrase meaning "note well"). What to mark is not as mysterious as some students believe. You should try to find main ideas by looking for clues: definitions and examples, enumerations, and emphasis words.

1 ***Definitions and examples:*** Definitions are often among the most important ideas in a selection. They are particularly significant in introductory courses in almost any subject area, where much of your learning involves mastering

the specialized vocabulary of that subject. In a sense, you are learning the "language" of psychology or business or whatever the subject might be.

Most definitions are abstract, and so they usually are followed by one or more examples to help clarify their meaning. Always mark off definitions and at least one example that makes a definition clear to you. In a psychology text, for example, we are told that "rationalization is an attempt to reduce anxiety by deciding that you have not really been frustrated." Several examples follow, among them: "A young man, frustrated because he was rejected when he asked for a date, convinces himself that the woman is not very attractive and is much less interesting than he had supposed."

2 *Enumerations:* Enumerations are lists of items (causes, reasons, types, and so on) that are numbered 1, 2, 3 . . . or that could easily be numbered in an outline. They are often signaled by addition words. Many of the paragraphs in this book, for instance, use words like *First of all, Another, In addition,* and *Finally* to signal items in a series. Other textbooks also use this very common and effective organizational method.

3 *Emphasis words:* Emphasis words tell you that an idea is important. Common emphasis words include phrases such as *a major event, a key feature, the chief factor, important to note, above all,* and *most of all.* Here is an example: "The most significant contemporary use of marketing is its application to nonbusiness areas, such as political parties."

Textbook Note-Taking

Next, you should take notes. Go through the chapter a second time, rereading the most important parts. Try to write down the main ideas in a simple outline form. For example, in taking notes on a psychology selection, under a main heading, "Defense Mechanisms," you might write down the subheadings "Definition" and "Kinds." Below the second subheading you would number and describe each kind and give an example of each.

> Defense Mechanisms
> a. Definition: unconscious attempts to reduce anxiety
> b. Kinds:
> (1) Rationalization: An attempt to reduce anxiety by deciding that you have not really been frustrated
>   Example: A man turned down for a date decides that the woman was not worth going out with anyway
> (2) Projection: Projecting onto other people motives or thoughts of one's own
>   Example: A wife who wants to have an affair accuses her husband of having one

Studying Your Text Notes

To study your notes, use the method of repeated self-testing. For example, look at the subheading "Kinds" under "Defense Mechanisms" and say to yourself, "What are the kinds of defense mechanisms?" When you can recite them, then say to yourself, "What is rationalization?" "What is an example of rationalization?" Then ask yourself, "What is projection?" "What is an example of projection?" After you learn each section, review it, and then go on to the next section.

Do not simply read your notes; keep looking away and seeing if you can recite them to yourself. This self-testing is the key to effective learning.

In conclusion, remember this sequence for dealing with a textbook: (1) previewing, (2) marking, (3) taking notes, (4) studying the notes. Approaching a textbook in this methodical way will give you very positive results. You will no longer feel bogged down in a swamp of words, unable to figure out what you are supposed to know. Instead, you will understand exactly what you have to do, and how to go about doing it.

Activity

Check your understanding by answering the following questions.

1. *True or false?* _____ Previewing a textbook means marking off definitions and examples.
2. A textbook writer might let you know an idea is important by using
   a. stars.
   b. emphasis signals.
   c. illustrations.
   d. addition signals.
3. Previewing a textbook selection includes
   a. reading the title.
   b. looking at diagrams.
   c. examining subheadings.
   d. all of the above.
4. *True or false?* _____ Headings are usually set off in larger type or different-colored ink.
5. Enumerations are
   a. definitions.
   b. emphasis signals.
   c. lists of items.
   d. examples.

Building a More Powerful Memory

Two Basic Steps in Remembering: Organization and Self-Testing

Effective studying and remembering require, first, that you organize the material to be learned. *Organization* means preparing study notes made up of headings and subheadings, definitions and examples, enumerations, and other important points. The very process of organizing material and condensing it to its main points will help you understand and remember it.

After you have organized your subject material, memorize it through repeated self-testing. Look at the first item in your notes; then look away and try to repeat it to yourself. When you can, look at the next item; then look away and try to repeat it. When you can repeat the second item, go back without looking at your notes and try to repeat both the first and the second items. This constant review is at the heart of self-testing. After you can repeat the first two items without looking at your notes, go on to the third item. When you learn it, try to repeat all three items without looking at your paper. After you learn each new item, go back and test yourself on all the previous items you have studied.

Six Aids to Memorization

1 *Intend to remember.* The first aid to memory is intending to remember. This bit of advice appears to be so obvious that many people overlook its value. But if you have made the decision to remember something, and you then work at mastering it, you will remember. Anyone can have a bear-trap memory by working at it; no one is born with a naturally poor memory.

2 *Overlearn.* Overlearning is a second memory aid. If you study a subject beyond the time needed for perfect recall, you will increase the length of time that you will remember it. The method of repeated self-testing used the principle of overlearning; you can also apply this principle by going over several times a lesson you have already learned perfectly.

3 *Space memory work.* Spacing memory work over several sessions, rather than a single long one, is the third aid. Just as with physical exercise, five two-hour sessions spaced over several days are more helpful than ten hours all at once. The spaced sessions allow material time to "sink in." (Psychologists would say that it "transfers from short-term to long-term memory.") Spacing the sessions also helps you "lock in" material you have studied in the first session but have begun to forget. Studies show that forgetting occurs most rapidly soon after learning ends—but that review within a day or two afterward prevents much memory loss.

4   **Study before bedtime.** A fourth aid in memorizing material is studying just before going to bed. Do not watch a late movie or allow any other interference between studying and sleep. Then be sure to review the material immediately when you get up in the morning. Set your clock a half hour earlier than usual so that you will have time to do this. The review in the morning will help "lock in" the material that you have studied the night before and that your mind has worked over during the night.

5   **Use keywords as "hooks."** A fifth helpful tool is using keywords in an outline as "hooks." Reduce your outline of a passage to a few keywords and memorize those words. The keywords you master will then serve as "hooks" that will help you pull back entire ideas into your memory.

6   **Use memory formulas.** Sixth and finally, another tool is using memory formulas to help you recall points under a main idea, items in a list, steps in a procedure, or other things arranged in a series. For example, you might remember the four methods used in behavior therapy (extinction, reinforcement, desensitization, and imitation) by writing down the first letter in each word (*e r d i*) and remembering the letters by forming an easily recalled catchphrase ("Ellen's rolling dice inside") or rearranging them to form an easily recalled word (*r i d e*). The letters serve as hooks that help you pull in words that are often themselves hooks for entire ideas.

Activity

Check your understanding by answering the following questions.

1. The two basic steps in remembering are organizing the material to be learned and

    a.   studying before bedtime.

    b.   testing yourself repeatedly.

    c.   preparing study notes.

    d.   memorizing definitions.

2. *True or false?* _____ Material is best studied in a single long session rather than spaced out over several sessions.

3. *True or false?* _____ Some people are born with a naturally poor memory.

4. Overlearning means

    a.   studying beyond the time needed for perfect recall.

    b.   transferring facts to short-term memory.

    c.   using memory formulas.

    d.   studying to the point of diminishing returns.

5. The first aid to memory is
   a. creating "hooks."
   b. self-testing.
   c. intending to remember.
   d. using study notes.

20 Writing an Exam Essay

Examination essays are among the most common types of writing that you will do in college. An exam essay includes one or more questions to which you must respond in detail, writing your answers in a clear, well-organized manner. This chapter describes five basic steps needed to prepare adequately for an essay test and to take the test. It is assumed, however, that you are already doing two essential things: first, attending class regularly and taking notes on what happens in class; second, reading your textbook and other assignments and taking notes on them. If you are not consistently going to class, reading your text, and taking notes in both cases, perhaps you should be asking yourself and talking with others (counselors, instructors, friends) about your feelings on being in school.

To write an effective exam essay, follow these five steps:

Step 1: Try to anticipate the probable questions on the exam.

Step 2: Prepare and memorize an informal outline answer for each question.

Step 3: Read exam directions and questions carefully, and budget your time.

Step 4: Prepare a brief outline before answering an essay question.

Step 5: Write a clear, well-organized essay.

Each step will be described on the pages that follow.

Step 1: Anticipate Probable Questions

Anticipating probable questions is not as hard as you might think. Because exam time is limited, the instructor can give you only several questions to answer. He or she will—reasonably enough—focus on questions dealing with the most important aspects of the subject. You can probably guess most of them if you make up a list of ten or more likely questions.

Your class notes are one key. What topics and ideas did your instructor spend a good deal of time on? Similarly, in your textbook, what ideas are emphasized? Usually the keys to the most important ideas are headings and subheadings, definitions and examples, enumerations, and ideas marked by emphasis signals. Also, take advantage of any study guides that may have been given out, any questions that you may have been given on quizzes, and any reviews that your instructor may have provided in class. You should, then, be able to determine the most important areas of the subject and make up questions that cover them.

335

Step 2: Prepare and Memorize an Informal Outline Answer and Keywords for Each Question

Write out each question you have made up and, under it, list the main points that need to be discussed. Put important supporting information in parentheses after each main point. You now have an informal outline that you can memorize.

Next, identify *keywords* in your outline. (See the discussion of keywords as memory "hooks" on page 333.) Circle one keyword in each entry in your outline.

As an additional memory aid, try combining the initial letters of your keywords to form a *catchword* or *catchphrase*—something you will be able to recall immediately. (See the discussion of memory formulas on page 333.)

Test yourself repeatedly on your outline, keywords, and catchword or catchphrase.

An Illustration of Step 2

One class was given a day to prepare for an essay exam. The students were told that the essay topic would be "Describe six aids to memory." One student, Teri, made up the following outline answer.

> Six Memory Aids
> 1. (Intend) to remember (personal decision is crucial)
> 2. (Overlearn) (helps you remember longer)
> 3. (Space) memory work (several sessions rather than one long session)
> 4. Time before (bed) as a study period (no interference; review the next morning)
> 5. Use (keywords) as "hooks" (help pull whole ideas into memory)
> 6. Memory (formulas) (letters serve as hooks to help you remember items in a series)
>
> IOSBKF (I often see Bill kicking footballs.)

Activity

See whether you can complete the following explanation of what Teri has done in preparing for the essay exam.

First, Teri wrote down the heading and numbered the different items under it.

Also, in parentheses beside each point she added _____.

_____. Next, she circled a keyword for each hint and wrote below her outline the first _____ of each keyword. She then used the first letter in each keyword to make up a catchphrase she could remember easily.

Finally, she _____ herself repeatedly until she could recall the keywords the letters stood for and the main points the keywords represented.

Step 3: Look at the Exam Carefully and Budget Your Time

First, read all test directions carefully. This point seems obvious, but people are often so anxious at the start of a test that they fail to read the instructions, and so they never understand clearly and completely just what they must do.

Second, read all the essay questions carefully, first noting the *direction word* or *words* in each question that tell you just what to do. For example, *enumerate,* or *list,* means "number 1, 2, 3, and so on"; *illustrate* means "explain by giving examples"; *compare* means "give similarities"; *contrast* means "give differences"; *summarize* means "give a condensed account of the main ideas."

Finally, budget your time, depending on the point value of each question and its difficulty for you. Write in the margin of the test the approximate time you give yourself to answer each question. This way you will not end the exam with too little time to respond to a question that you know you can answer.

An Illustration of Step 3

When Teri received the exam, she circled the direction word *Describe,* which she knew meant "Explain in detail." She also jotted "30" in the margin when the instructor said that students would have a half hour to write their answers.

Step 4: Prepare a Brief Outline before Answering an Essay Question

Too many students make the mistake of anxiously and blindly starting to write. Instead, you should first jot down the main points you want to discuss in an answer. (Use the margin of the exam or a separate piece of scratch paper.) Then decide how you will order the points in your essay. Write *1* in front of the first point, *2* beside the second, and so on. You now have an informal outline to guide you as you write your essay answer.

If there is a question on an exam which is similar to the questions you antici-pated and outlined at home, quickly write down the catchphrase that calls back the content of your outline. Below the catchphrase, write the keywords represented by each letter in it. The keywords, in turn, will remind you of the ideas they represent. If you have prepared properly, this step will take only a minute or so, and you will have before you the guide you need to write a focused, supported, organized answer.

An Illustration of Step 4

Teri first recited her catchphrase to herself, using it as a guide to write down her memory formula (IOSBKF) at the bottom of the test sheet. The letters in the for-mula helped her call into memory the keywords in her study outline, and she wrote down those words. Then in parentheses beside each word she added the support-ing points she remembered.

By investing only a couple of minutes, Teri was able to reconstruct her study outline and give herself a clear and solid guide to use in writing her answer.

Step 5: Write a Clear, Well-Organized Essay

If you have followed the suggestions to this point, you have done all the prelim-inary work needed to write an effective essay. Be sure not to wreck your chances of getting a good grade by writing carelessly. Instead, as you prepare your response, keep in mind the principles of good writing: unity, support, coherence, and clear, error-free sentences.

First, start your essay with a sentence that clearly states what your paper will be about. Then make sure that everything in your paper relates to your opening statement.

Second—although you must obviously take time limitations into account—provide as much support as possible for each of your main points.

Third, use transitions to guide your reader through your answer. Words such as *first, next, then, however,* and *finally* make it easy for the reader to follow your train of thought.

Last, leave time to edit your essay for sentence-skills mistakes you may have made while you concentrated on writing your answer. Look for words omitted, mis-written, or misspelled (if it is possible, bring a dictionary with you); look for awk-ward phrasings or misplaced punctuation marks; and look for whatever else may prevent the reader from understanding your thought. Cross out any mistakes and make your corrections neatly above the errors. To make a short insertion, use a *caret* (∧) and write the insertion above the line. For longer insertions—if you want to change or add to some point—insert an asterisk at the appropriate spot, put another asterisk at the bottom of the page, and add the corrected or additional material there.

An Illustration of Step 5

Read through Teri's answer, reproduced here, and then do the activity that follows.

	There are six aids to memory. One aid is to intend to remember.
	An important part of success is making the ~~decison~~ decision that you are truly
	going to remember something. A second aid is overlearning. ~~Studing~~
	Studying a lesson several more times after you know it will help you
	remember it longer. Also, space study over several sessions rather than ^just
	one long one.* Another aid is to study just before bedtime and not
	watch TV or do anything else after study. The mind ~~ad~~ absorbs the
	material during the night. ~~The most~~ You should then review the material
	the next morning. A fifth memory aid is ^to use keywords as hooks. For
	example, the keyword "bed" helped me remember the entire idea
	about the value of studying right before sleep. A final aid to memory is
	memory formulas. I used the catchphrase "I often see Bill kicking
	footballs" and IOSBKF to recall the first letters of the six memory aids.
	*You need time in between for material to "sink in."

Activity

The following sentences comment on Teri's essay. Fill in the missing word or words in each case.

1. Teri begins with a sentence that clearly states what her paper _____.
   Always begin with such a clear signal!

2. The six transitions that Teri used to guide her reader, and herself, through the
   six points of her answer are:

   _____   _____   _____

   _____   _____   _____

3. Notice the various _____ that Teri made when writing and proof-reading her paper. She neatly crossed out miswritten or unwanted words; she used her _____ after she had finished her essay to correct a misspelled word; she used insertion signs, or carets (∧), to add omitted words; and she used an asterisk (*) to add an omitted detail.

Practice in Writing an Exam Essay

Activity 1

Check your understanding of the chapter by answering the following questions.

1. When you receive an exam essay in class, you should first
   a.   tackle the easiest question.
   b.   write a brief outline of each question.
   c.   read all test directions carefully.
   d.   memorize a catchphrase.

2. *True or false?* _____ Because of time limits, you do not have worry about the four bases of good writing on an exam essay.

3. *True or false?* _____ It is possible to anticipate essay exam questions.

4. Clues to possible essay exam questions are
   a.   enumerations.
   b.   ideas marked by emphasis signals.
   c.   reviews in class.
   d.   all of the above.

5. A catchphrase can help you
   a.   recall an informal outline prepared for a test question.
   b.   proofread your essay for sentence-skills mistakes.
   c.   budget your time on an essay.
   d.   use transitions to guide the reader through your answer.

Activity 2

As the assignment for your next class, your instructor may ask you to study pages 321–323 so that you will be ready to write an in-class paper in response to the direction, "Describe five hints that will make you a better note-taker."

You should do well on this paper if you follow the five basic steps in writing an effective exam essay that have been presented in this chapter.

Activity 3

1. Make up five questions you might be expected to answer on an essay exam in a social science or physical science course (sociology, psychology, biology, or some other).

2. Then, for each of the five questions, make up an outline answer comparable to the one on memory training.

3. Finally, write a full essay answer, in complete sentences, for one of the questions. Your outline will serve as your guide.

Be sure to begin your essay with a statement that makes the direction of your answer clear. For example, "The six different kinds of defense mechanisms are defined and illustrated below." If you are explaining in detail the different causes of, reasons for, or characteristics of something, you may want to develop each point in a separate paragraph. For instance, if you were answering a question in sociology about the primary functions of the family unit, you could start with the statement, "There are three primary functions of the family unit," and then go on to develop and describe each function in a separate paragraph.

You will turn in the essay answer to your English instructor, who will evaluate it using the standards for effective writing applied to your other written assignments.

21 Writing a Summary

At some point in a course, your instructor may ask you to write a summary of a book, an article, a TV show, or the like. In a *summary* (also referred to as a *précis* or an *abstract*), you reduce material in an original work to its main points and key supporting details. Thus a summary is something like an outline. Unlike an outline, however, a summary does not use symbols such as I, A, 1, 2, and so on to indicate the relationships among parts of the original material.

A summary may consist of a single word, a phrase, several sentences, or one or more paragraphs. The length of the summary you prepare will depend on your instructor's expectations and the length of the original work. Most often, you will be asked to write a summary of one or more paragraphs.

Writing a summary brings together a number of important reading, study, and writing skills. To condense the original matter, you must preview, read, evaluate, organize, and perhaps outline the material. Summarizing, then, can be a real aid to understanding; you must "get inside" the material and realize fully what is being said before you can reduce its meaning to a few words.

How to Summarize an Article

To write a summary of an article, follow the steps described below. If the assigned material is a TV show or film, adapt the suggestions accordingly.

1   Take a few minutes to preview the work. You can preview an article in a magazine by taking a quick look at the following:

    a   ***Title.*** The title often summarizes what the article is about. Think about the title for a minute, and about how it may condense the meaning of the article.

    b   ***Subtitle.*** A subtitle, if given, is a short summary appearing under or next to the title. For example, in a *Newsweek* article titled "Splitting Up the Family," the following caption appeared: "The courts are changing rules of divorce and child custody—and often making things worse." The subtitle, the caption, or any other words in large print under or next to the title often provide a quick insight into the meaning of an article.

    c   ***First and last several paragraphs.*** In the opening paragraphs, the author may introduce you to the subject and state the purpose of the article. In the

343

closing paragraphs, the writer may present conclusions or a summary. In either case, you get a quick overview of what the entire article is about.

d **Other items.** Note any headings or subheadings that appear in the article. They often provide clues to the main points and give an immediate sense of what each section is about. Look carefully at any pictures, charts, or diagrams that accompany the article. Page space in a magazine or journal is limited, and such visual aids are generally used only when they help illustrate important points in the article. Note any words or phrases set off in *italic type* or **boldface type;** such words have probably been emphasized because they deal with important points.

2 Read the article quickly for general understanding the first time through. Do not slow down or turn back. Mark off what seem to be main points and key supporting points. Pay special attention to all the items noted in the preview. Look for definitions, examples, and enumerations (lists), since these often indicate key ideas. Also, try to identify important information by turning any headings and subheadings into questions and by reading to find answers to those questions.

3 Go back and reread more carefully the areas you have identified as most important. Also, focus on other key points you may have missed in your first reading.

4 Keep the following in mind when working on the rough drafts of your summary.

a Express the author's ideas in your own words. Do not imitate the original work or stay too close to its style.

b Do not write an overly detailed summary. Remember that the purpose of a summary is to reduce the original work to its main points and essential supporting points. A paragraph summary should be between 150 and 200 words in length.

c Do not use expressions like "the author says." Equally important, do not introduce your own opinions into the summary; that is, don't make comments like "another good point made by the author." Instead, concentrate on presenting the author's main ideas directly and briefly.

d Preserve the balance and proportion of the original work. If the original devoted 70 percent of its space to one idea and only 30 percent to another, your summary should reflect that emphasis.

e As you work on the summary, pay attention to the principles of effective writing (unity, support, coherence, and clear, error-free sentences) explained in Part One.

f Write the final draft of the summary.

A Model Summary

Here is a model summary for a magazine article.

In "Dyslexia and the New Science of Reading" (<u>Newsweek</u>, November 22, 1999), Barbara Kantrowitz and Anne Underwood report on advances made in understanding and treating dyslexia in children. Dyslexia is marked by difficulty in processing written language and particularly in breaking words down into their separate sounds. Even though many people, including some famous intellectuals, have suffered from dyslexia, it has been misunderstood, misdiagnosed, and mistreated until recently. Now it is being studied by scientists in much more sophisticated ways, the most effective of which is brain imaging. Using this procedure, scientists measure the brain activity of patients performing language-related activities. Recent scientific findings about the complexity of dyslexia show the need for creative and informed classroom strategies for teaching children to read. Educators and researchers are focusing on early detection of the problem, and new screening tests are being used in select school systems across the country. At the same time, parents must raise their own awareness about how to identify and overcome this disorder. Parents can reduce the negative affects of dyslexia by playing word games with their very young children and by closely following their children's progress in school. Most important, parents need to provide strong moral support to dyslexic children, helping them overcome frustration and creating positive feelings about learning.

How to Summarize a Book

To write a summary of a book, first preview the book by briefly looking at the following:

1 **Title.** The title is often the shortest possible summary of what a book is about. Think about the title for a minute, and how it may summarize the meaning of the work.

2 **Table of contents.** The contents will tell you the number of chapters in the book and the subject of each chapter. Use the contents to get a general sense of how the book is organized. You should also note the number of pages in each chapter. If thirty pages are devoted to one episode or idea in the book and an average of fifteen pages to other episodes or ideas, you should probably give more space in your summary to the contents of the longer chapter.

3 **Preface.** Here you will probably find out why the author wrote the book. Also, the preface may summarize the main ideas developed in the book and may describe briefly how the book is organized.

4   ***First and last chapters.*** In these chapters, the author may preview and review important ideas and themes developed in the book.

5   ***Other items.*** Note how the author has used headings and subheadings to organize information. Check the opening and closing paragraphs of each chapter to see if they contain introductions or summaries. Look quickly at charts, diagrams, and pictures, since they are probably there to illustrate key points. Note any special features (index, glossary, appendixes) that may appear at the end of the book.

After previewing the book, use steps 2 through 4 above as a guide in preparing a summary.

Practice in Writing a Summary

Activity 1

Check your understanding of the chapter by answering the following questions.

1. Key ideas in an article may be signaled by the
   a.   table of contents.
   b.   title and subtitle.
   c.   preface.
   d.   index.

2. After previewing an article, you should
   a.   read the article.
   b.   take notes on the material.
   c.   write a first draft of your summary.
   d.   quote from the material.

3. *True or false?* _____ Use expressions such as "the author says" when writing your summary.

4. The table of contents in a book will give you an idea of
   a.   how much space in the book is devoted to a particular idea.
   b.   why the author wrote the book.
   c.   the conclusions the author has reached.
   d.   all of the above.

5. *True or false?* _____ A summary should include the key supporting points of a selection.

Activity 2

Use the guidelines in this chapter to write a one-paragraph summary of one of the following sections of the chapter "Developing Key Study Skills":

Controlling Your Time
Developing Concentration
Studying Textbooks Systematically
Building a More Powerful Memory

Your summary should be no fewer than 100 words and no more than 125 words. A summary of one section is given below as a model.

A Summary of "Taking Effective Classroom Notes"

The following hints can help you take better notes in your classes. First, attend class faithfully. Copying another student's notes cannot substitute for hearing the ideas in person. Another important hint is to develop a system of abbreviations. Using abbreviations for often-used words and special terms will speed note-taking. Putting a key to abbreviations at the top of the page will prevent confusion. In addition, be alert for signals of importance: anything written on the board, definitions, enumerations, emphasis words, and repeated ideas. Writing down examples and connections between ideas is also essential. Next, review your notes after class to clarify and expand them. Finally, take notes in every class you attend. Otherwise, you are sure to forget most of what you hear.

Activity 3

Write a one-paragraph summary of an article of interest to you in a weekly or monthly magazine. Be sure to use the guidelines in this chapter when reading the article and preparing the summary. Hand in a copy of the article along with your summary.

Activity 4

Watch a television show. Then prepare a summary of the show. In your first sentence, give basic information about the show by using a format such as the following: "The January 30, 2001, broadcast of CBS's *60 Minutes* examined. . . ."

22 Writing a Report

Each semester, you will probably be asked by at least one instructor to read a book or an article (or watch a TV show or a film) and write a paper responding to the material. In these reports, or reaction papers, your instructor will most likely expect you to do two things: (1) summarize the material and (2) detail your reaction to it. The following pages explain both parts of a report.

Part 1 of a Report: A Summary of the Work

To develop the first part of a report, do the following.

1 Identify the author and title of the work and include in parentheses the publisher and publication date. An example follows on page 351. For magazines, give the date of publication.

2 Write an informative summary of the material. Condense the content of the work by highlighting its main points and key supporting points. (See pages 345–347 for a complete discussion of summarizing techniques.) Use direct quotations from the work to illustrate important ideas.

   Do not discuss any single aspect of the work in great detail while neglecting to mention other equally important points. Summarize the material so that the reader gets a general sense of *all* key aspects of the original work. Also, keep the summary objective and factual. Do not include in the first part of the paper your personal reaction to the work; your subjective impression will form the basis of the second part of the paper.

Part 2 of a Report: Your Reaction to the Work

To develop the second part of a report, do the following:

1 Focus on any or all of the following questions. (Check with your instructor to see if he or she wants you to emphasize specific points.)

   a How is the assigned work related to ideas and concerns discussed in the course for which you are preparing the paper? For example, what points made in the course textbook, class discussions, or lectures are treated more fully in the work?

   b How is the work related to problems in our present-day world?

   c How is the material related to your life, experiences, feelings, and ideas? For instance, what emotions did the work arouse in you? Did the work increase your understanding of an issue? Did it change your perspective?

2 Evaluate the merit of the work: the importance of its points, its accuracy, its completeness, its organization, and so on. You should also indicate here whether or not you would recommend the work to others, and why.

Points to Keep in Mind When Writing a Report

Here are some important matters to consider as you prepare a report.

1 Apply the four bases of effective writing: unity, support, coherence, and clear, error-free sentences.

   a Make sure each major paragraph presents and then develops a single main point. For example, in the model report in the next section, the first paragraph summarizes the book, and the three paragraphs that follow detail three separate reactions of the student writer. The student then closes the report with a short concluding paragraph.

   b Support your general points or attitudes with specific reasons and details. Statements such as "I agreed with many ideas in this article" and "I found the book very interesting" are meaningless without specific evidence that shows why you feel as you do. Look at the model report closely to see how the main point or topic sentence of each paragraph is developed by specific supporting evidence.

   c Organize the material in the paper. Follow this basic plan of organization: a *summary* of one or more paragraphs, a *reaction* of two or more paragraphs, and a *conclusion*. Also, use *transitions* to make the relationships among ideas in the paper clear.

   d Edit the paper carefully for errors in grammar, mechanics, punctuation, word use, and spelling.

2 Document quotations from the work by giving the page number in parentheses after the quoted material. Look at the example in the first paragraph of the model report. You may use quotations in both parts of your paper—summary and reaction—but do not rely on quotations too much. Use them only to emphasize key ideas.

A Model Report

Here is a report written by a student in an introductory psychology course. Look at the paper closely to see how it follows the guidelines for report writing described in this chapter.

A Report on <u>Man's Search for Meaning</u>

**PART 1:
SUMMARY**
Topic
sentence
for
summary
paragraph

Dr. Viktor Frankl's book <u>Man's Search for Meaning</u> (New York: Washington Square Press, 1985) is both an autobiographical account of his years as a prisoner in Nazi concentration camps and a presentation of his ideas about the meaning of life. The three years of deprivation and suffering he spent at Auschwitz and other Nazi camps led to the development of his theory of logotherapy, which, very briefly, states that the primary force in human beings is "a striving to find a meaning in one's life" (154). Without a meaning in life, Frankl feels, we experience emptiness and loneliness that lead to apathy and despair. This need for meaning was demonstrated to Frankl time and again with both himself and other prisoners who were faced with the horrors of camp existence. Frankl was able to sustain himself partly through the love he felt for his wife. In a moment of spiritual insight, he realized that this love was stronger and more meaningful than death and would be a real and sustaining force within him even if he knew his wife was dead. Frankl's comrades also had reasons to live that gave them strength. One had a child waiting for him; another was a scientist who was working on a series of books that needed to be finished. Finally, both Frankl and his friends found meaning through their decision to accept and bear their fate with courage. He says that the words of Dostoyevsky came frequently to mind: "There is one thing that I dread: not to be worthy of my suffering." When Frankl's prison experience was over and he returned to his profession—psychiatry—he found that his theory of meaning held true not only for the prisoners but for all people. He has since had great success in working with patients by helping them locate in their own lives meanings of love, work, and suffering.

**PART 2:
REACTION**
Topic
sentence
for first
reaction
paragraph

One of my reactions to the book was the relationship I saw between the "Capos" and ideas about anxiety, standards, and aggression discussed in our psychology class. The Capos were prisoners who acted as trustees, and Frankl says they acted more cruelly toward the other prisoners than the guards or the SS men. Several psychological factors help explain this cruelty. The Capos must have been suppressing intense anxiety about "selling out" to the Nazis in return for small favors. Frankl and other prisoners must have been a constant reminder to the Capos of the courage and integrity they themselves lacked. When our behavior and values are threatened by someone else who is acting in a different way, we may react with anger and aggression. The Capos are an extreme example of how, in certain situations, we may be capable of great cruelty to those whose actions threaten our standards.

Topic
sentence
for second
reaction
paragraph

    I think that Frankl's idea that meaning is the most important force in human beings helps explain some of the disorder and discontent in the world today. Many people are unhappy because they are caught in jobs where they have no responsibility or creativity; their work lacks meaning. Many are also unhappy because our culture seems to stress sexual technique in social relationships rather than human caring. People buy popular books that may help them become better partners in bed, but that may not make them more sensitive to each other's human needs. Where there is no real care, there is no meaning. To hide the inner emptiness that results from impersonal work and sex, people busy themselves accumulating material things. With television sets, stereos, cars, expensive clothes, and the like, they try to forget that their lives lack true meaning. Instead of working or going to school to get a meaningful job, or trying to be decent human beings and friends with the people around them, or accepting their troubles with quiet determination and dignity, they frantically buy, buy, buy to distract themselves from the lack of real meaning within.

Topic
sentence
for third
reaction
paragraph

    I have also found that Frankl's idea that suffering can have meaning helps me understand the behavior of people I know. I have a friend named Jim who was always poor and did not have much of a family—only a stepmother who never cared for him as much as for her own children. What Jim did have, though, was determination. He worked at two jobs to save money to go to school, and then he worked and went to school at the same time. The fact that his life was hard seemed to make him bear down all the more. On the other hand, I can think of a man in my neighborhood who for all the years I've known him has done nothing with his life. He spends whole days standing on his front porch, or on the sidewalk, or on the street corner, smoking and looking at cars go by. He is burned out. Somewhere in the past his problems must have become too much for him, and he gave up. He could have found meaning in his life by deciding to fight his troubles like Jim, but he didn't, and now he is a sad shadow of a man. Without determination or the desire to face his hardships, he lost his chance to make his life meaningful.

Concluding
paragraph

    In conclusion, I would strongly recommend Frankl's book to people who care about why they are alive, and who truly want to think about the purpose and meaning of their lives.

Practice in Writing a Report

Activity 1

Check your understanding of the chapter by answering the following questions.

1. *True or false?* _____ Each major paragraph in a report should develop a single main point.

2. A summary of a work should
   a. be opinionated.
   b. focus on one key idea.
   c. be objective and factual.
   d. show how the work relates to your life.

3. *True or false?* _____ Quotations should be documented by giving the page number in parentheses after the quoted material.

4. The two basic parts of a report are
   a. summary and supporting details.
   b. summary and reaction.
   c. plan of organization and quotations.
   d. reaction and a final draft.

5. A reaction to a work could include how the work relates to
   a. a certain course.
   b. current problems.
   c. your own life.
   d. all of the above.

Activity 2

Read a magazine article that interests you. Then write a report on the article. Include a one-paragraph summary, a reaction consisting of one or more paragraphs, and a brief concluding paragraph. You may, if you like, quote briefly from the article. Be sure to enclose in quotation marks the words that you take from the article and give the page number in parentheses at the end of the quoted material.

Activity 3

Read a book suggested by your instructor. Then write a report on the book. Include a summary of at least one paragraph, a reaction consisting of two or more paragraphs, and a brief concluding paragraph. Make sure that each major paragraph in your report develops a single main point. You may quote some sentences from the book, but they should be only a small part of your report. When you quote material, follow the directions in Activity 2 above.

23 Writing a Résumé and Job Application Letter

When applying for a job, you will almost always need to submit a résumé. If you're applying by mail, you should send both your résumé and a job application letter.

Résumé

A *résumé* is a summary of your personal background and your qualifications for a job. It helps a potential employer see at a glance whether you are suited for a job opening. A sample résumé is shown on the next page.

Points to Note about the Résumé

1 Your résumé, along with your letter of application, is your introduction to a potential employer. First impressions count; thus it is extremely important that you make the résumé neat!

 a If possible, type the résumé on good-quality letter paper (8½ by 11 inches). Keep at least a 1-inch margin on all sides.

 b Edit and proofread very carefully for sentence-skills and spelling mistakes. A potential employer may regard such mistakes as signs of carelessness in your character. You might even want to get someone else to proofread the résumé for you.

 c If possible, be brief and to the point: use only one page.

 d Use a format like that of the model résumé. (See also the variations described below.) Balance your résumé on the page so that you have (as noted above) at least a 1-inch margin on all sides.

 e Note that you should start with your most recent education or job experience and work backward in time.

A Sample Résumé

ROBERTA LYONS
715 Baltic Avenue
Atlantic City, New Jersey 08401
609-821-8715

Education

1998–present	Atlantic Cape Community College Mays Landing, New Jersey 08330

By June I will have completed my Associate of Science degree, including twenty-four hours of courses in my major, hotel-motel management. In addition, I will have taken twelve hours of courses in accounting. At present I have a B+ average in my major and a B in my other courses.

1994–1998	Pleasantville High School Pleasantville, New Jersey 08310

Job Experience

1998–present	Checker and Assistant to the Manager, A & P Supermarket, Atlantic City, New Jersey 08401

During holiday periods in the two years I have worked at A & P, I have served as an assistant to the manager by supervising the preparation of party trays.

1997–1998	Clerk, Seven-Eleven Food Store, Absecon, New Jersey 08300 My job also included some bookkeeping and stock inventory.

Special Training

As part of one of my courses, Seminar in Hospitality Management, I have helped plan and supervise the preparation of luncheons for several college affairs. I have also privately catered several baptisms and weddings for relatives and friends.

References

My references are available upon request from the Placement Office at Atlantic Cape Community College, Mays Landing, New Jersey 08330.

2   Your résumé should point up strengths, not weaknesses.

   a   Do not include "Special Training" if you have had none. Don't refer to your grade-point average if it is a low C.

   b   On the other hand, include a main heading like "Extracurricular Activities" if the activities or awards seem relevant. For example, if Roberta Lyons had been a member of the Management Club or vice president of the Hospitality Committee in high school or college, she should have mentioned these facts.

   c   If you have no work experience related to the job for which you are applying, then list the jobs you have had. Any job that shows a period of responsible employment may favorably impress a potential employer.

3   You may list the names of your references directly on the résumé. Be sure to get the permission of people you cite before listing their names. You can also give the address of a placement office file that holds references, as shown on the model report. Or you can simply say that you yourself will provide references on request.

Job Application Letter

The purpose of the letter of application that goes with your résumé is to introduce yourself briefly and to try to make an employer interested in you. You should include only the high points of the information about yourself given in the résumé.

    Shown on the next page is the letter of application that Roberta Lyons sent with her résumé.

Points to Note about the Job Application Letter

1   Your letter should do the following:

   a   In the first paragraph, state that you are an applicant for a job and note the source through which you learned about the job.

       Here is how Roberta's letter might have opened if her source had been a newspaper: "I would like to apply for the position of Assistant Banquet Manager which was advertised in yesterday's *Philadelphia Inquirer*."

       Sometimes an ad will list only a box number (such as Y-140) to reply to. Your inside address should then be:

> Y-140
> <u>Philadelphia Inquirer</u>
> Philadelphia, Pennsylvania 19101
>
> Dear Sir or Madam:

   b   In the second paragraph, state briefly your qualifications for the job and refer the reader to your résumé.

A Sample Job Application Letter

715 Baltic Avenue
Atlantic City, New Jersey 08401
March 3, 2000

Mr. Philip McGuire
Banquet Manager
Sheraton Hotel
1725 John F. Kennedy Boulevard
Philadelphia, Pennsylvania 19103

Dear Mr. McGuire:

I learned through the Placement Office at Atlantic Cape Community College of the Assistant Banquet Manager position at the Sheraton Hotel. I would like to be considered as a candidate for the job.

I will graduate from Atlantic Cape Community College in June with an Associate of Science degree in hotel-motel management. The degree will include twenty-four hours of courses related to the hospitality industry and twelve hours of accounting. Also, you will see from my résumé that I have work-related experience, including two years as an assistant to the manager at an A & P supermarket.

If my qualifications and experience are of interest to you, I will be happy to come for an interview at your convenience. I think you will find me eager, motivated, able, and truly interested in working in the hospitality field.

Sincerely yours,

Roberta Lyons

Roberta Lyons

c   In the last paragraph, state your willingness to come for an interview. If you can be available for an interview only at certain times, indicate this.

2   As with the résumé, neatness is crucial. Follow the same hints for the letter as for the résumé:

a   Type the letter on good-quality letter paper (8½ by 11 inches).

b Proofread very carefully for sentence-skills and spelling mistakes. Use the checklist of sentence skills on the inside front cover.

c Be brief and to the point: use no more than one page.

d Use a format like the model letter. Keep at least a 1-inch margin on all sides.

e Use punctuation and spelling in the model letter as a guide. For example:

Skip two spaces between the inside address and the salutation ("Dear Mr. McGuire").

Use a colon after the salutation.

Sign your name at the bottom, in addition to typing it.

Practice in Writing a Résumé and Job Application Letter

Activity 1

Check your understanding of the chapter by answering the following questions.

1. *True or false?* _____ A job application letter should tell an employer about your family and hobbies.

2. A résumé should always list
   a. names of references.
   b. previous jobs.
   c. height and weight.
   d. your grades.

3. *True or false?* _____ A résumé should be brief: one page if possible.

4. On a résumé, you should
   a. admit your weak areas.
   b. list your most recent job last.
   c. highlight your strengths.
   d. do all of the above.

5. The purpose of a job application letter is to
   a. try to make an employer interested in you.
   b. repeat all the information in your résumé.
   c. take the place of an interview.
   d. do all of the above.

Activity 2

Clip a job listing from a newspaper or copy a job description posted in your school placement office. The job should be one that you feel you are already qualified for or that you will be qualified for in the future.

Write a résumé and a letter of application for the job. Use the models as guides. Your instructor may let you invent some of the specific supporting material needed to make you appear a strong candidate for the job.

Use the checklist of the four bases on the inside front cover as a guide for your writing. Be sure to edit and proofread both the résumé and the application letter carefully, and give them to someone else to check as well. Each should be nothing less than perfect, because a prospective employer will use them as a first indication of whether you are a good candidate for a job.

24 Using the Library and the Internet

This chapter provides the basic information you need to use your college library and the Internet with confidence. You will learn that for most research topics there are two basic steps you should take:

1 Find books on your topic.
2 Find articles on your topic.

You will learn, too, that while using the library is the traditional way of doing such research, a home computer with an online service and Internet access now enables you to investigate any topic.

Using the Library

Most students seem to know that libraries provide study space, word-processing facilities, and copying machines. They are also aware of a library's reading area, which contains recent copies of magazines and newspapers. But the true heart of a library is the following: a *main desk,* the library's *catalog(s) of holdings, book stacks,* and the *periodicals storage area.* Each of these will be discussed on the pages that follow.

Main Desk

The main desk is usually located in a central spot. Check at the main desk to see if there is a brochure that describes the layout and services of the library. You might also ask if the library staff provides tours of the library. If not, explore your library to find each of the areas described below.

Activity

Make up a floor plan of your college library. Label the main desk, catalog(s), book stacks, and periodicals area.

Library Catalog

The *library catalog* will be your starting point for almost any research project. The *catalog* is a list of all the holdings of the library. It may still be an actual card catalog: a file of cards alphabetically arranged in drawers. More likely, however, the catalog is computerized and can be accessed on computer terminals located at different spots in the library. And increasingly, local and college libraries can be accessed online, so you may be able to check their book holdings on your home computer.

Finding a Book—Author, Title, and Subject

Whether you use an actual file of cards, use a computer terminal, or visit your library's holdings online, it is important for you to know that there are three ways to look up a book. You can look it up according to *author, title,* or *subject.* For example, suppose you wanted to see if the library has the book *Amazing Grace,* by Jonathan Kozol. You could check for the book in any of three ways:

1 You could do an *author* search and look it up under *Kozol, Jonathan.* An author is always listed under his or her last name.

2 You could do a *title* search and look it up under *Amazing Grace.* Note that you always look up a book under the first word in the title, excluding the words *A, An,* or *The.*

3 If you know the subject that the book deals with—in this case, "poor children"— you could do a *subject* search look it up under *Poor children.*

Here is the author entry in a computerized catalog for Kozol's book *Amazing Grace:*

Author:	Kozol, Jonathan
Title:	Amazing Grace
Publisher:	New York: Crown, 1995
LC Subjects:	1. Poor children—New York (N.Y.) 2. Racism and racial segregation—New York (N.Y.) 3. Children of minorities—New York (N.Y.) 4. AIDS, asthma, illnesses of children.
Call Number:	362.709 Koz
Material:	Book
Location:	Cherry Hill
Status:	Available

Note that in addition to giving you the publisher (Crown) and year of publication (1995), the entry also tells you the *call number*—where to find the book in the library. If the computerized catalog is part of a network of libraries, you may also learn at what branch or location the book is available. If the book is not at your library, you can probably arrange for an interlibrary loan.

Using **Subject** Headings to Research a Topic

Generally if you are looking for a particular book, it is easier to search by *author* or *title.* On the other hand, if you are researching a topic, then you should search by *subject.*

The subject section performs three valuable functions:

- It will give you a list of books on a given topic.
- It will often provide related topics that might have information on your subject.
- It will suggest to you more limited topics, helping you narrow your general topic.

Chances are you will be asked to do a research paper of about five to fifteen pages. You do not want to choose a topic so broad that it could be covered only by an entire book or more. Instead, you want to come up with a limited topic that can be adequately supported in a relatively short paper. As you search the subject section, take advantage of ideas that it might offer on how you can narrow your topic.

Activity

Part A: Answer the following questions about your library's catalog.

1. Is your library's catalog an actual file of cards in drawers, or is it computerized?

2. Which type of catalog search will help you research and limit a topic?

Part B: Use your library's catalog to answer the following questions.

1. What is the title of one book by Alice Walker?

2. What is the title of one book by George Will?

3. Who is the author of *The Making of the President?* (Remember to look up the title under *Making*, not *The.*)

    _____

4. Who is the author of *Angela's Ashes?* _____

5. List two books and their authors dealing with the subject of adoption:

    a. _____

        _____

    b. _____

        _____

6. Look up a book titled *The Road Less Traveled* or *Passages* or *The American Way of Death* and give the following information:

    a. Author _____

    b. Publisher _____

    c. Date of publication _____

    d. Call number _____

    e. Subject headings: _____

7. Look up a book written by Barbara Tuchman or Russell Baker or Bruce Catton and give the following information:

    a. Title _____

    b. Publisher _____

    c. Date of publication _____

    d. Call number _____

    e. Subject headings: _____

Book Stacks

The *book stacks* are the library shelves where books are arranged according to their call numbers. The *call number*, as distinctive as a social security number, always appears on the catalog entry for any book. It is also printed on the spine of every book in the library.

If your library has open stacks (ones that you are permitted to enter), here is how to find a book. Suppose you are looking for *Amazing Grace*, which has the call number HV[875] / N48 / K69 in the Library of Congress system. (Libraries using the Dewey decimal system have call letters made up entirely of numbers rather than letters and numbers. However, you use the same basic method to locate a book.) First, you go to the section of the stacks that holds the H's. After you locate the H's, you look for the HV's. After that, you look for HV875. Finally, you look for HV875 / N48 /K69, and you have the book.

If your library has *closed stacks* (ones you are not permitted to enter), you will have to write down the title, author, and call number on a request form. (Such forms will be available near the card catalog or computer terminals.) You'll then give the form to a library staff person, who will locate the book and bring it to you.

Activity

Use the book stacks to answer one of the following sets of questions. Choose the questions that relate to the system of classifying books used by your library.

Library of Congress System (letters and numbers)

1. Books in the BF21 to BF833 area deal with
   a. philosophy.
   b. sociology.
   c. psychology.
   d. history.

2. Books in the HV580 to HV5840 area deal with which type of social problem?
   a. Drugs
   b. Suicide
   c. White-collar crime
   d. Domestic violence

3. Books in the PR4740 to PR 4757 area deal with
   a. James Joyce.
   b. Jane Austen.
   c. George Eliot.
   d. Thomas Hardy.

Dewey Decimal System (numbers)

1. Books in the 320 area deal with:
   a. self-help.
   b. divorce.
   c. science.
   d. politics.

2. Books in the 636 area deal with:
   a. animals.
   b. computers.
   c. marketing.
   d. senior citizens.

3. Books in the 709 area deal with
   a. camping.
   b. science fiction.
   c. art.
   d. poetry.

Periodicals

The first step in researching a topic is to check for relevant books; the second step is to locate relevant periodicals. *Periodicals* (from the word *periodic*, which means "at regular periods") are magazines, journals, and newspapers. Periodicals often contain recent information about a given subject, or very specialized information about a subject, which may not be available in a book.

The library's catalog lists the periodicals that it holds, just as it lists its book holdings. To find articles in these periodicals, however, you will need to consult a *periodicals index.* Three indexes widely used in libraries are *Readers' Guide to Periodical Literature, Magazine Index Plus,* and *Ebscohost.*

Readers' Guide to Periodical Literature

The old-fashioned way to do research is to use the familiar green volumes of the *Readers' Guide*, found in just about every library. They list articles published in more than one hundred popular magazines, such as *Newsweek, Health, People, Ebony, Redbook,* and *Popular Science.* Articles appear alphabetically under both subject and author. For example, if you wanted to learn the names of articles published on the subject of child abuse within a certain time span, you would look under the heading "Child abuse."

Here is a typical entry from the *Guide:*

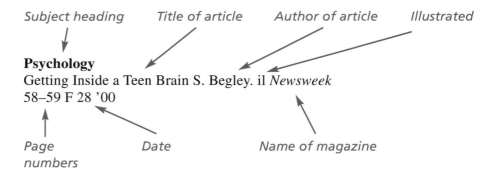

Note the sequence in which information is given about the article:

1 Subject heading.
2 Title of the article. In some cases, there will be bracketed words [ ] after the title that help make clear just what the article is about.
3 Author (if it is a signed article). The author's first name is always abbreviated.
4 Whether the article has a bibliography (*bibl*) or is illustrated with pictures (*il*). Other abbreviations sometimes used are shown in the front of the *Readers' Guide.*

5 Name of the magazine. A short title like *Time* is not abbreviated, but longer titles are. For example, the magazine *Popular Science* is abbreviated *Pop Sci.* Refer to the list of magazines in the front of the index to identify abbreviations.

6 Page numbers on which the article appears.

7 Date when the article appeared. Dates are abbreviated: for example, *Mr* stands for *March*, *Ag* for *August*, *O* for *October*. Other abbreviations are shown in the front of the *Guide.*

The *Readers' Guide* is published in monthly supplements. At the end of a year, a volume is published covering the entire year. You will see in your library large green volumes that say, for instance, *Readers' Guide 1998* or *Readers' Guide 2000.* You will also see the small monthly supplements for the current year.

The drawback of *Readers' Guide* is that it gives you only a list of articles; you must then go to your library's catalog to see if the library actually has copies of the magazines that contain those articles. If you're lucky and it does, you must take the time to locate the relevant issue, and then to read and take notes on the articles or make copies of them.

Readers' Guide is also available in a much more useful form on CD-ROM (compact disc, read-only memory). Using a computer terminal that accesses the CD-ROM, you can quickly search for articles on a given subject. You do this by typing into a box provided a keyword or phrase that will enable the computer to search for articles on your subject.

Magazine Index Plus

Magazine Index Plus is a computerized file that lists articles published over the last several years in about four hundred general-interest magazines, in addition to the *New York Times.* Once again, by sitting at a computer terminal and typing in a keyword or -words for your subject, you can rapidly locate relevant articles.

Ebscohost

Many libraries now provide an online computer search service such as *InfoTrac, Dialog,* or *Ebscohost.* Sitting at a terminal and using *Ebscohost,* for instance, you will be able to use keywords to quickly search many hundreds of periodicals for full-text articles on your subject. When you find articles that are relevant for your purpose, you can either print them off using a library printer (libraries may charge you about ten cents a page) or e-mail those articles to your home computer and run them off on your own printer. Obviously, if an online resource is available, that is the way you should conduct your research.

Activity 1

At this point in the chapter, you now know the two basic steps in researching a topic in the library. What are the steps?

1. _____

   _____

2. _____

   _____

Activity 2

1. Look up a recent article on Internet shopping using one of your library's periodicals indexes and fill in the following information:

   a. Name of the index you used _____

   b. Article title _____

   c. Author (if given) _____

   d. Name of magazine _____

   e. Pages _____   f. Date _____

2. Look up a recent article on violence in schools using one of your library's periodicals indexes and fill in the following information:

   a. Name of the index you used _____

   b. Article title _____

   c. Author (if given) _____

   d. Name of magazine _____

   e. Pages _____   f. Date _____

Specialized Indexes

Either through CD-ROM or online, your library will make available to you a number of specialized indexes. Your instructors may expect you to consult one or more of these indexes to obtain more specialized and professional information on a given subject. Listed here are representative indexes.

General
Biography Index
Humanities Index

New York Times Index
Social Sciences Index
Speech Index

Art/Literature
Art Index
Book Review Index
MLA Index
Music Index
New York Times Book Review Index

Business
Business Periodicals Index

Education
Education Index
ERIC

History/Political Science
Historical Abstracts
Public Affairs Information Service

Philosophy/Religion
Religion Index

Sciences
Applied Science and Technology Index
Biological Abstracts
Environment Index

Women's and Ethnic Studies
Hispanic American Periodicals Index
Index to Periodical Articles by and about Blacks
Women's Resources International

Using the Internet

The *Internet* is dramatic proof that a computer revolution has occurred in our lives. It is a giant network that connects computers at tens of thousands of educational, scientific, government, and commercial agencies around the world. Existing within the Internet is the World Wide Web, a global information system which got its name because countless individual websites contain *links* to other sites, forming a kind of web.

To use the Internet, you need a personal computer with a *modem*—a device that sends or receives electronic data over a telephone line for no more than the cost of a local telephone call. You also need to subscribe to an online service provider such as America Online or Earthlink. If you have an online service as well as a printer for your computer, you can do a good deal of your research for a paper at home. As you would in a library, you should proceed by searching for books and articles on your topic.

Before you begin searching the Internet on your own, though, take the time to learn whether your local or school library is online. If it is, visit its online address to find out exactly what sources and databases it has available. You may be able to do all your research using the online resources available through your library. If, on the other hand, your library's resources are limited, you can turn on your own to the Internet to search for material on any topic, as explained on the pages that follow.

Find Books on Your Topic

To find current books on your topic, go online and type in the address of one of the large commercial online booksellers:

Amazon at *www.amazon.com.*
Barnes and Noble Books at *www.bn.com*

The easy-to-use search facilities of both Amazon and Barnes and Noble are free, and you are under no obligation to buy books from them.

In some cases, you may not have to type the *www.* (for *World Wide Web*); the search program you are using may provide it for you. Note, by the way, that *.com* in the two addresses above is simply an abbreviation for *commercial*, referring to a business. Common abbreviations and examples are shown in the box on the next page.

Abbreviation	What It Indicates	Examples
.com	commerical organization; business	*www.mhhe.com* (McGraw-Hill Higher Education)
.edu	educational institution	*www.atlantic.edu* (Atlantic Cape Community College)
.gov	government agency	*www.whitehouse.gov* (President of the United States)
		www.usps.gov (United States Postal Service)
.mil	military agency	*www.defenselink.mil* (United States Department of Defense)
.net	Internet service provider; commercial organization	*www.earthlink.net* (Earthlink Network)
.org	nonprofit organization	*www.redcross.org* (American Red Cross)
		www.pbs.org (Public Broadcasting System)

Use the "Browse Subjects" Box

After you arrive at the Amazon or Barnes and Noble website (or the online library site of your choice), go to the "Browse Subjects" or "Keywords" box. You'll then get a list of categories where you might locate books on your general subject. For example, if your assignment was to report on the development of the modern telescope, you would notice that one of the subject listings is "science and nature." Upon choosing "science and nature," you would get several subcategories, one of which is "astronomy." Clicking on that will offer you still more subcategories, including one called "telescopes." When you choose that, you would get a list of recent books on the topic of telescopes. You could then click on each title for information about each book. All this browsing and searching can be done very easily and will help you research your topic quickly.

Use the "Keyword" Box

If your assignment is to prepare a paper on some aspect of photography, type in the word "photography" in the keyword search box. You'll then get a list of books on that subject. Just looking at the list may help you narrow your subject and decide on a specific topic you might want to develop. For instance, one student typed in "photography" as her keyword on Barnes and Noble's site and got back a list of thirteen thousand books on the subject. Considering just part of that list helped her realize that she wanted to write on some aspect of photography during the U.S. Civil War. She typed "Civil War Photography" and got back a list of twenty-six titles. After looking at information about those books, she was able to decide on a limited topic for her paper.

A Note on the Library of Congress

The commercial bookstore sites described are especially quick and easy to use. But you should know that to find additional books on your topic, you can also visit the Library of Congress website (*www.loc.gov*). The Library of Congress, in Washington, D.C., has copies of all books published in the United States. Its online catalog contains about twelve million entries. You can browse this catalog by subject or search by keywords. The search form permits you to check just those books that interest you and then print the list or e-mail it to yourself. Clicking on "Full Record" provides publication information about a book, as well as its call numbers. You can then try to find the book in your college library or through an interlibrary loan.

Other Points to Note

Remember that at any time, you can use your printer to quickly print out information presented on the screen. (For example, the student planning a paper on photography in the Civil War could print out a list of the twenty-six books, along with sheets of information about individual books.) You could then go to your library knowing just what books you want to borrow. If your own local or school library is accessible online, you can visit in advance to find out whether it has the books you want. Also, if you have time and money and if some of the books are available in paperback, you may want to purchase them from the online bookstore, which typically ships books in two to three days.

Find Articles on Your Topic

There are many online sources that will help you find articles on your subject. Following are descriptions of some of them.

A Resource for Magazines and Newspaper Articles

One online research resource that you can use at home is the Electric Library; it's available at *www.elibrary.com*. Chances are you may get a free thirty-day trial subscription, or you'll be able to enroll on a monthly basis at a modest cost. The Electric Library contains millions of newspaper and magazine articles as well as many thousands of book chapters and television and radio transcripts. After typing in one or more keywords, you'll get long lists of articles that may relate to your subject. When you then click on a given title, the full text of the article appears. If it fits your needs, you can print it out right away on your printer. Very easily, then, you can research a full range of magazine and newspaper articles.

For instance, one student wanted to write about the general topic of earthquakes. He typed in the keyword "earthquakes" and indicated that he wanted to see sixty documents. (In Electric Library, the user can indicate how many documents he or she wishes to see; the documents are ranked by the number of times the search term appears in each document.) In return, he got four magazine articles, four book excerpts, forty-seven newspaper articles, and five radio transcripts. Reading through the titles of these documents helped him decide that he would focus his research on the science of predicting earthquakes. When he typed in the keywords "predicting earthquakes" and asked for thirty documents, he received a variety of newspaper and magazine articles, book excerpts, and radio transcripts dealing specifically with that topic.

Here are three other good sources for magazine and newspaper articles.

America Online Newspaper Directory at *www.aol.com/directories/newspaper/html*

The Internet Public Library at *www.ipl.org/reading/news* and *www.ipl.org/reading/serials*

The Magazine Rack at *www.magazine-rack.com*

Search Directories and Search Engines

A number of search directories and search engines will help you find information quickly on the Internet; the box below shows some popular ones and their addresses.

AltaVista at *www.altavista.com*

America Online Search at *http://search.aol.com*

GoTo at *www.goto.com*

Lycos at *www.lycos.com*

Excite at *www.excite.com*

Hotbot at *www.hotbot.com*

Infoseek at *www.infoseek.com*

Yahoo at *www.yahoo.com*

My Virtual Reference Desk at *www.refdesk.com*

Web Search at *http://websearch.about.com*

A *search directory* organizes websites by categories. For example, on the next page is a picture of Yahoo's opening screen, also known as its *home page*. (Websites change their home pages all the time, so what appears on your computer screen may differ from what you see here.) You'll see that there are a number of subject areas you might visit, ranging from "Arts & Humanities" to "Society & Culture," depending on the area you want to research.

Each category is presented as a *link*—a stepping-stone that will take you to other sites. Typically, a link shows up as an underlined word or phrase that is a different color from the type elsewhere on the page. When you click on a link, you're automatically transported to a related site. There you are often presented with a more detailed list of websites and pages to choose from. As you move from link to link, you move from the general topic to more specific aspects of the topic.

If, for instance, you felt you wanted to do a research paper on some aspect of animals, you could click on the category "animals." Doing so would bring up more than fifty subcategories, including "Marine Life," "Animal Rights," "Veterinary Medicine," and "Prehistoric Animals." Let's say you wanted to explore possible topics in the area of marine life. Simply click on that item and you get a list of fourteen subgroupings, including "Squids," "Public Aquariums," "Underwater Photography," "Sharks," and "Jellyfish." In other words, Yahoo or any other search directory can help you discover a limited topic that you might want to research.

A *search engine* uses keywords to comb through the vast amount of information on the Web for sites or articles on particular topics. You activate a search engine by typing in a keyword or keywords that tell the engine what to look for. It then provides you with a list of "hits," or links, to sites or pages that contain your keywords. For example, a student planning a paper on threatened extinction of animal species first typed the words "animal species extinction" into the Search box on the Yahoo home page and within seconds got back a list of five website matches. Each of these sites brought up many individual articles on the extinction and animal species. The student was also given the option of learning about Web page matches. Upon clicking this option, he was given a list of 13,353 different articles he could access!

The overwhelming amount of information helped him realize that his research topic was far too broad, and he decided then to narrow his topic to extinction and the peregrine falcon. He typed in those keywords, which resulted in 689 Web page matches. As he read those articles and printed out the most relevant ones, he was able to further narrow his research.

Very often your challenge with searches will be getting too much information rather than too little. Most search engines include a *help* feature that will provide you with suggestions on ways to limit your search. Also, you might try another search engine. It may pitch a subject in a different way and give you other ideas for exploring your subject.

All the information, including categories and subcategories and related sites and pages, may seem overwhelming at first. But the very process of considering all of this information can help you think actively and creatively about just what you want your topic to be and how to limit that topic.

Final Internet Pointers

1 ***Creating bookmarks.*** When you find a helpful website that you may want to visit again, save its address. The program you are using will probably have a "Bookmark" or "Favorite Places" option. With the click of a mouse, you can "bookmark" a site. You will then be able to return to it simply by clicking on its name, rather than having to remember and type an address.

2 ***Evaluating Internet sources.*** Keep in mind that the quality and reliability of information you find on the Internet may vary widely. Anyone with a bit of computer know-how can create a website and post information there. That person may be a Nobel prize winner, a high school student, or a crackpot. Be careful, then, to look closely at your electronic source:

- *Electronic address:* Who is sponsoring the website? Is it an organization, a business, a government agency, a lobbying group, or an individual? Does the sponsor have reason to push a single point of view? If so, use this material with caution.
- *Author:* What credentials (if any) does the author have? Do these credentials qualify the author to provide information on the topic? Does the author provide an e-mail address so that you can request more information?
- *Internal evidence:* Does the author refer to studies or to other authors you can investigate? If the author does not name other sources or points of view, the information may be opinionated and one-sided.
- *Date:* Is the information cited recent and up-to-date? Check at the top or bottom of the document for copyright date, publication date, revision date, or all three. Having these dates will help you decide whether the material is recent enough for your purposes.

Practice in Using the Library and the Internet

Activity

Use your library or the Internet to research a subject that interests you. Select one of the following areas, or (with your teacher's permission) one of your own choice:

Assisted suicide	Computer use and carpal tunnel syndrome
Interracial adoptions	Noise control
Best job prospects today	Animals nearing extinction
Sexual harassment	Animal rights movement
Home schooling	Antigay violence
Greenhouse effect	Drug treatment programs for adolescents
Nursing home costs	Fertility drugs
Pro-choice movement today	Witchcraft today
Pro-life movement today	New treatments for AIDS
Attention deficit disorder (ADD)	Mind-body medicine

Drinking water pollution	Habitat for Humanity
Problems of retirement	Hazardous substances in the home
Cremation	Teenage fathers
Road rage	Gambling and youth
Prenatal care	Nongraded schools
Acid rain	Earthquake forecasting
New aid for the handicapped	Ethical aspects of hunting
New remedies for allergies	Vegetarianism
Censorship on the Internet	Recent consumer frauds
New prison reforms	Stress reduction in the workplace
Drug treatment programs	Global warming
Sudden infant death syndrome (SIDS)	Everyday addictions
New treatments for insomnia	Toxic waste disposal
Organ donation	Self-help groups
Child abuse	Telephone crimes
Voucher system in schools	Date rape
Food poisoning (salmonella)	Heroes for today
Alzheimer's disease	Eating disorders
Holistic healing	Surrogate mothers
Adoptions: Open records or closed?	Computer crime

Research the topic first through a subject search in your library's catalog or that of an online bookstore. Then research the topic through a periodicals index (print or online), or an online search directory or search engine. On a separate sheet of paper, provide the following information:

1. Topic
2. Three books that either cover the topic directly or at least in some way touch on the topic. Include these items:

    Author

    Title

    Place of publication

    Publisher

    Date of publication

3. Three articles on the topic published in 1996 or later. Include these items:

   Title of article

   Author (if given)

   Title of magazine

   Date

   Page(s) (if given)

4. Finally, include a paragraph describing just how you went about researching your topic. In addition, include a photocopy or printout of one of the three articles.

25 Writing a Research Paper

The process of writing a research paper can be divided into six steps:

1 Select a topic that you can readily research.
2 Limit your topic and make the purpose of your paper clear.
3 Gather information on your limited topic.
4 Plan your paper and take notes on your limited topic.
5 Write the paper.
6 Use an acceptable format and method of documentation.

This chapter explains and illustrates each of these steps and then provides a model research paper.

Step 1: Select a Topic That You Can Readily Research

Researching at a Local Library

First of all, do a *subject* search of your library's catalog (as described on page 363) and see whether there are several books on your general topic. For example, if you initially choose the broad topic of "divorce," try to find at least three books on the topic of divorce. Make sure that the books are actually available on the library shelves.

Next, go to a *periodicals index* in your library (see pages 366–369) to see if there are a fair number of magazine, newspaper, or journal articles on your subject. For instance, when Sarah Hughes, author of the model research paper "Divorce Mediation," visited her local library, she found a CD-ROM index called *Magazine Index Plus* (see page 367), which indexes all the articles published over a three- to four-year period in over four hundred popular magazines. When Sarah typed in the search term "divorce," *Magazine Index Plus* came back with hundreds of "hits"—titles, locations, and brief descriptions of articles about divorce. The index also marked those articles that were in magazines available in Sarah's library.

Researching on the Internet

If you have access to the Internet on a home or library computer, you can use it to determine if resources are available for your topic.

The first step is to go to the *subjects* section of a large online bookseller or library catalog to find relevant books. (Don't worry—you don't have to buy the books; you're just browsing for information.) As mentioned in Chapter 24, two of the largest online booksellers are Barnes and Noble and Amazon.

Sarah Hughes checked out both Barnes and Noble *(www.bn.com)* and Amazon *(www.amazon.com)*. "Both sites were easy to use," she reported. "All I had to do to get started was look at their 'browse subject' options and click on the subjects that seemed most relevant.

"At Barnes and Noble, the category I clicked on first was called 'Parenting and Families.' Under that was a bunch of subcategories, including one on 'Divorce.' I clicked on 'Divorce' and that brought up a list of 733 books! I spent some time scrolling through those titles and saw that there were lots of different themes: mostly 'how to survive your own divorce' books, but also books on all kinds of other topics, like 'how to keep sane while your boyfriend is going through a divorce' and 'how to stay involved in your children's lives when you're not living with them.' Others were about all kinds of emotional, legal, and financial aspects of divorce. There were clearly plenty of divorce-related books available, but I still didn't know what my paper's focus was going to be." At this point Sarah was feeling frustrated. She would return to Barnes and Noble a little later, but first she decided to try something else: searching online for newspaper and magazine articles.

There are several ways to determine if magazine or newspaper articles on your topic are available online. Your Internet service provider (such as America Online) has a built-in "engine" that allows you to search the Internet for any topic you like. When you type in a keyword or keywords related to your topic, you'll get back a listing of sources, or "hits," on the Internet. Sarah relates her experience searching the Internet in this way:

"First I typed in the word 'divorce' in the keyword box," she said. "I got more than a hundred thousand hits! When I looked at the first twenty or thirty sites, I saw that most of them were useless to me—they were advertisements from divorce lawyers, or information about divorce law in one particular state, etc. Now I was *really* frustrated. How was I ever going to narrow this topic down?"

Sarah turned to her instructor, asking how she could find magazine and newspaper articles about divorce. Her instructor recommended Electric Library, an online research service that the college subscribed to. (See more about Electric Library on pages 372–373.) This is what happened next: "I typed in the search word 'divorce,' clicked on the newspaper and magazine icons to indicate where I wanted to search, and asked to see 150 documents—the maximum number

Electric Library offers," says Sarah. "In a few seconds I was looking at headlines of 150 recent articles about divorce. I started clicking and reading, skimming each article for its main ideas, and finally I felt I was making some progress. I noticed the title of a *USA Today* article—'A Kinder, Gentler Divorce?'—that really grabbed my attention. I read it carefully and came across a phrase I hadn't heard before: 'divorce mediation.' In that article, I learned that divorce mediation helps people divorce without becoming bitter enemies in the process. To me, it definitely sounded like a topic worth exploring. So I went back to the Electric Library search box and typed in 'divorce mediation,' asking for 30 articles. I began to read them and realized I had struck gold. I'd narrowed the huge topic of 'divorce' down to a much more specific one. Now I was beginning to have a focus."

Encouraged, Sarah returned to Barnes and Noble and asked to see books on "divorce mediation." That brought up a manageable list of just 41 books. As Sarah clicked on their titles, she instantly saw on the screen information about those books—the titles and authors, reviews, sometimes even summaries and tables of contents. Reading about those books helped Sarah narrow her focus even further: she decided her paper would be about the advantages of divorce mediation over traditional divorce. With that idea in mind, she was able to choose ten books that sounded most relevant to her paper. She went to her local library and found six of those books, then bought one more that was available in paperback at a nearby bookstore. (If you find relevant books in your online search that your local library does not own, ask your research librarian if he or she can obtain them from another library through an interlibrary loan program.)

However you choose to do your research, the outcome is the same: If both books and articles are available, pursue your topic. Otherwise, you may have to choose another topic. You cannot write a paper on a topic for which research materials are not readily available.

Step 2: Limit Your Topic and Make the Purpose of Your Paper Clear

A research paper should *thoroughly* develop a *limited* topic. It should be narrow and deep rather than broad and shallow. Therefore, as you read through books and articles on your general topic, look for ways to limit the topic.

For instance, as Sarah read through materials on the general topic "divorce," she chose to limit her paper to divorce mediation. Furthermore, she decided to limit it even more by focusing on the advantages of divorce mediation over more traditional adversarial divorces. The general topic "violence in the media" might be narrowed to instances of copycat crimes inspired by movies or TV. After doing some reading on protests against the death penalty, you might decide to limit your paper to cases in which executed people were later proved innocent. The broad subject "learning disabilities" could be reduced to the widespread use of the drug Ritalin or possible causes of dyslexia. "AIDS" might be limited to federal funding to fight the disease; "personal debt" could be narrowed to the process an individual goes through in declaring bankruptcy.

The subject headings in your library's catalog and periodicals index will give you helpful ideas about how to limit your subject. For example, under the subject heading "Divorce" in the book file at Sarah's library were titles suggesting many limited directions for research: helping children cope with divorce, cooperative parenting after a divorce, the financial toll of divorce, fathers and custody rights. Under the subject heading "Divorce" in the library's periodicals index were subheadings and titles of many articles which suggested additional limited topics that a research paper might explore: how women can learn more about family finances in the event of a divorce, how parents can move past their own pain to focus on children's welfare, becoming a divorce mediator, divorce rates in second marriages. The point is that *subject headings and related headings, as well as book and article titles, may be of great help to you in narrowing your topic.* Take advantage of them.

Do not expect to limit your topic and make your purpose clear all at once. You may have to do quite a bit of reading as you work out the limited focus of your paper. Note that many research papers have one of two general purposes. Your purpose might be to make and defend a point of some kind. (For example, your purpose in a paper might be to provide evidence that gambling should be legalized.) Or, depending on the course and the instructor, your purpose might simply be to present information about a particular subject. (For instance, you might be asked to write a paper describing the most recent scientific findings about what happens when we dream.)

Step 3: Gather Information on Your Limited Topic

After you have a good sense of your limited topic, you can begin gathering information that is relevant to it. A helpful way to proceed is to sign out the books that you need from your library. In addition, make copies of all relevant articles from magazines, newspapers, or journals. If your library has an online periodicals database, you may be able to print those articles out.

In other words, take the steps needed to get all your key source materials together in one place. You can then sit and work on these materials in a quiet, unhurried way in your home or some other place of study.

Step 4: Plan Your Paper and Take Notes on Your Limited Topic

Preparing a Scratch Outline

As you carefully read through the material you have gathered, think constantly about the specific content and organization of your paper. Begin making decisions about exactly what information you will present and how you will arrange it. Prepare a scratch outline for your paper that shows both its thesis and the areas of support for the thesis. It may help to try to plan at least three areas of support.

Thesis: _____

Support: 1. _____

2. _____

3. _____

Here, for example, is the brief outline that Sarah Hughes prepared for her paper on divorce mediation:

Thesis: Divorce mediation is an alternative to the painful, expensive process of a traditional divorce.

Support: 1. Saves time and money

2. Produces less hostility

3. Produces more acceptable agreement between ex-spouses

Note-Taking

With a tentative outline in mind, you can begin taking notes on the information that you expect to include in your paper. Write your notes on four- by six-inch or five- by eight-inch cards, on sheets of loose-leaf paper, or in a computer file. The notes you take should be in the form of *direct quotations, summaries in your own words,* or both. (At times you may also *paraphrase*—use an equal number of your own words in place of someone else's words. Since most research involves condensing information, you will summarize much more than you will paraphrase.)

A *direct quotation* must be written *exactly* as it appears in the original work. But as long as you don't change the meaning, you may omit words from a quotation if they are not relevant to your point. Show such an omission with three bracketed spaced periods (known as an *ellipsis)* in place of the deleted words:

Original Passage

If you choose to follow the traditional path through this adversarial system, you will each hire lawyers who will fight on your behalf like ancient knights, charging each other with lances. Each knight, highly skilled in the intricacies of jousting but untrained in other ways to resolve conflict, will try to win by seizing for his client as much booty (children and property) as possible.

Direct Quotation with Ellipses

"[Y]ou will each hire lawyers who will fight on your behalf like ancient knights, charging each other with lances. Each knight [. . .] will try to win by seizing for his client as much booty (children and property) as possible."

(Note that the capital letter in brackets shows that the word was capitalized by the student, but did not begin the sentence in the original source. Similarly, the brackets around the three periods indicate that the student inserted these ellipses.)

In a *summary*, you condense the original material by expressing it in your own words. Summaries may be written as lists, as brief paragraphs, or both. Following is one of Sarah Hughes's summary note cards:

> Abusive spouse
> If there has been a recent history of physical abuse, mediation should not be attempted. If the abuse has been mental/verbal, mediation may not be successful if abused partner is very intimidated.
>
> Butler/Walker, 46–47

Keep in mind the following points about your research notes:

- Write on only one side of each card or sheet of paper.
- Write only one kind of information, from one source, on any one card or sheet. For example, the sample card above has information on only one idea (abusive spouse) from one source (Butler/Walker).

- At the top of each card or sheet, write a heading that summarizes its content. This will help you organize the different kinds of information that you gather.
- Identify the source and page number at the bottom.

Whether you quote or summarize, be sure to record the exact source and page from which you take each piece of information. In a research paper, you must document all information that is not common knowledge or a matter of historical record. For example, the birth and death dates of Dr. Martin Luther King, Jr., are established facts and do not need documenting. On the other hand, the number of adoptions granted to single people in 2000 is a specialized fact that should be documented. As you read several sources on a subject, you will develop a sense of what authors regard as generally shared or common information and what is more specialized information that must be documented.

A Note on Plagiarism

If you do not document information that is not your own, you will be stealing. The formal term is *plagiarizing*—using someone else's work as your own, whether you borrow a single idea, a sentence, or an entire essay. Plagiarism is a direct violation of academic code; if you pass someone else's work off as your own, you risk being failed or even expelled. Also, plagiarism undermines the money, time, and energy you have spent in school, cheating you out of an education.

With the accessibility of the Internet—especially websites targeting students— comes new temptation to plagiarize. But just remember that those sites are just as accessible to your instructor as they are to you. Many writing teachers are aware of these Internet "resources" and can spot "recycled" work.

If you use another person's material, *you must acknowledge your source.* When you cite a source properly, you give credit where it is due, you provide your readers with a way to locate the original material on their own, and you demonstrate that your work is carefully researched.

Step 5: Write the Paper

After you have finished reading and note-taking, you should have a fairly clear idea of the plan of your paper. Make a *final outline* and use it as a guide to write your first full draft. If your instructor requires an outline as part of your paper, you should prepare either a *topic outline*, which contains your thesis plus supporting words and phrases; or a *sentence outline,* which contains all complete sentences. In the model paper shown on pages 392–402, a topic outline appears on page 393. You will note that roman numerals are used for first-level headings, capital letters for second-level headings, and numbers for third-level headings.

In your *introduction,* include a thesis statement expressing the purpose of your paper and indicate the plan of development that you will follow. The section on writing an introductory paragraph for an essay (pages 296–298) is also appropriate for the introductory section of a research paper.

As you move from *introduction* to *main body* to *conclusion*, strive for unity, support, and coherence so that your paper will be clear and effective. Repeatedly ask, "Does each of my supporting paragraphs develop the thesis of my paper?" Use the checklist on the inside front cover of this book to make sure that your paper touches all four bases of effective writing.

Step 6: Use an Acceptable Format and Method of Documentation

Format

The model paper on pages 392–402 shows acceptable formats for a research paper, including the style recommended by the Modern Language Association (MLA). Be sure to note carefully the comments and directions set in small print in the margins of each page.

Documentation of Sources

You must tell the reader the sources (books, articles, and so on) of the borrowed material in your paper. Whether you quote directly or summarize ideas in your own words, you must acknowledge your sources. In the past, you may have used footnotes and a bibliography to cite your sources. Here you will learn a simplifed and widely accepted documentation style used by the Modern Language Association.

Citations within a Paper

When citing a source, you must mention the author's name and the relevant page number. The author's name may be given either in the sentence you are writing or in parentheses following the sentence. Here are two examples:

Paula James, the author of <u>The Divorce Mediation Handbook,</u> has witnessed the divorce process from both sides—actually, <u>three</u> sides. First, she went through a traditional divorce herself. In her words, "we simply turned our destinies over to our two attorneys. [. . .] Many thousands of dollars later we were divorced, but with resentment and distrust and no lidea of how we would jointly raise our child" (xvi).

As the authors of <u>The Divorce Mediation Answer Book</u> say, a mediated agreement is "future focused. In mediation, as contrasted to litigation, each of you is empowered to control your own future, and since you have shared in the negotiation process, you are more likely to abide by the agreement" (Butler and Walker 5).

There are several points to note about citations within the paper:

- When an author's name is provided within the parentheses, only the last name is given.
- There is no punctuation between the author's name and the page number.
- The parenthetical citation is placed after the borrowed material but before the period at the end of the sentence.
- If you are using more than one work by the same author, include a shortened version of the title within the parenthetical citation. For example, suppose you were using two books by Paula James and you included a second quotation from her book *The Divorce Mediation Handbook*. Your citation within the text would be:

  (James, <u>Handbook</u> 39).

  Note that a comma separates the author's last name from the abbreviated title and page number.

Citations at the End of a Paper

Your paper should end with a list of "Works Cited" which includes all the sources actually used in the paper. (Don't list any other sources, no matter how many you have read.) Look at "Works Cited" in the model research paper (page 402) and note the following points:

- The list is organized alphabetically according to the authors' last names. (If no author is given, the entry is alphabetized by title.) Entries are not numbered.
- Entries are double-spaced, with no extra space between entries.
- After the first line of each entry, there is a half-inch indentation for each additional line in the entry.
- Use the abbreviation *qtd. in* when citing a quotation from another source. For example, a quotation from Lynn Jacob on page 3 of the paper is from a work written not by her but by Ann Field. The citation is therefore handled as follows:

  As pointed out by Lynn Jacob, president of the Academy of Family Mediators, "the legal system is designed so that the more the couples fight, the more money the lawyers earn" (qtd. in Field 136).

Model Entries for a List of "Works Cited"

Model entries of "Works Cited" are given below. Use these entries as a guide when you prepare your own list.

Book by One Author

Nuland, Sherwin B. <u>How We Die: Reflections on Life's Final Chapter</u>. New

　　York: Vintage, 1995.

Note that the author's name is reversed.

　　In addition, when citing *any* book, always provide the full title, which you should copy from the inside title page. Include any subtitle by placing a colon after the main title and then copying the subtitle, word for word.

Two or More Entries by the Same Author

---. <u>The Mysteries Within: A Surgeon Reflects on Medical Myths</u>. New York:

　　Simon & Schuster, 2000.

If you cite two or more entries by the same author (in the example above, a second book by Sherwin B. Nuland is cited), do not repeat the author's name. Instead, begin with a line made up of three hyphens followed by a period. Then give the remaining information as usual. Arrange the works by the same author alphabetically by title. The words *A, An,* and *The* are ignored in alphabetizing by title.

Book by Two or More Authors

Baxandall, Rosalyn, and Elizabeth Ewen. <u>Picture Windows: How the</u>

　　<u>Suburbs Happened</u>. New York: Basic Books, 2000.

For a book with two or three authors, give all the authors' names but reverse only the first name. For a book with more then three authors, cite only the first author's name, followed by a comma and the phrase *et al.*

Magazine Article

Chin, Paula. "You Were a Good Man, Charlie Brown." <u>People</u> 28 Feb. 2000:

　　52–59.

Write the date of the issue as follows: day, month (abbreviated in most cases to three or four letters), and year, followed by a colon. The final number or numbers refer to the pages of the issue on which the article appears.

Newspaper Article

Zoroya, Gregg. "A Hunger for Heroes." <u>USA Today</u> 28 Feb. 2000: D1–2.

The final letter and number refer to pages 1 and 2 of section D.

    If the article is not printed on consecutive pages, simply list the first page, followed by a plus sign "+" (in that case, the above example would read "D1+").

    In addition, when citing newspaper titles, omit the introductory *The* (for example, *Boston Globe*, not *The Boston Globe*).

Editorial

"Drugs and Preschoolers." Editorial. <u>Philadelphia Inquirer</u> 28 Feb.

    2000: A10.

List an editorial as you would any signed or unsigned article, but indicate the nature of the piece by adding *Editorial* or *Letter* after the article's title.

Selection in an Edited Collection

Feist, Raymond E. "The Wood Boy." <u>Legends: Short Novels by the Masters</u>

    <u>of Modern Fantasy</u>. Ed. Robert Silverberg. New York: Tor Books, 1998.

    176–211.

Revised or Later Edition

Davis, Mark H. <u>Social Psychology</u>. 4th ed. New York: McGraw-Hill, 2000.

Note: The abbreviations *Rev. ed., 2nd ed., 3rd ed.,* and so on, are placed right after the title.

Chapter or Section in a Book by One Author

Secunda, Victoria. "A New Sense of Family." <u>Losing Your Parents, Finding</u>

    <u>Yourself: The Defining Turning Point of Adult Life</u>. New York:

    Hyperion, 2000. 242–59.

Pamphlet

<u>Heart and Stroke Facts</u>. New York: American Heart Association, 2000.

Television Program

"Smoke Screen." 60 Minutes. Narr. Lesley Stahl. Prod. Rome Hartman. CBS.
    11 Nov. 1998.

Film

Music of the Heart. Dir. Wes Craven. Miramax, 1999.

Sound Recording

Chapman, Tracy. "Speak the Word." Telling Stories. Elektra Entertainment,
    2000.

Videocassette

"To the Moon." Nova. Narr. Liev Schrieber. Videocassette. PBS Video, 1999.

Personal Interview

Anderson, Robert B. Personal interview. 17 Sept. 2000.

Online Source in a Reference Database

"Heredity." Britannica Online. Sept. 1999. Encyclopaedia Britannica.
    2 Mar. 2000 <http://www.britannica.com/bcom/eb/article/4/0,
    5716,120934,00.html#Article>.

The first date refers to the online publication date; the second refers to the exact
day when the student researcher accessed the information and should *not* be followed by a period.

Online Article

Ehrenreich, Barbara. "Will Women Still Need Men?" Time Online 21 Feb.
    2000. 15 Apr. 2000 <http://www.time.com/time/reports/v21/live/
    men_mag.html>.

Activity

On a separate sheet of paper, convert the information in each of the following references into the correct form for a list of "Works Cited." Use the appropriate model above as a guide.

1. An article by Susan Sachs titled "Egypt's Women Win Equal Rights to Divorce" on pages A1 and A5 of the March 1, 2000 issue of the *New York Times*.

2. An article by Nancy Franklin titled "Nonsense and Sensibility" on pages 96–97 of the March 6, 2000 issue of the *New Yorker*.

3. A book by Francis McInerney and Sean White called *Futurewealth: Investing in the Second Great Wave of Technology* and published in New York by St. Martin's in 2000.

4. A book by Ellen N. Junn and Chris Boyatzis titled *Child Growth and Development* and published in a seventh edition by McGraw-Hill in New York in 2000.

5. An article by Yahlin Chang titled "Grace Under Pressure" found on March 2, 2000 at <http://newsweek.com/issue/09_00a/focus/grace.htm> in the February 28, 2000 online issue of *Newsweek*.

Model Paper

Model Title Page

The title should begin about one-third of the way down the page. Center the title. Double-space between lines of the title and your name. Also center and double-space the instructor's name and the date.

While the *MLA Handbook* does not require a title page or an outline for a paper, your instructor may ask you to include one or both. Here is a model title page.

Divorce Mediation: A Better Alternative

by

Sarah Hughes

English 101

Professor Martinez

8 March 2000

Model First Page with a Top Heading

Double-space between lines. Leave a one-inch margin on all sides.

Papers written in MLA style use the simple format shown below. There is no title page or outline.

½ inch

1 inch

Hughes 1

Sarah Hughes

Professor Martinez

English 101

8 March 2000

Divorce Mediation: A Better Alternative

    Divorce is never easy. Even if two people both want to part, ending a marriage is a painful experience. In order to become divorced, most people go through a process that increases this pain. Starting with the lawsuit that one partner has to file against the other, the two take on the roles of enemies. . . .

Model Outline Page

After the title page, number all pages in upper-right corner—a half-inch from the top. Place your name before the page number. Use small Roman numerals on outline pages. Use arabic numbers on pages following the outline.

The word *Outline* (without underlining or quotation marks) is centered one inch from the top. Double-space between lines. Leave a one-inch margin on all sides.

Use this format if your instructor asks you to submit an outline of your paper.

Hughes i

Outline

Thesis: Divorce mediation offers several advantages over the traditional process of divorce.

I. Introduction

   A. Traditional divorce

      1. Casts divorcing couple in the role of enemies

      2. Expensive and painful

   B. Mediation

      1. Description of mediation process

      2. Growing popularity of mediation

II. Mediation's advantages in terms of money and time

   A. Traditional divorce

      1. Lawyers' fees charged for every step

      2. Lawyers' and courts' involvement slows process down

   B. Mediation

      1. Mediators' fees lower than lawyers'

      2. Couple controls costs of case

      3. Mediated divorces completed more quickly

III. Mediation's emotional benefits

   A. Traditional divorce

      1. Pits clients against one another

      2. Produces hostility and distrust

   B. Mediation encourages clients to work cooperatively

IV. Mediation's advantages in terms of divorce agreement

   A. Traditional divorce leaves clients with attorney-negotiated agreement that may not work well for them

   B. Mediation creates agreement that both clients can live with

V. Who shouldn't use mediation

VI. Conclusion

Here is a full model paper. It assumes the writer has included a title page.

Hughes 1

Divorce Mediation: A Better Alternative

Divorce is never easy. Even if two people both want to break up, ending a marriage is a painful experience. In order to become divorced, most people go through a process that increases this pain. Starting with the lawsuit that one partner files against the other, the two take on the roles of enemies. As author Paula James describes it,

> You will each hire lawyers who will fight on your behalf like ancient knights, charging each other with lances. Each knight [. . .] will try to win by seizing for his client as much booty (children and property) as possible. You will stand on the sidelines wringing your hands while you watch the battle— and, of course, pay your knight a high hourly fee. One peculiarity of this battle is that the wounds inflicted don't appear on the other warrior; they appear on you, your spouse, and your children. (3)

But there is an alternative to this traditional, ugly divorce process. It is called divorce mediation. Couples who use divorce mediation find that it saves them time and money, it produces less hostility, and it leaves them with an agreement they can respect.

What is divorce mediation? According to a 1997 USA Today article, it is a process in which "the couple, rather than a judge, decides who gets the kids, the house, the cars, and other marital assets. The mediator serves as coach, counselor, consensus builder and occasional referee" (Valente B7). That mediator, who is usually a lawyer or a therapist, helps the couple hammer out a divorce agreement they both find acceptable. This is done in as few or as

Left margin annotations:

Double-space between lines of the text. Leave a one-inch margin all the way around the page. Your name and the page number should be typed one-half inch from the top of the page.

Source is identified by name

Direct quotations of five typed lines or more are indented ten spaces from the left margin. Quotation marks are not used.

The bracketed spaced periods (ellipsis) show that material from the original source has been omitted.

Only the page number is needed, as the author has already been named in the text.

Thesis, followed by plan of development.

Citation for a signed newspaper article. The letter and number refer to section B, page 7.

Hughes 2

many meetings as necessary. Each spouse will probably hire a personal lawyer to review the agreement before it is made final. But the spouses, not "hired gun" lawyers, are responsible for creating it. During the process, the mediator doesn't favor one partner over the other. Instead the mediator maintains, in the words of the lawyer and mediator Gary Friedman, an attitude of "positive neutrality." Friedman explains the term by saying, "While I am largely neutral as to outcome [. . .] I am not neutral as to process. On the contrary, I am actively engaged in trying to insure that each party takes responsibility for him- or herself, and making sure that all decisions are sound for both of them" (26).

Once the couple is satisfied with the agreement, it is filed in court and approved by a judge in a brief hearing. In many states, the couple does not even need to attend that hearing. Couples can thus complete a divorce without ever seeing the inside of a courtroom. There are no official statistics to tell how many divorcing couples use mediation, but it is definitely becoming a popular option. According to the Academy of Family Mediators in Boston, the number of mediators has jumped in recent years from just 100 to over 3,600 (Valente B7). And courts in twenty-five states now require couples involved in child-custody disputes to work with a mediator (Field 136).

One practical advantage of mediation is that it is less expensive and time-consuming. In a traditional divorce, after each partner retains a lawyer and sets the divorce machine in motion, costs mount up quickly. A lawyer's fee "may range from $125 to $500 per hour [. . .] for each spouse" ("Avoiding the War"). The lawyers bill their clients

Source is identified by name and area of expertise

This typical citation is made up of the author's last name and the relevant page number. "Works Cited" then provides full information about the source.

Citation for an on-line source. No page number is given because the online document does not provide it.

for every phone call made, every letter written, every hearing attended, every meeting held to iron out another wrinkle in the process. In addition, when people divorce, they must make decisions about countless details. Even if the spouses are not far apart in their thinking, those decisions take time. If the husband and wife are deeply divided, the bills can become staggering. According to Field, "An uncontested, amiable divorce may cost $5,000 per partner and drag on for more than a year. [. . .] A warring duo [. . .] could wind up spending $30,000 apiece, and the case might span an entire Presidential administration" (136). The couple's financial welfare is not the top concern of courts and attorneys. As pointed out by Lynn Jacob, president of the Academy of Family Mediators, "the legal system is designed so that the more the couples fight, the more money the lawyers earn" (qtd. in Field 136).

By contrast, mediation costs are far more reasonable. Most mediators charge between $100 and $350 an hour (Friedman 19). Because both spouses are present for all mediating sessions, they are in control of how high the costs mount. Although there is no "typical" divorce, it is clear that mediated divorces tend to be much less expensive than others. In Friedman's experience, a mediated divorce in which there is "substantial disagreement" costs between $2,000 and $5,000 (19). Ken Waldron, a mediator with the Madison (Wisconsin) Center for Divorce Mediation, estimates that most mediated divorces end up costing one-half to one-third less than an attorney-negotiated divorce (Schuetz 10). Mediator

The abbreviation *qtd.* means *quoted.* The quoted material is not capitalized because the student has blended it into a sentence with an introductory phrase.

Quotation marks acknowledge that the phrase is copied from the previous citation.

Hughes 4

and author Paula James describes mediated divorces as costing "a fraction" of attorney-negotiated ones (60).

Second, mediated divorces are finalized much more quickly than ones fought out in the courts. Couples divorcing in the traditional way spend a long time going through the following cycle: meet with attorney, wait for attorney to talk with spouse's attorney, wait for spouse's attorney to talk with spouse, wait for spouse's attorney to return with response. Mediating couples don't have to do any of that. They also don't have the ordeal of endless hearings, court delays, and their attorneys' own schedule problems. Mediating couples can do a large part of the work of their divorce agreement outside their meetings with the mediator. Most mediating couples really want to get their agreement finished, for both financial and emotional reasons. Because they have the guidance of a professional to help them work through difficult points, they tend to work efficiently. According to Meg Lundstrum's writing in <u>Business Week</u>, most mediated divorces are completed in four to eight sessions, or six to twenty-four hours (228). Gary Friedman's estimate is about the same: four to six meetings spaced over a period of two to three months (18). A typical mediation center advertising online, Divorce Solutions of New York, N.Y., says, "The entire divorce process takes approximately 2–3 months, as opposed to 2–3 years in the adversarial process" ("Mediation: How It Works").

A third important point is that mediated divorces leave less hostility behind them. It's true that a divorce produces feelings of grief, anger, and frustration for almost everyone. But mediation can

Citation for an online source.

help people deal with these feelings. By contrast, an attorney-fought divorce seems designed to make the splitting partners hate each other as much as possible. Paula James, the author of <u>The Divorce Mediation Handbook</u>, has witnessed the divorce process from both sides—actually, <u>three</u> sides. First, she went through a traditional divorce herself. In her words, "we simply turned our destinies over to our two attorneys. [. . .] Many thousands of dollars later we were divorced, but with resentment and distrust and no idea of how we would jointly raise our child" (xvi).

Later, Paula James became an attorney herself and represented clients in traditional divorces. She describes how she and her colleagues routinely dug for dirt about possible affairs, alcohol abuse, shady business dealings, child neglect, and any other personal weaknesses they could use as ammunition in court. By the end of such an ordeal, she writes, couples were "deeply in debt, very angry, and distrustful of one another" (10).

And finally, Paula James began working as a divorce mediator. As a mediator she works with many clients who may no longer be the best of friends, but who want to remain on decent terms with their ex-spouses, for their own sake as well as for the sake of any children. One such client, Terri, expressed the feelings of many people who want a mediated divorce. She called James after having talked with an attorney. Terri was horrified by the attorney's fee ($5,000 to start) and what he told her. " 'He said that Eli and I are now adversaries, that I must do everything I can to protect myself from him and to get as much money as possible . . . ,' Terri said. 'That's not what I want. I'm

Single quotation marks are used for a quotation within a quotation.

Hughes 6

sorry that our marriage hasn't worked out, but I'm not trying to take Eli to the cleaners' " (10). Terri and Eli then started working with James. By listening carefully to them both, and stepping in occasionally to help them explain their fears and priorities rather than attack one another, James helped Terri and Eli work out an agreement in a short amount of time and for a reasonable fee. "They left my office looking more relaxed than when they had entered," she reported (15). According to the Divorce Law Information Service Center's home page, "In family law disputes, mediation is often preferred over litigation because it facilitates future communication between the parties which is necessary when the future of the children is at stake."

In the long run, the biggest advantage of mediated divorce is that it helps couples develop an agreement they will be willing to live with. As the authors of The Divorce Mediation Answer Book say, a mediated agreement is "future focused. In mediation, as contrasted to litigation, each of you is empowered to control your own future, and since you have shared in the negotiation process, you are more likely to abide by the agreement" (Butler and Walker 5). Attorney-negotiated agreements tend to fall into rigid, traditional patterns: she gets the house; he gets the car; the kids spend every other weekend and six weeks in the summer with him. But mediated agreements are generally more creative and in tune with the divorcing couple's lives. One couple described in the Cosmopolitan article had been fighting bitterly over the mail-order business they had built together. Each insisted that he or she should take over the business entirely.

Quoted from an on-line source. Since the source has been named in the text, no further citation is necessary.

Without lawyers, judges, or formal courtroom rules to get in the way, the mediator got Vivian and Bill to agree on a general plan whereby one spouse would keep the business, buy out the other, and lend him or her enough money to start a new venture. Then he instructed them to calculate their company's net worth. Finally, the material helped them realize on their own that Vivian, who'd had more contact with overseas suppliers, should keep the business; Bill, who was more aggressive, would do better taking the loan and launching a new product line. (Field 137)

Once they are used to the idea, most couples like the idea of creating an agreement that really works for them. In the words of Paula James, "[The divorcing couple] aren't ignorant children who must be silenced while their lawyers do the talking" (xvii).

Although mediation has clear advantages, it is not right for everyone. Most mediation experts agree with Butler and Walker, who say that mediation "would not be an appropriate way to negotiate a fair settlement" if one of the divorcing partners feels unable or too frightened to stand up to the other. Examples are situations characterized by "intimidation or fear of violence," "a recent history of domestic violence or child abuse," or "severe intellectual or emotional limitations" (6). In such cases, it is probably best for the weaker partner if an attorney does his or her negotiating.

In conclusion, while divorce is never a pleasant experience, divorce mediation can save a couple time and money, help them keep a civil relationship, and produce an agreement that they both feel is

Brackets indicate that the words inside them were supplied by the student and did not appear in the original source.

The conclusion provides a summary and restates the thesis.

Hughes 8

reasonable. According to the Academy of Family Mediators, 70 to 90 percent of couples are satisfied with the terms of their mediated divorces (Lundstrum 228). This high figure shows that mediation is a more civilized and respectful way to achieve a divorce than the traditional courtroom method.

A mediating couple, Sam and Jane, said it best:

> [Sam said,] "I really do appreciate your help. This was a lot easier than I thought it would be."
>
> Jane smiled. "We both thought we were going to end up in a huge fight. Doing it this way was so much better." (Qtd. in James xi)

Works cited should be double-spaced. Titles of books, magazines, and the like should be underlined.

Include the date you accessed a Web source—in this case, February 18, 2000.

Works Cited

"Avoiding the War." Divorce Mediation Services. 18 Feb. 2000

<http://www.divorcewithoutwar.com/avoiding.htm>.

Butler, Carol A., and Dolores D. Walker. <u>The Divorce Mediation</u>

<u>Answer Book</u>. New York: Kodansha America, 1999.

<u>The Divorce Law Information Center Home Page</u>. The Divorce Law

Information Center. 18 Feb. 2000

<http://www.divorcelawinfo.com/mediation/intromed.htm>.

Field, Ann. "Divorce Mediation and Other (Cheap) Ways to Split."

<u>Cosmopolitan</u> Aug. 1995: 136–37.

Friedman, Gary J. <u>A Guide to Divorce Mediation</u>. New York: Workman,

1993.

James, Paula. <u>The Divorce Mediation Handbook</u>. San Francisco: Jossey-

Bass, 1997.

Lundstrom, Meg. "A Way to 'Take the War' Out of Divorce." <u>Business</u>

<u>Week</u> 16 Nov. 1998: 228.

"Mediation: How It Works." <u>Divorce Solutions Home Page</u>. Mar. 1999.

18 Feb. 2000 <http://www.divorcesolutions.com/mediation.html>.

Schuetz, Lisa. "Mediation Offers an Alternative When Dealing with

Divorce." <u>Wisconsin State Journal</u> 31 May 1998: 10.

Valente, Judith. "A Kinder, Gentler Divorce?" <u>USA Today</u> 25 Aug.

1997: B7.

Three of the above sources (*The Divorce Law Information Center Home Page* and the articles "Avoiding the War" and "Mediation: How It Works") are online. By going online and typing the letters after *www.* in each citation, you can access any of the sources. For example, you could type *divorcewithoutwar.com/avoiding.htm* to call up the first online article cited.

Part Five

Handbook of Sentence Skills

PREVIEW

As explained in Part One, there are four steps, or bases, in effective writing. Part Five is concerned with the fourth step: the ability to write clear, error-free sentences. First a diagnostic test is provided so that you can check your present understanding of important sentence skills. Then the skills themselves appear under the general headings "Grammar," "Mechanics," "Punctuation," and "Word Use." Next come mastery tests and then editing tests that reinforce many basic writing skills and give you practice in editing and proofreading. Closing out Part Five are an achievement test that helps you measure your improvement in important sentence skills and a chapter that presents pointers and brief activities for ESL students.

Sentence-Skills Diagnostic Test

Part 1

This test will help you check your knowledge of important sentence skills. Certain parts of the following word groups are underlined. Write X in the answer space if you think a mistake appears at the underlined part. Write C in the answer space if you think the underlined part is correct.

A series of headings ("Fragments," "Run-Ons," and so on) will give you clues to the mistakes to look for. However, you do not have to understand the label to find a mistake. What you are checking is your own sense of effective written English.

Fragments

_____ 1. Until his mother called him twice. Barry did not get out of bed. He had stayed up too late the night before.

_____ 2. After I slid my aching bones into the hot water of the tub, I realized there was no soap. I didn't want to get out again.

_____ 3. I spent two hours on the phone yesterday. Trying to find a garage to repair my car. Eventually I had to have the car towed to a garage in another town.

_____ 4. Sweating under his heavy load. Brian staggered up the stairs to his apartment. He felt as though his legs were crumbling beneath him.

_____ 5. I love to eat and cook Italian food, especially lasagna and ravioli. I make everything from scratch.

_____ 6. One of my greatest joys in life is eating desserts. Such as blueberry cheese-cake and vanilla cream puffs. Almond fudge cake makes me want to dance.

Run-Ons

_____ 7. He decided to stop smoking, for he didn't want to die of lung cancer.

_____ 8. The window shade snapped up like a gunshot her cat leaped four feet off the floor.

_____ 9. Billy is the meanest little kid on his block, he eats only the heads of animal crackers.

_____ 10. He knew he had flunked the driver's exam, he ran over a stop sign.

_____ 11. My first boyfriend was five years <u>old. We</u> met every day in the playground sandbox.

_____ 12. The store owner watched the shopper <u>carefully, she</u> suspected him of stealing from her before.

Standard English Verbs

_____ 13. Jed <u>tows</u> cars away for a living and is ashamed of his job.

_____ 14. You <u>snored</u> like a chain saw last night.

_____ 15. When I was about to finish work last night, a man <u>walk</u> into the restaurant and ordered two dozen hamburgers.

_____ 16. Charlotte <u>react</u> badly whenever she gets caught in a traffic jam.

Irregular Verbs

_____ 17. I <u>gived</u> a twenty-dollar bill to the cashier and waited for my change.

_____ 18. I had <u>eaten</u> so much food at the buffet dinner that I went into the bathroom just to loosen my belt.

_____ 19. When the mud slide started, the whole neighborhood <u>began</u> going downhill.

_____ 20. Juan has <u>rode</u> the bus to school for two years while saving for a car.

Subject-Verb Agreement

_____ 21. There <u>is</u> long lines at the checkout counter.

_____ 22. The little girl <u>have</u> a painful ear infection.

_____ 23. One of the crooked politicians <u>was</u> jailed for a month.

_____ 24. The cockroaches behind my stove <u>gets</u> high on Raid.

Consistent Verb Tense

_____ 25. My brother and I played video games for an hour before we <u>start</u> to do homework.

_____ 26. The first thing Jerry does every day is weigh himself. The scale <u>informs</u> him what kind of meals he can eat that day.

_____ 27. Sandy eats a nutritional breakfast, <u>skips</u> lunch, and then enjoys a big dinner.

_____ 28. His parents stayed together for his sake; only after he <u>graduates</u> from college were they divorced.

Pronoun Agreement, Reference, and Point of View

_____ 29. I get my hair cut by a barber who talks to <u>you</u> constantly.

_____ 30. I enjoy movies like _The Return of the Vampire_ that frighten <u>me</u>.

_____ 31. Every guest at the party dressed like <u>their</u> favorite cartoon character.

_____ 32. Persons camping in those woods should watch <u>their</u> step because of wild dogs.

_____ 33. Angry because he had struck out, Tony hurled the baseball bat at the fence and broke <u>it</u>.

_____ 34. I love Parmesan cheese, but <u>it</u> does not always agree with me.

Pronoun Types

_____ 35. Alfonso and <u>me</u> take turns driving to work.

_____ 36. No one is a better cook than <u>she</u>.

Adjectives and Adverbs

_____ 37. Bonnie ran <u>quick</u> up the steps, taking them two at a time.

_____ 38. Larry is <u>more better</u> than I am at darts.

Misplaced Modifiers

_____ 39. He swatted the wasp that stung him <u>with a newspaper</u>.

_____ 40. Charlotte returned the hamburger <u>that was spoiled</u> to the supermarket.

_____ 41. Jamal test-drove a car at the dealership <u>with power windows and a sunroof</u>.

_____ 42. I adopted a dog from a junkyard <u>which is very close to my heart</u>.

Dangling Modifiers

_____ 43. <u>Tapping a pencil on the table</u>, Ms. Garcia asked for the students' attention.

_____ 44. <u>Flunking out of school</u>, my parents demanded that I get a job.

_____ 45. <u>While I was waiting for the bus</u>, rain began to fall.

_____ 46. <u>Braking the car suddenly</u>, the shopping bags tumbled onto the floor.

Faulty Parallelism

_____ 47. Jeff enjoys hunting for rabbits, socializing with friends, and <u>to read the comics</u>.

_____ 48. The recipe instructed me to chop onions, to peel carrots, and <u>to boil a pot of water</u>.

_____ 49. When I saw my roommate with my girlfriend, I felt worried, angry, and <u>embarrassment as well</u>.

_____ 50. Frances enjoys shopping for new clothes, <u>trying different cosmetics</u>, and reading beauty magazines.

Capital Letters

_____ 51. Sitting in the hot, stuffy classroom, I couldn't stop thinking about a cold pepsi.

_____ 52. During july, Frank's company works a four-day week.

_____ 53. A woman screamed, "He's stolen my purse!"

_____ 54. On Summer days I like to sit in the backyard and sunbathe.

Apostrophe

_____ 55. The Wolfman's bite is worse than his bark.

_____ 56. Clydes quick hands reached out to break his son's fall.

_____ 57. I'll be with you shortly if youll just wait a minute.

_____ 58. We didn't leave the rude waiter any tip.

Quotation Marks

_____ 59. Mark Twain once said, "The more I know about human beings, the more I like my dog."

_____ 60. Say something tender to me, "whispered Tony to Lola."

_____ 61. "I hate that commercial, he muttered."

_____ 62. "If you don't leave soon," he warned, "you'll be late for work."

Comma

_____ 63. My favorite sandwich includes turkey tomatoes lettuce and mayonnaise on whole-wheat bread.

_____ 64. Although I have a black belt in karate I decided to go easy on the demented bully who had kicked sand in my face.

_____ 65. All the tree branches, which were covered with ice, glittered like diamonds.

_____ 66. We could always tell when our instructor felt disorganized for his shirt would not be tucked into his pants.

_____ 67. You, my man, are going to get yours.

_____ 68. His father shouted "Why don't you go out and get a job?"

Commonly Confused Words

_____ 69. Some stores will accept your credit cards but not you're money.

_____ 70. Since he's lost weight, most of Max's clothes are to big for him.

_____ 71. They're planning to trade in their old car.

_____ 72. Its important to get this job done properly.

_____ 73. Will you <u>except</u> this job if it's offered to you, or keep looking for something better?

_____ 74. <u>Who's</u> the culprit who left the paint can on the table?

Effective Word Choice

_____ 75. Because the school was flooded, the dance had to be <u>postponed until a later date</u>.

_____ 76. The movie was a <u>real bomb</u>, so we left early.

_____ 77. The victims of the car accident were shaken but <u>none the worse for wear</u>.

_____ 78. Anne is <u>of the opinion that</u> the death penalty should be abolished.

Answers are on page 629.

Part 2 (Optional)

Do Part 2 at your instructor's request. This second part of the test will provide more detailed information about skills you need to know. On separate paper, number and correct all the items you have marked with an X. For example, suppose you had marked the following word groups with an X. (Note that these examples are not taken from the test.)

4. <u>If football games disappeared entirely from television</u>. I would not even miss them. Other people in my family would perish.

7. The kitten suddenly saw her reflection in the <u>mirror, she</u> jumped back in surprise.

15. I wanted to get close enough to see the tag on the stray <u>dogs</u> collar.

29. When we go out to a <u>restaurant we</u> always order something we would not cook for ourselves.

Here is how you should write your corrections on a separate sheet of paper.

4. television, I

7. mirror, and

15. dog's

29. restaurant, we

There are over forty corrections to make in all.

26 Subjects and Verbs

The basic building blocks of English sentences are subjects and verbs. Understanding them is an important first step toward mastering a number of sentence skills.

Every sentence has a subject and a verb. Who or what the sentence speaks about is called the <u>subject</u>; what the sentence says about the subject is called the <u>verb</u>.

> The children laughed.
> Several branches fell.
> Most students passed the test.
> That man is a crook.

A Simple Way to Find a Subject

To find a subject, ask *who* or *what* the sentence is about. As shown below, your answer is the subject.

> *Who* is the first sentence about? Children
> *What* is the second sentence about? Several branches
> *Who* is the third sentence about? Most students
> *Who* is the fourth sentence about? That man

A Simple Way to Find a Verb

To find a verb, ask what the sentence *says about* the subject. As shown below, your answer is the verb.

> What does the first sentence *say about* the children? They laughed.
> What does the second sentence *say about* the branches? They fell.
> What does the third sentence *say about* the students? They passed.
> What does the fourth sentence *say about* that man? He is (a crook).

A second way to find the verb is to put *I, you, we, he, she, it,* or *they* (whichever form is appropriate) in front of the word you think is a verb. If the result makes sense, you have a verb. For example, you could put *they* in front of *laughed* in the first sentence above, with the result, *they laughed,* making sense. Therefore you know that *laughed* is a verb. You could use *they* or *he,* for instance, to test the other verbs as well.

Finally, it helps to remember that most verbs show action. In the sentences already considered, the three action verbs are *laughed, fell,* and *passed.* Certain other verbs, known as *linking verbs,* do not show action. They do, however, give information about the subject. In "That man is a crook," the linking verb *is* tells us that the man is a crook. Other common linking verbs include *am, are, was, were, feel, appear, look, become,* and *seem.*

Activity

In each of the following sentences, draw one line under the subject and two lines under the verb.

1. A sudden thunderstorm ended the baseball game.
2. Small stones pinged onto the windshield.
3. The test directions confused the students.
4. Cotton shirts feel softer than polyester ones.
5. The fog rolled into the cemetery.
6. Yoko invited her friends to dinner.
7. A green fly stung her on the ankle.
8. Every other night, garbage trucks rumble down my street on their way to the river.
9. The elderly man sat for a few minutes on the park bench.
10. With their fingers, the children drew pictures on the steamed window.

More about Subjects and Verbs

1 A pronoun (a word like *he, she, it, we, you,* or *they* used in place of a noun) can serve as the subject of a sentence. For example:

He seems like a lonely person.

They both like to gamble.

Without a surrounding context (so that we know who *He* or *They* refers to), such sentences may not seem clear, but they *are* complete.

2 A sentence may have more than one verb, more than one subject, or several subjects and verbs:

My heart skipped and pounded.
The radio and tape player were stolen from the car.
Dave and Ellen prepared the report together and presented it to the class.

3 The subject of a sentence never appears within a prepositional phrase. A *prepositional phrase* is simply a group of words that begins with a preposition. Following is a list of common prepositions:

about	before	by	inside	over
above	behind	during	into	through
across	below	except	of	to
among	beneath	for	off	toward
around	beside	from	on	under
at	between	in	onto	with

Cross out prepositional phrases when you are looking for the subject of a sentence.

~~Under my pillow~~ I found a quarter left by the tooth fairy.
One ~~of the yellow lights at the school crossing~~ began flashing.
The comics pages ~~of the newspaper~~ have disappeared.
~~In spite of my efforts,~~ Bob dropped out of school.
~~During a rainstorm,~~ I sat in my car reading magazines.

4 Many verbs consist of more than one word. Here, for example, are some of the many forms of the verb *smile*.

smile	smiled	should smile
smiles	were smiling	will be smiling
does smile	have smiled	can smile
is smiling	had smiled	could be smiling
are smiling	had been smiling	must have smiled

Notes

a Words like *not, just, never, only,* and *always* are not part of the verb, although they may appear within the verb.

Larry did not finish the paper before class.

The road was just completed last week.

b No verb preceded by *to* is ever the verb of a sentence.

My car suddenly began to sputter on the freeway.

I swerved to avoid a squirrel on the road.

c No -*ing* word by itself is ever the verb of a sentence. (It may be part of the verb, but it must have a helping verb in front of it.)

They leaving early for the game. (not a sentence, because the verb is not complete)

They are leaving early for the game. (a sentence)

Activity

Draw a single line under the subjects and a double line under the verbs in the following sentences. Be sure to include all parts of the verb.

1. A burning odor from the wood saw filled the room.
2. At first, sticks of gum always feel powdery on your tongue.
3. Vampires and werewolves are repelled by garlic.
4. Three people in the long bank line looked impatiently at their watches.
5. The driving rain had pasted wet leaves all over the car.
6. She has decided to buy a condominium.
7. The trees in the mall were glittering with tiny white lights.
8. The puppies slipped and tumbled on the vinyl kitchen floor.
9. Tony and Lola ate at Pizza Hut and then went to a movie.
10. We have not met our new neighbors in the apartment building.

■ Review Test

Draw a single line under subjects and a double line under verbs. Crossing out prepositional phrases may help to find the subjects.

1. A cloud of fruit flies hovered over the bananas.
2. Candle wax dripped onto the table and hardened into pools.
3. Nick and Fran are both excellent Frisbee players.
4. The leaves of my dying rubber plant resembled limp brown rags.
5. During the first week of vacation, Ken slept until noon every day.
6. They have just decided to go on a diet together.
7. Psychology and word processing are my favorite subjects.
8. The sofa in the living room has not been cleaned for over a year.
9. The water stains on her suede shoes did not disappear with brushing.
10. Fred stayed in bed too long and, as a result, arrived late for work.

27 Sentence Sense

What Is Sentence Sense?

As a speaker of English, you already possess the most important of all sentence skills. You have *sentence sense*—an instinctive feel for where a sentence begins, where it ends, and how it can be developed. You learned sentence sense automatically and naturally, as part of learning the English language, and you have practiced it through all the years that you have been speaking English. It is as much a part of you as your ability to speak and understand English is a part of you.

Sentence sense can help you recognize and avoid fragments and run-ons, two of the most common and most serious sentence-skills mistakes in written English. Sentence sense will also help you to place commas, spot awkward and unclear phrasing, and add variety to your sentences.

You may ask, "If I already have this 'sentence sense,' why do I still make mistakes in punctuating sentences?" One answer could be that your past school experiences in writing were unrewarding or unpleasant. English courses may have been a series of dry writing topics and heavy doses of "correct" grammar and usage, or they may have given no attention at all to sentence skills. For any of these reasons, or perhaps for other reasons, the instinctive sentence skills you practice while *speaking* may turn off when you start *writing*. The very act of picking up a pen may shut down your natural system of language abilities and skills.

Turning On Your Sentence Sense

Chances are that you don't *read a paper aloud* after you write it, or you don't do the next best thing: read it "aloud" in your head. But reading aloud is essential to turn on the natural language system within you. By reading aloud, you will be able to hear the points where your sentences begin and end. In addition, you will be able to pick up any trouble spots where your thoughts are not communicated clearly and well.

The activities that follow will help you turn on and rediscover the enormous language power within you. You will be able to see how your built-in sentence sense can guide your writing just as it guides your speaking.

Activity

Each item that follows lacks basic punctuation. There is no period to mark the end of one sentence and no capital letter to mark the start of the next. Read each item aloud (or in your head) so that you "hear" where each sentence begins and ends. Your voice will tend to drop and pause at the point of each sentence break. Draw a light slash mark (/) at every point where you hear a break. Then go back and read the item a second time. If you are now sure of each place where a split occurs, insert a period and change the first small letter after it to a capital. Minor pauses are often marked in English by commas; these are already inserted. Part of item 1 is done for you as an example.

1. I take my dog for a walk on Saturdays in the big park, by the lake/I do this very early in the morning before children come to the park that way I can let my dog run freely he jumps out the minute I open the car door and soon sees the first innocent squirrel, then he is off like a shot and doesn't stop running for a least half an hour.

2. Lola hates huge tractor trailers that sometimes tailgate her Honda Civic, the enormous smoke-belching machines seem ready to swallow her small car, she shakes her fist at the drivers, and she rips out a lot of angry words, recently she had a very satisfying dream, she broke into an army supply depot and stole a bazooka she then became the first person in history to murder a truck.

3. When I sit down to write, my mind is blank, all I can think of is my name, which seems to me the most boring name in the world, often I get sleepy and tell myself I should take a short nap, other times I start daydreaming about things I want to buy, sometimes I decide I should make a telephone call to someone I know the piece of paper in front of me is usually still blank when I leave to watch my favorite television show.

4. One of the biggest regrets of my life is that I never told my father I loved him. I resented the fact that he had never been able to say the words "I love you" to his children even during the long period of my father's illness, I remained silent and unforgiving then one morning he was dead, with my words left unspoken a guilt I shall never forget tore a hole in my heart I determined not

to hold in my feelings with my daughters they know they are loved, because I both show and tell them this all people, no matter who they are, want to be told that they are loved.

5. Two days ago, Greg killed seven flying ants in his bedroom he also sprayed a column of ants forming a colony along the kitchen baseboard yesterday he picked the evening newspaper off the porch and two black army ants scurried onto his hand this morning, he found an ant crawling on a lollipop he had left in his shirt pocket if any more insects appear, he is going to call Orkin Pest Control he feels like the victim in a Hitchcock movie called *The Ants* he is half afraid to sleep the darkness may be full of tiny squirming things waiting to crawl all over him.

Summary: Using Sentence Sense

You probably did well in locating the end stops in these selections—proving to yourself that you *do* have sentence sense. This instinctive sense will help you deal with fragments and run-ons, perhaps the two most common sentence-skills mistakes.

Remember the importance of *reading your paper aloud.* By reading aloud, you turn on the natural language skills that come from all your experience of speaking English. The same sentence sense that helps you communicate effectively in speaking will help you communicate effectively in writing.

28 Fragments

Introductory Project

Every sentence must have a subject and a verb and must express a complete thought. A word group that lacks a subject or a verb and that does not express a complete thought is a fragment. Underline the statement in each numbered item that you think is *not* a complete sentence.

1. Because I could not sleep. I turned on my light and read.
2. Calling his dog's name. Todd walked up and down the street.
3. My little sister will eat anything. Except meat, vegetables, and fruit.
4. The reporter turned on her laptop computer. Then began to type quickly.

Understanding the answers: Read and complete each explanation.

1. *Because I could not sleep* is not a complete sentence. The writer does not complete the _____ by telling us what happened because he could not sleep. Correct the fragment by joining it to the sentence that follows it:

   Because I could not sleep, I turned on my light and read.

2. *Calling his dog's name* is not a complete sentence. This word group has no _____ and no verb, and it does not express a complete thought. Correct the fragment by adding it to the sentence that follows it:

   Calling his dog's name, Todd walked up and down the street.

3. *Except meat, vegetables, and fruit* is not a complete sentence. Again, the word group has no subject and no _____, and it does not express a complete thought. Correct the fragment by adding it to the sentence that comes before it:

   My little sister will eat anything except meat, vegetables, and fruit.

4. *Then began to type quickly* is not a complete sentence. This word group has no _____. One way to correct the fragment is to add the subject *she:*

   Then she began to type quickly.

Answers are on page 630.

What Are Fragments?

Every sentence must have a subject and a verb and must express a complete thought. A word group that lacks a subject or a verb and does not express a complete thought is a *fragment*. The most common types of fragments are:

1   Dependent-word fragments
2   *-ing* and *to* fragments
3   Added-detail fragments
4   Missing-subject fragments

Once you understand what specific kinds of fragments you write, you should be able to eliminate them from your writing. The following pages explain all four types of fragments.

Dependent-Word Fragments

Some word groups that begin with a dependent word are fragments. Here is a list of common dependent words:

Dependent Words		
after	if, even if	when, whenever
although, though	in order that	where, wherever
as	since	whether
because	that, so that	which, whichever
before	unless	while
even though	until	who, whoever
how	what, whatever	whose

Whenever you start a sentence with one of these words, you must be careful that a fragment does not result.

The word group beginning with the dependent word *After* in the example below is a fragment.

After I learned the price of new cars. I decided to keep my old Buick.

A *dependent statement*—one starting with a dependent word like *After*—cannot stand alone. It depends on another statement to complete the thought. "After I learned the price of new cars" is a dependent statement. It leaves us hanging. We expect to find out—in the same sentence—*what happened after* the writer learned the price of new cars. When a writer does not follow through and complete a thought, a fragment results.

To correct the fragment, simply follow through and complete the thought:

After I learned the price of new cars, I decided to keep my old Buick.

Remember, then, that *dependent statements by themselves are fragments*. They must be attached to a statement that makes sense standing alone.

Here are two other examples of dependent-word fragments:

My daughter refused to stop smoking. Unless I quit also.

Tommy made an appointment. Which he did not intend to keep.

"Unless I quit also" is a fragment; it does not make sense standing by itself. We want to know—in the same statement—*what would not happen unless* the writer quit also. The writer must complete the thought. Likewise, "Which he did not intend to keep" is not in itself a complete thought. We want to know in the same statement what *which* refers to.

Correcting a Dependent-Word Fragment

In most cases you can correct a dependent-word fragment by attaching it to the sentence that comes after it or the sentence that comes before it:

After I learned the price of new cars, I decided to keep my old Buick.
(*The fragment has been attached to the sentence that comes after it.*)
My daughter refused to quit smoking unless I quit also.
(*The fragment has been attached to the sentence that comes before it.*)
Tommy made an appointment which he did not intend to keep.
(*The fragment has been attached to the sentence that comes before it.*)

Another way of connecting a dependent-word fragment is simply to eliminate the dependent word by rewriting the sentence:

I learned the price of new cars and decided to keep my old Buick.

She wanted me to quit also.

He did not intend to keep it.

Do not use this method of correction too frequently, however, for it may cut down on interest and variety in your writing style.

Notes

1   Use a comma if a dependent-word group comes at the beginning of a sentence (see also page 537):

After I learned the price of new cars, I decided to keep my old Buick.

However, do not generally use a comma if the dependent-word group comes at the end of a sentence:

My daughter refused to stop smoking unless I quit also.

Tommy made an appointment which he did not intend to keep.

2   Sometimes the dependent words *who, that, which,* or *where* appear not at the very start, but near the start, of a word group. A fragment often results:

The town council decided to put more lights on South Street. <u>A place where several people have been mugged.</u>

"A place where several people have been mugged" is not in itself a complete thought. We want to know in the same statement *where the place was* that several people were mugged. The fragment can be corrected by attaching it to the sentence that comes before it:

The town council decided to put more lights on South Street, a place where several people have been mugged.

Activity 1

Turn each of the following dependent-word groups into a sentence by adding a complete thought. Put a comma after the dependent-word group if a dependent word starts the sentence.

Examples   Although I arrived in class late

> *Although I arrived in class late, I still did well on the test.*

The little boy who plays with our daughter

> *The little boy who plays with our daughter just came down with German measles.*

1. Because the weather is bad

2. If I lend you twenty dollars

_____

_____

3. The car that we bought

_____

_____

4. Since I was tired

_____

_____

5. Before the instructor entered the room

_____

_____

Activity 2

Underline the dependent-word fragment or fragments in each item. Then correct each fragment by attaching it to the sentence that comes before or the sentence that comes after—whichever sounds more natural. Put a comma after the dependent-word group if it starts the sentence.

1. When my neighbor and I both use our cordless telephones. We hear one another's conversations. One of us needs to get a different phone.

_____

_____

_____

2. Bill always turns on the radio in the morning to hear the news. He wants to be sure that World War III has not started. Before he gets on with his day.

_____

_____

_____

3. Although Mr. Simon is over eighty years old. He walks briskly to work every day. He seems like a much younger man. Since he is so active and involved in life.

_____

_____

_____

4. My dog ran in joyous circles on the wide beach. Until she found a dead fish. Before I had a chance to drag her away. She began sniffing and nudging the smelly remains.

    _____

    _____

    _____

5. When the air conditioner broke down. The temperature was over ninety degrees. I then found an old fan. Which turned out to be broken also.

    _____

    _____

    _____

-ing and *to* Fragments

When an *-ing* word appears at or near the start of a word group, a fragment may result. Such fragments often lack a subject and part of the verb. Underline the word groups in the examples below that contain *-ing* words. Each is a fragment.

Example 1

I spent almost two hours on the phone yesterday. Trying to find a garage to repair my car. Eventually I had to have it towed to a garage in another town.

Example 2

Maggie was at first very happy with the blue sports car she had bought for only five hundred dollars. Not realizing until a week later that the car averaged seven miles per gallon of gas.

Example 3

He looked forward to the study period at school. It being the only time he could sit unbothered and dream about his future. He imagined himself as a lawyer with lots of money and women to spend it on.

People sometimes write *-ing* fragments because they think the subject in one sentence will work for the next word group as well. Thus, in the first example, the writer thinks that the subject *I* in the opening sentence will also serve as the subject for "Trying to find a garage to repair my car." But the subject must actually be *in* the sentence.

Correcting *-ing* Fragments

1 Attach the *-ing* fragment to the sentence that comes before it or the sentence that comes after it, whichever makes sense. Example 1 could read: "I spent almost two hours on the phone yesterday, trying to find a garage to repair my car."

2 Add a subject and change the *-ing* verb part to the correct form of the verb. Example 2 could read: "She did not realize until a week later that the car averaged seven miles per gallon of gas."

3 Change *being* to the correct form of the verb *be (am, are, is, was, were)*. Example 3 could read: "It was the only time he could sit unbothered and dream about his future."

Correcting *to* Fragments

When *to* appears at or near the start of a word group, a fragment sometimes results:

> I plan on working overtime. To get this job finished. Otherwise, my boss may get angry at me.

The second word group is a fragment and can be corrected by adding it to the preceding sentence:

> I plan on working overtime to get this job finished.

Activity 1

Underline the *-ing* fragment in each of the items that follow. Then make it a sentence by rewriting it, using the method described in parentheses.

Example   A thunderstorm was brewing. A sudden breeze shot through the windows.
<u>Driving the stuffiness out of the room.</u>
(Add the fragment to the preceding sentence.)

A sudden breeze shot through the windows, driving the stuffiness out of the room.

(In the example, a comma is used to set off "driving the stuffiness out of the room," which is extra material placed at the end of the sentence.)

1. Sweating under his heavy load. Brian staggered up the stairs to his apartment. He felt as though his legs were crumbling beneath him.
   (Add the fragment to the sentence that comes after it.)

   _____

   _____

2. He works 10 hours a day. Then going to class for 2½ hours. It is no wonder he writes fragments.
   (Connect the fragment by adding the subject *he* and changing *going* to the proper form of the verb, *goes.*)

   _____

   _____

3. Charlotte loved the movie *Gone with the Wind,* but Clyde hated it. His chief objection being that it lasted four hours.
   (Correct the fragment by changing *being* to the proper verb form, *was.*)

   _____

   _____

Activity 2

Underline the *-ing* or *to* fragment or fragments in each item. Then rewrite each item, using one of the methods of correction described on pages 424–425.

1. A mysterious package arrived on my porch yesterday. Bearing no return address. I half expected to find a bomb inside.

   _____

   _____

   _____

2. Jack bundled up and went outside on the bitterly cold day. To saw wood for his fireplace. He returned half frozen with only two logs.

   _____

   _____

   _____

3. Looking tired and drawn. The little girl's parents sat in the waiting room. The operation would be over in a few minutes.

   _____

   _____

   _____

4. Sighing with resignation. Jill switched on her television set. She knew that the picture would be snowy and crackling with static. Her house being in a weak reception area.

_____

_____

_____

5. Jabbing the ice with a screwdriver. Luis attempted to speed up the defrosting process in his freezer. However, he used too much force. The result being a freezer compartment riddled with holes.

_____

_____

_____

Added-Detail Fragments

Added-detail fragments lack a subject and a verb. They often begin with one of the following words:

also	except	including
especially	for example	such as

See if you can locate and underline the one added-detail fragment in each of the examples that follow:

Example 1

I love to cook and eat Italian food. <u>Especially spaghetti and lasagna.</u> I make everything from scratch.

Example 2

The class often starts late. <u>For example, yesterday at a quarter after nine instead of at nine sharp.</u> Today the class started at five after nine.

Example 3

He failed a number of courses before he earned his degree. <u>Among them, English I, Economics, and General Biology.</u>

People often write added-detail fragments for much the same reason they write *-ing* fragments. They think the subject and verb in one sentence will serve for the next word group as well. But the subject and verb must be in *each* word group.

Correcting Added-Detail Fragments

1   Attach the fragment to the complete thought that precedes it. Example 1 could read: "I love to cook and eat Italian food, especially spaghetti and lasagna."

2   Add a subject and a verb to the fragment to make it a complete sentence. Example 2 could read: "The class often starts late. For example, yesterday it began at a quarter after nine instead of at nine sharp."

3   Change words as necessary to make the fragment part of the preceding sentence. Example 3 could read: "Among the courses he failed before he earned his degree were English I, Economics, and General Biology."

Activity 1

Underline the fragment in each of the items below. Then make it a sentence by rewriting it, using the method described in parentheses.

Example   I am always short of pocket money. Especially for everyday items like magazines and sodas. Luckily my friends often have change.
(Add the fragment to the preceding sentence.)

I am always short of pocket money, especially for everyday items

like magazines and sodas.

1. There are many little things wrong with this apartment. For example, defective lights and leaking faucets. The landlord is not good about making repairs.
(Correct the fragment by adding the subject and verb *it has.*)

_____

_____

2. I could feel Bill's anger building. Like a land mine ready to explode. I was silent because I didn't want to be the one to set it off.
(Add the fragment to the preceding sentence.)

_____

_____

3. We went on vacation without several essential items. Among other things, our sneakers and sweat jackets.
(Correct the fragment by adding the subject and verb *we forgot.*)

_____

_____

Activity 2

Underline the added-detail fragment in each item. Then rewrite that part of the item needed to correct the fragment. Use one of the three methods of correction described above.

1. It's always hard for me to get up for work. Especially on Mondays after a holiday weekend. However, I always wake up early on free days.

_____

_____

_____

2. Tony has enormous endurance. For example, the ability to run five miles in the morning and then play basketball all afternoon.

_____

_____

_____

3. A counselor gives you a chance to talk about your problems. With your family or the boss at work. You learn how to cope better with life.

_____

_____

_____

4. Fred and Martha do most of their shopping through mail-order catalogs. Especially the J. C. Penney catalog.

_____

_____

_____

5. One of my greatest joys in life is eating desserts. Such as cherry cheesecake and vanilla cream puffs. Almond fudge cake makes me want to dance.

_____

_____

_____

Missing-Subject Fragments

In each example below, underline the word group in which the subject is missing.

Example 1

The truck skidded on the rain-slick highway. <u>But missed a telephone pole on the side of the road.</u>

Example 2

Michelle tried each of the appetizers on the table. <u>And then found that, when the dinner arrived, her appetite was gone.</u>

People write missing-subject fragments because they think the subject in one sentence will apply to the next word group as well. But the subject, as well as the verb, must be in *each* word group to make it a sentence.

Correcting Missing-Subject Fragments

1 Attach the fragment to the preceding sentence. Example 1 could read: "The truck skidded on the rain-slick highway but missed a telephone pole on the side of the road."

2 Add a subject (which can often be a pronoun standing for the subject in the preceding sentence). Example 2 could read: "She then found that, when the dinner arrived, her appetite was gone."

Activity

Underline the missing-subject fragment in each item. Then rewrite that part of the item needed to correct the fragment. Use one of the two methods of correction described above.

1. I tried on an old suit hanging in our basement closet. And discovered, to my surprise, that it was too tight to button.

   _____

   _____

   _____

2. When Mary had a sore throat, friends told her to gargle with salt water. Or suck on an ice cube. The worst advice she got was to avoid swallowing.

_____

_____

_____

3. One of my grade-school teachers embarrassed us with her sarcasm. Also, seated us in rows from the brightest student to the dumbest. I can imagine the pain the student in the last seat must have felt.

_____

_____

_____

A Review: How to Check for Fragments

1 Read your paper aloud from the *last* sentence to the *first.* You will be better able to see and hear whether each word group you read is a complete thought.

2 If you think a word group is a fragment, ask yourself: Does this contain a subject and a verb and express a complete thought?

3 More specifically, be on the lookout for the most common fragments:
   - Dependent-word fragments (starting with words like *after, because, since, when,* and *before)*
   - *-ing* and *to* fragments (*-ing* or *to* at or near the start of a word group)
   - Added-detail fragments (starting with words like *for example, such as, also,* and *especially)*
   - Missing-subject fragments (a verb is present but not the subject)

■   Review Test 1

Turn each of the following word groups into a complete sentence. Use the spaces provided.

Example   With sweaty palms
            With sweaty palms, I walked in for the job interview.
            _____

            Even when it rains
            The football teams practice even when it rains.
            _____

1. When the alarm sounded

   _____

   _____

2. In order to save some money

   _____

   _____

3. Were having a party

   _____

   _____

4. To pass the course

   _____

   _____

5. Geraldo, who is very impatient

   _____

   _____

6. During the holiday season

   _____

   _____

7. The store where I worked

   _____

   _____

8. Before the movie started

   _____

   _____

9. Down in the basement

   _____

   _____

10. Feeling very confident

   _____

   _____

■ Review Test 2

1. _____
2. _____
3. __✓__
4. _____
5. __✓__
6. _____
7. _____
8. __✓__
9. _____
10. __✓__
11. __✓__
12. _____
13. __✓__
14. _____
15. _____
16. __✓__
17. _____
18. __✓__
19. _____
20. _____

Each word group in the student paragraph below is numbered. In the space provided, write C if a word group is a *complete sentence;* write F if it is a *fragment.* You will find seven fragments in the paragraph.

A Disastrous First Date

¹My first date with Donna was a disaster. ²I decided to take her to a small Italian restaurant. ³That my friends told me had reasonable prices. ⁴I looked over the menu and realized I could not pronounce the names of the dishes. ⁵Such as "veal piccante" and "fettucini Alfredo." ⁶Then, I noticed a burning smell. ⁷The candle on the table was starting to blacken. ⁸And scorch the back of my menu. ⁹Trying to be casual, I quickly poured half my glass of water onto the menu. ¹⁰When the waiter returned to our table. ¹¹He asked me if I wanted to order some wine. ¹²I ordered a bottle of Blue Nun. ¹³The only wine that I had heard of and could pronounce. ¹⁴The waiter brought the wine, poured a small amount into my glass, and waited. ¹⁵I said, "You don't have to stand there. We can pour the wine ourselves." ¹⁶After the waiter put down the wine bottle and left. ¹⁷Donna told me I was supposed to taste the wine. ¹⁸Feeling like a complete fool. ¹⁹I managed to get through the dinner. ²⁰However, for weeks afterward, I felt like jumping out of a tenth-story window.

On separate paper, correct the fragments you have found. Attach each fragment to the sentence that comes before or after it, or make whatever other change is needed to turn the fragment into a sentence.

■ Review Test 3

Underline the two fragments in each item. Then rewrite the item in the space provided, making the changes needed to correct the fragments.

Example   The people at the diner save money. <u>By watering down the coffee. Also, using the cheapest grade of hamburger.</u> Few people go there anymore.

The people at the diner save money by watering down the coffee.

Also, they use the cheapest grade of hamburger. . . .

1. Gathering speed with enormous force, The plane was suddenly in the air. Then it began to climb sharply, And several minutes later leveled off.

_____

_____

_____

2. Before my neighbors went on vacation, They asked me to watch their house.
   I agreed to check the premises once a day, Also, to take in their mail.

   and also to

   _____

   _____

   _____

3. Running untouched into the end zone, The halfback raised his arms in triumph.
   Then he slammed the football to the ground, And did a little victory dance.

   and

   _____

   _____

   _____

4. It's hard to keep up with bills, Such as the telephone, gas, and electricity. After
   you finally mail the checks, New bills seem to arrive a day or two later.

   _____

   _____

   _____

5. While a woman ordered twenty pounds of cold cuts, Customers at the deli
   counter waited impatiently. The woman explained that she was in charge of
   a school picnic, And apologized for taking up so much time.

   and

   _____

   _____

   _____

■ Review Test 4

Write quickly for five minutes about what you like to do in your leisure time.
Don't worry about spelling, punctuation, finding exact words, or organizing your
thoughts. Just focus on writing as many words as you can without stopping.

   After you have finished, go back and make whatever changes are needed to
correct any fragments in your writing.

29 Run-Ons

Introductory Project

A run-on occurs when two sentences are run together with no adequate sign given to mark the break between them. Shown below are four run-ons and four correctly marked sentences. See if you can complete the statement that explains how each run-on is corrected.

1. He is the meanest little kid on his block he eats only the heads of animal crackers. *Run-on*

    He is the meanest little kid on his block. He eats only the heads of animal crackers. *Correct*

    The run-on has been corrected by using a _____ and a capital letter to separate the two complete thoughts.

2. Fred Grencher likes to gossip about other people, he doesn't like them to gossip about him. *Run-on*

    Fred Grencher likes to gossip about other people, but he doesn't like them to gossip about him. *Correct*

    The run-on has been corrected by using a joining word, comma splice, to connect the two complete thoughts.

3. The chain on my bike likes to chew up my pants, it leaves grease marks on my ankle as well. *Run-on*

    The chain on my bike likes to chew up my pants; it leaves grease marks on my ankles as well. *Correct*

    The run-on has been corrected by using a _____ to connect the two closely related thoughts.

4. The window shade snapped up like a gunshot, her cat leaped four feet off the floor. *Run-on*

    When the window shade snapped up like a gunshot, her cat leaped four feet off the floor. *Correct*

    The run-on has been corrected by using the subordinating word _____ to connect the two closely related thoughts.

Answers are on page 630.

What Are Run-Ons?

A *run-on* is two complete thoughts that are run together with no adequate sign given to mark the break between them.* Some run-ons have no punctuation at all to mark the break between the thoughts. Such run-ons are known as *fused sentences:* they are fused, or joined together, as if they were only one thought.

Fused Sentences

My grades are very good this semester my social life rates only a C.

Our father was a madman in his youth he would do anything on a dare.

In other run-ons, known as *comma splices,* a comma is used to connect, or "splice" together, the two complete thoughts. However, a comma alone is *not enough* to connect two complete thoughts. Some stronger connection than a comma alone is needed.

Comma Splices

My grades are very good this semester, my social life rates only a C.

Our father was a madman in his youth, he would do anything on a dare.

Comma splices are the most common kind of run-on. Students sense that some kind of connection is needed between two thoughts and so put a comma at the dividing point. But the comma alone is not sufficient: a stronger, clearer mark is needed between the two thoughts.

A Warning about Words That Can Lead to Run-Ons: People often write run-ons when the second complete thought begins with one of the following words:

I	we	there	now
you	they	this	then
he, she, it		that	next

Remember to be on the alert for run-ons whenever you use one of these words in writing a paper.

*Notes:
1 Some instructors feel that the term *run-ons* should be applied only to fused sentences, not to comma splices. But for many other instructors, and for our purposes in this book, the term *run-on* applies equally to fused sentences and comma splices. The bottom line is that you do not want either fused sentences or comma splices in your writing.
2 Some instructors refer to each complete thought in a run-on as an *independent clause. A clause* is simply a group of words having a subject and a verb. A clause may be *independent* (expressing a complete thought and able to stand alone) or *dependent* (not expressing a complete thought and not able to stand alone). A run-on is two independent clauses that are run together with no adequate sign given to mark the break between them.

Correcting Run-Ons

Here are four common methods of correcting a run-on:

1 Use a period and a capital letter to break the two complete thoughts into separate sentences.

My grades are very good this semester. My social life rates only a C.
Our father was a madman in his youth. He would do anything on a dare.

2 Use a comma plus a joining word (*and, but, for, or, nor, so, yet*) to connect the two complete thoughts.

My grades are very good this semester, but my social life rates only a C.
Our father was a madman in his youth, for he would do anything on a dare.

3 Use a semicolon to connect the two complete thoughts.

My grades are very good this semester; my social life rates only a C.
Our father was a madman in his youth; he would do anything on a dare.

4 Use subordination.

Although my grades are very good this semester, my social life rates only a C.
Because my father was a madman in his youth, he would do anything on a dare.

The following pages will give you practice in all four methods of correcting a run-on. The use of subordination is explained on pages 109–111.

Method 1: Period and a Capital Letter

One way of correcting a run-on is to use a period and a capital letter at the break between the two complete thoughts. Use this method especially if the thoughts are not closely related or if another method would make the sentence too long.

Activity 1

Locate the split in each of the following run-ons. Each is a *fused sentence*—that is, each consists of two sentences that are fused, or joined together, with no punctuation at all between them. Reading each fused sentence aloud will help you "hear" where a major break or split in the thought occurs. At such a point, your voice will probably drop and pause.

Correct the run-on by putting a period at the end of the first thought and a capital letter at the start of the next thought.

Example   Martha Grencher shuffled around the apartment in her slippers, _Hher husband couldn't stand their slapping sound on the floor.

1. A felt-tip pen is easy to ruin just leave, _{It}it lying around without its cap.

2. Phil cringed at the sound of the dentist's drill it buzzed like a fifty-pound mosquito.

3. Last summer no one swam in the lake, _Aa little boy had dropped his pet piranhas into the water.

4. A horse's teeth never stop growing. _{They}they will eventually grow outside the horse's mouth.

5. Sue's doctor told her he was an astrology nut. _{She}she did not feel good about learning that.

6. Ice water is the best remedy for a burn using. _{Butter}butter is like adding fat to a flame.

7. In the apartment the air was so dry that her skin felt parched the heat was up to eighty degrees.

8. My parents bought me an ant farm it's going to be hard to find tractors that small.

9. Lobsters are cannibalistic this is one reason they are hard to raise in captivity.

10. Julia placed an egg timer next to the phone she did not want to talk more than three minutes on her long-distance calls.

Activity 2

Locate the split in each of the following run-ons. Some of the run-ons are fused sentences, and some are *comma splices*—run-ons spliced, or joined together, with only a comma. Correct each run-on by putting a period at the end of the first thought and a capital letter at the start of the next thought.

1. A bird got into the house through the chimney. _{We}we had to catch it before our cat did.

2. Some so-called health foods are not so healthy, many are made with oils that raise cholesterol levels.

3. We sat only ten feet from the magician, ^we we still couldn't see where all the birds came from.

4. Jerome needs only five hours of sleep each night his wife needs at least seven.

5. Our image of dentistry will soon change dentists will use lasers instead of drills.

6. Gale entered her apartment and jumped with fright someone was leaving through her bedroom window.

7. There were several unusual hairstyles at the party one woman had bright green braids.

8. Todd saves all his magazines, once a month, he takes them to a nearby nursing home.

9. The doctor seemed to be in a rush, I still took time to ask all the questions that were on my mind.

10. When I was little, my brother tried to feed me flies, he told my they were raisins.

Activity 3

Write a second sentence to go with each of the sentences that follow. Start the second sentence with the word given in italics. Your sentences can be serious or playful.

Example *She* Jackie works for the phone company. _She climbs telephone poles in all kinds of weather._

It   1. The alarm clock is unreliable. _____

_____

He   2. My uncle has a peculiar habit. _____

_____

Then   3. Lola studied for the math test for two hours. _____

_____

It   4. I could not understand why the car would not start. _____

_____

There   5. We saw all kinds of litter on the highway. _____

_____

Method 2: Comma and a Joining Word

A second way of correcting a run-on is to use a comma plus a joining word to connect the two complete thoughts. Joining words (also called *conjunctions*) include *and, but, for, or, nor, so,* and *yet.* Here is what the four most common joining words mean:

and　in addition to, along with

His feet hurt from the long hike, and his stomach was growling.

(*And* means "in addition": His feet hurt from the long hike; *in addition,* his stomach was growling.)

but　however, except, on the other hand, just the opposite

I remembered to get the cocoa, but I forgot the marshmallows.

(*But* means "however": I remembered to get the cocoa; *however,* I forgot the marshmallows.)

for　because, the reason why, the cause of something

She was afraid of not doing well in the course, for she had always had bad luck with English before.

(*For* means "because" or "the reason why": She was afraid of not doing well in the course; *the reason why* was that she had always had bad luck with English before.)

Note:　If you are not comfortable using *for,* you may want to use *because* instead of *for* in the activities that follow. If you do use *because,* omit the comma before it.

so　as a result, therefore

The windshield wiper was broken, so she was in trouble when the rain started.

(*So* means "as a result": The windshield wiper was broken; *as a result,* she was in trouble when the rain started.)

Activity 1

Insert the joining word *(and, but, for, so)* that logically connects the two thoughts in each sentence.

1. The couple wanted desperately to buy the house, __but__ they did not qualify for a mortgage.

2. A lot of men today get their hair styled, __and__ they use perfume and other cosmetics as well.

3. Clyde asked his wife if she had any bandages, __for__ he had just sliced his finger with a paring knife.

4. The computer's mouse was not behaving correctly, __so__ Rita took it apart and cleaned it.

5. The restaurant was beautiful, __but__ the food was overpriced.

Activity 2

Add a complete and closely related thought to go with each of the following statements. Use a comma plus the italicized joining word when you write the second thought.

Example   *for*   Lola spent the day walking barefoot, *for the heel of one of her shoes had come off.*

but   1. She wanted to go to the party _____

_____

and   2. Tony washed his car in the morning _____

_____

so   3. The day was dark and rainy _____

_____

for   4. I'm not going to eat in the school cafeteria anymore _____

_____

but   5. I asked my brother to get off the telephone _____

_____

Method 3: Semicolon

A third method of correcting a run-on is to use a semicolon to mark the break between two thoughts. A *semicolon* (;) is made up of a period above a comma and is sometimes called a *strong comma*. The semicolon signals more of a pause than a comma alone but not quite the full pause of a period.

Semicolon Alone   Here are some earlier sentences that were connected with a comma plus a joining word. Notice that a semicolon alone, unlike a comma alone, can be used to connect the two complete thoughts in each sentence:

> A lot of men today get their hair styled; they use perfume and other cosmetics as well.
>
> She was afraid of not doing well in the course; she had always had bad luck with English before.
>
> The restaurant was beautiful; the food was overpriced.

The semicolon can add to sentence variety. For some people, however, the semicolon is a confusing mark of punctuation. Keep in mind that if you are not comfortable using it, you can and should use one of the first two methods of correcting a run-on.

Activity

Insert a semicolon where the break occurs between the two complete thoughts in each of the following run-ons.

Example   I missed the bus by seconds;there would not be another for half an hour.

1. I spend eight hours a day in a windowless office it's a relief to get out into the open air after work.
2. The audience howled with laughter;the comedian enjoyed a moment of triumph.
3. It rained all week;parts of the highway were flooded.
4. Tony never goes to a certain gas station anymore he found out that the service manager overcharged him for a valve job.
5. The washer shook and banged with its unbalanced load then it began to walk across the floor.

Semicolon with a Transitional Word   A semicolon is sometimes used with a transitional word and a comma to join two complete thoughts.

We were short of money; therefore, we decided not to eat out that weekend.

The roots of a geranium have to be crowded into a small pot; otherwise, the plants may not flower.

I had a paper to write; however, my brain had stopped working for the night.

Following is a list of common transitional words (also known as *adverbial conjunctions*). Brief meanings are given for the words.

Transitional Word	Meaning
however	but
nevertheless	but
on the other hand	but
instead	as a substitute
meanwhile	in the intervening time
otherwise	under other conditions
indeed	in fact
in addition	and
also	and
moreover	and
furthermore	and
as a result	in consequence
thus	as a result
consequently	as a result
therefore	as a result

Activity 1

Choose a logical transitional word from the list in the box and write it in the space provided. Put a semicolon *before* the connector and a comma *after* it.

Example   Exams are over _____; however,_____ I still feel tense and nervous.

1. I did not understand her point ____; in fact____ I asked her to repeat it.

2. Janis spent several minutes trying to pry open the case of her new CD __*; However,*__ she didn't succeed until she attacked it with a hammer.

3. Post offices are closed for today's holiday __*; therefore,*__ no mail will be delivered.

4. Mac and Alana didn't have a fancy wedding __*; instead*__ they used their money for a nice honeymoon.

5. I had to skip lunch __*; otherwise,*__ I would have been late for class.

Activity 2

Punctuate each sentence by using a semicolon and a comma.

Example   My brother's asthma was worsening; as a result, he quit the soccer team.

1. My brother ate an entire pizza for supper in addition he had a big chunk of pound cake for dessert.

2. The man leaned against the building in obvious pain however no one stopped to help him.

3. Our instructor was absent therefore the test was postponed.

4. I had no time to type up the paper instead I printed it out neatly in black ink.

5. Lola loves the velvety texture of cherry Jell-O moreover she loves to squish it between her teeth.

Method 4: Subordination

A fourth method of joining related thoughts is to use subordination. *Subordination* is a way of showing that one thought in a sentence is not as important as another thought.

Here are three earlier sentences that have been recast so that one idea is subordinated to (made less important than) the other idea:

When the window shade snapped up like a gunshot, her cat leaped four feet off the floor.

Because it rained all week, parts of the highway were flooded.

Although my grades are very good this year, my social life rates only a C.

Notice that when we subordinate, we use dependent words like *when,* *because,* and *although.* Here is a brief list of common dependent words:

Common Dependent Words		
after	before	unless
although	even though	until
as	if	when
because	since	while

Subordination is explained on pages 109–111.

Activity

Choose a logical dependent word from the box above and write it in the space provided.

Example   _____*Because*_____ I had so much to do, I never even turned on the TV last night.

1. _____After_____ we emerged from the darkened theater, it took several minutes for our eyes to adjust to the light.

2. _____Although_____ "All Natural" was printed in large letters on the yogurt carton, the fine print listing the ingredients told a different story.

3. I can't study for the test this weekend _____because_____ my boss wants me to work overtime.

4. _____when , eventhough_____ the vampire movie was over, my children were afraid to go to bed.

5. _____Unless , eventhough_____ you have a driver's license and two major credit cards, that store will not accept your check.

A Review: How to Check for Run-Ons

1 To see if a sentence is a run-on, read it aloud and listen for a break marking two complete thoughts. Your voice will probably drop and pause at the break.

2 To check an entire paper, read it aloud from the *last* sentence to the *first*. Doing so will help you hear and see each complete thought.

3 Be on the lookout for words that can lead to run-on sentences:

I	he, she, it	they	this	next
you	we	there	that	then

4 Correct run-on sentences by using one of the following methods:
   - Period and capital letter
   - Comma and joining word *(and, but, for, or, nor, so, yet)*
   - Semicolon
   - Subordination

■ Review Test 1

Some of the run-ons that follow are fused sentences, having no punctuation between the two complete thoughts; others are comma splices, having only a comma between the two complete thoughts. Correct the run-ons by using one of the following three methods:

- Period and capital letter
- Comma and joining word
- Semicolon

Do not use the same method of correction for every sentence.

Example   Three people did the job, _{but} I could have done it alone.

1. The impatient driver tried to get a jump on the green light he kept edging his car into the intersection.   *,so or ;therefor.*

2. The course on the history of UFOs sounded interesting, it turned out to be very dull.   *,but*

3. That clothing store is a strange place to visit *·You* you keep walking up to dum- ~~*beause*~~ mies that look like real people.

4. Everything on the menu of the Pancake House sounded delicious.·they *,·therefore·;* *·they* wanted to order the entire menu.

5. Chung pressed a cold washcloth against his eyes; *·it* it helped relieve his headache.

6. Marc used to be a fast-food junkie *·Now* now he eats only vegetables and sunflower seeds.

7. I knew my term paper was not very good, *;so* I placed it in a shiny plastic cover to make it look better.

8. The boy smiled joyously, his silver braces flashed in the sun.

9. My boss does not know what he is doing half the time then he tries to tell me what to do.

10. In the next minute, 100 people will die, over 240 babies will be born.

■ Review Test 2

Correct each run-on by using subordination. Choose from among the following dependent words:

after	before	unless
although	even though	until
as	if	when
because	since	while

Example   My eyes have been watering all day, I can tell the pollen count is high.

Because my eyes have been watering all day, I can tell the pollen

count is high.

1. There are a number of suits and jackets on sale, they all have very noticeable flaws.

_____

_____

2. Rust has eaten a hole in the muffler, my car sounds like a motorcycle.

_____

_____

3. I finished my household chores, I decided to do some shopping.

_____

_____

4. The power went off for an hour during the night, all the clocks in the house must be reset.

_____

_____

5. Self-cleaning public toilets are available, few American cities have installed them.

_____

_____

■ Review Test 3

There are two run-ons in each passage. Correct them by using one of the following methods.

- Period and capital letter
- Comma and one of these joining words: *and, but,* or *so*
- One of these dependent words: *although, because,* or *when*

1. The dog raced into the house it was happy to be among people. Its owner bent down to pet it he drew back in disgust. The dog had rolled in something with a horrible smell.

_____

_____

_____

2. Small feet were admired in ancient China, some female infants had their feet tightly bound. The feet then grew into a tiny, deformed shape. The women could barely walk their feet were crippled for life.

_____

_____

_____

3. Davie insisted on dressing himself for nursery school. It was a cold winter day, he put on shorts and a tank top. He also put on cowboy boots over his bare feet. He liked his image in the mirror his mother made him change.

_____

_____

_____

4. A stimulating scent such as peppermint can help people concentrate better. The idea has practical applications, studies have shown that students do better on tests when peppermint is in the air. Maybe scented air could improve students' performance, it might help office workers be more alert, too.

_____

_____

_____

■ **Review Test 4**

Write quickly for five minutes about what you did this past weekend. Don't worry about spelling, punctuation, finding exact words, or organizing your thoughts. Just focus on writing as many words as you can without stopping.

After you have finished, go back and make whatever changes are needed to correct any run-ons in your writing.

30 Standard English Verbs

Underline what you think is the correct form of the verb in each of the sentences below:

As a boy, he (enjoy, enjoyed) watching nature shows on television.
He still (enjoy, enjoys) watching such shows today as an adult.

When my car was new, it always (start, started) in the morning.
Now it (start, starts) only sometimes.

A couple of years ago, when Alice (cook, cooked) dinner, you needed an antacid tablet.
Now, when she (cook, cooks), neighbors invite themselves over to eat with us.

On the basis of the above examples, see if you can complete the following statements:

1. The first example in each pair refers to a (past, present) action, and the regular verb ends in _____.

2. The second example in each pair refers to a (past, present) action, and the regular verb ends in _____.

Answers are on page 630.

Many people have grown up in communities where nonstandard verb forms are used in everyday life. Such forms include *I thinks, he talk, it done, we has, you was,* and *she don't.* Community dialects have richness and power but are a drawback in college and the world at large, where standard English verb forms must be used. Standard English helps ensure clear communication among English-speaking people everywhere, and it is especially important in the world of work.

This chapter compares community dialect and standard English forms of one regular verb and three common irregular verbs.

Regular Verbs: Dialect and Standard Forms

The chart below compares community dialect (nonstandard) and standard English forms of the regular verb *smile.*

Smile

Community Dialect (Do not use in your writing)		*Standard English* (Use for clear communication)	
Present tense			
~~I smiles~~	~~we smiles~~	I smile	we smile
you smiles	you smiles	you smile	you smile
~~he, she,~~ it smile	~~they smiles~~	he, she, it smiles	they smile
Past tense			
~~I smile~~	~~we smile~~	I smiled	we smiled
you smile	you smile	you smiled	you smiled
~~he, she,~~ it smile	~~they smile~~	he, she, it smiled	they smiled

One of the most common nonstandard forms results from dropping the endings of regular verbs. For example, people might say, "David never *smile* anymore" instead of "David never *smiles* anymore." Or they will say, "Before he lost his job, David *smile* a lot," instead of, "Before he lost his job, David *smiled* a lot." To avoid such nonstandard usage, memorize the forms shown above for the regular verb *smile.* Then use the activities that follow to help make a habit of including verb endings when you write.

Present Tense Endings

The verb ending -*s* or -*es* is needed with a regular verb in the present tense when the subject is *he, she, it,* or any *one person* or *thing.* Consider the following examples of present tense endings.

He	He yell*s*.
She	She throw*s* things.
It	It really anger*s* me.
One person	Their son storm*s* out of the house.
One person	Their frightened daughter crouch*es* behind the bed.
One thing	At night the house shake*s*.

Activity 1

All but one of the ten sentences that follow need -*s* or -*es* verb endings. Cross out the nonstandard verb forms and write the standard forms in the spaces provided. Mark the one sentence that needs no change with a *C* for *correct.* One example is given for you.

Example   ___*wants*___ Dana always ~~want~~ the teacher's attention.

_____   1. That newspaper print nothing but bad news.

_____   2. Don't eat a fish that smell funny.

_____   3. Claire plan to enter the contest.

_____   4. Whole-wheat bread taste better to me than rye bread.

_____   5. Bob weaken his lungs by smoking so much.

_____   6. The sick baby scream whenever her mother puts her down.

_____   7. You make me angry sometimes.

_____   8. Troy run faster than anybody else on the track team.

_____   9. She live in a rough section of town.

_____   10. Martha like mystery novels better than romances.

Activity 2

Rewrite the short passage below, adding present -*s* or -*es* verb endings wherever needed.

Terri work in a big office downtown. Her cubicle sit right next to another worker's. This worker drive Terri crazy. He make more noise than you can imagine. Every day he bring a bag of raw carrots to work. The crunching noise fill the air. After he eat the carrots, he chew gum. He pop it so loud it sound like gunfire.

_____

_____

_____

_____

_____

Past Tense Endings

The verb ending -*d* or -*ed* is needed with a regular verb in the past tense.

A midwife deliver*ed* my baby.
The visitor puzzl*ed* over the campus map.
The children watch*ed* cartoons all morning.

Activity 1

All but one of the ten sentences that follow need -*d* or -*ed* verb endings. Cross out the nonstandard verb forms and write the standard forms in the spaces provided. Mark the one sentence that needs no change with a *C*.

Example   ___*failed*___ Yesterday I ~~fail~~ a chemistry quiz.

_____ 1. Lily carefully color her mouth with red lipstick.

_____ 2. The Vietnamese student struggle with the new language.

_____ 3. The sick little boy start to cry again.

_____ 4. The tired mother turned on the TV for him.

_____ 5. I miss quite a few days of class early in the semester.

_____ 6. The weather forecaster promise blue skies, but rain began early this morning.

_____ 7. Sam attempt to put out the candle flame with his finger.

_____ 8. However, he end up burning himself.

_____ 9. On the bus, Yolanda listen to music through the headphones of her Walkman.

_____ 10. As the photographer was about to take a picture of the smiling baby, a sudden noise frighten the child and made her cry.

Activity 2

Rewrite the short passage on the next page, adding past tense -*d* or -*ed* verb endings wherever needed.

I smoke for two years and during that time suffer no real side effects. Then my body attack me. I start to have trouble falling asleep, and I awaken early every morning. My stomach digest food very slowly, so that at lunchtime I seem to be still full with breakfast. My lips and mouth turn dry, and I swallow water constantly. Also, mucus fill my lungs and I cough a lot. I decide to stop smoking when my wife insist I take out more life insurance for our family.

_____

_____

_____

_____

_____

_____

Three Common Irregular Verbs: Dialect and Standard Forms

The following charts compare community dialect and standard English forms of the common irregular verbs *be, have,* and *do.* (For more on irregular verbs, see pages 459–467.)

Be

Community Dialect (Do not use in your writing)		Standard English (Use for clear communication)	
Present tense			
I be (or is)	we be	I am	we are
you be	you be	you are	you are
he, she, it be	they be	he, she, it is	they are
Past tense			
I were	we was	I was	we were
you was	you was	you were	you were
he, she, it were	they was	he, she, it was	they were

Have

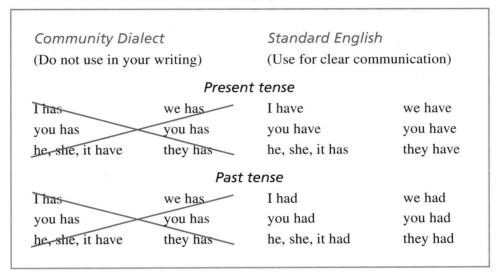

Community Dialect		Standard English	
(Do not use in your writing)		(Use for clear communication)	
Present tense			
I has	we has	I have	we have
you has	you has	you have	you have
he, she, it have	they has	he, she, it has	they have
Past tense			
I has	we has	I had	we had
you has	you has	you had	you had
he, she, it have	they has	he, she, it had	they had

Do

Community Dialect		Standard English	
(Do not use in your writing)		(Use for clear communication)	
Present tense			
I does	we does	I do	we do
you does	you does	you do	you do
he, she, it do	they does	he, she, it does	they do
Past tense			
I done	we done	I did	we did
you done	you done	you did	you did
he, she, it done	they done	he, she, it did	they did

Note: Many people have trouble with one negative form of *do*. They will say, for example, "He don't agree" instead of "He doesn't agree," or they will say, "The door don't work," instead of "The door doesn't work." Be careful to avoid the common mistake of using *don't* instead of *doesn't*.

Activity 1

Underline the standard form of *be, have,* or *do.*

1. Crystal (have, has) such a nice singing voice that she often sings solos at our choir concerts.
2. The children (is, are) ready to go home.
3. Whenever we (do, does) the laundry, our clothes are spotted with blobs of undissolved detergent.
4. Rod and Arlene (was, were) ready to leave for the movies when the baby began to wail.
5. Our art class (done, did) the mural on the wall of the cafeteria.
6. If I (have, has) the time later, I will help you set up your new laser printer.
7. Jesse (be, is) the best Ping-Pong player in the college.
8. My mom always goes to the same hair stylist because she (do, does) Mom's hair just the way Mom likes.
9. The mice in our attic (have, has) chewed several holes in our ceiling.
10. The science instructor said that the state of California (be, is) ready for a major earthquake any day.

Activity 2

Fill in each blank with the standard form of *be, have,* or *do.*

1. My car _____ a real personality.
2. I think it _____ almost human.
3. On cold mornings, it _____ not want to start.
4. Like me, the car _____ a problem dealing with freezing weather.
5. I don't want to get out of bed, and my car _____ not like leaving the garage.
6. Also, we _____ the same feeling about rainstorms.
7. I hate driving to school in a downpour, and so _____ the car.
8. When the car _____ stopped at a light, it stalls.
9. The habits my car _____ may be annoying.
10. But they _____ understandable.

■ **Review Test 1**

Underline the standard verb form.

1. Alex (argue, argues) just to hear himself talk.
2. Manuel and Yvonne (do, does) their grocery shopping first thing in the morning when the store is nearly empty.
3. The cheap ballpoint pen (leak, leaked) all over the lining of my pocketbook.
4. Dan (climb, climbed) up on the roof to see where the water was coming in.
5. If you (has, have) any trouble with the assignment, give me a call.
6. As soon as she gets home from work, Missy (boil, boils) some water to make tea.
7. My daughter often (watch, watches) TV after the rest of the family is in bed.
8. Two of the players (was, were) suspended from the league for ten games for using drugs.
9. Jeannie (has, have) only one eye; she lost the other years ago after falling on some broken glass.
10. I remember how my wet mittens (use, used) to steam on the hot school radiator.

■ **Review Test 2**

Cross out the two nonstandard verb forms in each sentence below. Then write the standard English verbs in the spaces provided.

Example   ___*is*___   When our teacher ~~be~~ angry, his eyelid ~~begin~~ to twitch.
                begins

_____   1. My mother work for the local newspaper; she take classified ads over the
_____   phone.
_____   2. Last week the city tow away my car; this morning I paid sixty dollars and pick
_____   it up from the towing company.
_____   3. When my wife be late for work, she rush around the house like a speeded-up
_____   cartoon character.
_____   4. Henry love to go camping until two thieves in the campground remove his
_____   cooler, stove, and sleeping bag from his tent.

_____   5. If the baby have a bad cold, I takes her into a steamy bathroom for a while to
_____   ease her breathing.

_____   6. Although my little girls knows they shouldn't tease the cat, they often dresses
_____   up the animal in doll clothes.

_____   7. When my brothers watches their favorite *Star Trek* reruns, they knows
_____   exactly what Captain Kirk is going to say next.

_____   8. The hot, sweaty children jumps into the cool water of the pool and splashes
_____   around like a couple of happy seals.

_____   9. I show the receipt to the manager to prove that the clerk had accidentally
_____   overcharge me.

_____   10. As far as our son be concerned, oatmeal taste like soggy cardboard.

_____

31 Irregular Verbs

Introductory Project

You may already have a sense of which common English verbs are regular and which are not. To test yourself, fill in the past tense and past participle of the verbs below. Five are regular verbs and so take *-d* or *-ed* in the past tense and past participle. (The item at the top is an example.) Five are irregular verbs and will probably not sound right when you try to add *-d* or *-ed*. Write *I* for *irregular* in front of these verbs. Also, see if you can write in their irregular verb forms.

Present	Past	Past Participle
shout	shouted	shouted
1. crawl		
2. bring		
3. use		
4. do		
5. give		
6. laugh		
7. go		
8. scare		
9. dress		
10. see		

Answers are on page 630.

A Brief Review of Regular Verbs

Every verb has four principal parts: present, past, past participle, and present participle. These parts can be used to build all the verb tenses (the times shown by a verb).

The past and past participle of a regular verb are formed by adding *-d* or *-ed* to the present. The *past participle* is the form of the verb used with the helping verbs *have, has,* or *had* (or some form of *be* with passive verbs). The *present participle* is formed by adding *-ing* to the present. Here are the principal forms of some regular verbs:

Present	*Past*	*Past Participle*	*Present Participle*
crash	crashed	crashed	crashing
shiver	shivered	shivered	shivering
kiss	kissed	kissed	kissing
apologize	apologized	apologized	apologizing
tease	teased	teased	teasing

Most verbs in English are regular.

List of Irregular Verbs

Irregular verbs have irregular forms in the past tense and past participle. For example, the past tense of the irregular verb *know* is *knew;* the past participle is *known.*

Almost everyone has some degree of trouble with irregular verbs. When you are unsure about the form of a verb, you can check the following list of irregular verbs. (The present participle is not shown on this list, because it is formed simply by adding *-ing* to the base form of the verb.) Or you can check a dictionary, which gives the principal parts of irregular verbs.

Present	*Past*	*Past Participle*
arise	arose	arisen
awake	awoke *or* awaked	awoken *or* awaked
be (am, are, is)	was (were)	been
become	became	become
begin	began	begun
bend	bent	bent
bite	bit	bitten
blow	blew	blown
break	broke	broken
bring	brought	brought
build	built	built
burst	burst	burst
buy	bought	bought
catch	caught	caught
choose	chose	chosen
come	came	come
cost	cost	cost
cut	cut	cut
do (does)	did	done
draw	drew	drawn
drink	drank	drunk
drive	drove	driven
eat	ate	eaten
fall	fell	fallen
feed	fed	fed
feel	felt	felt
fight	fought	fought
find	found	found
fly	flew	flown
freeze	froze	frozen
get	got	got *or* gotten
give	gave	given
go (goes)	went	gone
grow	grew	grown

Present	Past	Past Participle
have (has)	had	had
hear	heard	heard
hide	hid	hidden
hold	held	held
hurt	hurt	hurt
keep	kept	kept
know	knew	known
lay	laid	laid
lead	led	led
leave	left	left
lend	lent	lent
let	let	let
lie	lay	lain
lose	lost	lost
make	made	made
meet	met	met
pay	paid	paid
ride	rode	ridden
ring	rang	rung
run	ran	run
say	said	said
see	saw	seen
sell	sold	sold
send	sent	sent
shake	shook	shaken
shrink	shrank	shrunk
shut	shut	shut
sing	sang	sung
sit	sat	sat
sleep	slept	slept
speak	spoke	spoken
spend	spent	spent
stand	stood	stood
steal	stole	stolen

Present	Past	Past Participle
stick	stuck	stuck
sting	stung	stung
swear	swore	sworn
swim	swam	swum
take	took	taken
teach	taught	taught
tear	tore	torn
tell	told	told
think	thought	thought
wake	woke *or* waked	woken *or* waked
wear	wore	worn
win	won	won
write	wrote	written

Activity 1

Cross out the incorrect verb form in each of the following sentences. Then write the correct form of the verb in the space provided.

Example   _drew_ The little boy ~~drawed~~ on the marble table with permanent ink.

_____ 1. Tomatoes were once thought to be poisonous, and they were growed only as ornamental shrubs.

_____ 2. On the last day of swim class, every student swimmed the whole length of the pool.

_____ 3. My cats have tore little holes in all my good wool sweaters.

_____ 4. The pipes in the bathroom freezed last winter, and they burst when they thawed.

_____ 5 Every time my telephone has rang today, there has been bad news on the line.

_____ 6. Only seven people have ever knowed the formula for Coca-Cola.

_____ 7. Amy blowed up animal-shaped balloons for her son's birthday party.

_____ 8. I shaked the bottle of medicine before I took a teaspoonful of it.

_____ 9. While waiting for the doctor to arrive, I sitted in a plastic chair for over two hours.

_____ 10. The pile of bones on the plate showed how much chicken the family had ate.

Activity 2

For each of the italicized verbs, fill in the three missing forms in the following order:

---

a Present tense, which takes an *-s* ending when the subject is *he, she, it,* or any *one person* or *thing* (see pages 451–452)

b Past tense

c Past participle—the form that goes with the helping verb *have, has,* or *had*

Example   My uncle likes to *give* away certain things. He *(a)* ___*gives*___ old, threadbare clothes to the Salvation Army. Last year he *(b)* ___*gave*___ me a worthless television set whose picture tube was burned out. He has *(c)* ___*given*___ away stuff that a junk dealer would reject.

1. I like to *freeze* Hershey bars. A Hershey bar *(a)* _____ in half an hour. Once I *(b)* _____ a bottle of Pepsi. I put it in the freezer to chill and then forgot about it. Later I opened the freezer and discovered that it had *(c)* _____ and exploded.

2. Natalie *speaks* French. She *(a)* _____ German too. Her grand-mother *(b)* _____ both languages and taught them to her. Since she was a baby, Natalie has *(c)* _____ them both as well as she speaks English.

3. An acquaintance of mine is a shoplifter, although he knows it's wrong to *steal*. He *(a)* _____ candy bars from supermarkets. Last month he *(b)* _____ a Sony Walkman and was caught by a detective. He has *(c)*_____ pants and shirts by wearing several layers of clothes out of a store.

4. I *go* to parties a lot. Often Camille *(a)* _____ with me. She *(b)* _____ with me just last week. I have *(c)* _____ to parties every Friday for the past month.

5. My brother likes to *throw* things. Sometimes he *(a)* _____ socks into his bureau drawer. In high school he *(b)* _____ footballs while quarterbacking the team. And he has *(c)* _____ Frisbees in our backyard for as long as I can remember.

6. I would like to *see* a UFO. I spend hours looking at the night sky, hoping to *(a)* _____ one. A neighbor of ours claims he *(b)* _____ one last month. But he says he has *(c)* _____ the Abominable Snowman, too.

7. I often *lie* down for a few minutes after a hard day's work. Sometimes my cat *(a)* _____ down near me. Yesterday was Saturday, so I *(b)* _____ in bed all morning. I probably would have *(c)* _____ in bed all afternoon, but I wanted to get some planting done in my vegetable garden.

8 I *do* not understand the assignment. It simply *(a)* _____ not make sense to me. I was surprised to learn that Shirley *(b)* _____ understand it. In fact, she had already *(c)* _____ the assignment.

9. I often find it hard to *begin* writing a paper. The assignment that I must do *(a)* _____ to worry me while I'm watching television, but I seldom turn off the set. Once I waited until the late movie had ended before I *(b)* _____ to write. If I had *(c)* _____ earlier, I would have gotten a decent night's sleep.

10. Martha likes to *eat*. She (a)_____ as continuously as some people smoke. Once she *(b)* _____ a large pack of cookies in half an hour. Even if she has *(c)* _____ a heavy meal, she often starts munching snacks right afterward.

■ Review Test 1

Underline the correct verb in the parentheses.

1. As I began my speech, my hands (shaked, shook) so badly I nearly dropped my notes.

2. Chico came into the gym and (began, begun) to practice on the parallel bars.

3. Over half the class has (taken, took) this course on a pass-fail basis.

4. Even though my father (teached, taught) me how to play baseball, I never enjoyed any part of the game.

5. Because I had (lended, lent) him money, I had a natural concern about what he did with it.

6. The drugstore clerk (gave, gived) him the wrong change.

7. Lola (brang, brought) a sweatshirt with her, for she knew the mountains got cold at night.

8. My sister (was, be) at school when a stranger came asking for her at our home.

9. The mechanic (did, done) an expensive valve job on my engine without getting my permission.

10. The basketball team has (broke, broken) the school record for most losses in one year.

11. Someone (leaved, left) his or her books in the classroom.

12. That jacket was (tore, torn) during the football game.

13. If I hadn't (threw, thrown) away the receipt, I could have gotten my money back.

14. I would have (become, became) very angry if you had not intervened.

15. As the flowerpot (fell, falled) from the windowsill, the little boy yelled, "Bombs away!"

■ Review Test 2

Write short sentences that use the form requested for the following irregular verbs.

Example   Past of *grow* *I grew eight inches in one year.*

1. Past of *know* _____

   _____

2. Past participle of *take* _____

   _____

3. Past of *give* _____

   _____

4. Past participle of *write* _____

   _____

5. Past of *bring* _____

   _____

6. Past participle of *speak* _____

_____

7. Past of *begin* _____

_____

8. Past of *go* _____

_____

9. Past participle of *see* _____

_____

10. Past of *drive* _____

_____

32 Subject-Verb Agreement

Introductory Project

As you read each pair of sentences below, write a check mark beside the sentence that you think uses the underlined word correctly.

There was too many people talking at once. _____

There were too many people talking at once. __✓__

The onions in that spaghetti sauce gives me heartburn. __✓__

The onions in that spaghetti sauce give me heartburn. _____

The mayor and her husband attends our church. __✓__

The mayor and her husband attend our church. _____

Everything seem to slow me down when I'm in a hurry. __✓__

Everything seems to slow me down when I'm in a hurry. _____

Answers are on page 630.

A verb must agree with its subject in number. A *singular subject* (one person or thing) takes a singular verb. A *plural subject* (more than one person or thing) takes a plural verb. Mistakes in subject-verb agreement are sometimes made in the situations listed below (each situation is explained on the following pages):

1   When words come between the subject and the verb

2   When a verb comes before the subject

3   With compound subjects

4   With indefinite pronouns

Words between Subject and Verb

Words that come between the subject and the verb do not change subject-verb agreement. In the sentence

The tomatoes in this salad are brown and mushy.

the subject (tomatoes) is plural, and so the verb (are) is plural. The words *in this salad* that come between the subject and the verb do not affect subject-verb agreement.

To help find the subject of certain sentences, you should cross out prepositional phrases (see page 413):

Nell, ~~with her three dogs close behind~~, runs around the park every day.

The seams ~~in my new coat~~ have split after only two wearings.

Activity

Underline the correct verb form in the parentheses.

1. The decisions of the judge (seem, seems) questionable.
2. The flakes in this cereal (taste, tastes) like sawdust.
3. The woman with the dark sunglasses (is, are) our mayor.
4. Many people in Europe (speak, speaks) several languages.
5. A hamburger with a double order of french fries (is, are) my usual lunch.
6. That silk flower by the candles (look, looks) real.
7. One of my son's worst habits (is, are) leaving an assortment of dirty plates on the kitchen counter.

8. The rust spots on the back of Emily's car (need, needs) to be cleaned with a special polish.

9. The collection of medicine bottles in my parents' bathroom (overflow, overflows) the cabinet shelves.

10. A tired-looking student in my classes often (sleep, sleeps) through most of the lectures.

Verb before Subject

A verb agrees with its subject even when the verb comes *before* the subject. Words that may precede the subject include *there, here,* and, in questions, *who, which, what,* and *where.*

> On Glen's doorstep were two police officers.
> There are many pizza places in our town.
> Here is your receipt.
> Where are they going to sleep?

If you are unsure about the subject, look at the verb and ask *who* or *what.* With the first example above, you might ask, "*Who* were on the doorstep?" The answer, *police officers,* is the subject.

Activity

Write the correct form of the verb in the space provided.

is, are   1. What __is__ your middle name?

was, were   2. Among the guests __were__ a private detective.

do, does   3. Where __do__ you go when you want to be alone?

is, are   4. There __are__ many hungry people in American cities.

rest, rests   5. In that grave __rest__ the bones of my great-grandfather.

was, were   6. There __were__ too many people in the room for me to feel comfortable.

is, are   7. Why __are__ the lights turned off?

stand, stands   8. Across the street __stand__ the post office.

is, are   9. Here _____ the tickets for tonight's game.

was, were   10. Stuffed into the mailbox __were__ ten pieces of junk mail and three ripped magazines.

Compound Subjects

Subjects joined by *and* generally take a plural verb.

Maple syrup and sweet butter taste delicious on pancakes.

Fear and ignorance have a lot to do with hatred.

When subjects are joined by *either . . . or, neither . . . nor, not only . . . but also,* the verb agrees with the subject closer to the verb.

Either the Oak Ridge Boys or Mary Chapin Carpenter deserves the award for the best country album of the year.

The nearer subject, *Mary Chapin Carpenter,* is singular, and so the verb is singular.

Activity

Write the correct form of the verb in the space provided.

stays, stay ✓ 1. Our cats and dog _stay_ at a neighbor's house when we go on vacation.

Is, Are 2. _Are_ the birthday cake and ice cream ready to be served?

holds, hold 3. Staples and Scotch tape _holds_ all our old photo albums together.

was, were 4. Rent and car insurance _were_ my biggest expenses last month.

wants, *singer* 5. Neither the students nor the instructor _want_ to postpone the final exam
want *plural*   till after the holidays.

is, are 6. An egg and a banana _____ required for the recipe.

was, were 7. Owning a car and having money in my pocket _____ the chief ambitions
of my adolescence.

visits, visit 8. My aunt and uncle from Ireland _____ us every other summer.

was, were 9. Before they saw a marriage therapist, Peter and Jenny _____ planning
to get divorced.

acts, act 10. Not only the landlady but also her children _____ unfriendly to us.

Indefinite Pronouns

The following words, known as *indefinite pronouns*, always take singular verbs:

(-one words)	*(-body words)*	*(-thing words)*	
one	nobody	nothing	each
anyone	anybody	anything	either
everyone	everybody	everything	neither
someone	somebody	something	

Note: *Both* always takes a plural verb.

Activity

Write the correct form of the verb in the space provided.

is, are

feel, feels

knows, know

needs, need

sounds, sound

pitches, pitch

was, were

provides, provide

likes, like

steals, steal

1. Everybody at my new school _____ friendly.

2. Neither of those mattresses _____ comfortable.

3. Nobody in my family _____ how to swim.

4. Each of the children _____ some attention.

5. Something about Robbie's story _____ suspicious.

6. If each of us _____ in, we can finish this job in an hour.

7. Everybody in the theater _____ getting up and leaving before the movie ended.

8. Neither of the restaurants _____ facilities for the handicapped.

9. No one in our family _____ housecleaning, but we all take a turn at it.

10. Someone in our neighborhood _____ vegetables from people's gardens.

■ Review Test 1

Underline the correct verb in parentheses.

1. Lettuce in most of the stores in our area now (costs, cost) almost three dollars a head.
2. Nobody in the class of fifty students (understands, understand) how to solve
   the equation on the blackboard.
3. The packages in the shopping bag (was, were) a wonderful mystery to the
   children.
4. My exercise class of five students (meets, meet) every Thursday afternoon.
5. Anyone who (steals, steal) my purse won't find much inside it.
6. Business contacts and financial backing (is, are) all that I need to establish
   my career as a dress designer.
7. Each of those breakfast cereals (contains, contain) a high proportion of sugar.
8. The serious look in that young girl's eyes (worries, worry) me.
9. All of the cars on my block (has, have) to be moved one day a month for street
   cleaning.
10. Some people (know, knows) more about their favorite TV characters than they
    do about the members of their own family.

■ Review Test 2

Each of the following passages contains *two* mistakes in subject-verb agreement.
Find these two mistakes and cross them out. Then write the correct form of each
verb in the space provided.

1. Few people recalls seeing baby pigeons. The reason is simple. Baby pigeons
   in the nest eats a huge amount of food each day. Upon leaving the nest, they
   are close to the size of their parents.

   a. _____

   b. _____

2. Everything in the mall stores are on sale today. Customers from all over are
   crowding the aisles. There is terrific bargains in many departments.

   a. _____

   b. _____

3. All the neighbors meets once a year for a block party. Everyone talks and dances far into the night. Huge bowls of delicious food sits on picnic tables. Afterward, everyone goes home and sleeps all day.

   a. _____

   b. _____

4. The members of the swimming team paces nervously beside the pool. Finally, an official blows a whistle. Into the pool dive a swimmer with thick, tan arms. He paddles quickly through the water.

   a. _____

   b. _____

4. When Lin Soo comes home from school each day, her work is just beginning. The members of her family all works in their small restaurant. Nobody rest until the last customer is served. Only then do Lin Soo and her brother start their homework.

   a. _____

   b. _____

33 Pronoun Agreement and Reference

Introductory Project

Read each pair of sentences below. Then write a check mark beside the sentence that you think uses the underlined word or words correctly.

Someone in my neighborhood lets <u>their</u> dog run loose. _____

Someone in my neighborhood lets <u>his or her</u> dog run loose. _____

After Tony reviewed his notes with Bob, <u>he</u> passed the exam with ease. _____

After reviewing his notes with Bob, <u>Tony</u> passed the exam with ease. _____

Answers are on page 630.

Pronouns are words that take the place of nouns (persons, places, or things). In fact, the word *pronoun* means "for a noun." Pronouns are shortcuts that keep you from unnecessarily repeating words in writing. Here are some examples of pronouns:

> Shirley had not finished *her* paper. (*Her* is a pronoun that takes the place of *Shirley's*.)
>
> Tony swung so heavily on the tree branch that *it* snapped. (*It* replaces *branch*.)
>
> When the three little pigs saw the wolf, *they* pulled out cans of Mace. (*They* is a pronoun that takes the place of *pigs*.)

This section presents rules that will help you avoid two common mistakes people make with pronouns. The rules are as follows:

1 A pronoun must agree in number with the word or words it replaces.

2 A pronoun must refer clearly to the word it replaces.

Pronoun Agreement

A pronoun must agree in number with the word or words it replaces. If the word a pronoun refers to is singular, the pronoun must be singular; if that word is plural, the pronoun must be plural. (Note that the word a pronoun refers to is also known as the *antecedent*.)

Barbara agreed to lend me (her) Willie Nelson CDs.

People walking the trail must watch (their) step because of snakes.

In the first example, the pronoun *her* refers to the singular word *Barbara;* in the second example, the pronoun *their* refers to the plural word *People.*

Activity

Write the appropriate pronoun *(their, they, them, it)* in the blank space in each of the following sentences.

Example   I lifted the pot of hot potatoes carefully, but __*it*__ slipped out of my hand.

1. People should try to go into a new situation with _____ minds open, not with opinions already firmly formed.

2. Fred never misses his daily workout; he believes _____ keeps him healthy.

3. Sometimes, in marriage, partners expect too much from _____ mates.

4. For some students, college is often their first experience with an undisciplined learning situation, and _____ are not always ready to accept the responsibility.

5. Our new neighbors moved in three months ago, but I have yet to meet _____ .

Indefinite Pronouns

The following words, known as *indefinite pronouns,* are always singular.

(-one words)	*(-body words)*	
one	nobody	each
anyone	anybody	either
everyone	everybody	neither
someone	somebody	

If a pronoun in a sentence refers to one of the above singular words, the pronoun should be singular.

Each father felt that his child should have won the contest.

One of the women could not find her purse.

Everyone must be in his seat before the instructor takes the roll.

In each example, the circled pronoun is singular because it refers to one of the special singular words.

Note: The last example is correct if everyone in the class is a man. If everyone in the class is a woman, the pronoun would be *her.* If the class has both women and men, the pronoun form would be *his or her:*

Everyone must be in his or her seat before the instructor takes the roll.

Some writers follow the traditional practice of using *his* to refer to both women and men. Many now use *his or her* to avoid an implied sexual bias. To avoid using *his* or the somewhat awkward *his or her,* a sentence can often be rewritten in the plural:

> Students must be in their seats before the instructor takes the roll.

Activity

Underline the correct pronoun.

1. Someone has blocked the parking lot exit with (his or her, their) car.
2. Everyone in the women's group has volunteered some of (her, their) time for the voting drive.
3. Neither of the men arrested as terrorists would reveal (his, their) real name.
4. Not one of the women coaches will be returning to (her, their) job next year.
5. Each of the president's advisers offered (his or her, their) opinion about the airline strike.

Pronoun Reference

A sentence may be confusing and unclear if a pronoun appears to refer to more than one word, or if the pronoun does not refer to any specific word. Look at this sentence:

> Joe almost dropped out of high school, for he felt *they* emphasized discipline too much.

Who emphasized discipline too much? There is no specific word that *they* refers to. Be clear:

> Joe almost dropped out of high school, for he felt *the teachers* emphasized discipline too much.

Here are sentences with other kinds of faulty pronoun reference. Read the explanations of why they are faulty and look carefully at how they are corrected.

Faulty

June told Margie that *she* lacked self-confidence.
(*Who* lacked self-confidence: June or Margie? Be clear.)

Clear

June told Margie, "You lack self-confidence."
(Quotation marks, which can sometimes be used to correct an unclear reference, are explained on pages 528–534.)

Nancy's mother is a hairdresser, but Nancy is not interested in *it*.
(There is no specific word that *it* refers to. It would not make sense to say, "Nancy is not interested in hairdresser.")

Nancy's mother is a hairdresser, but Nancy is not interested in becoming one.

Ron blamed the police officer for the ticket, *which* was foolish.
(Does *which* mean that the officer's giving the ticket was foolish, or that Ron's blaming the officer was foolish? Be clear.)

Foolishly, Ron blamed the police officer for the ticket.

Activity

Rewrite each of the following sentences to make the vague pronoun reference clear. Add, change, or omit words as necessary.

Example   Our cat was friends with our hamster until he bit him.
                Until the cat bit the hamster, the two were friends.

1. Maria's mother let her wear her new earrings to school.

   _____

2. When I asked why I failed my driver's test, he said I drove too slowly.

   _____

3. Dad ordered my brother to paint the garage because he didn't want to do it.

   _____

4. Herb dropped his psychology courses because he thought they assigned too much reading.

   _____

5. I love Parmesan cheese on veal, but it does not always digest well.

   _____

■ Review Test 1

Cross out the pronoun error in each sentence and write the correction in the space provided at the left. Then circle the letter that correctly describes the type of error that was made.

Examples

his (or her)   Each player took ~~their~~ position on the court.

Mistake in: (a.) pronoun agreement.   b. pronoun reference.

the store   I was angry when ~~they~~ wouldn't give me cash back when I returned the sweater I had bought.

Mistake in: a. pronoun agreement.   (b.) pronoun reference.

_____   1. Dan asked Mr. Sanchez if he could stay an extra hour at work today.

    Mistake in: a. pronoun agreement.   b. pronoun reference.

_____   2. Both the front door and the back door of the abandoned house had fallen off its hinges.

    Mistake in: a. pronoun agreement.   b. pronoun reference.

_____   3. I've been taking cold medicine, and now it is better.

    Mistake in: a. pronoun agreement.   b. pronoun reference.

_____   4. Norm was angry when they raised the state tax on cigarettes.

    Mistake in: a. pronoun agreement.   b. pronoun reference.

_____   5. Every one of those musicians who played for two hours in the rain truly earned their money last night.

    Mistake in: a. pronoun agreement.   b. pronoun reference.

_____   6. An annual flu shot is a good idea; they will help children and older people stay healthy.

    Mistake in: a. pronoun agreement.   b. pronoun reference.

_____   7. Each of the beauty queens is asked a thought-provoking question and then judged on their answer.

    Mistake in: a. pronoun agreement.   b. pronoun reference.

_____   8. Indira could not believe that they had changed the immigration laws again.

    Mistake in: a. pronoun agreement.   b. pronoun reference.

_____   9. At the dental office, I asked him if it was really necessary to take X rays of my mouth again.

   Mistake in: a. pronoun agreement.   b. pronoun reference.

_____   10. Every ant in the bustling anthill has their own job to do that helps support the entire community.

   Mistake in: a. pronoun agreement.   b. pronoun reference.

■ Review Test 2

Underline the correct word in parentheses.

1. Cindy is the kind of woman who will always do (their, her) best.

2. Hoping to be first in line when (they, the ushers) opened the doors, we arrived two hours early for the concert.

3. If a person really wants to appreciate good coffee, (he or she, they) should drink it black.

4. My children are hooked on science fiction stories because (they, the stories) allow readers to escape to other worlds.

5. Lois often visits the reading center in school, for she finds that (they, the tutors) give her helpful instruction.

6. Nobody seems to know how to add or subtract without (his or her, their) pocket calculator anymore.

7. As the room got colder, everybody wished for (his or her, their) coat.

8. Each of my brothers has had (his, their) apartment broken into.

9. If someone is going to write a composition, (he or she, they) should prepare at least one rough draft.

10. My wife and I both need thick glasses, so I imagine our children won't escape (it, needing glasses).

34 Pronoun Types

This chapter describes some common types of pronouns: subject and object pronouns, possessive pronouns, and demonstrative pronouns.

Subject and Object Pronouns

Pronouns change their form depending on the purpose they serve in a sentence. In the box that follows is a list of subject and object pronouns.

Subject Pronouns	Object Pronouns
I	me
you	you (*no change*)
he	him
she	her
it	it (*no change*)
we	us
they	them

Subject Pronouns

Subject pronouns are subjects of verbs.

She is wearing blue nail polish on her toes. (*She* is the subject of the verb *is wearing*)

They ran up three flights of steps. (*They* is the subject of the verb *ran*).

We children should have some privacy too. (*We* is the subject of the verb *should have.*)

Rules for using subject pronouns, and several kinds of mistakes people sometimes make with subject pronouns, are explained below.

Rule 1   Use a subject pronoun in spots where you have a compound (more than one) subject.

Incorrect	*Correct*
Sally and *me* are exactly the same size.	Sally and *I* are exactly the same size.
Her and *me* share our wardrobes with each other.	*She* and *I* share our wardrobes with each other.

Hint   If you are not sure what pronoun to use, try each pronoun by itself in the sentence. The correct pronoun will be the one that sounds right. For example, "her shares her wardrobe" does not sound right. "She shares her wardrobe" does.

Rule 2   Use a subject pronoun after forms of the verb *be*. Forms of *be* include *am, are, is, was, were, has been,* and *have been.*

It was *I* who called you a minute ago and then hung up.

It may be *they* entering the diner.

It was *he* who put the white tablecloth into the washing machine with a red sock.

The sentences above may sound strange and stilted to you because they are seldom used in conversation. When we speak with one another, forms such as "It was me," "It may be them," and "It is her" are widely accepted. In formal writing, however, the grammatically correct forms are still preferred.

Hint   To avoid having to use the subject pronoun form after *be,* you can simply reword a sentence. Here is how the preceding examples could be reworded:

I was the one who called you a minute ago and then hung up.

They may be the ones entering the diner.

He put the white tablecloth into the washing machine with a red sock.

Rule 3   Use subject pronouns after *than* or *as.* The subject pronoun is used because a verb is understood after the pronoun.

Mark can hold his breath longer than *I* (can). (The verb *can* is understood after *I*.)

Her thirteen-year-old daughter is as tall as *she* (is). (The verb *is* is understood after *she.)*

You drive much better than *he* (drives). (The verb *drives* is understood after *he*.)

Hint   Avoid mistakes by mentally adding the "missing" verb at the end of the sentence.

Object Pronouns

Object pronouns *(me, him, her, us, them)* are the objects of verbs or prepositions. (*Prepositions* are connecting words like *for, at, about, to, before, by, with,* and *of.* See also page 413.)

Lee pushed *me.* (*Me* is the object of the verb *pushed.*)

We dragged *them* all the way home. (*Them* is the object of the verb *dragged.*)

She wrote all about *us* in her diary. (*Us* is the object of the preposition *about.*)

Vera passed a note to *him* as she walked to the pencil sharpener. (*Him* is the object of the preposition *to.*)

People are sometimes uncertain about which pronoun to use when two objects follow the verb.

Incorrect	*Correct*
I argued with his sister and *he.*	I argued with his sister and *him.*
The cashier cheated Rick and *I.*	The cashier cheated Rick and *me.*

Hint   If you are not sure which pronoun to use, try each pronoun by itself in the sentence. The correct pronoun will be the one that sounds right. For example, "I argued with he" does not sound right; "I argued with him" does.

Activity

Underline the correct subject or object pronoun in each of the following sentences. Then show whether your answer is a subject or an object pronoun by circling S or O in the margin. The first one is done for you as an example.

Ⓢ   O   1. Darcy and (<u>she</u>, her) kept dancing even after the band stopped playing.

S   O   2 The letters Mom writes to Estelle and (I, me) are always typed in red.

S   O   3. Pilar is good at bowling, but her little sister is even better than (she, her).

S   O   4. Their relay team won because they practiced more than (we, us).

S   O   5. (We, Us) choir members get to perform for the governor.

S   O   6. The rest of (they, them) came to the wedding by train.

S   O   7. (She, Her) and Sammy got divorced and then remarried.

S   O   8. Since we were both taking a tough statistics course, it was a long, hard semester for my best friend and (me, I).

S   O   9. Tony and (he, him) look a lot alike, but they're not even related.

S   O   10. Our neighbors asked Rosa and (I, me) to help with their parents' surprise party.

Possessive Pronouns

Possessive pronouns show ownership or possession.

> Using a small branch, Stu wrote *his* initials in the wet cement.
> The furniture is *mine,* but the car is *hers.*

Here is a list of possessive pronouns:

my, mine	our, ours
your, yours	your, yours
his	their, theirs
her, hers	
its	

Note   A possessive pronoun *never* uses an apostrophe. (See also page 523.)

Incorrect	*Correct*
That earring is *her's.*	That earring is *hers.*
The orange cat is *theirs'.*	The orange cat is *theirs.*

Activity

Cross out the incorrect pronoun form in each of the sentences below. Write the correct form in the space at the left.

Example   *ours*   The house with the maroon shutters is ~~ours'~~.

_____ 1. A porcupine has no quills on it's belly.

_____ 2. The PowerBook on that table is theirs'.

_____ 3. You can easily tell which team is ours' by when we cheer.

_____ 4. My dog does not get along with her's.

_____ 5. Grandma's silverware and dishes will be yours' when you get married.

Demonstrative Pronouns

Demonstrative pronouns point to or single out a person or thing. There are four demonstrative pronouns:

this	these
that	those

Generally speaking, *this* and *these* refer to things close at hand; *that* and *those* refer to things farther away. These four pronouns are commonly used in the role of demonstrative adjectives as well.

    This milk has gone sour.

    My son insists on saving all *these* hot rod magazines.

    I almost tripped on *that* roller skate at the bottom of the steps.

    Those plants in the corner don't get enough light.

Note   Do not use *them, this here, that there, these here,* or *those there* to point out. Use only *this, that, these,* or *those.*

Activity

Cross out the incorrect form of the demonstrative pronoun and write the correct form in the space provided.

Example   ___*Those*___   ~~Those there~~ tires look worn.

_____   1. This here child has a high fever.

_____   2. These here pants I'm wearing are so tight I can hardly breathe.

_____   3. Them kids have been playing in the alley all morning.

_____   4. That there umpire won't stand for any temper tantrums.

_____   5. I save them old baby clothes for my daughter's dolls.

■ Review Test

Underline the correct word in the parentheses.

1. If I left dinner up to (he, him), we'd have Cheerios every night.
2. The vase on my dresser belonged to my grandmother, and the candlesticks on the windowsill were (hers', hers) as well.
3. My boyfriend offered to drive his mother and (I, me) to the mall to shop for his birthday present.
4. (Them, Those) little marks on the floor are scratches, not crumbs.
5. I took a picture of my brother and (I, me) looking into the hallway mirror.
6. When Lin and (she, her) drove back from the airport, they talked so much that they missed their exit.
7. (That there, That) orange juice box says "Fresh," but the juice is made from concentrate.
8. Eliot swears that he dreamed about (she, her) and a speeding car the night before Irina was injured in a car accident.
9. The waitress brought our food to the people at the next table and gave (theirs, theirs') to us.
10. Since it was so hot out, Lana and (he, him) felt they had a good excuse to study at the beach.

35 Adjectives and Adverbs

Adjectives

What Are Adjectives?

Adjectives describe nouns (names of persons, places, or things) or pronouns.

> Ernie is a *rich* man. (The adjective *rich* describes the noun *man.*)
> He is also *generous*. (The adjective *generous* describes the pronoun *he.*)
> Our *gray* cat sleeps a lot. (The adjective *gray* describes the noun *cat.*)
> She is *old.* (The adjective *old* describes the pronoun *she.*)

Adjectives usually come before the word they describe (as in *rich man* and *gray cat*). But they also come after forms of the verb *be (is, are, was, were,* and so on). They also follow verbs such as *look, appear, seem, become, sound, taste,* and *smell*.

> That speaker was *boring.* (The adjective *boring* describes the speaker.)
> The Petersons are *homeless. (*The adjective *homeless* describes the Petersons.)
> The soup looked *good.* (The adjective *good* describes the soup.)
> But it tasted *salty.* (The adjective *salty* describes the pronoun *it.*)

Using Adjectives to Compare

For all one-syllable adjectives and some two-syllable adjectives, add *-er* when comparing two things and *-est* when comparing three or more things.

> My sister's handwriting is *neater* than mine, but Mother's is the *neatest*.
> Canned juice is sometimes *cheaper* than fresh juice, but frozen juice is often the *cheapest.*

For some two-syllable adjectives and all longer adjectives, add *more* when comparing two things and *most* when comparing three or more things.

Typing something is *more efficient* than writing it out by hand, but the *most efficient* way to write is on a computer.

Jeans are generally *more comfortable* than slacks, but sweat pants are the *most comfortable* of all.

You can usually tell when to use *more* and *most* by the sound of a word. For example, you can probably tell by its sound that "carefuller" would be too awkward to say and that *more careful* is thus correct. In addition, there are many words for which both -*er* or -*est* and *more* or *most* are equally correct. For instance, either "a more fair rule" or "a fairer rule" is correct.

To form negative comparisons, use *less* and *least.*

When kids called me "Dum-dum," I tried to look *less* hurt than I felt.

They say men gossip *less* than women do, but I don't believe it.

Suzanne is the most self-centered, *least* thoughtful person I know.

Points to Remember about Comparing

Point 1   Use only one form of comparison at a time. In other words, do not use both an -*er* ending and *more* or both an -*est* ending and *most.*

Incorrect	*Correct*
My Southern accent is always *more stronger* after I visit my family in Georgia.	My Southern accent is always *stronger* after I visit my family in Georgia.
My *most luckiest* day was the day I met my wife.	My *luckiest* day was the day I met my wife.

Point 2   Learn the irregular forms of the words shown below.

	Comparative (for Comparing Two Things)	*Superlative (for Comparing Three or More Things)*
bad	worse	worst
good, well	better	best
little (in amount)	less	least
much, many	more	most

Do not use both *more* and an irregular comparative or *most* and an irregular superlative.

Incorrect	*Correct*
It is *more better* to stay healthy than to have to get healthy.	It is *better* to stay healthy than to have to get healthy.
Yesterday I went on the *most best* date of my life—and all we did was go on a picnic.	Yesterday I went on the *best* date of my life—and all we did was go on a picnic.

Activity

Add to each sentence the correct form of the word in the margin.

bad

Examples   The _____*worst*_____ scare I ever had was the time when I thought my son was on an airplane that had crashed.

wonderful

The day of my divorce was even ___*more wonderful*___ than the day of my wedding.

good

1. The Grammy awards are given to the _____ recording artists of each year.

popular

2. Vanilla ice cream is even _____ than chocolate ice cream.

bad

3. One of the _____ things you can do to people is ignore them.

light

4. A pound of feathers is no _____ than a pound of stones.

little

5. The _____ expensive way to accumulate a wardrobe is by buying used clothing whenever possible.

Adverbs

What Are Adverbs?

Adverbs—which usually end in *-ly*—describe verbs, adjectives, or other adverbs.

The referee *suddenly* stopped the fight. (The adverb *suddenly* describes the verb *stopped*.)

Her yellow rosebushes are *absolutely* beautiful. (The adverb *absolutely* describes the adjective *beautiful*.)

The auctioneer spoke so *terribly* fast that I couldn't understand him. (The adverb *terribly* describes the adverb *fast*.)

A Common Mistake with Adverbs and Adjectives

People often mistakenly use an adjective instead of an adverb after a verb.

Incorrect	*Correct*
I jog *slow.*	I jog *slowly.*
The nervous witness spoke *quiet.*	The nervous witness spoke *quietly.*
The first night I quit smoking, I wanted a cigarette *bad.*	The first night I quit smoking, I wanted a cigarette *badly.*

Activity

Underline the adjective or adverb needed. (Remember that adjectives describe nouns, and adverbs describe verbs, adjectives, or other adverbs.)

1. During a quiet moment in class, my stomach rumbled (loud, loudly).
2. I'm a (slow, slowly) reader, so I have to put aside more time to study than some of my friends.
3. Thinking no one was looking, the young man (quick, quickly) emptied his car's ashtray onto the parking lot.
4. The kitchen cockroaches wait (patient, patiently) in the shadows; at night they'll have the place to themselves.
5. I hang up the phone (immediate, immediately) whenever the speaker is a recorded message.

Well and *Good*

Two words that are often confused are *well* and *good*. *Good* is an adjective; it describes nouns. *Well* is usually an adverb; it describes verbs. *Well* (rather than *good)* is also used to refer to a person's health.

Activity

Write *well* or *good* in each of the sentences that follow.

1. I could tell by the broad grin on Della's face that the news was _____.
2. They say my grandfather sang so _____ that even the wind stopped to listen.
3. The food at the salad bar must not have been too fresh, because I didn't feel _____ after dinner.

4. When I want to do a really _____ job of washing the floor, I do it on my hands and knees.

5. The best way to get along _____ with our boss is to stay out of his way.

■ Review Test

Underline the correct word in the parentheses.

1. In Egypt, silver was once (more valued, most valued) than gold.
2. The doctor predicted that Ben would soon be (good, well) enough to go home.
3. The (little, less) coffee I drink, the better I feel.
4. Light walls make a room look (more large, larger) than dark walls do.
5. One of the (unfortunatest, most unfortunate) men I know is a millionaire.
6. The moth's (continuous, continuously) thumping against the screen got on my nerves.
7. The Amish manage (good, well) without radios, telephones, or television.
8. When the store owner caught the little boys stealing, he scolded them (bad, badly) and called their parents.
9. It is (good, better) to teach people to fish than to give them fish.
10. Today a rocket can reach the moon more (quick, quickly) than it took a stage-coach to travel from one end of England to the other.

36 Misplaced Modifiers

Introductory Project

Because of misplaced words, each of the sentences below has more than one possible meaning. In each case, see if you can explain the intended meaning and the unintended meaning. Also, circle the words that you think create the confusion because they are misplaced.

1. The sign in the restaurant window reads, "Wanted: Young Man—To Open Oysters with References."

   Intended meaning: _____

   _____

   Unintended meaning: _____

   _____

2. Clyde and Charlotte decided to have two children on their wedding day.

   Intended meaning: _____

   _____

   Unintended meaning: _____

   _____

3. The students no longer like the math instructor who failed the test.

   Intended meaning: _____

   _____

   Unintended meaning: _____

   _____

Answers are on page 630.

What Misplaced Modifiers Are and How to Correct Them

Modifiers are descriptive words. *Misplaced modifiers* are words that, because of awkward placement, do not describe the words the writer intended them to describe. Misplaced modifiers often obscure the meaning of a sentence. To avoid them, place words as close as possible to what they describe.

Misplaced Words	*Correctly Placed Words*
Tony bought an old car from a crooked dealer *with a faulty transmission.* (The *dealer* had a faulty transmission?)	Tony bought an old car with a faulty transmission from a crooked dealer. (The words describing the old car are now placed next to "car.")
I *nearly* earned a hundred dollars last week. (You just missed earning a hundred dollars, but in fact earned nothing?)	I earned nearly a hundred dollars last week. (The meaning—that you earned a little under a hundred dollars—is now clear.)
Bill yelled at the howling dog *in his underwear.* (The *dog* wore underwear?)	Bill, in his underwear, yelled at the howling dog. (The words describing Bill are placed next to "Bill.")

Activity

Underline the misplaced word or words in each sentence. Then rewrite the sentence, placing related words together and thereby making the meaning clear.

Examples   The suburbs <u>nearly</u> had five inches of rain.

The suburbs had nearly five inches of rain.

We could see the football stadium <u>driving across the bridge.</u>

Driving across the bridge, we could see the football stadium.

1. I saw mountains of uncollected trash walking along the city streets.

_____

_____

2. I almost had a dozen job interviews after I sent out my résumé.

_____

_____

3. The child stared at the movie monster with huge, innocent eyes.

_____

_____

4. Joanne decided to live with her grandparents while she attended college to save money.

_____

_____

5. Charlotte returned the hamburger to the supermarket that was spoiled.

_____

_____

6. Roger visited the old house still weak with the flu.

_____

_____

7. The phone almost rang fifteen times last night.

_____

_____

8. My uncle saw a kangaroo at the window under the influence of whiskey.

_____

_____

9. We decided to send our daughter to college on the day she was born.

_____

_____

10. Fred always opens the bills that arrive in the mailbox with a sigh.

_____

_____

■ Review Test

Write *M* for *misplaced modifier* or *C* for *correct* in front of each sentence.

_____   1. Rita found it difficult to mount the horse wearing tight jeans.

_____   2. Rita, wearing tight jeans, found it difficult to mount the horse.

_____   3. I noticed a crack in the window walking into the delicatessen.

_____   4. Walking into the delicatessen, I noticed a crack in the window.

_____ 5. The biology teacher told us there would be a pop quiz with an evil grin.

_____ 6. With an evil grin, the biology teacher told us there would be a pop quiz.

_____ 7. I almost caught a hundred lightning bugs.

_____ 8. I caught almost a hundred lightning bugs.

_____ 9. In a secondhand store, Willie found a television set that had been stolen from me last month.

_____ 10. Willie found a television set in a secondhand store that had been stolen from me last month.

_____ 11. Willie found, in a secondhand store, a television set that had been stolen from me last month.

_____ 12. In his shrillest voice, the reporter yelled a question at the departing mayor.

_____ 13. The reporter yelled a question at the departing mayor in his shrillest voice.

_____ 14. The president was quoted on the *NBC Evening News* as saying that the recession was about to end.

_____ 15. The president was quoted as saying that the recession was about to end on the *NBC Evening News*.

37 Dangling Modifiers

Introductory Project

Because of dangling words, each of the sentences below has more than one possible meaning. In each case, see if you can explain the intended meaning and the unintended meaning.

1. While smoking a pipe, my dog sat with me by the crackling fire.

   Intended meaning: _____

   Unintended meaning: _____

2. Looking at the leather-skirted woman, his sports car went through a red light.

   Intended meaning: _____

   Unintended meaning: _____

3. After baking for several hours, Grandmother removed the beef pie from the oven.

   Intended meaning: _____

   Unintended meaning: _____

Answers are on page 630.

What Dangling Modifiers Are and How to Correct Them

A modifier that opens a sentence must be followed immediately by the word it is meant to describe. Otherwise, the modifier is said to be *dangling*, and the sentence takes on an unintended meaning. For example, in the sentence

While smoking a pipe, my dog sat with me by the crackling fire.

the unintended meaning is that the *dog* was smoking the pipe. What the writer meant, of course, was that *he,* the writer, was smoking the pipe. The dangling modifier could be corrected by placing *I*, the word being described, directly after the opening modifier and revising as necessary:

While smoking a pipe, *I sat with* my dog by the crackling fire.

The dangling modifier could also be corrected by placing the subject within the opening word group:

While *I was* smoking my pipe, my dog sat with me by the crackling fire.

Here are other sentences with dangling modifiers. Read the explanations of why they are dangling and look carefully at how they are corrected.

Dangling	*Correct*
Swimming at the lake, a rock cut Sue's foot. (*Who* was swimming at the lake? The answer is not *rock* but *Sue.* The subject *Sue* must be added.)	Swimming at the lake, Sue cut her foot on a rock. *Or:* When Sue was swimming at the lake, she cut her foot on a rock.
While eating my sandwich, five mosquitoes bit me. (*Who* is eating the sandwich? The answer is not *five mosquitoes,* as it unintentionally seems to be, but *I.* The subject *I* must be added.)	While *I* was eating my sandwich, five mosquitoes bit me. *Or:* While eating my sandwich, *I* was bitten by five mosquitoes.
Getting out of bed, the tile floor was so cold that Yoko shivered all over. (*Who* got out of bed? The answer is not *tile floor* but *Yoko.* The subject *Yoko* must be added.)	Getting out of bed, *Yoko* found the tile floor so cold that she shivered all over. *Or:* When *Yoko* got out of bed, the tile floor was so cold that she shivered all over.

Dangling

To join the team, a C average or better is necessary.
(*Who* is to join the team? The answer is not *C average* but *you.* The subject *you* must be added.)

Correct

To join the team, *you* must have a C average or better.
Or: For *you* to join the team, a C average or better is necessary.

The preceding examples make clear the two ways of correcting a dangling modifier. Decide on a logical subject and do one of the following:

1   Place the subject *within* the opening word group.

When Sue was swimming at the lake, she cut her foot on a rock.

Note   In some cases an appropriate subordinating word such as *When* must be added, and the verb may have to be changed slightly as well.

2   Place the subject right *after* the opening word group.

Swimming at the lake, Sue cut her foot on a rock.

Activity

Ask *Who?* as you look at the opening words in each sentence. The subject that answers the question should be nearby in the sentence. If it is not, provide the logical subject by using either method of correction described above.

Example   While sleeping at the campsite, a Frisbee hit Derek on the head.

While Derek was sleeping at the campsite, a Frisbee hit him on the

head.

or   *While sleeping at the campsite, Derek was hit on the head by a*

Frisbee.

1. Watching the horror movie, goose bumps covered my spine.

_____

_____

2. After putting on a corduroy shirt, the room didn't seem as cold.

_____

_____

3. Flunking out of school, my parents demanded that I get a job.

   _____

   _____

4. Covered with food stains, my mother decided to wash the tablecloth.

   _____

   _____

5. Joining several college clubs, Antonio's social life became more active.

   _____

   _____

6. While visiting the Jungle Park Safari, a baboon scrambled onto the hood of their car.

   _____

   _____

7. Under attack by beetles, Charlotte sprayed her roses with insecticide.

   _____

   _____

8. Standing at the ocean's edge, the wind coated my glasses with a salty film.

   _____

   _____

9. Braking the car suddenly, my shopping bags tumbled off the seat.

   _____

   _____

10. Using binoculars, the hawk was clearly seen following its prey.

   _____

   _____

■ Review Test

Write *D* for *dangling* or *C* for *correct* in the blank next to each sentence. Remember that the opening words are a dangling modifier if they have no nearby logical subject to modify.

_____   1. Advertising in the paper, Ian's car was quickly sold.

_____   2. By advertising in the paper, Ian quickly sold his car.

_____   3. After painting the downstairs, the house needed airing to clear out the fumes.

_____   4. After we painted the downstairs, the house needed airing to clear out the fumes.

_____   5. Frustrated by piles of homework, Wanda was tempted to watch television.

_____   6. Frustrated by piles of homework, Wanda's temptation was to watch television.

_____   7. After I waited patiently in the bank line, the teller told me I had filled out the wrong form.

_____   8. After waiting patiently in the bank line, the teller told me I had filled out the wrong form.

_____   9. When dieting, desserts are especially tempting.

_____   10. When dieting, I find desserts especially tempting.

_____   11. Looking through the telescope, I saw a brightly lit object come into view.

_____   12. As I was looking through the telescope, a brightly lit object came into view.

_____   13. Looking through the telescope, a brightly lit object came into my view.

_____   14. Tossed carelessly over the arm of a chair, Mildred saw her new raincoat slide onto the floor.

_____   15. Mildred saw her new raincoat, which had been tossed carelessly over the arm of a chair, slide onto the floor.

38 Paper Format

When you hand in a paper for any of your courses, probably the first thing you will be judged on is its format. It is important, then, that you do certain things to make your papers look attractive, neat, and easy to read.

Here are guidelines to follow in preparing a paper for an instructor:

1 Use full-size theme or typewriter paper, 8½ by 11 inches.

2 Leave wide margins (1 to 1½ inches) on all four sides of each page. In particular, do not crowd the right-hand or bottom margin. The white space makes your paper more readable; also, the instructor has room for comments.

3 If you write by hand:

   a Use a pen with blue or black ink (*not* a pencil).

   b Be careful not to overlap letters or to make decorative loops on letters. On narrow-ruled paper, write only on every other line.

   c Make all your letters distinct. Pay special attention to *a, e, i, o,* and *u*— five letters that people sometimes write illegibly.

   d Keep your capital letters clearly distinct from small letters. You may even want to print all the capital letters.

   e Make commas, periods, and other punctuation marks firm and clear. Leave a slight space after each period.

4 Center the title of your paper on the first line of page 1. Do *not* put quotation marks around the title, do not underline it, and do not put a period after it. Capitalize all the major words in a title, including the first word. Short connecting words within a title like *of, for, the, in,* and *to* are not capitalized. Skip a line between the title and the first line of your text.

5 Indent the first line of each paragraph about five spaces (half an inch) from the left-hand margin.

6 When you type or word-process, use double-spacing between lines. Also double-space after a period.

7 Whenever possible, avoid breaking (hyphenating) words at the end of lines. If you must break a word, break only between syllables (see page 551). Do not break words of one syllable.

8 Write your name, the date, and the course number where your instructor asks for them.

Also keep in mind these important points about the *title* and *first sentence* of your paper:

9 The title should simply be several words that tell what the paper is about. It should usually *not* be a complete sentence. For example, if you are writing a paper about one of the most frustrating jobs you have ever had, the title could be just "A Frustrating Job."

10 Do not rely on the title to help explain the first sentence of your paper. The first sentence must be independent of the title. For instance, if the title of your paper is "A Frustrating Job," the first sentence should *not* be "It was working as a baby-sitter." Rather, the first sentence might be "Working as a baby-sitter was the most frustrating job I ever had."

Activity 1

Identify the mistakes in format in the following lines from a student theme. Explain the corrections in the spaces provided. One correction is provided as an example.

	"an unpleasant dining companion"
	My little brother is often an unpleasant dining companion. Last
	night was typical. For one thing, his appearance was disgusting.
	His shoes were not tied, and his shirt was unbuttoned and han-
	ging out of his pants, which he had forgotten to zip up. Traces
	of his afternoon snack of grape juice and chocolate cookies were

1. Hyphenate only between syllables. _____

2. _____

3. _____

4. _____

5. _____

6. _____

Activity 2

As already stated, a title should tell in several words (but *not* a complete sentence) what a paper is about. Often a title can be based on the topic sentence—the sentence that expresses the main idea of the paper. Following are five topic sentences from student papers. Write a suitable and specific title for each paper, basing the title on the topic sentence. (Note the example.)

Example   <u>Compromise in a Relationship   </u>
Learning how to compromise is essential to a good relationship.

1. *Title:* _____
Some houseplants are dangerous to children and pets.

2. *Title:* _____
A number of fears haunted me when I was a child.

3. *Title:* _____
You don't have to be a professional to take good photographs if you keep a few guidelines in mind.

4. *Title:* _____
My husband is compulsively neat.

5. *Title:* _____
There are a number of drawbacks to having a roommate.

Activity 3

As has already been stated, you must *not* rely on the title to help explain your first sentence. In four of the five sentences that follow, the writer has, inappropriately, used the title to help explain the first sentence.

Rewrite these four sentences so that they stand independent of the title. Write *Correct* under the one sentence that is independent of the title.

Example   *Title:* My Career Plans
First sentence: They have changed in the last six months.
Rewritten: <u>My career plans have changed in the last six months.</u>

1. *Title:* Contending with Dogs
First sentence: This is the main problem in my work as a mail carrier.

Rewritten : _____

_____

2. *Title:* Study Skills
First sentence: They are necessary if a person is to do well in college.

Rewritten : _____

_____

3. *Title:* Summer Vacation
First sentence: Contrary to popular belief, a summer vacation can be the most miserable experience of the year.

Rewritten : _____

_____

4. *Title:* My Wife and the Sunday Newspaper
First sentence: My wife has a peculiar way of reading it.

Rewritten : _____

_____

5. *Title:* Cell Phones
First sentence: Many motorists have learned the hard way just how dangerous these handy tools can be.

Rewritten : _____

_____

■   ## Review Test

In the space provided, rewrite the following sentences from a student paper. Correct the mistakes in format.

	"disciplining our children"
	My husband and I are becoming experts in disciplining our child-
	ren. We have certain rules that we insist upon, and if there are
	any violations, we are swift to act. When our son simply doesn't
	do what he is told to do, he must write that particular action
	twenty times. For example, if he doesn't brush his teeth, he
	writes, "I must brush my teeth." If a child gets home after the

39 Capital Letters

Introductory Project

Items 1–13: You probably know a good deal about the uses of capital letters. Answering the questions below will help you check your knowledge.

1. Write the full name of a person you know: _____

2. In what city and state were you born? _____

3. What is your present street address? _____

4. Name a country where you would like to travel: _____

5. Name a school that you attended: _____

6. Give the name of a store where you buy food: _____

7. Name a company where someone you know works: _____

8. What day of the week gives you the best chance to relax? _____

9. What holiday is your favorite? _____

10. What brand of toothpaste do you use? _____

11. Write the brand name of a candy or gum you like: _____

12. Name a song or a television show you enjoy: _____

13. Write the title of a magazine you read: _____

Items 14–16: Three capital letters are needed in the lines below. Underline the words that you think should be capitalized. Then write them, capitalized, in the spaces provided.

the masked man reared his silvery-white horse, waved good-bye, and rode out of town. My heart thrilled when i heard someone say, "that was the Lone Ranger. You don't see his kind much, anymore."

14. _____   15. _____   16. _____

Answers are on page 630.

Main Uses of Capital Letters

Capital letters are used with:

1 The first word in a sentence or direct quotation
2 Names of persons and the word *I*
3 Names of particular places
4 Names of days of the week, months, and holidays
5 Names of commercial products
6 Names of organizations such as religious and political groups, associations, companies, unions, and clubs
7 Titles of books, magazines, newspapers, articles, stories, poems, films, television shows, songs, papers that you write, and the like

Each use is illustrated on the pages that follow.

First Word in a Sentence or Direct Quotation

The panhandler touched me and asked, "Do you have any change?"

(Capitalize the first word in the sentence.)   (Capitalize the first word in the direct quotation.)

"If you want a ride," said Tawana, "get ready now. Otherwise, I'm going alone."

(*If* and *Otherwise* are capitalized because they are the first words of sentences within a direct quotation. But *get* is not capitalized because it is part of the first sentence within the quotation.)

Names of Persons and the Word *I*

Last night I ran into Tony Curry and Lola Morrison.

Names of Particular Places

Charlotte graduated from Fargone High School in Orlando, Florida. She then moved with her parents to Bakersfield, California, and worked for a time there at Alexander's Gift House. Eventually she married and moved with her husband to the Naval Reserve Center in Atlantic County, New Jersey. She takes courses two nights a week at Stockton State College. On weekends she and her family often visit the nearby Wharton State Park and go canoeing on the

Mullica River. She does volunteer work at Atlantic City Hospital in connection with the First Christian Church. In addition, she works during the summer as a hostess at Convention Hall and the Holiday Inn.

But: Use small letters if the specific name of a place is not given.

Charlotte sometimes remembers her unhappy days in high school and at the gift shop where she worked after graduation. She did not imagine then that she would one day be going to college and doing volunteer work for a church and a hospital in the community where she and her husband live.

Names of Days of the Week, Months, and Holidays

I was angry at myself for forgetting that Sunday was Mother's Day.

During July and August, Fred works a four-day week, and he has Mondays off.

Bill still has a scar on his ankle from a cherry bomb that exploded near him on a Fourth of July and a scar on his arm where he stabbed himself with a fishhook on a Labor Day weekend.

But: Use small letters for the seasons—summer, fall, winter, spring.

Names of Commercial Products

Clyde uses Scope mouthwash, Certs mints, and Dentyne gum to drive away the taste of the Marlboro cigarettes and White Owl cigars that he always smokes.

My sister likes to play Monopoly and Sorry; I like chess and poker; my brother likes Scrabble, baseball, and table tennis.

But: Use small letters for the *type* of product (mouthwash, mints, gum, cigarettes, and so on).

Names of Organizations Such as Religious and Political Groups, Associations, Companies, Unions, and Clubs

Fred Grencher was a Lutheran for many years but converted to Catholicism when he married. Both he and his wife, Martha, are members of the Democratic Party. Both belong to the American Automobile Association. Martha works part time as a refrigerator salesperson at Sears. Fred is a mail carrier and belongs to the Postal Clerks' Union.

Tony met Lola when he was a Boy Scout and she was a Campfire Girl; she asked him to light her fire.

Titles of Books, Magazines, Newspapers, Articles, Stories, Poems, Films, Television Shows, Songs, Papers That You Write, and the Like

On Sunday Lola read the first chapter of *I Know Why the Caged Bird Sings*, a book required for her writing course. She looked through her parents' copy of the *New York Times*. She then read an article titled "Thinking about a Change in Your Career" and a poem titled "Some Moments Alone" in *Cosmopolitan* magazine. At the same time she played an old Beatles album, *Abbey Road*. In the evening she watched *60 Minutes* on television and a movie, *Sudden Impact*, starring Clint Eastwood. Then from 11 P.M. to midnight she worked on a paper titled "Uses of Leisure Time in Today's Culture" for her sociology class.

Activity

Cross out the words that need capitals in the following sentences. Then write the capitalized forms of the words in the spaces provided. The number of spaces tells you how many corrections to make in each case.

Example   I brush with ~~crest~~ toothpaste but get cavities all the time. ____*Crest*____

1. A spokesperson for general motors announced that the prices of all chevrolets will rise next year.

    _____ _____ _____

2. In may 2000 mario's family moved here from brownsville, Texas.

    _____ _____ _____

3. The mild-mannered reporter named clark kent said to the Wolfman, "you'd better think twice before you mess with me, Buddy."

    _____ _____ _____

4. While watching television, Spencer drank four pepsis, ate an entire package of ritz crackers, and finished a bag of oreo cookies.

    _____ _____ _____

5. A greyhound bus almost ran over Tony as he was riding his yamaha to a friend's home in florida.

    _____ _____ _____

6. Before I lent my polaroid camera to Janet, I warned her, "be sure to return it by friday."

    _____ _____ _____

7. Before christmas George took his entire paycheck, went to sears, and bought a twenty-inch zenith color television.

_____ _____ _____

8. On their first trip to New York City, Fred and Martha visited the empire State Building and Times square. They also saw the New York mets play at Shea Stadium.

_____ _____ _____

9. Clyde was listening to Tina Turner's recording of "Proud mary," Charlotte was reading an article in *Reader's digest* titled "let's Stop Peddling Sex," and their son was watching *sesame Street.*

_____ _____ _____ _____

10. When a sign for a howard johnson's rest stop appeared on the turnpike, anita said, "let's stop here and stretch our legs for a bit."

_____ _____ _____

Other Uses of Capital Letters

Capital letters are also used with:

1 Names that show family relationships
2 Titles of persons when used with their names
3 Specific school courses
4 Languages
5 Geographic locations
6 Historical periods and events
7 Races, nations, and nationalities
8 Opening and closing of a letter

Each use is illustrated on the pages that follow.

Names That Show Family Relationships

I got Mother to baby-sit for me.
I went with Grandfather to the church service.
Uncle Carl and Aunt Lucy always enclose twenty dollars with birthday cards.

But: Do not capitalize words like *mother, father, grandmother, aunt,* and so on, when they are preceded by a possessive word (*my, your, his, her, our, their*).

I got my mother to baby-sit for me.

I went with my grandfather to the church service.

My uncle and aunt always enclose twenty dollars with birthday cards.

Titles of Persons When Used with Their Names

I wrote to Senator Grabbel and Congresswoman Punchie.

Professor Snorrel sent me to Chairperson Ruck, who sent me to Dean Rappers.

He drove to Dr. Helen Thompson's office after the cat bit him.

But: Use small letters when titles appear by themselves, without specific names.

I wrote to my senator and my congresswoman.

The professor sent me to the chairperson, who sent me to the dean.

He drove to the doctor's office after the cat bit him.

Specific School Courses

I got an A in both Accounting I and Small Business Management, but I got a C in Human Behavior.

But: Use small letters for general subject areas.

I enjoyed my business courses but not my psychology or language courses.

Languages

She knows German and Spanish, but she speaks mostly American slang.

Geographic Locations

I grew up in the Midwest. I worked in the East for a number of years and then moved to the West Coast.

But: Use small letters for directions.

A new high school is being built at the south end of town.

Because I have a compass in my car, I know that I won't be going east or west when I want to go north.

Historical Periods and Events

Hector did well answering an essay question about the Second World War, but he lost points on a question about the Great Depression.

Races, Nations, and Nationalities

The research study centered on African Americans and Hispanics.

They have German knives and Danish glassware in the kitchen, an Indian wood carving in the bedroom, Mexican sculptures in the study, and an Oriental rug in the living room.

Opening and Closing of a Letter

Dear Sir:

Dear Madam:

Sincerely yours,

Truly yours,

Note: Capitalize only the first word in a closing.

Activity

Cross out the words that need capitals in the following sentences. Then write the capitalized forms of the words in the spaces provided. The number of spaces tells you how many corrections to make in each case.

1. Although my grandfather spoke german and polish, my mother never learned either language.

   _____   _____

2. The chain letter began, "dear friend—You must mail twenty copies of this letter if you want good luck."

   _____   _____

3. Tomorrow in our history class, dr. connalley will start lecturing on the civil war.

   _____   _____   _____   _____

4. aunt Sarah and uncle Hal, who are mormons, took us to their church services when we visited them in the midwest.

———————   ———————   ———————   ———————

5. While visiting san francisco, Liza stopped in at a buddhist temple and talked to a chinese nun there.

———————   ———————   ———————   ———————

Unnecessary Use of Capitals

Many errors in capitalization are caused by using capitals where they are not needed.

Activity

Cross out the incorrectly capitalized words in the following sentences. Then write the correct forms of the words in the spaces provided. The number of spaces tells you how many corrections to make in each sentence.

1. The old man told the Cabdriver, "I want to go out to the Airport, and don't try to cheat me."

———————   ———————

2. When I see Nike Ads that say, "Just do it," I always think, "Why should a Sneaker tell Me what to do?"

———————   ———————   ———————

3. A front-page Newspaper story about the crash of a commercial Jet has made me nervous about my Overseas trip.

———————   ———————   ———————

4. During a Terrible Blizzard in 1888, People froze to Death on the streets of New York.

———————   ———————   ———————   ———————

5. I asked the Bank Officer at Citibank, "How do I get an identification Card to use the automatic teller machines?"

———————   ———————   ———————

■ Review Test 1

Cross out the words that need capitals in the following sentences. Then write the capitalized forms of the words in the spaces provided. The number of spaces tells you how many corrections to make in each sentence.

1. wanda and i agreed to meet on saturday before the football game.

   _____   _____   _____

2. Between Long island and the atlantic Ocean lies a long, thin sandbar called fire island.

   _____   _____   _____   _____

3. When I'm in the supermarket checkout line, it seems as if every magazine on display has an article called "how You Can Lose Twenty pounds in two weeks."

   _____   _____   _____   _____

4. At the bookstore, each student received a free sample pack of bayer aspirin, arrid deodorant, and pert shampoo.

   _____   _____   _____

5. "can't you be quiet?" I pleaded. "do you always have to talk while I'm watching *general hospital* on television?"

   _____   _____   _____   _____

6. On father's day, the children drove home and took their parents out to dinner at the ramada inn.

   _____   _____   _____   _____

7. I will work at the holly Day School on mondays and fridays for the rest of september.

   _____   _____   _____   _____

8. glendale bank, where my sister Amber works, is paying for her night course, business accounting I.

   _____   _____   _____   _____

9. I subscribe to one newspaper, the *daily planet,* and two magazines, *people* and *glamour.*

   _____   _____   _____   _____

10. On thanksgiving my brother said, "let's hurry and eat so i can go watch the football game on our new sony TV."

    _____   _____   _____   _____

■ Review Test 2

On separate paper,

1. Write seven sentences demonstrating the seven main uses of capital letters.
2. Write eight sentences demonstrating the eight additional uses of capital letters.

40 Numbers and Abbreviations

Numbers

1 Spell out numbers that can be expressed in one or two words. Otherwise, use numerals—the numbers themselves.

During the past five years, over twenty-five barracuda have been caught in the lake.

The parking fine was ten dollars.

In my grandmother's attic are eighty-four pairs of old shoes.

But

Each year about 250 baby trout are added to the lake.

My costs after contesting a parking fine in court were $135.

Grandmother has 382 back copies of *Reader's Digest* in her attic.

2 Be consistent when you use a series of numbers. If some numbers in a sentence or paragraph require more than two words, then use numerals throughout the selection:

During his election campaign, State Senator Mel Grabble went to 3 county fairs, 16 parades, 45 cookouts, and 112 club dinners, and delivered the same speech 176 times.

3 Use numerals for dates, times, addresses, percentages, and parts of a book.

The letter was dated April 3, 1872.

My appointment was at 6:15. (*But:* Spell out numbers before *o'clock*. For example: The doctor didn't see me until seven o'clock.)

He lives at 212 West 19th Street.

About 20 percent of our class has dropped out of school.

Turn to page 179 in Chapter 8 and answer questions 1–10.

Activity

Cross out the mistakes in numbers and write the corrections in the spaces provided.

1. Pearl Harbor was attacked on December the seventh, nineteen forty-one.

   _____

   _____

2. When the 2 children failed to return from school, over 50 people volunteered to search for them.

   _____

   _____

3. At 1 o'clock in the afternoon last Thursday, an earthquake destroyed at least 20 buildings in the town.

   _____

   _____

Abbreviations

While abbreviations are a helpful time-saver in note-taking, you should avoid most abbreviations in formal writing. Listed below are some of the few abbreviations that can be used acceptably in compositions. Note that a period is used after most abbreviations.

1 Mr., Mrs., Ms., Jr., Sr., Dr. when used with proper names:

Mr. Tibble   Dr. Stein   Ms. O'Reilly

2 Time references:

A.M. or a.m.   P.M. or p.m.   B.C. or A.D.

3 First or middle name in a signature:

R. Anthony Curry   Otis T. Redding   J. Alfred Prufrock

4 Organizations and common terms known primarily by their initials:

FBI   UN   CBS   FM   VCR

Activity

Cross out the words that should not be abbreviated and correct them in the spaces provided.

1. On a Sat. morning I will never forget, Jan. 15, 2000, at ten min. after eight o'clock, I came downstairs and discovered that I had been robbed.

   _____   _____   _____

2. For six years I lived at First Ave. and Gordon St. right next to Shore Memorial Hosp., in San Fran., Calif.

   _____   _____   _____   _____   _____

3. Before her biol. and Eng. exams, Linda was so nervous that her doc. gave her a tranq.

   _____   _____   _____   _____

■ Review Test

Cross out the mistakes in numbers and abbreviations and correct them in the spaces provided.

1. At three-fifteen P.M., an angry caller said a bomb was planted in a bus stat. locker.

   _____   _____

2. Page eighty-two is missing from my chem. book.

   _____   _____

3. Martha has over 200 copies of *People* mag.; she thinks they may be worth money someday.

   _____   _____

4. When I was eight yrs. old, I owned three cats, two dogs, and 4 rabbits.

   _____   _____

5. Approx. half the striking workers returned to work on Nov. third, nineteen ninety-nine.

   _____   _____   _____   _____

41 Apostrophe

Introductory Project

1. Larry's motorcycle
   my sister's boyfriend
   Grandmother's shotgun
   the men's room

   What is the purpose of the *'s* in the examples above?

   _____

2. They didn't mind when their dog bit people, but now they're leashing him because he's eating all their garden vegetables.

   What is the purpose of the apostrophe in *didn't, they're,* and *he's?*

   _____

3. I used to believe that vampires lived in the old coal bin of my cellar.
   The vampire's whole body recoiled when he saw the crucifix.
   Fred ate two baked potatoes.
   One baked potato's center was still hard.

   In each of the sentence pairs above, why is the *'s* used in the second sentence but not in the first?

   _____

   _____

Answers are on page 630.

The two main uses of the apostrophe are:

1 To show the omission of one or more letters in a contraction

2 To show ownership or possession

Each use is explained on the pages that follow.

Apostrophe in Contractions

A *contraction* is formed when two words are combined to make one word. An apostrophe is used to show where letters are omitted in forming the contraction. Here are two contractions:

> have + not = haven't (*o* in *not* has been omitted)
> I + will = I'll (*wi* in *will* has been omitted)

The following are some other common contractions:

I	+ am	= I'm	it	+ is	= it's
I	+ have	= I've	it	+ has	= it's
I	+ had	= I'd	is	+ not	= isn't
who	+ is	= who's	could	+ not	= couldn't
do	+ not	= don't	I	+ would	= I'd
did	+ not	= didn't	they	+ are	= they're

Note Will + not has an unusual contraction: won't.

Activity 1

Combine the following words into contractions. One is done for you.

1. we + are = ___we're___   6. you + have = _____

2. are + not = _____   7. has + not = _____

3. you + are = _____   8. who + is = _____

4. they + have = _____   9. does + not = _____

5. would + not = _____   10. there + is = _____

Activity 2

Write the contractions for the words in parentheses. One is done for you.

1. (Are not) ___*Aren't*___ you coming with us to the concert?

2. (I am) _____ going to take the car if (it is) _____ all right with you.

3. (There is) _____ an extra bed upstairs if (you would) _____ like to stay here for the night.

4. (I will) _____ give you the name of the personnel director, but there (is not) _____ much chance that (he will) _____ speak to you.

5. Denise (should not) _____ complain about the cost of food if (she is) _____ not willing to grow her own by planting a backyard garden.

Note   Even though contractions are common in everyday speech and in written dialogue, usually it is best to avoid them in formal writing.

Apostrophe to Show Ownership or Possession

To show ownership or possession, we can use such words as *belongs to, possessed by, owned by,* or (most commonly) *of.*

> the jacket that *belongs to* Tony
> the grades *possessed by* James
> the gas station *owned by* our cousin
> the footprints *of* the animal

But often the quickest and easiest way to show possession is to use an apostrophe plus *s* (if the word is not a plural ending in *-s*). Thus we can say:

> Tony's jacket
> James's grades
> our cousin's gas station
> the animal's footprints

Points to Remember

1 The *'s* goes with the owner or possessor (in the examples given, *Tony, James, cousin, the animal*). What follows is the person or thing possessed (in the examples given, *the jacket, grades, gas station, footprints*).

2 When *'s* is handwritten, there should always be a break between the word and the *'s*.

Tony's   not   Tony's
Yes   No

3 A singular word ending in *-s* (such as *James* in the earlier example) also shows possession by adding an apostrophe plus *s (James's)*.

Activity 1

Rewrite the italicized part of each of the sentences below, using *'s* to show possession. Remember that the *'s* goes with the owner or possessor.

Example   *The toys belonging to the children* filled an entire room.

    The children's toys

1. *The new sunglasses belonging to Elena* have been stolen.

2. *The visit of my cousin* lasted longer than I wanted it to.

3. *The owner of the pit bull* was arrested after the dog attacked a child.

4. *The prescription of a doctor* is needed for the pills.

5. *The jeep owned by Dennis* was recalled because of an engine defect.

6. Is this *the hat of somebody?*

7. The broken saddle produced a sore on *the back of the horse.*

8. *The cords coming from the computer* were so tangled they looked like spaghetti.

_____

9. *The energy level possessed by the little boy* is much higher than hers.

_____

10. *The foundation of the house* is crumbling.

_____

Activity 2

Add *'s* to each of the following words to make them the possessors or owners of something. Then write sentences using the words. Your sentences can be serious or playful. One is done for you.

1. parakeet ___*parakeet's*___   *The parakeet's cage needs cleaning.*___

_____

2. instructor _____   _____

_____

3. Lola _____   _____

_____

4. store _____   _____

_____

5. mother _____   _____

_____

Apostrophe versus Possessive Pronouns

Do not use an apostrophe with possessive pronouns. They already show ownership. Possessive pronouns include *his, hers, its, yours, ours,* and *theirs.*

Incorrect	*Correct*
The bookstore lost its' lease.	The bookstore lost its lease.
The racing bikes were theirs'.	The racing bikes were theirs.
The change is your's.	The change is yours.
His' problems are ours', too.	His problems are ours, too.
His' skin is more sunburned than her's.	His skin is more sunburned than hers.

Apostrophe versus Simple Plurals

When you want to make a word plural, just add an -*s* at the end of the word. Do *not* add an apostrophe. For example, the plural of the word *movie* is *movies,* not *movie's* or *movies'.* Look at this sentence:

Lola adores Tony's broad shoulders, rippling muscles, and warm eyes.

The words *shoulders, muscles,* and *eyes* are simple plurals, meaning *more than one shoulder, more than one muscle, more than one eye.* The plural is shown by adding only an -*s*. On the other hand, the *'s* after *Tony* shows possession—that Tony owns the shoulders, muscles, and eyes.

Activity

In the space provided under each sentence, add the one apostrophe needed and explain why the other word or words ending in *s* are simple plurals.

Example   Karens tomato plants are almost six feet tall.

Karens: *Karen's, meaning "belonging to Karen"*

plants: *simple plural meaning "more than one plant"*

1. The restaurants reputation brought hungry diners from miles around.

   restaurants: _____

   diners: _____

2. Phils job—slaughtering pigs—was enough to make him a vegetarian.

   Phils: _____

   pigs: _____

3. As Tinas skill at studying increased, her grades improved.

   Tinas: _____

   grades: _____

4. When I walked into my doctors office, there were six people waiting who also had appointments.

   doctors: _____

   appointments: _____

5. I asked the music store clerk for several blank cassette tapes and Lauryn Hills new CD.

   tapes: _____

   Hills: _____

6. After six weeks without rain, the nearby streams started drying up, and the lakes water level fell sharply.

weeks: _____

streams: _____

lakes: _____

7. Rebeccas hooded red cloak makes her look like a fairy-tale character, but her heavy black boots spoil the effect.

Rebeccas: _____

boots: _____

8. When the brakes failed on Eriks truck, he narrowly avoided hitting several parked cars and two trees.

brakes: _____

Eriks: _____

cars: _____

trees: _____

9. My familys favorite breakfast is bacon, eggs, and home-fried potatoes.

familys: _____

eggs: _____

potatoes: _____

10. My parents like Floridas winters, but they prefer to spend their summers back home in Maine.

Floridas: _____

winters: _____

summers: _____

Apostrophe with Plural Words Ending in -s

Plurals that end in -s show possession simply by adding the apostrophe (rather than an apostrophe plus s):

My *parents'* station wagon is ten years old.

The *students'* many complaints were ignored by the high school principal.

All the *Boy Scouts'* tents were damaged by the hailstorm.

Activity

In each sentence, cross out the one plural word that needs an apostrophe. Then write the word correctly, with the apostrophe, in the space provided.

Example   _soldiers'_   All the ~~soldiers~~ rifles were cleaned for inspection.

1. My parents car was stolen last night.

   _____

2. The transit workers strike has just ended.

   _____

3. Two of our neighbors homes are up for sale.

   _____

4. The door to the ladies room is locked.

   _____

5. When students gripes about the cafeteria were ignored, many started to bring their own lunches.

   _____

■ Review Test 1

In each sentence, cross out the two words that need apostrophes. Then write the words correctly in the spaces provided.

1. The contestants face fell when she learned that all she had won was a years supply of Ajax cleanser.

   _____   _____

2. Weve been trying for weeks to see that movie, but theres always a long line.

   _____   _____

3. Freds car wouldnt start until the baby-faced mechanic replaced its spark plugs and points.

   _____   _____

4. The citys budget director has trouble balancing his own familys checkbook.

   _____   _____

5. Taking Dianes elderly parents to church every week is one example of Pauls generous behavior.

   _____   _____

6. Heres a checklist of points to follow when youre writing your class reports.

   _____   _____

7. The curious child dropped his sisters makeup into the bedrooms hot-air vent.

   _____   _____

8. The cats babies are under my chair again; I cant find a way to keep her from bringing them near me.

   _____   _____

9. Because of a family feud, Julie wasnt invited to a barbecue at her only cousins house.

   _____   _____

10. Phyllis grade was the highest in the class, and Kevin grade was the lowest.

   _____   _____

■ **Review Test 2**

Make the following words possessive and then use at least five of them in a not-so-serious paragraph that tells a story. In addition, use at least three contractions in the paragraph.

mugger	restaurant	Tony	student
New York	sister	children	vampire
skunk	Jay Leno	boss	Oprah Winfrey
customer	bartender	police car	yesterday
instructor	someone	mob	Chicago

42 Quotation Marks

Read the following scene and underline all the words enclosed within quotation marks. Your instructor may also have you dramatize the scene, with one person reading the narration and two persons acting the two speaking parts—the young man and the old woman. The two speakers should imagine the scene as part of a stage play and try to make their words seem as real and true-to-life as possible.

An old woman in a Rolls-Royce was preparing to back into a parking space. Suddenly a small sports car appeared and pulled into the space. "That's what you can do when you're young and fast," the young man in the car yelled to the old woman. As he strolled away, laughing, he heard a terrible crunching sound. "What's that noise?" he said. Turning around, he saw the old woman backing repeatedly into his small car and crushing it. "You can't do that, old lady!" he yelled.

"What do you mean, I can't?" she chuckled, as metal grated against metal. "This is what you can do when you're old and rich."

1. On the basis of the above passage, what is the purpose of quotation marks?

   _____

2. Do commas and periods that come after a quotation go inside or outside the quotation marks?

   _____

Answers are on page 631.

The two main uses of quotation marks are:

1 To set off the exact words of a speaker or a writer

2 To set off the titles of short works

Each use is explained on the pages that follow.

Quotation Marks to Set Off Exact Words of a Speaker or Writer

Use quotation marks when you want to show the exact words of a speaker or a writer.

> "Say something tender to me," whispered Lola to Tony.
> (Quotation marks set off the exact words that Lola spoke to Tony.)

> Mark Twain once wrote, "The more I know about human beings, the more I like my dog."
> (Quotation marks set off the exact words that Mark Twain wrote.)

> "The only dumb question," the instructor said, "is the one you don't ask."
> (Two pairs of quotation marks are used to enclose the instructor's exact words.)

> Sharon complained, "I worked so hard on this paper. I spent two days getting information in the library and two days writing it. Guess what grade I got on it."
> (Note that the end quotation marks do not come until the end of Sharon's speech. Place quotation marks before the first quoted word of a speech and after the last quoted word. As long as no interruption occurs in the speech, do not use quotation marks for each new sentence.)

Punctuation Hint: In the four examples above, notice that a comma sets off the quoted part from the rest of the sentence. Also observe that commas and periods at the end of a quotation always go *inside* quotation marks.

Complete the following statements explaining how capital letters, commas, and periods are used in quotations. Refer to the four examples as guides.

1. Every quotation begins with a _____ letter.

2. When a quotation is split (as in the sentence above about dumb questions), the second part does not begin with a capital letter unless it is a

    _____ sentence.

3. _____ are used to separate the quoted part of a sentence from the rest of the sentence.

4. Commas and periods that come at the end of a quotation should go _____ the quotation marks.

The answers are *capital, new, Commas,* and *inside.*

Activity 1

Place quotation marks around the exact words of a speaker or writer in the sentences that follow.

1. The health-food store clerk said, Sucking on zinc lozenges can help you get over a cold.
2. How are you doing in school? my uncle always asks me.
3. An epitaph on a tombstone in Georgia reads, I told you I was sick!
4. Dave said, Let's walk faster. I think the game has already started.
5. Mark Twain once said, The man who doesn't read good books has no advantage over the man who can't.
6. Thelma said, My brother is so lazy that if opportunity knocked, he'd resent the noise.
7. It's extremely dangerous to mix alcohol and pills, Dr. Wilson reminded us. The combination could kill you.
8. Ice-cold drinks! shouted the vendor selling lukewarm drinks.
9. Be careful not to touch the fence, the guard warned. It's electrified.
10. Just because I'm deaf, Lynn said, many people treat me as if I were stupid.

Activity 2

1. Write a sentence in which you quote a favorite expression of someone you know. Identify the relationship of the person to you.

    Example   *One of my father's favorite expressions is, "Don't sweat the small stuff."*

    _____

    _____

    _____

2. Write a quotation that contains the words *Tony asked Lola.* Write a second quotation that includes the words *Lola replied.*

_____

_____

_____

_____

3. Copy a sentence or two that interest you from a book or magazine. Identify the title and author of the work.

Example In <u>Night Shift,</u> Stephen King writes, "I don't like to sleep with one leg sticking out. Because if a cool hand ever reached out from under the bed and grasped my ankle, I might scream."

_____

_____

_____

_____

Indirect Quotations

An indirect quotation is a rewording of someone else's comments, rather than a word-for-word direct quotation. The word *that* often signals an indirect quotation. Quotation marks are *not* used with indirect quotations.

Direct Quotation	*Indirect Quotation*
Fred said, "The distributor cap on my car is cracked."	Fred said that the distributor cap on his car was cracked.
(Fred's exact spoken words are given, so quotation marks are used.)	(We learn Fred's words indirectly, so no quotation marks are used.)
Sally's note to Jay read, "I'll be working late. Don't wait up for me."	Sally left a note for Jay saying she would be working late and he should not wait up for her.
(The exact words that Sally wrote in the note are given, so quotation marks are used.)	(We learn Sally's words indirectly, so no quotation marks are used.)

Activity

Rewrite the following sentences, changing words as necessary to convert the sentences into direct quotations. The first one is done for you as an example.

1. The instructor told everyone to take out a pen and sheet of paper.
   The instructor said, "Take out a pen and sheet of paper."

2. A student in the front row asked if this was a test.

   _____

3. The instructor replied that it was more of a pop quiz.

   _____

4. She added that anyone who did the homework would find it easy.

   _____

5. The student groaned that he was a dead man.

   _____

Quotation Marks to Set Off Titles of Short Works

Titles of short works are usually set off by quotation marks, while titles of long works are underlined. Use quotation marks to set off the titles of such short works as articles in books, newspapers, or magazines; chapters in a book; short stories; poems; and songs.

On the other hand, you should underline the titles of books, newspapers, magazines, plays, movies, record albums, and television shows.

Quotation Marks	*Underlines*
the article "The Mystique of Lawyers"	in the book <u>Verdicts on Lawyers</u>
the article "Getting a Fix on Repairs"	in the newspaper the <u>New York Times</u>
the article "Animal Facts and Fallacies"	in the magazine <u>Reader's Digest</u>
the chapter "Why Do Men Marry?"	in the book <u>Passages</u>
the story "The Night the Bed Fell"	in the book <u>A Thurber Carnival</u>
the poem "A Prayer for My Daughter"	in the book <u>Poems of W.B. Yeats</u>
the song "Beat It"	in the album <u>Thriller</u>
	the television show <u>Dateline NBC</u>
	the movie <u>Gone with the Wind</u>

Note   In printed works, titles of books, newspapers, and so on are set off by italics—slanted type that looks *like this*—instead of being underlined.

Activity

Use quotation marks or underlines as needed.

1. Whenever Gina sees the movie The Sound of Music, the song near the end, Climb Every Mountain, makes her cry.
2. No advertising is permitted in Consumer Reports, a nonprofit consumer magazine.
3. I printed out an article titled Too Much Homework? from the online version of Time to use in my sociology report.
4. Maddie's favorite television show is The Simpsons, and her favorite movie is Titanic.
5. Our instructor gave us a week to buy the textbook titled Personal Finance and to read the first chapter, Work and Income.
6. Every holiday season, our family watches the movie A Christmas Carol on television.
7. Looking around to make sure no one he knew saw him, Bob bought the newest National Enquirer in order to read the story called Man Explodes on Operating Table.
8. Edgar Allan Poe's short story The Murders in the Rue Morgue and his poem The Raven are in a paperback titled Great Tales and Poems of Edgar Allan Poe.
9. When Ling got her TV Guide, she read an article called Who Will Oscar Smile Upon? and thumbed through the listings to read the preview for Ally McBeal.
10. The night before his exam, he discovered with horror that the chapter Becoming Mature was missing from Childhood and Adolescence, the psychology text that he had bought secondhand.

Other Uses of Quotation Marks

1 Quotation marks are used to set off special words or phrases from the rest of a sentence:

Many people spell the words "a lot" as *one* word, "alot," instead of correctly spelling them as two words.

I have trouble telling the difference between "their" and "there."

Note   In printed works, *italics* are often used to set off special words or phrases. That is usually done in this book, for example.

2   Single quotation marks are used to mark off a quotation within a quotation.

> The instructor said, "Know the chapter titled 'Status Symbols' in *Adolescent Development* if you expect to pass the test."
>
> Lola said, "One of my favorite Mae West lines is 'I used to be Snow White, but I drifted.' "

■ Review Test 1

Insert quotation marks where needed in the sentences that follow.

1. Don't you ever wash your car? Lola asked Tony.
2. When the washer tilted and began to buzz, Martha shouted, Let's get rid of that blasted machine!
3. Take all you want, read the sign above the cafeteria salad bar, but please eat all you take.
4. After scrawling formulas all over the board with lightning speed, my math instructor was fond of asking, Any questions now?
5. Move that heap! the truck driver yelled. I'm trying to make a living here.
6. I did a summary of an article titled Aspirin and Heart Attacks in the latest issue of Time.
7. Writer's block is something that happens to everyone at times, the instructor explained. You simply have to keep writing to break out of it.
8. A passenger in the car ahead of Clyde threw food wrappers and empty cups out the window. That man, said Clyde to his son, is a human pig.
9. If you are working during the day, said the counselor, the best way to start college is with a night course or two.
10. I told the dentist that I wanted Novocain. Don't be a sissy, he said. A little pain won't hurt. I told him that a little pain wouldn't hurt him, but it would bother me.

■ Review Test 2

Go through the comics section of a newspaper to find a comic strip that amuses you. Be sure to choose a strip in which two or more characters are speaking to each other. Write a full description that will enable people who have not read the comic strip to visualize it clearly and appreciate its humor. Describe the setting and action in each panel, and enclose the words of the speakers in quotation marks.

43 Comma

Introductory Project

Commas often (though not always) signal a minor break, or pause, in a sentence. Each of the six pairs of sentences below illustrates one of the six main uses of the comma. Read each pair of sentences aloud and place a comma wherever you feel a slight pause occurs.

1. a. Frank's interests are Maria television and sports.
   b. My mother put her feet up sipped some iced tea and opened the newspaper.

2. a. Although the Lone Ranger used lots of silver bullets he never ran out of ammunition.
   b. To remove the cap of the aspirin bottle you must first press down on it.

3. a. Kitty Litter and Dredge Rivers Hollywood's leading romantic stars have made several movies together.
   b. Sarah who is my next-door neighbor just entered the hospital with an intestinal infection.

4. a. The wedding was scheduled for four o'clock but the bride changed her mind at two.
   b. Verna took three coffee breaks before lunch and then she went on a two-hour lunch break.

5. a. Lola's mother asked her "What time do you expect to get home?"
   b. "Don't bend over to pat the dog" I warned "or he'll bite you."

6. a. Roy ate seventeen hamburgers on July 29 1992 and lived to tell about it.
   b. Roy lives at 817 Cresson Street Detroit Michigan.

Answers are on page 631.

Six Main Uses of the Comma

Commas are used mainly as follows:

1 To separate items in a series

2 To set off introductory material

3 Before and after words that interrupt the flow of thought in a sentence

4 Before two complete thoughts connected by *and, but, for, or, nor, so, yet*

5 To set off a direct quotation from the rest of a sentence

6 For certain everyday material

Each use is explained on the pages that follow.

You may find it helpful to remember that the comma often marks a slight pause, or break, in a sentence. Read aloud the sentence examples given for each use, and listen for the minor pauses, or breaks, that are signaled by commas.

Comma between Items in a Series

Use commas to separate items in a series.

Do you drink tea with milk, lemon, or honey?

Today the dishwasher stopped working, the garbage bag split, and the refrigerator turned into an icebox.

The television talk shows enraged him so much he did not know whether to laugh, cry, or throw up.

Reiko awoke from a restless, nightmare-filled sleep.

Notes

a The final comma in a series is optional, but it is often used.

b A comma is used between two descriptive words in a series only if *and* inserted between the words sounds natural. You could say:

Reiko awoke from a restless *and* nightmare-filled sleep.

But notice in the following sentence that the descriptive words do not sound natural when *and* is inserted between them. In such cases, no comma is used.

Wanda drove a shiny blue Corvette. (A shiny *and* blue Corvette doesn't sound right, so no comma is used.)

Activity

Place commas between items in a series.

1. Superman believes in truth justice and the American way.
2. Jerry opened his textbook made sure his pencil was sharpened and fell asleep with his head on the desk.
3. Felipe added white wine mushrooms salt pepper and oregano to his spaghetti sauce.
4. Baggy threadbare jeans feel more comfortable than pajamas to me.
5. Carmen grabbed a tiny towel bolted out of the bathroom and ran toward the ringing phone.

Comma after Introductory Material

Use a comma to set off introductory material.

After punching the alarm clock with his fist, Bill turned over and went back to sleep.

Looking up at the sky, I saw a man who was flying faster than a speeding bullet.

Holding a baited trap, Clyde cautiously approached the gigantic mousehole.

In addition, he held a broom in his hand.

Also, he wore a football helmet in case a creature should leap out at his head.

Notes

a If the introductory material is brief, the comma is sometimes omitted. In the activities here, you should use the comma.

b A comma is also used to set off extra material at the end of a sentence. Here are two sentences where this comma rule applies:

A sudden breeze shot through the windows, driving the stuffiness out of the room.

I love to cook and eat Italian food, especially spaghetti and lasagna.

Activity

Place commas after introductory material.

1. When the president entered the room became hushed.

2. Feeling brave and silly at the same time Tony volunteered to go on stage and help the magician.

3. While I was eating my tuna sandwich the cats circled my chair like hungry sharks.

4. Because my parents died when I was young I have learned to look after myself. Even though I am now independent I still carry a special loneliness within me.

5. At first putting extra hot pepper flakes on the pizza seemed like a good idea. However I felt otherwise when flames seemed about to shoot out of my mouth.

Comma around Words Interrupting the Flow of Thought

Use commas before and after words or phrases that interrupt the flow of thought in a sentence.

My brother, a sports nut, owns over five thousand baseball cards.

That game show, at long last, has been canceled.

The children used the old Buick, rusted from disuse, as a backyard clubhouse.

Usually you can "hear" words that interrupt the flow of thought in a sentence. However, if you are not sure that certain words are interrupters, remove them from the sentence. If it still makes sense without the words, you know that the words are interrupters and the information they give is nonessential. Such nonessential information is set off with commas. In the sentence

Dody Thompson, who lives next door, won the javelin-throwing competition.

the words *who lives next door* are extra information, not needed to identify the subject of the sentence, *Dody Thompson*. Put commas around such nonessential information. On the other hand, in the sentence

The woman who lives next door won the javelin-throwing competition.

the words *who lives next door* supply essential information—information needed for us to identify the woman being spoken of. If the words were removed from the sentence, we would no longer know who won the competition. Commas are *not* used around such essential information.

Here is another example:

Wilson Hall, which the tornado destroyed, was ninety years old.

Here the words *which the tornado destroyed* are extra information, not needed to identify the subject of the sentence, *Wilson Hall.* Commas go around such nonessential information. On the other hand, in the sentence

The building which the tornado destroyed was ninety years old.

the words *which the tornado destroyed* are needed to identify the building. Commas are *not* used around such essential information.

As noted above, however, most of the time you will be able to "hear" words that interrupt the flow of thought in a sentence and will not have to think about whether the words are essential or nonessential.

Activity

Use commas to set off interrupting words.

1. On Friday my day off I went to get a haircut.
2. Dracula who had a way with women is Tony's favorite movie hero. He feels that the Wolfman on the other hand showed no class in handling women.
3. Many people forget that Franklin Roosevelt one of our most effective presidents was disabled.
4. Mowing the grass especially when it is six inches high is my least favorite job.
5. A jar of chicken noodle soup which was all there was in the refrigerator did not make a very satisfying meal.

Comma between Complete Thoughts

Use a comma between two complete thoughts connected by *and, but, for, or, nor, so, yet.*

The wedding was scheduled for four o'clock, but the bride changed her mind at two.

We could always tell when our instructor felt disorganized, for his shirt would not be tucked in.

Rich has to work on Monday nights, so he tapes the TV football game on his VCR.

Notes

a The comma is optional when the complete thoughts are short.

> Grace's skin tans and Mark's skin freckles.
>
> Her soda was watery but she drank it anyway.
>
> The day was overcast so they didn't go swimming.

b Be careful not to use a comma in sentences having *one* subject and a *double* verb. The comma is used only in sentences made up of two complete thoughts (two subjects and two verbs). In the following sentence, there is only one subject (*Kevin*) with a double verb (*will go* and *forget*). Therefore, no comma is needed:

> Kevin will go partying tonight and forget all about tomorrow's exam.

Likewise, the following sentence has only one subject (*Rita*) and a double verb (*was* and *will work*); therefore, no comma is needed:

> Rita was a waitress at the Holiday Inn last summer and probably will work there this summer.

Activity

Place a comma before a joining word that connects two complete thoughts (two subject-verb combinations). Remember, do *not* place a comma within sentences that have only one subject and a double verb.

1. The oranges in the refrigerator were covered with blue mold and the potatoes in the cupboard felt like sponges.
2. All the slacks in the shop were on sale but not a single pair was my size.
3. Martha often window-shops in the malls for hours and comes home without buying anything.
4. Tony left the dentist's office with his mouth still numb from Novocain and he talked with a lisp for two hours.
5. The whole family searched the yard inch by inch but never found Mom's missing wedding ring.
6. The car squealed down the entrance ramp and sped recklessly out onto the freeway.
7. The dancers in the go-go bar moved like wound-up Barbie dolls and the men in the audience sat as motionless as stones.

8. The aliens in the science fiction film visited our planet in peace but we greeted them with violence.

9. I felt like shouting at the gang of boys but didn't dare open my mouth.

10. Lenny claims that he wants to succeed in college but he has missed classes all semester.

Comma with Direct Quotations

Use a comma to set off a direct quotation from the rest of a sentence.

His father shouted, "Why don't you go out and get a job?"

"Our modern world has lost a sense of the sacredness of life," the speaker said.

"No," said Celia to Jerry. "I won't go to the roller derby with you."

"Can anyone remember," wrote Emerson, "when the times were not hard and money not scarce?"

Note   Commas and periods at the end of a quotation go inside quotation marks. See also page 529.

Activity

Use commas to set off quotations from the rest of the sentence.

1. Hassan came to the door and called out "Welcome to my home!"

2. My partner on the dance floor said "Don't be so stiff. You look as if you swallowed an umbrella."

3. The question on the anatomy test read "What human organ grows faster than any other, never stops growing, and always remains the same size?"

4. The student behind me whispered "The skin."

5. "My stomach hurts" Bruce said "and I don't know whether it was the hamburger or the math test."

Comma with Everyday Material

Use a comma with certain everyday material.

Persons Spoken To

Tina, go to bed if you're not feeling well.

Cindy, where did you put my shoes?

Are you coming with us, Owen?

Dates

March 4, 2000, is when Martha buried her third husband.

Addresses

Tony's grandparents live at 183 Roxborough Avenue, Cleveland, Ohio 44112.

Note   No comma is used to mark off the zip code.

Openings and Closings of Letters

Dear Santa,

Dear Larry,

Sincerely yours,

Truly yours,

Note   In formal letters, a colon is used after the opening: Dear Sir: *or* Dear Madam:

Numbers

The dishonest dealer turned the used car's odometer from 98,170 miles to 39,170 miles.

Activity

Place commas where needed.

1. I expected you to set a better example for the others Mike.
2. Janet with your help I passed the test.
3. The movie stars Kitty Litter and Dredge Rivers were married on September 12 2000 and lived at 3865 Sunset Boulevard Los Angeles California for one month.
4. They received 75000 congratulatory fan letters and were given picture contracts worth $3000000 in the first week of their marriage.
5. Kitty left Dredge on October 12 2000 and ran off with their marriage counselor.

■ Review Test 1

Insert commas where needed. In the space provided below each sentence, summarize briefly the rule that explains the use of the comma or commas.

1. The best features of my new apartment are its large kitchen its bay windows and its low rent.

   _____

2. Because we got in line at dawn we were among the first to get tickets for the concert.

   _____

3. "When will someone invent a telephone" Lola asked "that will ring only at convenient moments?"

   _____

4. Without opening his eyes Simon stumbled out of bed and opened the door for the whining dog.

   _____

5. I think Roger that you had better ask someone else for your $2500 loan.

   _____

6. Hot dogs are the most common cause of choking deaths in children for a bite-size piece can easily plug up a toddler's throat.

   _____

7. Tax forms though shortened and revised every year never seem to get any simpler.

   _____

8. Sandra may decide to go to college full-time or she may start by enrolling in a couple of evening courses.

   _____

9. I remember how with the terrible cruelty of children we used to make fun of the retarded girl who lived on our street.

   _____

10. Although that old man on the corner looks like a Skid Row bum he is said to have a Swiss bank account.

   _____

■ Review Test 2

Insert commas where needed.

1. My dog who is afraid of the dark sleeps with a night-light.
2. "Although men have more upper-body strength" said the lecturer "women are more resistant to fatigue."

3. The hot dogs at the ball park tasted delicious but they reacted later like delayed time bombs.

4. Janice attended class for four hours worked at the hospital for three hours and studied at home for two hours.

5. The old man as he gasped for air tried to assure the hospital clerk that he had an insurance card somewhere.

6. George and Ida sat down to watch the football game with crackers sharp cheese salty pretzels and two frosty bottles of beer.

7. Although I knew exactly what was happening the solar eclipse gave me a strong feeling of anxiety.

8. The company agreed to raise a senior bus driver's salary to $38000 by January 1 2001.

9. Even though King Kong was holding her at the very top of the Empire State Building Fay Wray kept yelling at him "Let me go!"

10. Navel oranges which Margery as a little girl called belly-button oranges are her favorite fruit.

■ Review Test 3

On separate paper, write six sentences, each demonstrating one of the six main comma rules.

44 Other Punctuation Marks

Introductory Project

Each of the sentences below needs one of the following punctuation marks:

;   —   -   ( )   :

See if you can insert the correct mark in each sentence. Each mark should be used once.

1. The following holiday plants are poisonous and should be kept away from children and pets holly, mistletoe, and poinsettias.
2. The freeze dried remains of Annie's canary were in the clear bottle on her bookcase.
3. William Shakespeare 1564–1616 married a woman eight years his senior when he was eighteen.
4. Grooming in space is more difficult than on Earth no matter how much astronauts comb their hair, for instance, it still tends to float loosely around their heads.
5. I opened the front door, and our cat walked in proudly with a live bunny hanging from his mouth.

Answers are on page 631.

Colon (:)

Use the colon at the end of a complete statement to introduce a list, a long quotation, or an explanation.

List

The following were my worst jobs: truck loader in an apple plant, assembler in a battery factory, and attendant in a state mental hospital.

Long Quotation

Thoreau explains in *Walden:* "I went to the woods because I wished to live deliberately, to front only the essential facts of life, and see if I could not learn what it had to teach, and not, when I came to die, discover that I had not lived."

Explanation

There are two softball leagues in our town: the fast-pitch league and the lob-pitch league.

Activity

Place colons where needed.

1. Foods that are high in cholesterol include the following eggs, butter, milk, cheese, shrimp, and well-marbled meats.

2. All the signs of the flu were present hot and cold spells, heavy drainage from the sinuses, a bad cough, and an ache through the entire body.

3. In his book *Illiterate America,* Jonathan Kozol has written "Twenty-five million American adults cannot read the poison warnings on a can of pesticide, a letter from their child's teacher, or the front page of a daily paper. An additional 35 million read only at a level which is less than equal to the full survival needs of our society. Together, these 60 million people represent more than one-third of the entire adult population."

Semicolon (;)

The main use of the semicolon is to mark a break between two complete thoughts, as explained on page 442. Another use of the semicolon is to mark off items in a series when the items themselves contain commas. Here are some examples:

Winning prizes at the national flower show were Roberta Collins, Alabama, azaleas; Sally Hunt, Kentucky, roses; and James Weber, California, Shasta daisies.

The following books must be read for the course: *The Color Purple,* by Alice Walker; *In Our Time,* by Ernest Hemingway; and *Man's Search for Meaning,* by Victor Frankl.

Activity

Place semicolons where needed.

1. The specials at the restaurant today are eggplant Parmesan, for $5.95 black beans and rice, for $4.95 and chicken potpie, for $6.95.
2. The top of the hill offered an awesome view of the military cemetery thousands of headstones were ranged in perfect rows.
3. Lola's favorite old movies are *To Catch a Thief,* starring Cary Grant and Grace Kelly *Animal Crackers,* a Marx Brothers comedy and *The Wizard of Oz,* with Judy Garland.

Dash (—)

A dash signals a pause longer than a comma but not as complete as a period. Use a dash to set off words for dramatic effect:

I didn't go out with him a second time—once was more than enough.

Some of you—I won't mention you by name—cheated on the test.

It was so windy that the VW passed him on the highway—overhead.

Notes

a The dash can be formed on a keyboard by striking the hyphen twice (--). In handwriting, the dash is as long as two letters would be.

b Be careful not to overuse dashes.

Activity

Place dashes where needed.

1. Riding my bike, I get plenty of exercise especially when dogs chase me.
2. I'm advising you in fact, I'm telling you not to bother me again.
3. The package finally arrived badly damaged.

Hyphen (-)

1 Use a hyphen with two or more words that act as a single unit describing a noun.

> The fast-talking salesman was so good that he went into politics. (*Fast* and *talking* combine to describe the salesman.)
>
> I both admire and envy her well-rounded personality.
>
> When the dude removed his blue-tinted shades, Lonnell saw the spaced-out look in his eyes.

2 Use a hyphen to divide a word at the end of a line of writing or typing. When you need to divide a word at the end of a line, divide it between syllables. Use your dictionary to be sure of correct syllable divisions (see also page 551).

> When Josh lifted up the hood of his Toyota, he realized that one of the radiator hoses had broken.

Notes

a Do not divide words of one syllable.

b Do not divide a word if you can avoid doing so.

Activity

Place hyphens where needed.

1. High flying jets and gear grinding trucks are constant sources of noise pollution in our neighborhood.

2. When Linda turned on the porch light, ten legged creatures scurried every where over the crumb filled floor.

3. Fred had ninety two dollars in his pocket when he left for the supermarket, and he had twenty two dollars when he got back.

Parentheses ( )

Parentheses are used to set off extra or incidental information from the rest of a sentence:

> The section of that book on the medical dangers of abortion (pages 35 to 72) is outdated.
>
> Yesterday at Hamburger House (my favorite place to eat), the guy who makes french fries asked me to go out with him.

Note   Do not use parentheses too often in your writing.

Activity

Add parentheses where needed.

1. Certain sections of the novel especially Chapter 5 made my heart race with suspense.
2. Did you hear that George Linda's first husband just got remarried?
3. Sigmund Freud 1856–1939 was the founder of psychoanalysis.

■ Review Test

At the appropriate spot, place the punctuation mark shown in the margin.

;
1. Efra's savings have dwindled to nothing she's been borrowing from me to pay her rent.

—
2. There's the idiot I'd know him anywhere who dumped trash on our front lawn.

-
3. Today's two career couples spend more money on eating out than their parents did.

:
4. Ben Franklin said "If a man empties his purse into his head, no man can take it away from him. An investment in knowledge always pays the best interest."

( )
5. One-fifth of our textbook pages 401–498 consists of footnotes and a bibliography.

45 Using the Dictionary

The dictionary is a valuable tool. To take advantage of it, you need to understand the main kinds of information that a dictionary gives about a word. Look at the information provided for the word *murder* in the following entry from the *American Heritage Dictionary of the English Language:**

Spelling and syllabication   Pronunciation   Part of speech

mur•der (mûr′dər) *n.* The unlawful killing of one human being by another, esp. with premeditated malice. —*v.* **1.** To kill (a human being) unlawfully. **2.** To mar or spoil by ineptness: *murder the English language.* **3.** *Slang.* To defeat decisively. [< OE *morthor.*] — **mur′der•er** *n.* — **mur′der•ess** *n.*

Meanings

Other forms of the word

Spelling

The first bit of information, in the boldface (heavy-type) entry itself, is the spelling of *murder.* You probably already know the spelling of *murder,* but if you didn't, you could find it by pronouncing the syllables in the word carefully and then looking it up in the dictionary.

Use your dictionary to correct the spelling of the following words:

compatable _____   insite _____

althogh _____   troble _____

aksident _____   untill _____

embelish _____	easyer _____
systimatise _____	prepostrous _____
shedule _____	comotion _____
attenshun _____	Vasaline _____
wierd _____	fatel _____
hurryed _____	busines _____
alright _____	jenocide _____
fony _____	poluted _____
kriterion _____	perpose _____
hetirosexual _____	chalange _____

Syllabication

The second bit of information that the dictionary gives, also in the boldface entry, is the syllabication of *murder.* Note that a dot separates the syllables.

Use your dictionary to mark the syllable divisions in the following words. Also indicate how many syllables are in each word.

j i t t e r   (_____ syllables)

m o t i v a t e   (_____ syllables)

o r a n g u t a n   (_____ syllables)

i n c o n t r o v e r t i b l e   (_____ syllables)

Noting syllable divisions will enable you to *hyphenate* a word: divide it at the end of one line of writing and complete it at the beginning of the next line. You can correctly hyphenate a word only at a syllable division, and you may have to check your dictionary to make sure of the syllable divisions.

Pronunciation

The third bit of information in the dictionary entry is the pronunciation of *murder:* (murder). You already know how to pronounce *murder,* but if you didn't, the information within the parentheses would serve as your guide. Use your dictionary to complete the following exercises that relate to pronunciation.

Vowel Sounds

You will probably use the pronunciation key in your dictionary mainly as a guide to pronouncing different vowel sounds (vowels are the letters *a, e, i, o,* and *u*). Here is a part of the pronunciation key in the *American Heritage Dictionary:*

ă pat / ā way / ĕ pet / ē bee / ĭ pit / ī pie

This key tells you, for example, that the sound of the short *a* is like the *a* in *pat,* the sound of the long *a* is like the *a* in *way,* and the sound of the short *e* is like the *e* in *pet.*

Now look at the pronunciation key in your own dictionary. The key is probably located in the front of the dictionary or at the bottom of alternate pages. What common word in the key tells you how to pronounce each of the following sounds?

ī _____   ŭ _____

ŏ _____   o͝o _____

ō _____   o͞o _____

(Note that a long vowel always has the sound of its own name.)

The Schwa (ə)

The symbol ə looks like an upside-down e. It is called a *schwa,* and it stands for the unaccented sound in such words as *ago, item, easily, gallop,* and *circus.* More approximately, it stands for the sound *uh*—like the *uh* that speakers sometimes make when they hesitate. Perhaps it would help to remember that *uh,* as well as ə, could be used to represent the schwa sound.

Here are some of the many words in which the schwa sound appears: *imitation* (im-uh-tā′shuhn or im-ə-tā′shən); *elevate* (el′uh-vāt or el′ə-vāt); *horizon* (huh-rī′zuhn or hə-rī′zən). Open your dictionary to any page, and you will almost surely be able to find three words that make use of the schwa in the pronunciation in parentheses after the main entry.

In the spaces below, write three words that make use of the schwa, and their pronunciations.

1. _____   (_____)

2. _____   (_____)

3. _____   (_____)

Accent Marks

Some words contain both a primary accent, shown by a heavy stroke ('), and a secondary accent, shown by a lighter stroke ('). For example, in the word *controversy* (kon'trə vûr'se), the stress, or accent, goes chiefly on the first syllable (*kon'*), and, to a lesser extent, on the third syllable (*vûr'*).

Use your dictionary to add stress marks to the following words:

preclude (pri klo͞od)

atrophy (at rə fē)

inveigle (in vā gəl)

ubiquitous (yo͞o bik wi təs)

prognosticate (prog nos ti kāt)

Full Pronunciation

Use your dictionary to write the full pronunciation (the information given in parentheses) for each of the following words.

1. inveigh _____

2. diatribe _____

3. raconteur _____

4. panacea _____

5. esophagus _____

6. cesarean _____

7. clandestine _____

8. vicarious _____

9. quiescent _____

10. parsimony _____

11. penchant _____

12. antipathy _____

13. capricious _____

14. schizophrenia _____

15. euphemism _____

16. internecine _____

17. amalgamate _____

18. quixotic _____

19. laissez-faire _____

20. antidisestablishmentarianism (This word is probably not in a paperback dictionary, but if you can say *establish* and if you break the rest of the word into indiviudal syllables, you should be able to pronounce it.)

_____

Now practice pronouncing each word. Use the pronunciation key in your dictionary as an aid to sounding out each syllable. *Do not* try to pronounce a word all at once; instead, work on mastering *one syllable at a time*. When you can pronounce each of the syllables in a word successfully, then say them in sequence, add the accent, and pronounce the entire word.

Parts of Speech

The next bit of information that the dictionary gives about *murder* is *n.* This abbreviation means that the meanings of *murder* as a noun will follow.

Use your dictionary if necessary to fill in the meanings of the following abbreviations:

v. = _____   sing. = _____

adj. = _____   pl. = _____

Principal Parts of Irregular Verbs

Murder is a regular verb and forms its principal parts by adding *-ed, -ed,* and *-ing* to the stem of the verb. When a verb is irregular, the dictionary lists its principal parts. For example, with *give* the present tense comes first (the entry itself, *give*). Next comes the past tense (*gave*), and then the past participle (*given*)—the form of the verb used with such helping words as *have, had,* and *was.* Then comes the present participle (*giving*)—the *-ing* form of the verb.

Look up the principal parts of the following irregular verbs and write them in the spaces provided. The first one has been done for you.

Present	Past	Past Participle	Present Participle
tear	*tore*	*torn*	*tearing*
go			
know			
steal			

Plural Forms of Irregular Nouns

The dictionary supplies the plural forms of all irregular nouns. (Regular nouns like *murder* form the plural by adding -*s* or -*es*). Give the plurals of the following nouns. If two forms are shown, write down both.

analysis _____

dictionary _____

criterion _____

activity _____

thesis _____

Meanings

When a word has more than one meaning, the meanings are numbered in the dictionary, as with the verb *murder*. In many dictionaries, the most common meanings of a word are presented first. The introductory pages of your dictionary will explain the order in which meanings are presented.

Use the sentence context to try to explain the meaning of the underlined word in each of the following sentences. Write your definition in the space provided. Then look up and record the dictionary meaning of the word. Be sure to select the meaning that fits the word as it is used in the sentence.

1. I spend an <u>inordinate</u> amount of time watching television.

   Your definition: _____

   Dictionary definition: _____

2. I appreciated her candid remark that my pants were so baggy they made me look like a clown.

Your definition: _____

Dictionary definition: _____

3. The FBI squelched the terrorists' plan to plant a bomb in the White House.

Your definition: _____

Dictionary definition: _____

4. One of the cardinal rules in our house was, "Respect other people's privacy."

Your definition: _____

Dictionary definition: _____

5. A special governor prevents the school bus from traveling more than fifty-five miles an hour.

Your definition: _____

Dictionary definition: _____

Etymology

Etymology refers to the origin and historical development of a word. Such information is usually enclosed in brackets and is more likely to be present in a hardbound desk dictionary than in a paperback one. Good desk dictionaries include the following:

American Heritage Dictionary of the English Language

Random House College Dictionary

Webster's New Collegiate Dictionary

Webster's New World Dictionary

A good desk dictionary will tell you, for example, that the word *berserk* derives from the name of a tribe of Scandanavian warriors who would work themselves into a frenzy during battle. The word is now a general term to describe someone whose actions are frenzied or crazed.

See if your dictionary says anything about the origins of the following words.

bikini _____

_____

_____

_____

sandwich _____

_____

_____

_____

tantalize _____

_____

_____

_____

breakfast _____

_____

_____

_____

Usage Labels

As a general rule, use only standard English words in your writing. If a word is not standard English (as is the case, for example, with the third meaning of *murder* as a verb), your dictionary will probably give it a usage label like one of the following: *informal, nonstandard, slang, vulgar, obsolete, archaic, rare.*

Look up the following words and record how your dictionary labels them. Remember that a recent hardbound desk dictionary will always be the best source of information about usage.

flunk _____

tough (meaning "unfortunate, too bad") _____

creep (meaning "an annoying person") _____

ain't _____

scam _____

Synonyms

A *synonym* is a word that is close in meaning to another word. Using synonyms helps you avoid unnecessary repetition of the same word in a paper. A paperback dictionary is not likely to give you synonyms for words, but a good desk dictionary will. (You might also want to own a *thesaurus,* a book that lists synonyms and antonyms. An *antonym* is a word approximately opposite in meaning to another word.)

Consult a desk dictionary that gives synonyms for the following words, and write the synonyms in the spaces provided.

heavy _____

escape _____

necessary _____

46 Improving Spelling

Poor spelling often results from bad habits developed in early school years. With work, you can correct such habits. If you can write your name without misspelling it, there is no reason why you can't do the same with almost any word in the English language. Following are six steps you can take to improve your spelling.

Step 1: Use the Dictionary

Get into the habit of using the dictionary. When you write a paper, allow yourself time to look up the spelling of all those words you are unsure about. Do not overlook the value of this step just because it is such a simple one. By using the dictionary, you can probably make yourself a 95 percent better speller.

Step 2: Keep a Personal Spelling List

Keep a list of words you misspell, and study these words regularly. Use the chart on page 634 as a starter. When you accumulate additional words, write them on the back page of a frequently used notebook or on a separate sheet of paper titled "Personal Spelling List."

To master the words on your list, do the following:

1 Write down any hint that will help you remember the spelling of a word. For example, you might want to note that *occasion* is spelled with two *c's* and one *s,* or that *all right* is two words, not one word.

2 Study a word by looking at it, saying it, and spelling it. You may also want to write out the word one or more times, or "air-write" it with your finger in large, exaggerated motions.

3 When you have trouble spelling a long word, try to break the word into syllables and see whether you can spell the syllables. For example, *inadvertent* can be spelled easily if you can hear and spell in turn its four syllables: *in ad ver tent.* And *consternation* can be spelled easily if you hear and spell in turn its four syllables: *con ster na tion.* Remember, then: try to see, hear, and spell long words syllable by syllable.

4 Keep in mind that review and repeated self-testing are the keys to effective learning. When you are learning a series of words, go back after studying each new word and review all the preceding ones.

Step 3: Master Commonly Confused Words

Master the meanings and spellings of the commonly confused words on pages 569–578. Your instructor may assign twenty words at a time for you to study and may give you a series of quizzes until you have mastered the words.

Step 4: Understand Basic Spelling Rules

Explained briefly here are three rules that may improve your spelling. While exceptions sometimes occur, the rules hold true most of the time.

Rule 1: *Changing y to i*   When a word ends in a consonant plus *y*, change *y* to *i* when you add an ending (but keep the *y* before *-ing*).

try + ed = tried	easy + er = easier
defy + es = defies	carry + ed = carried
ready + ness = readiness	penny + less = penniless

Rule 2: *Final Silent e*   Drop a final *e* before an ending that starts with a vowel (the vowels are *a, e, i, o,* and *u*).

create + ive = creative	believe + able = believable
nerve + ous = nervous	share + ing = sharing

Keep the final *e* before an ending that starts with a consonant.

extreme + ly = extremely	life + less = lifeless
hope + ful = hopeful	excite + ment = excitement

Rule 3: *Doubling a Final Consonant*   Double the final consonant of a word when all three of the following are true:

a   The word is one syllable or is accented on the last syllable.
b   The word ends in a single consonant preceded by a single vowel.
c   The ending you are adding starts with a vowel.

shop + er = shopper	thin + est = thinnest
equip + ed = equipped	submit + ed = submitted
swim + ing = swimming	drag + ed = dragged

Activity

Combine the following words and endings by applying the three rules above.

1. worry   + ed   = _____
2. write   + ing = _____
3. marry   + es   = _____
4. run   + ing = _____
5. terrify + ed   = _____
6. dry   + es   = _____
7. forget   + ing = _____
8. care   + ful = _____
9. control + ed   = _____
10. debate   + able = _____

Step 5: Study a Basic Word List

Study the spellings of the words in the following list. They are five hundred of the words most often used in English. Your instructor may assign twenty-five or fifty words for you to study at a time and give you a series of quizzes until you have mastered the list.

Five Hundred Basic Words

ability	all right	another	automobile
absent	almost	answer	autumn
accept	a lot	anxious	avenue
accident	already	appetite	awful
ache	also	apply	awkward
across	although	approach	back
address	always	approve	balance
advertise	amateur	argue	bargain
advice	American	around	beautiful
after	among	arrange	because
again	amount	attempt	become **50**
against	angry **25**	attention	been
agree	animal	August	before

begin	choose	disease	fight
being	church	distance	flower
believe	cigarette	doctor **125**	forehead
between	citizen	does	foreign
bicycle	city	dollar	forty
black	close	don't	forward
blue	clothing	doubt	found
board	coffee	down	fourteen
borrow	collect	dozen	Friday
bottle	college	during	friend
bottom	color	each	from
brake	come	early	gallon
breast	comfortable **100**	earth	garden
breathe	company	easy	general
brilliant	condition	education	get
brother	conversation	eight	good
building	copy	either	grammar
bulletin	daily	empty	great **175**
bureau	danger	English	grocery
business	daughter	enough	grow
came	daybreak	entrance	guess
can't	dear	evening	half
careful **75**	death	everything	hammer
careless	December	examine	hand
cereal	decide	except	handkerchief
certain	deed	exercise	happy
chair	dentist	exit	having
change	deposit	expect **150**	head
charity	describe	fact	heard
cheap	did	factory	heavy
cheat	died	family	high
cheek	different	far	himself
chicken	dinner	February	hoarse
chief	direction	few	holiday
children	discover	fifteen	home

hospital	light	needle	part
house	listen	neither	peace
however	little	never	pear **300**
hundred	loaf	newspaper	pencil
hungry	loneliness	nickel	penny
husband	long	niece	people
instead	lose	night	perfect
intelligence **200**	made	ninety	period
interest	making	noise	person
interfere	many	none	picture
interrupt	March	not	piece
into	marry	nothing	pillow
iron	match	November **275**	place
itself	matter	now	plain
January	may	number	please
July	measure	ocean	pocket
June	medicine	o'clock	policeman
just	men	October	possible
kindergarten	middle	offer	post office
kitchen	might	often	potato
knock	million	old	power
knowledge	minute	omit	prescription
labor	mistake **250**	once	president
laid	Monday	one	pretty
language	money	only	probably
last	month	operate	promise
laugh	more	opinion	psychology
learn	morning	opportunity	public **325**
led	mother	optimist	pursue
left	mountain	original	put
leisure	mouth	ought	quart
length	much	ounce	quarter
lesson **225**	must	overcoat	quick
letter	nail	pain	quiet
life	near	paper	quit

quite	since	tenant	understand
quiz	sister	tenth	United States
raise	sixteenth	than	until
read	sleep	Thanksgiving	upon
ready	smoke	that	used
really	soap	theater	usual
reason	soldier	them	valley
receive	something **375**	there	value
recognize	sometimes	they	variety
refer	soul	thing	vegetable
religion	soup	thirteen	very
remember	south	this	view
repeat	stamp	though	villain **450**
resource	state	thousand	visitor
restaurant	still	thread	voice
ribbon	stockings	three	vote
ridiculous	straight	through	wage
right **350**	street	Thursday	wagon
said	strong	ticket	waist
same	student	time	wait
sandwich	studying	tired	wake
Saturday	such	today	walk
say	suffer	together **425**	warm
school	sugar	tomorrow	warning
scissors	suit	tongue	Washington
season	summer	tonight	watch
see	Sunday	touch	water
sentence	supper	toward	wear
September	sure	travel	weather
service	sweet	trouble	Wednesday
seventeen	take	trousers	week
several	teach	truly	weigh
shoes	tear **400**	twelve	welcome
should	telegram	uncle	well
sight	telephone	under	went

were	whose	won't	wrong
what	wife	work	year
whether **475**	window	world	yesterday
which	winter	worth	yet
while	without	would	young
white	woman	writing	your
whole	wonder	written	you're **500**

Note   Two spelling mistakes that students often make are to write *a lot* as one word (*alot*) and to write *all right* as one word (*alright*). Do not write either *a lot* or *all right* as one word.

Step 6: Use Electronic Aids

There are three electronic aids that may help your spelling. First, most *electronic typewriters* can be set to beep automatically when you misspell a word. They include built-in dictionaries that will then give you the correct spelling. Second, *electronic spell-checks* are pocket-size devices that look much like the pocket calculators you may use in math class. Electronic spellers can be found in almost any electronics store. The checker includes a tiny keyboard. You type out the word the way you think it is spelled, and the checker quickly provides you with the correct spelling of related words. Finally, *a computer with a spell-checker* as part of its word processing program will identify incorrect words and suggest correct spellings. If you know how to write on the computer, you will have little trouble learning how to use the spell-check feature.

47 Vocabulary Development

A good vocabulary is a vital part of effective communication. A command of many words will make you a better writer, speaker, listener, and reader. Studies have shown that students with a strong vocabulary, and students who work to improve a limited vocabulary, are more successful in school. And one research study found that *a good vocabulary, more than any other factor, was common to people enjoying successful careers.* This section will describe three ways of developing your word power: (1) regular reading, (2) vocabulary wordsheets, and (3) vocabulary study books. You should keep in mind from the start, however, that none of the approaches will help unless you truly decide that vocabulary development is an important goal. Only when you have this attitude can you begin doing the sustained work needed to improve your word power.

Regular Reading

Through reading a good deal, you will learn words by encountering them a number of times in a variety of sentences. Repeated exposure to a word in context will eventually make it a part of your working language.

You should develop the habit of reading a daily newspaper and one or more weekly magazines like *Time, Newsweek,* or even *People,* as well as monthly magazines suited to your interests. In addition, you should try to read some books for pleasure. This may be especially difficult at times when you also have textbook reading to do. Try, however, to redirect a regular half hour to one hour of your recreational time to reading books, rather than watching television, listening to music, or the like. Doing so, you may eventually reap the rewards of an improved vocabulary *and* discover that reading can be truly enjoyable. If you would like some recommendations, ask your instructor for a copy of the "List of Interesting Books" in the Instructor's Manual that accompanies *English Skills.*

Vocabulary Wordsheets

Vocabulary wordsheets are another means of vocabulary development. Whenever you read, you should mark off words that you want to learn. After you have accumulated a number of words, sit down with a dictionary and look up basic information about each of them. Put this information on a wordsheet like the one shown below. Be sure also to write down a sentence in which each word appears. A word is always best learned not in a vacuum but in the context of surrounding words.

Study each word as follows. To begin with, make sure you can correctly pronounce the word and its derivations. (Pages 551–554 explain the dictionary pronunciation key that will help you pronounce each word properly.) Next, study the main meanings of the word until you can say them without looking at them. Finally, spend a moment looking at the example of the word in context. Follow the same process with the second word. Then, after testing yourself on the first and the second words, go on to the third word. After you learn each new word, remember to continue to test yourself on all the words you have studied. Repeated self-testing is a key to effective learning.

Activity

In your reading, locate four words that you would like to master. Enter them in the spaces on the vocabulary wordsheet below and fill in all the needed information. Your instructor may then check your wordsheet and perhaps give you a quick oral quiz on selected words.

You may receive a standing assignment to add five words a week to a wordsheet and to study the words. Note that you can create your own wordsheets using loose-leaf paper, or your instructor may give you copies of the wordsheet that appears below.

Vocabulary Wordsheet

1. Word: _____formidable_____ Pronunciation: _____(fôr′ mi də bəl)_____

   Meanings: _____1. feared or dreaded_____

   _____2. extremely difficult_____

   _____

   Other forms of the word: _____formidably   formidability_____

   Use of the word in context: _____Several formidable obstacles stand between_____

   _____Matt and his goal._____

2. Word: _____ Pronunciation: _____

   Meanings: _____

   _____

   _____

   Other forms of the word: _____

   Use of the word in context: _____

   _____

3. Word: _____   Pronunciation: _____

    Meanings: _____

    _____

    _____

    Other forms of the word: _____

    Use of the word in context: _____

    _____

4. Word: _____   Pronunciation: _____

    Meanings: _____

    _____

    _____

    Other forms of the word: _____

    Use of the word in context: _____

    _____

5. Word: _____   Pronunciation: _____

    Meanings: _____

    _____

    _____

    Other forms of the word: _____

    Use of the word in context: _____

    _____

Vocabulary Study Books

A third way to increase your word power is to use vocabulary study books. Many vocabulary books and programs are available. The best are those that present words in one or more contexts and then provide several reinforcement activities for each word. These books will help you increase your vocabulary if you have the determination required to work with them on a regular basis.

48 Commonly Confused Words

Introductory Project

Circle the five words that are misspelled in the following passage. Then see if you can write the correct spellings in the spaces provided.

You're mind and body are not as separate as you might think. Their is a lot of evidence, for instance, that if you believe a placebo (a substance with no medicine) will help you, than it will. One man is said too have rapidly recovered from an advanced case of cancer after only one dose of a drug that he believed was highly effective. Its not clear just how placebos work, but they do show how closely the mind and body are related.

1. _____

2. _____

3. _____

4. _____

5. _____

Answers are on page 631.

Homonyms

The commonly confused words on the following pages have the same sounds but different meanings and spellings; such words are known as *homonyms*. Complete the activity for each set of homonyms, and check off and study the words that give you trouble.

all ready completely prepared
already previously; before

> We were *all ready* to start the play, but the audience was still being seated.
> I have *already* called the police.

Fill in the blanks: I am _____ for the economics examination because I have _____ studied the chapter three times.

brake stop; the stopping device in a vehicle
break come apart

> His car bumper has a sticker reading, "I *brake* for animals."
> "I am going to *break* up with Bill if he keeps seeing other women," said Rita.

Fill in the blanks: When my car's emergency _____ slipped, the car rolled back and demolished my neighbor's rose garden, causing a _____ in our good relations with each other.

coarse rough
course part of a meal; a school subject; direction; certainly (as in *of course*).

> By the time the waitress served the customers the second *course* of the meal, she was aware of their *coarse* eating habits.

Fill in the blanks: Ted felt that the health instructor's humor was too _____ for his taste and was glad when he finished the _____.

hear perceive with the ear
here in this place

> "The salespeople act as though they don't see or *hear* me, even though I've been standing *here* for fifteen minutes," the woman complained.

Fill in the blanks: "Did you _____ about the distinguished visitor who just came into town and is staying _____ at this very hotel?"

hole   an empty spot
whole   entire

"I can't believe I ate the *whole* pizza," moaned Ralph. "I think it's going to make a *hole* in my stomach lining."

Fill in the blanks: The _____ time I was at the party I tried to conceal the _____ I had in my pants.

its   belonging to it
it's   shortened form of *it is* or *it has*

The car blew *its* transmission (the transmission belonging to it, the car).
It's (it has) been raining all week and *it's* (it is) raining now.

Fill in the blanks: _____ hot and unsanitary in the restaurant kitchen I work in, and I don't think the restaurant deserves _____ good reputation.

knew   past form of *know*
new   not old

"I had *new* wallpaper put up," said Sarah.
"I *knew* there was some reason the place looked better," said Bill.

Fill in the blanks: Lola _____ that getting her hair cut would give her face a _____ look.

know   to understand
no   a negative

"I don't *know* why my dog Fang likes to attack certain people," said Martha. "There's *no* one thing the people have in common."

Fill in the blanks: I _____ of _____ way of telling whether that politician is honest or not.

pair   set of two
pear   fruit

"What a great *pair* of legs Tony has," said Lola to Vonnie. Tony didn't hear her, for he was feeling very sick after munching on a green *pear.*

Fill in the blanks: In his lunch box was a _____ of _____s.

passed   went by; succeeded in; handed to
past   time before the present; beyond, as in "We worked past closing time."

Someone *passed* him a wine bottle; it was the way he chose to forget his unhappy *past.*

Fill in the blanks: I walked _____ the instructor's office but was afraid to ask her whether or not I had _____ the test.

peace   calm
piece   part

Nations often risk world *peace* by fighting over a *piece* of land.

Fill in the blanks; Martha did not have any _____ until she gave her dog a _____ of meat loaf.

plain   simple
plane   aircraft

The *plain,* unassuming young man on the *plane* suddenly jumped up with a grenade in his hand and announced, "We're all going to Tibet."

Fill in the blanks: The game-show contestant opened the small box wrapped in _____ brown paper and found inside the keys to his own jet _____.

principal   main; a person in charge of a school
principle   law, standard, or rule

Pete's high school *principal* had one *principal* problem: Pete. This was because there were only two *principles* in Pete's life: rest and relaxation.

Fill in the blanks: The _____ reason she dropped out of school was that she believed in the _____ of complete freedom of choice.

Note   It might help to remember that the *e* in *principle* is also in *rule*—the meaning of *principle.*

right   correct; opposite of *left*
write   put words on paper

   If you have the *right* course card, I'll *write* your name on the class roster.

Fill in the blanks: Eddie thinks I'm weird because I _____ with both my _____ and my left hand.

than   used in comparisons
then   at that time

   When we were kids, my friend Elaine had prettier clothes *than* I did. I really envied her *then.*

Fill in the blanks: Marge thought she was better _____ the rest of us, but _____ she got the lowest grade on the history test.

Note   It might help to remember that th*e*n (with an *e*) is also a tim*e* signal.

their   belonging to them
there   at that place; neutral word used with verbs like *is, are, was, were, have,* and *had*
they're   shortened form of *they are*

   Two people own that van over *there* (at that place). *They're* (they are) going to move out of *their* apartment (the apartment belonging to them) and into the van, in order to save money.

Fill in the blanks: _____ not going to invite us to _____ table because _____ is no room for us to sit down.

threw   past form of *throw*
through   from one side to the other; finished

   The fans *threw* so much litter onto the field that the teams could not go *through* with the game.

Fill in the blanks: When Mr. Jefferson was _____ screaming about the violence on television, he _____ the newspaper at his dog.

to	verb part, as in *to smile;* toward, as in "I'm going *to* heaven"
too	overly, as in "The pizza was *too* hot"; also, as in "The coffee was hot, *too.*"
two	the number 2

Tony drove *to* the park *to* be alone with Lola. (The first *to* means "toward"; the second *to* is a verb part that goes with *be.)*

Tony's shirt is *too* tight, *too.* (The first *too* means "overly"; the second *too* means "also.")

You need *two* hands (2 hands) to handle a Whopper.

Fill in the blanks: _____ times tonight, you have been _____ ready _____ make assumptions without asking questions first.

wear	to have on
where	in what place

Fred wanted to *wear* his light pants on the hot day, but he didn't know *where* he had put them.

Fill in the blanks: Exactly _____ on my leg should I _____ this elastic bandage?

weather	atmospheric conditions
whether	if it happens that; in case; if

Some people go on vacations *whether* or not the *weather* is good.

Fill in the blanks: I always ask Bill _____ or not we're going to have a storm, for his bad knee can feel rainy _____ approaching.

whose	belonging to whom
who's	shortened form of *who is* and *who has*

Who's the instructor *whose* students are complaining?

Fill in the blanks: _____ the guy _____ car I saw you in?

your   belonging to you
you're shortened form of *you are*

> *You're* (meaning "you are") not going to the fair unless *your* brother (the brother belonging to you) goes with you.

Fill in the blanks: _____ going to have to put aside individual differences and play together for the sake of _____ team.

Other Words Frequently Confused

Following is a list of other words that people frequently confuse. Complete the activities for each set of words, and check off and study the words that give you trouble.

a, an Both *a* and *an* are used before other words to mean, approximately, "one."

Generally you should use *an* before words starting with a vowel *(a, e, i, o, u)*:

    an ache   an experiment   an elephant   an idiot   an ox

Generally you should use *a* before words starting with a consonant (all other letters):

    a Coke   a brain   a cheat   a television   a gambler

Fill in the blanks: The girls had _____ argument over _____ former boyfriend.

accept (ăk sĕpt′) receive; agree to
except (ĕk sĕpt′) exclude; but

> "I would *accept* your loan," said Bill to the bartender, "*except* that I'm not ready to pay 25 percent interest."

Fill in the blanks: _____ for the fact that she can't _____ any criticism, Lori is a good friend.

advice (ăd vīs′) noun meaning "an opinion"
advise (ăd vīz′) verb meaning "to counsel, to give advice"

I *advise* you to take the *advice* of your friends and stop working so hard.

Fill in the blanks: I _____ you to listen carefully to any

_____ you get from your boss.

affect (uh fĕkt′)   verb meaning "to influence"
effect (i fĕkt′)   verb meaning "to bring about something"; noun meaning
                      "result"

The full *effects* of marijuana and alcohol on the body are only partly known; however, both drugs clearly *affect* the brain in various ways.

Fill in the blanks: The new tax laws go into _____ next month,

and they are going to _____ your income tax deductions.

among   implies three or more
between   implies only two

We had to choose from *among* fifty shades of paint but *between* only two fabrics.

Fill in the blanks: The layoff notices distributed _____ the

unhappy workers gave them a choice _____ working for another month at full pay and leaving immediately with two weeks' pay.

beside   along the side of
besides   in addition to

I was lucky I wasn't standing *beside* the car when it was hit.
Besides being unattractive, these uniforms are impractical.

Fill in the blanks: _____ the alarm system hooked up to the door,

our neighbors keep a gun _____ their beds.

desert (dĕz′ərt)   stretch of dry land; (dĭ zûrt′) to abandon one's post or duty
dessert (dĭ zûrt′)   last part of a meal

Sweltering in the *desert,* I was tormented by the thought of an icy *dessert.*

Fill in the blanks: After their meal, they carried their _____ into the living room so that they would not miss the start of the old

_____ movie about Lawrence of Arabia.

fewer   used with things that can be counted
less   refers to amount, value, or degree

There were *fewer* than seven people in all my classes today.
I seem to feel *less* tired when I exercise regularly.

Fill in the blanks: With _____ people driving large cars, we are importing _____ oil than we used to.

loose (lōōs)   not fastened; not tight-fitting
lose (lōōz)   misplace; fail to win

Phil's belt is so *loose* that he always looks ready to *lose* his pants.

Fill in the blanks: At least once a week our neighbors _____ their dog; it's because they let him run _____.

quiet (kwī′ ĭt) peaceful
quite (kwīt)   entirely; really; rather

After a busy day, the children are now *quiet,* and their parents are *quite* tired.

Fill in the blanks: The _____ halls of the church become _____ lively during square-dance evenings.

though (thō)   despite the fact that
thought (thôt)   past form of *think*

Even *though* she worked, she *thought* she would have time to go to school.

Fill in the blanks: Yoshiko _____ she would like the job, but even _____ the pay was good, she hated the traveling involved.

■ Review Test 1

Underline the correct word in the parentheses. Don't try to guess. If necessary, look back at the explanations of the words.

1. Please take my (advice, advise) and (where, wear) something warm and practical, rather (than, then) something fashionable and flimsy.

2. Glen felt that if he could (loose, lose) twenty pounds, the (affect, effect) on his social life might be dramatic.

3. (Their, There, They're) going to show seven horror films at (their, there, they're) Halloween festival; I hope you'll be (their, there, they're).

4. (Your, You're) going to have to do (a, an) better job on (your, you're) final exam if you expect to pass the (coarse, course).

5. Those (to, too, two) issues are (to, too, two) hot for any politician (to, too, two) handle.

6. Even (though, thought) the (brakes, breaks) on my car were worn, I did not have (quiet, quite) enough money to get them replaced (right, write) away.

7. (Accept, Except) for the fact that my neighbor receives most of his mail in (plain, plane) brown wrappers, he is (know, no) stranger (than, then) anyone else in this rooming house.

8. Because the Randalls are so neat and fussy, (its, it's) hard (to, too, two) feel comfortable when (your, you're) in (their, there, they're) house.

9. (Whose, Who's) the culprit who left the paint can on the table? The paint has ruined a (knew, new) tablecloth, and (its, it's) soaked (threw, through) the linen and (affected, effected) the varnish.

10. I would have been angry at the car that (passed, past) me at ninety miles an hour on the highway, (accept, except) that I (knew, new) it would not get (passed, past) the speed trap (to, too, two) miles down the road.

■ Review Test 2

On a separate paper, write short sentences using the ten words shown below.

their	principal
its	except
you're	past
too	through
then	who's

49 Effective Word Choice

Introductory Project

Put a check mark beside the sentence in each pair that makes more effective use of words.

1. I flipped out when Faye broke our date. _____

   I got very angry when Faye broke our date. _____

2. Doctors as dedicated as Dr. Curtin are few and far between. _____

   Doctors as dedicated as Dr. Curtin are rare. _____

3. Yesterday I ascertained that Elena and Wes broke up. _____

   Yesterday I found out that Elena and Wes broke up. _____

Now see if you can circle the correct number in each case:

Pair (1, 2, 3) contains a sentence with slang.

Pair (1, 2, 3) contains a sentence with a cliché.

Pair (1, 2, 3) contains a sentence with a pretentious word.

Answers are on page 631.

Choose your words carefully when you write. Always take the time to think about your word choices rather than simply using the first word that comes to mind. You want to develop the habit of selecting words that are appropriate and exact for your purposes. One way you can show sensitivity to language is by avoiding slang, clichés, and pretentious words.

Slang

We often use slang expressions when we talk because they are so vivid and colorful. However, slang is usually out of place in formal writing. Here are some examples of slang expressions:

My girlfriend *got straight* with me by saying she wanted to see other men.

Rick spent all Saturday *messing around* with his stereo.

My boss keeps *riding* me about coming to work late.

The tires on the Corvette make the car look like *something else.*

The crowd was *psyched up* when the game began.

Slang expressions have a number of drawbacks: they go out of date quickly, they become tiresome if used excessively in writing, and they may communicate clearly to some readers but not to others. Also, the use of slang can be a way of evading the specific details that are often needed to make one's meaning clear in writing. For example, in "The tires on the Corvette make the car look like something else," the writer has not provided the specific details about the tires necessary for us to understand the statement clearly. In general, then, you should avoid slang in your writing. If you are in doubt about whether an expression is slang, it may help to check a recently published hardbound dictionary.

Activity

Rewrite the following sentences, replacing the italicized slang words with more formal ones.

Example   The movie was a real bomb, so we cut out early.
The movie was terrible, so we left early.
_____

1. My roommate told me he was going to quit school and *hit the road*, but later he admitted he was just *messing with my mind.*

_____

_____

2. The car was a *steal* until the owner *jacked up* the price.

_____

_____

3. If the instructor stops *hassling* me, I am going to *get my act together* in the course.

_____

_____

Clichés

A *cliché* is an expression that has been worn out through constant use. Some typical clichés are listed below:

Clichés

all work and no play	saw the light
at a loss for words	short but sweet
better late than never	sigh of relief
drop in the bucket	singing the blues
easier said than done	taking a big chance
had a hard time of it	time and time again
in the nick of time	too close for comfort
in this day and age	too little, too late
it dawned on me	took a turn for the worse
it goes without saying	under the weather
last but not least	where he (she) is coming from
make ends meet	word to the wise
on top of the world	work like a dog
sad but true	

Clichés are common in speech but make your writing seem tired and stale. Also, clichés—like slang—are often a way of evading the specific details that you must work to provide in your writing. You should, then, avoid clichés and try to express your meaning in fresh, original ways.

Activity

Underline the cliché in each of the following sentences. Then substitute specific, fresh words for the trite expression.

Example   I passed the test <u>by the skin of my teeth.</u>
           I barely passed the test.
           _____

1. Hal decided not to eat anything because he was feeling under the weather.

    _____

2. Judy doesn't make any bones about her ambition.

    _____

3. I met with my instructor to try to iron out the problems in my paper.

    _____

Pretentious Words

Some people feel they can improve their writing by using fancy, elevated words rather than simple, natural words. They use artificial and stilted language that more often obscures their meaning than communicates it clearly.

Here are some unnatural-sounding sentences:

I comprehended her statement.

While partaking of our morning meal, we engaged in an animated conversation.

I am a stranger to excessive financial sums.

Law enforcement officers directed traffic when the lights malfunctioned.

The same thoughts can be expressed more clearly and effectively by using plain, natural language, as below:

I understood what she said.

While eating breakfast, we had a lively talk.

I have never had much money.

Police officers directed traffic when the lights stopped working.

Activity

Cross out the pretentious words in each sentence. Then substitute clear, simple language for the artificial words.

Example   The manager ~~reproached~~ me for my ~~tardiness~~.
           The manager criticized me for being late.
           _____

1. One of Colleen's objectives in life is to accomplish a large family.

   _____

   _____

2. Upon entering our residence, we detected smoke in the atmosphere.

   _____

   _____

3. I am not apprehensive about the test, which encompasses five chapters of the book.

   _____

   _____

■ Review Test

Certain words are italicized in the following sentences. In the space provided, identify the words as *slang* (S), *clichés* (C), or *pretentious words* (PW). Then rewrite the sentences, replacing the words with more effective diction.

_____   1. We're *psyched* for tonight's concert, which is going to be *totally awesome.*

            _____

            _____

_____   2. Getting good grades in college courses is sometimes *easier said than done.*

            _____

            _____

_____   3. I *availed myself* of the chance to *participate in* the computer course.

            _____

            _____

_____   4. The victims of the car accident were shaken but *none the worse for wear.*

            _____

            _____

_____   5. My roommate *pulled an all-nighter* and almost *conked out* during the exam.

_____

_____

_____   6. Be sure to *deposit* your trash in the appropriate *receptacle*.

_____

_____

_____   7. Fred has to *work like a dog* in his advanced math class.

_____

_____

_____   8. My sister's constant criticism *drives me up a wall*.

_____

_____

_____   9. Everyone in our family *congregates* at Miriam's house for the annual Thanksgiving *repast*.

_____

_____

_____   10. Carlos *totally lost it* when the clerk told him that she didn't have any blue shirts in his size.

_____

_____

50 Combined Mastery Tests

Fragments and Run-Ons

■ Combined Mastery Test 1

The word groups below are numbered 1 through 20. In the space provided for each, write C if a word group is a complete sentence, write F if it is a fragment, and write RO if it is a run-on. Then correct the errors.

1. _____

2. _____

3. _____

4. _____

5. _____

6. _____

7. _____

8. _____

9. _____

10. _____

11. _____

12. _____

13. _____

14. _____

15. _____

16. _____

17. _____

18. _____

19. _____

20. _____

[1]I had a frightening dream last night, I dreamed that I was walking high up on an old railroad trestle. [2]It looked like the one I used to walk on recklessly. [3]When I was about ten years old. [4]At that height, my palms were sweating, just as they did when I was a boy. [5]I could see the ground out of the corners of my eyes, I felt a swooning, sickening sensation. [6]Suddenly, I realized there were rats below. [7]Thousands upon thousands of rats. [8]They knew I was up on the trestle, they were laughing. [9]Because they were sure they would get me. [10]Their teeth glinted in the moonlight, their red eyes were like thousands of small reflectors. [11]That almost blinded my sight. [12]Sensing that there was something even more hideous behind me. [13]I kept moving forward. [14]Then I realized that I was coming to a gap in the trestle. [15]There was no way I could stop or go back I would have to cross over that empty gap. [16]I leaped out in despair. [17]Knowing I would never make it. [18]And felt myself falling helplessly down to the swarm of rejoicing rats. [19]I woke up bathed in sweat. [20]Half expecting to find a rat in my bed.

Score Number correct _____ × 5 = _____ percent

585

Fragments and Run-Ons

■ Combined Mastery Test 2

The word groups below are numbered 1 through 20. In the space provided for each, write C if a word group is a complete sentence, write F if it is a fragment, and write RO if it a run-on. Then correct the errors.

1. _____

2. _____

3. _____

4. _____

5. _____

6. _____

7. _____

8. _____

9. _____

10. _____

11. _____

12. _____

13. _____

14. _____

15. _____

16. _____

17. _____

18. _____

19. _____

20. _____

[1]My sister asked my parents and me to give up television for two weeks. [2]As an experiment for her psychology class. [3]We were too embarrassed to refuse, we reluctantly agreed. [4]The project began on Monday morning. [5]To help us resist temptation. [6]My sister unplugged the living room set. [7]That evening the four of us sat around the dinner table much longer than usual, we found new things to talk about. [8]Later we played board games for several hours, we all went to bed pleased with ourselves. [9]Everything went well until Thursday evening of that first week. [10]My sister went out after dinner. [11]Explaining that she would be back about ten o'clock. [12]The rest of us then decided to turn on the television. [13]Just to watch the network news. [14]We planned to unplug the set before my sister got home. [15]And pretend nothing had happened. [16]We were settled down comfortably in our respective chairs, unfortunately, my sister walked in at that point and burst out laughing. [17]"Aha! I caught you," she cried. [18]She explained that part of the experiment was to see if we would stick to the agreement. [19]Especially during her absence. [20]She had predicted we would weaken, it turned out she was right.

| **Score**   Number correct _____ × 5 = _____ percent |

Verbs

■ Combined Mastery Test 3

Each sentence contains a mistake involving (1) standard English or irregular verb forms, (2) subject-verb agreement, or (3) consistent verb tense. Circle the letter that identifies the mistake. Then cross out the incorrect verb and write the correct form in the space provided.

_____ 1. One of my apartment neighbors always keep the radio on all night.

   Mistake in: a. Subject-verb agreement   b. Verb tense

_____ 2. The more the instructor explained the material and the more he wroted on the board, the more confused I got.

   Mistake in: a. Irregular verb form   b. Verb tense

_____ 3. I grabbed the last carton of skim milk on the supermarket shelf, but when I checks the date on it, I realized it was not fresh.

   Mistake in: a. Subject-verb agreement   b. Verb tense

_____ 4. This morning my parents argued loudly, but later they apologized to each other and embrace.

   Mistake in: a. Subject-verb agreement   b. Verb tense

_____ 5. When the bell rang, Mike takes another bite of his sandwich and then prepared for class.

   Mistake in: a. Irregular verb form   b. Verb tense

_____ 6. Someone called Marion at the office to tell her that her son had been bit by a stray dog.

   Mistake in: a. Irregular verb form   b. Verb tense

_____ 7. Because I had throwed away the sales slip, I couldn't return the microwave.

   Mistake in: a. Irregular verb form   b. Verb tense

_____ 8. My dog and cat usually ignores each other, but once in a while they fight.

   Mistake in: a. Subject-verb agreement   b. Verb tense

_____ 9. From the back of our neighborhood bakery comes some of the best smells in the world.

   Mistake in: a. Subject-verb agreement   b. Verb tense

_____ 10. The cost of new soles and heels are more than those old shoes are worth.

   Mistake in: a. Subject-verb agreement   b. Verb tense

Score   Number correct _____ × 5 = _____ percent

Verbs

■ Combined Mastery Test 4

Each sentence contains a mistake involving (1) standard English or irregular verb forms, (2) subject-verb agreement, or (3) consistent verb tense. Circle the letter that identifies the mistake. Then cross out the incorrect verb and write the correct form in the space provided.

_____   1. My friend's bitter words had stinged me deeply.

        Mistake in: a. Irregular verb form   b. Verb tense

_____   2. After she poured the ammonia into the bucket, Karen reels backward because the strong fumes made her eyes tear.

        Mistake in: a. Subject-verb agreement   b. Verb tense

_____   3. Flying around in space is various pieces of debris from old space satellites.

        Mistake in: a. Subject-verb agreement   b. Verb tense

_____   4. Eileen watched suspiciously as a strange car drived back and forth in front of her house.

        Mistake in: a. Irregular verb form   b. Verb tense

_____   5. Both crying and laughing helps us get rid of tension.

        Mistake in: a. Subject-verb agreement   b. Verb tense

_____   6. All my clothes were dirty, so I stayed up late and washes a load for tomorrow.

        Mistake in: a. Subject-verb agreement   b. Verb tense

_____   7. McDonald's has selled enough hamburgers to reach to the moon.

        Mistake in: a. Irregular verb form   b. Verb tense

_____   8. When Chen peeled back the bedroom wallpaper, he discovered another layer of wallpaper and uses a steamer to get that layer off.

        Mistake in: a. Subject-verb agreement   b. Verb tense

_____   9. Rosie searched for the fifty-dollar bill she had hid somewhere in her dresser.

        Mistake in: a. Irregular verb form   b. Verb tense

_____   10. The realistic yellow tulips on the gravestone is made of a weather-resistant fabric.

        Mistake in: a. Subject-verb agreement   b. Verb tense

> *Score*   Number correct _____ × 5 = _____ percent

Capital Letters and Punctuation

■ **Combined Mastery Test 5**

Each of the following sentences contains an error in capitalization or punctuation. Refer to the box below and write, in the space provided, the letter identifying the error. Then correct the error.

> a. missing capital letter   c. missing quotation marks
> b. missing apostrophe   d. missing comma

_____ 1. Maggie's aerobics class has been canceled this week so she's decided to go running instead.

_____ 2. "One of the striking differences between a cat and a lie, wrote Mark Twain, "is that a cat has only nine lives."

_____ 3. My uncles checks are printed to look like Monopoly money.

_____ 4. Did you know someone is turning the old school on ninth Street into a restaurant named Home Economics?

_____ 5. My parents always ask me where Im going and when I'll be home.

_____ 6. She doesn't talk about it much, but my aunt has been a member of alcoholics Anonymous for ten years.

_____ 7. The sweating straining horses neared the finish line.

_____ 8. Whenever he gave us the keys to the car, my father would say, Watch out for the other guy."

_____ 9. If you're going to stay up late be sure to turn down the heat before going to bed.

_____ 10. I decided to have a glass of apple juice rather than order a pepsi.

> *Score* Number correct _____ × 5 = _____ percent

Capital Letters and Punctuation

■ **Combined Mastery Test 6**

Each of the following sentences contains an error in capitalization or punctuation. Refer to the box below and write, in the space provided, the letter identifying the error. Then correct the error.

a. missing capital letter	c. missing quotation marks
b. missing apostrophe	d. missing comma

_____   1. Even though I hadn't saved the receipt I was able to return the blender to Sears.

_____   2. "The diners food is always reliable," said Stan. "It's consistently bad."

_____   3. Some people are surprised to hear that manhattan is an island.

_____   4. "To love oneself, said Oscar Wilde, "is the beginning of a lifelong romance."

_____   5. The airplane was delayed for more than three hours and the passengers were getting impatient.

_____   6. Leslie said to the woman behind her in the theater, "will you stop talking, please?"

_____   7. Walters arthritis is as good a predictor of the weather as the TV weather report.

_____   8. "Before you can reach your goals," says my grandfather, you have to believe you can reach them."

_____   9. There is little evidence that king Arthur, the legendary hero, really existed.

_____   10. My cousin learned to cook when he was an Army cook during World war II.

Score Number correct _____ × 5 = _____ percent	

Word Use

■ **Combined Mastery Test 7**

Each of the following sentences contains a mistake identified in the left-hand margin. Underline the mistake and then correct it in the space provided.

Slang

1. Because Nicole has a lot of pull at work, she always has first choice of vacation time.

_____

Wordiness

2. Truthfully, I've been wishing that the final could be postponed to a much later date sometime next week.

_____

Cliché

3. Kate hoped her friends would be green with envy when they saw her new boyfriend.

_____

Pretentious language

4. Harold utilizes old coffee cans to water his houseplants.

_____

Adverb error

5. The sled started slow and then picked up speed as the icy hill became steeper.

_____

Error in comparison

6. When the weather is dry, my sinus condition feels more better.

_____

Confused word

7. If you neglect your friends, their likely to become former friends.

_____

Confused word

8. She's the neighbor who's dog is courting my dog.

_____

Confused word

9. If you don't put cans, jars, and newspapers on the curb for recycling, the township won't pick up you're garbage.

_____

Confused word

10. "Its the most economical car you can buy," the announcer said.

_____

Score Number correct _____ × 5 = _____ percent

Word Use

■ Combined Mastery Test 8

Each of the following sentences contains a mistake identified in the left-hand margin. Underline the mistake and then correct it in the space provided.

Slang

1. After coming in to work late all last week, Sheila was canned.

_____

Wordiness

2. At this point in time, I'm not really sure what my major will be.

_____

Cliché

3. Jan and Alan knew they could depend on their son in their hour of need.

_____

Pretentious language

4. I plan to do a lot of comparison shopping before procuring a new dryer.

_____

Adverb error

5. The children sat very quiet as their mother read the next chapter of *Charlie and the Chocolate Factory*.

_____

Error in comparison

6. The respectfuller you treat people, the more they are likely to deserve your respect.

_____

Confused word

7. The dog has lost its' flea collar.

_____

Confused word

8. "My advise to you," said my grandmother, "is to focus on your strengths, not your fears."

_____

Confused word

9. The principle advantage of the school cafeteria is that it's three blocks from a Wendy's.

_____

Confused word

10. My parents mean well, but there goals for me aren't my goals.

_____

Score   Number correct _____ × 5 = _____ percent

51 Editing Tests

The twelve editing tests in this chapter will give you practice in revising for sentence-skills mistakes. Remember that if you don't edit carefully, you run the risk of sabotaging much of the work you have put into a paper. If readers see too many surface flaws, they may assume you don't place much value on what you have to say, and they may not give your ideas a fair hearing. Revising to eliminate sentence-skills errors is a basic part of clear, effective writing.

In half of the tests, the spots where errors occur have been underlined; your job is to identify and correct each error. In the rest of the tests, you must locate as well as identify and correct the errors.

Following are hints that can help you edit the next-to-final draft of a paper for sentence-skills mistakes:

Editing Hints

1 Have at hand two essential tools: a good dictionary (see page 550) and a handbook (you can use Chapter 5 and Part Five of this book).

2 Use a sheet of paper to cover your essay so that you will expose only one sentence at a time. Look for errors in grammar, spelling, and typing. It may help to read each sentence out loud. If it does not read clearly and smoothly, chances are something is wrong.

3 Pay special attention to the kinds of errors you yourself tend to make. For example, if you tend to write run-ons or fragments, be especially on the lookout for those errors.

4 Proofreading symbols that may be of particular help are the following:

	omit	in the the meantime
^	insert missing letter or word	beleve
cap, lc	Add a capital (or a lowercase) letter	cap My persian Cat lc

■ Editing Test 1

Identify the five mistakes in paper format in the student paper that follows. From the box below, choose the letters that describe the five mistakes and write those letters in the spaces provided.

---

a. The title should not be underlined.
b. The title should not be set off in quotation marks.
c. There should not be a period at the end of a title.
d. All the major words in a title should be capitalized.
e. The title should be a phrase, not a complete sentence.
f. The first line of a paper should stand independent of the title.
g. A line should be skipped between the title and the first line of the paper.
h. The first line of a paragraph should be indented.
i. The right-hand margin should not be crowded.
j. Hyphenation should occur only between syllables.

"my candy apple adventure"

It was the best event of my day. I loved the sweetness that filled my mouth as I bit into the sugary coating. With my second bite, I munched contentedly on the apple underneath. Its crunchy tartness was the perfect balance to the smooth sweet-ness of the outside. Then the apple had a magical effect on me. Suddenly I remembered when I was seven years old, walking through the county fair grounds, holding my father's hand. We stopped at a refreshment stand, and he bought us each a candy apple. I had never had one before, and I asked him what it was. "This is a very special fruit," he said. "If you ever feel sad, all you have to do is eat a candy apple, and it will bring you sweetness." Now, years later, his words came back to me, and as I ate my candy apple, I felt the world turn sweet once more.

---

1. _____   2. _____   3. _____   4. _____   5. _____

Editing Test 2

Identify the sentence-skills mistakes at the underlined spots in the paragraph that follows. From the box below, choose the letter that describes each mistake and write it in the space provided. The same mistake may appear more than once.

a. fragment	d. apostrophe mistake
b. run-on	e. faulty parallelism
c. mistake in subject-verb agreement	

Looking Out for Yourself

It's sad but true: "If you don't look out for yourself, no one else will." For example, some people have a false idea about the power of a college degree, they think that once they possesses the degree, the world will be waiting on their doorstep. In fact, nobody is likely to be on their doorstep unless, through advance planning, they has prepared themselves for a career. The kind in which good job opportunities exist. Even after a person has landed a job, however, a healthy amount of self-interest is needed. People who hide in corners or with hesitation to let others know about their skills doesn't get promotions or raises. Its important to take credit for a job well done, whether the job involves writing a report, organized the office filing system, or calming down an angry customer. Also, people should feel free to ask the boss for a raise. If they work hard and really deserve it. Those who look out for themselves get the rewards, people who depend on others to help them along get left behind.

1. _____ 2. _____ 3. _____ 4. _____ 5. _____

6. _____ 7. _____ 8. _____ 9. _____ 10. _____

■ Editing Test 3

Identify the sentence-skills mistakes at the underlined spots in the paragraph that follows. From the box below, choose the letter that describes each mistake and write it in the space provided. The same mistake may appear more than once.

a. fragment	e. missing commas around an interrupter
b. run-on	f. mistake with quotation marks
c. mistake in verb tense	g. apostrophe mistake
d. mistake in irregular verb	

Deceptive Appearances

Appearances can be deceptive. While looking through a library window yesterday, I saw a neatly groomed woman walk by. Her clothes were skillfully tailored her makeup was
<u>   </u>
                                                                                    1
perfect. Then thinking no one was looking she crumpled a piece of paper in her hand.
      <u>   </u>
                                  2
And tossed it into a nearby hedge. Suddenly she no longer looks attractive to me. On
<u>   </u>   <u>   </u>
                    3   4
another occasion, I started talking to a person in my psychology class named Eric. Eric seemed to be a great person. He always got the class laughing with his jokes, on the days
                                                                          <u>   </u>
                                                                                  5
when Eric was absent, I think even the professor missed his lively personality. Eric asked me "if I wanted to get a Coke in the cafeteria," and I felt happy he had chose me to be
   <u>   </u>   <u>   </u>
                      6   7
a friend. While we were sitting in the cafeteria. Eric took out an envelope with several
         <u>   </u>
                            8
kinds of pills inside. "Want one?" he asked. "They're uppers." I didn't want one, I felt
                                                                               <u>   </u>
                                                                                    9
disappointed. Erics terrific personality was the product of the pills he took.
              <u>   </u>
                10

1. _____   2. _____   3. _____   4. _____   5. _____

6. _____   7. _____   8. _____   9. _____   10. _____

■ Editing Test 4

Identify the sentence-skills mistakes at the underlined spots in the paragraph that follows. From the box below, choose the letter that describes each mistake and write it in the space provided. The same mistake may appear more than once.

a. fragment	e. apostrophe mistake
b. run-on	f. dangling modifier
c. irregular verb mistake	g. missing quotation marks
d. missing comma after introductory words	

A Horrifying Moment

The most horrifying moment of my life occurred in the dark hallway of my building. Which led to my apartment. Though the hallway light was out I managed to find my apartment door. However, I could not find the keyhole with my door key. I then pulled a book of matches from my pocket. Trying to strike a match, the entire book of matches bursted into flames. I flicked the matches away but not before my coat sleeve catched fire. Within seconds, my arm was like a torch. Struggling to unsnap the buttons of my coat, flames began to sear my skin. I was quickly going into shock. And began screaming in pain. A neighbors door opened and a voice cried out, My God! I was pulled through an apartment and put under a bathroom shower, which extinguished the flames. I suffered third-degree burns on my arm, I felt lucky to escape with my life.

1. _____   2. _____   3. _____   4. _____   5. _____

6. _____   7. _____   8. _____   9. _____   10. _____

■ Editing Test 5

Identify the sentence-skills mistakes at the underlined spots in the paragraph that follows. From the box below, choose the letter that describes each mistake and write it in the space provided. The same mistake may appear more than once.

a. fragment	e. faulty parallelism
b. run-on	f. apostrophe mistake
c. missing capital letter	g. missing quotation mark
d. mistake in subject-verb agreement	h. missing comma after introductory words

Why I Didn't Go to Church

In my boyhood years, I almost never attended church. There was an unwritten code that the guys on the corner <u>was</u> not to be seen in <u>churches'</u>. Although there <u>was</u> many days
  1   2   3
when I wanted to attend a church, I felt I had no choice but to stay away. If the guys had heard I had gone to church, they would have said things like, <u>"hey</u>, angel, when are you
                                                                          4
going to <u>fly?</u> With my group of friends, <u>its</u> amazing that I developed any religious feeling
         5   6
at all. Another reason for not going to church was my father. When he was around the house <u>he</u> told my mother, "Mike's not going to church. No boy of mine is a sissy." My
        7
mother and sister went to <u>church,</u> I sat with my father and read the Sunday paper or
                                              8
<u>watching television.</u> I did not start going to church until years later. <u>When I no longer hung</u>
          9   10
<u>around with the guys on the corner or let my father have power over me.</u>

1. _____   2. _____   3. _____   4. _____   5. _____

6. _____   7. _____   8. _____   9. _____   10. _____

■ Editing Test 6

Identify the sentence-skills mistakes at the underlined spots in the paragraph that follows. From the box below, choose the letter that describes each mistake and write it in the space provided. The same mistake may appear more than once.

---

a. fragment

b. run-on

c. faulty parallelism

d. missing apostrophe

e. missing quotation mark

f. missing comma between two complete thoughts

g. missing comma after introductory words

h. misspelled word

Anxiety and the Telephone

Not many of us would want to do without our <u>telephone but</u>¹ there are times when the phone is a source of anxiety. For example, you might be walking up to your front door. <u>When you hear the phone ring.</u>² You struggle to find your key, to unlock the door, and <u>getting</u>³ to the phone quickly. You know the phone will stop ringing the instant you pick up <u>the receiver, then</u>⁴ you wonder if you missed the call that would have made you a <u>millionare</u>⁵ or introduced you to the love of your life. Another time, you may have called in sick to work with a phony excuse. All day long, <u>youre</u>⁶ afraid to leave the house in case the boss calls back. <u>And asks himself why you were feeling well enough to go out.</u>⁷ In addition, you worry that you might unthinkingly pick up the phone and say in a cheerful voice, <u>"Hello,</u>⁸ completely <u>forgeting</u>⁹ to use your fake cough. In cases like <u>these having</u>¹⁰ a telephone is more of a curse than a blessing.

1. _____   2. _____   3. _____   4. _____   5. _____

6. _____   7. _____   8. _____   9. _____   10. _____

■ Editing Test 7

See if you can locate and correct the ten sentence-skills mistakes in the following passage. The mistakes are listed in the box below. As you locate each mistake, write the number of the word group containing that mistake. Use the spaces provided. Then (on separate paper) correct the mistakes.

5 fragments	_____	_____	_____	_____	_____
5 run-ons	_____	_____	_____	_____	_____

Family Stories

¹When I was little, my parents invented some strange stories to explain everyday events to me, my father, for example, told me that trolls lived in our house. ²When objects such as scissors or pens were missing. ³My father would look at me and say, "The trolls took them." ⁴For years, I kept a flashlight next to my bed. ⁵Hoping to catch the trolls in the act as they carried away our possessions. ⁶Another story I still remember is my mother's explanation of pussy willows. ⁷After the fuzzy gray buds emerged in our backyard one spring. ⁸I asked Mom what they were. ⁹Pussy willows, she explained, were cats who had already lived nine lives, in this tenth life, only the tips of the cats' tails were visible to people. ¹⁰All the tails looked alike. ¹¹So that none of the cats would be jealous of the others. ¹²It was also my mother who created the legend of the birthday fairy, this fairy always knew which presents I wanted. ¹³Because my mother called up on a special invisible telephone. ¹⁴Children couldn't see these phones, every parent had a direct line to the fairy. ¹⁵My parents' stories left a great impression on me, I still feel a surge of pleasure when I think of them.

■ Editing Test 8

See if you can locate and correct the ten sentence-skills mistakes in the following passage. The mistakes are listed in the box below. As you locate each mistake, write the number of the word group containing that mistake. Use the spaces provided. Then (on separate paper) correct the mistakes.

---

1 fragment _____   2 missing commas between items

1 run-on _____   in a series _____   _____

1 nonstandard verb _____   2 apostrophe mistakes _____   _____

1 missing comma around   1 capital letter mistake _____

   an interrupter _____   1 homonym mistake _____

Search for the Perfect Pajama Bottoms

[1]I met a strange character in my job as an Orderly at a state mental hospital. [2]Jacks illness was such that it led to a strange behavior. [3]Jack, a middle-aged man spent most of the day obsessed with pajama bottoms. [4]He seemed to think that someone might have a better pair of pajama bottoms than his. [5]He would sneak into other patients rooms. [6]And steal there pajama bottoms. [7]Other times, he would undress a distracted patient to try on his pajamas. [8]He would try them on find they were not perfect and discard them. [9]Some days, I'd come upon three or four patients with no pajama bottoms on, I'd know Jack was on the prowl again. [10]He were tireless in his search for the perfect pair of pajama bottoms. [11]It was clearly a search that would never end in success.

■ Editing Test 9

See if you can locate and correct the ten sentence-skills mistakes in the following passages. The mistakes are listed in the box below. As you locate each mistake, write the number of the word group containing that mistake. Use the spaces provided. Then (on separate paper) correct the mistakes.

---

2 fragments _____ _____   1 missing comma after introductory

1 run-on _____   words _____

1 irregular verb mistake _____   2 apostrophe mistakes _____ _____

1 missing comma between   1 faulty parallelism _____

  items in a series _____   1 missing quotation mark _____

Fred's Funeral

[1]Sometimes when Fred feels undervalued and depression, he likes to imagine his own funeral. [2]He pictures all the people who will be there. [3]He hears their hushed words sees their tears, and feels their grief. [4]He glows with warm sadness as the minister begins a eulogy by saying, Fred Grencher was no ordinary man . . . " [5]As the minister talks on Freds eyes grow moist. [6]He laments his own passing and feels altogether appreciated and wonderful.

Feeding Time

[7]Recently I was at the cat house in the zoo. [8]Right before feeding time. [9]The tigers and lions were lying about on benches and little stands. [10]Basking in the late-afternoon sun. [11]They seemed tame and harmless. [12]But when the meat was brung in, a remarkable change occurred. [13]All the cats got up and moved toward the food. [14]I was suddenly aware of the rippling muscles' of their bodies and their large claws and teeth. [15]They seemed three times bigger, I could feel their power.

■ Editing Test 10

See if you can locate and correct the ten sentence-skills mistakes in the following passage. The mistakes are listed in the box below. As you locate each mistake, write the number of the word group containing that mistake. Use the spaces provided. Then (on separate paper) correct the mistakes.

---

1 run-on _____   2 missing commas around

1 mistake in subject-verb   an interrupter _____ _____

   agreement _____   1 missing comma between items

1 missing comma after   in a series _____

   introductory words _____   2 apostrophe mistakes _____ _____

                                  2 missing quotation marks _____ _____

Walking Billboards

[1]Many Americans have turned into driving, walking billboards. [2]As much as we all claim to hate commercials on television we dont seem to have any qualms about turning ourselves into commercials. [3]Our car bumpers for example advertise lake resorts underground caverns, and amusement parks. [4]Also, we wear clothes marked with other peoples initials and slogans. [5]Our fascination with the names of designers show up on the backs of our sneakers, the breast pockets of our shirts, and the right rear pockets of our blue jeans. [6]And we wear T-shirts filled with all kinds of advertising messages. [7]For instance, people are willing to wear shirts that read, "Dillon Construction," "Nike," or even I Got Crabs at Ed's Seafood Palace. [8]In conclusion, we say we hate commercials, we actually pay people for the right to advertise their products.

■ Editing Test 11

See if you can locate and correct the ten sentence-skills mistakes in the following passage. The mistakes are listed in the box below. As you locate each mistake, write the number of the word group containing that mistake. Use the spaces provided. Then (on separate paper) correct the mistakes.

3 fragments _____	1 mistake in pronoun point
_____ _____	of view _____
2 run-ons _____ _____	1 dangling modifier _____
1 irregular verb mistake _____	1 missing comma between two
1 faulty parallelism _____	complete thoughts _____

Too Many Cooks

¹The problem in my college dining hall was the succession of incompetent cooks who were put in charge. ²During the time I worked there, I watched several cooks come and go. ³The first of these was Irving. ⁴He was skinny and greasy like the undercooked bacon he served for breakfast. ⁵Irving drank, by late afternoon he begun to sway as he cooked. ⁶Once, he looked at the brightly colored photograph on the orange juice machine. ⁷And asked why the TV was on. ⁸Having fired Irving, Lonnie was hired. ⁹Lonnie had a soft, round face that resembled the Pillsbury Doughboy's but he had the size and temperament of a large bear. ¹⁰He'd wave one paw and growl if you entered the freezers without his permission. ¹¹He also had poor eyesight. ¹²This problem caused him to substitute flour for sugar and using pork for beef on a regular basis. ¹³After Lonnie was fired, Enzo arrived. ¹⁴Because he had come from Italy only a year or two previously. ¹⁵He spoke little English. ¹⁶In addition, Enzo had trouble with seasoning and spices. ¹⁷His vegetables were too salty, giant bay leaves turned up in everything. ¹⁸Including the scrambled eggs. ¹⁹The cooks I worked for in the college dining hall would have made Julia Child go into shock.

■ Editing Test 12

See if you can locate and correct the ten sentence-skills mistakes in the following passage. The mistakes are listed in the box below. As you locate each mistake, write the number of the word group containing that mistake. Use the spaces provided. Then (on separate paper) correct the mistakes.

2 fragments _____ _____

2 run-ons _____ _____

1 mistake in pronoun
  point of view _____

1 apostrophe mistake _____

1 missing comma between two
  complete thoughts _____

1 missing quotation mark _____

1 missing comma between items in
  a series _____

1 misspelled word _____

My Ideal Date

¹Here are the ingredients for my ideal date, first of all, I would want to look as stunning as possible. ²I would be dressed in a black velvet jumpsuit. ³That would fit me like a layer of paint. ⁴My accessories would include a pair of red satin spike heels a diamond hair clip, and a full-length black mink coat. ⁵My boyfriend, Tony, would wear a sharply tailored black tuxedo, a white silk shirt, and a red bow tie. ⁶The tux would emphasize Tony's broad shoulders and narrow waist, and you would see his chest muscles under the smooth shirt fabric. ⁷Tony would pull up to my house in a long, shiney limousine, then the driver would take us to the most exclusive and glittery nightclub in Manhattan. ⁸All eyes would be on us as we entered and photographers would rush up to take our picture for *People* magazine. ⁹As we danced on the lighted floor of the club, everyone would step aside to watch us perform our moves. ¹⁰After several bottles of champagne, Tony and I would head for the top floor of the World Trade Center. ¹¹As we gazed out over the light's of the city, Tony would hand me a small velvet box containing a fifty-carat ruby engagement ring. ¹²And ask me to marry him. ¹³I would thank Tony for a lovely evening and tell him gently, "Tony, I don't plan to marry until I'm thirty.

Sentence-Skills Achievement Test

Part 1

This test will help you measure your improvement in important sentence skills. Certain parts of the following word groups are underlined. Write X in the answer space if you think a mistake appears at the underlined part. Write C in the answer space if you think the underlined part is correct.

The headings ("Fragments," Run-Ons," and so on) will give you clues to the mistakes to look for.

Fragments

_____ 1. After a careless driver hit my motorcycle, I decided to buy a car. At least I would have more protection against other careless drivers.

_____ 2. I was never a good student in high school. Because I spent all my time socializing with my group of friends. Good grades were not something that my group really valued.

_____ 3. The elderly couple in the supermarket were not a pleasant sight. Arguing with each other. People pretended not to notice them.

_____ 4. Using a magnifying glass, the little girls burned holes in the dry leaf. They then set some tissue paper on fire.

_____ 5. My brother and I seldom have fights about what to watch on television. Except with baseball games. I get bored watching this sport.

_____ 6. My roommate and I ate, talked, danced, and sang at a fish-fry party the other night. Also, we played cards until 3 A.M. As a result, we both slept until noon the next day.

Run-Ons

_____ 7. She decided to quit her high-pressured job, she didn't want to develop heart trouble.

_____ 8. His car's wheels were not balanced properly, for the car began to shake when he drove over forty miles an hour.

_____ 9. I got through the interview without breaking out in a sweat <u>mustache, I</u> also managed to keep my voice under control.

_____ 10. The craze for convenience in our country has gone too <u>far. There</u> are drive-in banks, restaurants, and even churches.

_____ 11. My most valued possession is my stoneware <u>cooker, I</u> can make entire meals in it at a low cost.

_____ 12. The shopping carts outside the supermarket seemed welded <u>together, Rita</u> could not separate one from another.

Standard English Verbs

_____ 13. I am going to borrow my father's car if he <u>agree</u>.

_____ 14. For recreation he sets up hundreds of dominoes, and then he <u>knocks</u> them over.

_____ 15. He <u>stopped</u> taking a nap after supper because he then had trouble sleeping at night.

_____ 16. There was no bread for sandwiches, so he <u>decided</u> to drive to the store.

Irregular Verbs

_____ 17. I learned that Dennis had <u>began</u> to see someone else while he was still going out with me.

_____ 18. That woman has never <u>ran</u> for political office before.

_____ 19. I <u>knowed</u> the answer to the question, but I was too nervous to think of it when the instructor called on me.

_____ 20. They had <u>ate</u> the gallon of natural vanilla ice cream in just one night.

Subject-Verb Agreement

_____ 21. Her watchband <u>have</u> to be fixed.

_____ 22. There <u>is</u> two minutes left in the football game.

_____ 23. He believes films that feature violence <u>is</u> a disgrace to our society.

_____ 24. The plastic slipcovers that she bought <u>have</u> begun to crack.

Consistent Verb Tense

_____ 25. Myra wanted to watch the late movie, but she was so tired she <u>falls</u> asleep before it started.

_____ 26. When the mailman arrived, I <u>hoped</u> the latest issue of _People_ magazine would be in his bag.

_____ 27. Juan ran down the hall without looking and <u>trips</u> over the toy truck lying on the floor.

_____ 28. Debbie enjoys riding her bike in the newly built park, which <u>features</u> a special path for bikers and runners.

Pronoun Agreement, Reference, and Point of View

_____ 29. At the Saturday afternoon movie we went to, children were making so much noise that <u>you</u> could not relax.

_____ 30. We did not return to the amusement park, for <u>we</u> had to pay too much for the rides and meals.

_____ 31. Drivers should check the oil level in <u>their</u> cars every three months.

_____ 32. At the hospital, I saw mothers with tears in their eyes wandering down the hall, hoping that <u>her</u> child's operation was a success.

_____ 33. Sharon's mother was overjoyed when <u>Sharon</u> became pregnant.

_____ 34. You must observe all the rules of the game, even if you do not always agree with <u>it</u>.

Pronoun Types

_____ 35. Nancy and <u>her</u> often go to singles bars.

_____ 36. No one in the class is better at computers than <u>he</u>.

Adjectives and Adverbs

_____ 37. The little girl spoke so <u>quiet</u> I could hardly hear her.

_____ 38. Lola looks <u>more better</u> than Gina in a leather coat.

Misplaced Modifiers

_____ 39. I saw sharks <u>scuba-diving</u>.

_____ 40. <u>With a mile-wide grin</u>, Betty turned in her winning raffle ticket.

_____ 41. I bought a beautiful blouse in a local store <u>with long sleeves and French cuffs</u>.

_____ 42. I first spotted the turtle <u>playing tag on the back lawn</u>.

Dangling Modifiers

_____ 43. <u>When seven years old</u>, Jeff's father taught him to play ball.

_____ 44. <u>Running across the field</u>, I caught the Frisbee.

_____ 45. <u>Turning on the ignition</u>, the car backfired.

_____ 46. <u>Looking at my watch</u>, a taxi nearly ran me over.

Faulty Parallelism

_____ 47. Much of my boyhood was devoted to getting into rock fights, crossing railway trestles, and <u>the hunt for rats in drainage tunnels.</u>

_____ 48. I put my books in my locker, changed into my gym clothes, and <u>hurried to the playing field.</u>

_____ 49. Ruth begins every day with warm-up exercises, a half-hour run, and <u>taking a hot shower.</u>

_____ 50. In the evening I plan to write a paper, <u>to watch a movie,</u> and to read two chapters in my biology text.

Capital Letters

_____ 51. When the can of <u>drano</u> didn't unclog the sink, Hal called a plumber.

_____ 52. I asked Cindy, "<u>what</u> time will you be leaving?"

_____ 53. I have to get an allergy shot once a <u>Week.</u>

_____ 54. Mother ordered a raincoat from the catalog on <u>Monday,</u> and it arrived four days later.

Apostrophe

_____ 55. I asked the clerk if the store had Stevie <u>Wonders</u> latest CD.

_____ 56. <u>He's</u> failing the course because he doesn't have any confidence in his ability to do the work.

_____ 57. Clyde was incensed at the dentist who charged him fifty dollars to fix his <u>son's</u> tooth.

_____ 58. I <u>cant</u> believe that she's not coming to the dance.

Quotation Marks

_____ 59. <u>"Don't forget to water the grass, my sister said.</u>

_____ 60. Martha said to Fred at bedtime, "Why is it that men's pajamas always have such baggy <u>bottoms?" "You</u> look like a circus clown in that flannel outfit."

_____ 61. The red sign on the door <u>read, "Warning</u>—open only in case of an emergency."

_____ 62. "I can't stand that commercial," said Sue. "<u>Do you mind if I turn off the television?"</u>

Comma

_____ 63. Hard-luck Sam needs a <u>loan, a good-paying job, and</u> someone to show an interest in him.

_____ 64. Even though I was <u>tired I</u> agreed to go shopping with my parents.

_____ 65. <u>Power, not love or money, is</u> what most politicians want.

_____ 66. The heel on one of Lola's shoes came <u>off, so</u> she spent the day walking barefoot.

_____ 67. "Thank goodness I'm almost <u>done" I</u> said aloud with every stroke of the broom.

_____ 68. I hated to ask <u>Anita who is a very stingy person to</u> lend me the money.

Commonly Confused Words

_____ 69. To succeed in the job, you must learn how to control <u>your</u> temper.

_____ 70. Fortunately, I was not driving very fast when my car lost <u>it's</u> brakes.

_____ 71. Put your packages on the table over <u>their.</u>

_____ 72. There are <u>too</u> many steps in the math formula for me to understand it.

_____ 73. The counseling center can <u>advise</u> you on how to prepare for an interview.

_____ 74. <u>Who's</u> white Eldorado is that in front of the house?

Effective Word Use

_____ 75. The teacher called to discuss Ron's <u>social maladjustment difficulties.</u>

_____ 76. I thought the course would be a <u>piece of cake,</u> but a ten-page paper was required.

_____ 77. When my last class ended, I felt <u>as free as a bird.</u>

_____ 78. Spike gave away his television <u>owing to the fact that</u> it distracted him from studying.

Part 2 (Optional)

Do Part 2 at your instructor's request. This second part of the test will provide more detailed information about your improvement in sentence skills. On separate paper, number and correct all the items you have marked with an X. For example, suppose you had marked the word groups below with an X. (Note that these examples are not taken from the test.)

4. <u>If football games disappeared entirely from television.</u> I would not even miss them. Other people in my family would perish.

7. The kitten suddenly saw her reflection in the <u>mirror, she</u> jumped back in surprise.

15. The tree in my <u>cousins</u> front yard always sheds its leaves two weeks before others on the street.

29. When we go out to a <u>restaurant we</u> always order something we would not cook for ourselves.

Here is how you should write your corrections on a separate sheet of paper.

4. television, I
7. mirror, and
15. cousin's
29. restaurant, we

There are over forty corrections to make in all.

52 ESL Pointers

This section covers rules that most native speakers of English take for granted but that are useful for speakers of English as a second language (ESL).

Articles

Articles are noun markers—they signal that a noun will follow. There are two kinds of articles: indefinite and definite. The indefinite articles are *a* and *an*. Use *a* before a word that begins with a consonant sound:

> **a c**arrot, **a p**ig, **a u**niform
>
> (*A* is used before *uniform* because the *u* in that word sounds like the consonant *y* plus *u,* not a vowel sound.)

Use *an* before a word beginning with a vowel sound:

> **an e**xcuse, **an o**nion, **an h**onor
>
> (*Honor* begins with a vowel because the *h* is silent.)

The definite article is *the.*

> **the** lemon, **the** fan

An article may come right before a noun:

> **a** circle, **the** summer

Or an article may be separated from the noun by words that describe the nouns:

> **a** large circle, **the** long hot summer.

Note   There are various other noun markers, including quantity words (*a few, many, a lot of*), numerals (*one, ten, 120*), demonstrative adjectives (*this, these*), adjectives (*my, your, our*), and possessive nouns (*Vinh's, the school's*).

Articles with Count and Noncount Nouns

To know whether to use an article with a noun and which article to use, you must recognize count and noncount nouns. (A *noun* is a word used to name something—a person, place, thing, or idea.)

Count nouns name people, places, things, or ideas that can be counted and made into plurals, such as *window, table*, and *principal* (*one window, two tables, three principals*).

Noncount nouns refer to things or ideas that cannot be counted and therefore cannot be made into plurals, such as *weather, anger*, and *happiness*. The box below lists and illustrates common types of noncount nouns.

Common Noncount Nouns

Abstractions and emotions: joy, humor, patience, mercy, curiosity

Activities: soccer, gardening, reading, writing, searching

Foods: sugar, spaghetti, fudge, chicken, lettuce

Gases and vapors: air, nitrogen, oxygen, smoke, steam

Languages and areas of study: Laotian, German, social studies, calculus, biology

Liquids: coffee, gasoline, soda, milk, water

Materials that come in bulk or mass form: lumber, soil, dust, detergent, hay

Natural occurrences: gravity, hail, snow, thunder, rust

Other things that cannot be counted: clothing, furniture, homework, machinery, money, news, transportation, vocabulary, work

---

The quantity of a noncount noun can be expressed with a word or words called a *qualifier*, such as *some, more, a unit of*, and so on. In the following two examples, the qualifiers are shown in *italic* type, and the noncount nouns are shown in **boldface** type.

I hear *a little* **anger** in your voice.

The pea soup had gotten thick overnight, so Kala added *more* **water** to it.

Some words can be either count or noncount nouns, depending on whether they refer to one or more individual items or to something in general:

The yearly **rains** in India are called monsoons.

(This sentence refers to individual rains; *rains* in this case is a count noun.)

Rain is something that farmers cannot live without.

(This sentence refers to rain in general; in this case, *rain* is a noncount noun.)

Using *a* or *an* with Nonspecific Singular Count Nouns

Use *a* or *an* with singular nouns that are nonspecific. A noun is nonspecific when the reader doesn't know its specific identity.

A penguin cannot fly; it uses its "wings" to "fly" through the water.

(The sentence refers to any penguin, not a specific one.)

There was **a** fire today in our neighborhood.

(The reader isn't familiar with the fire. This is the first time it is mentioned.)

Using *the* with Specific Nouns

In general, use *the* with all specific nouns—specific singular, plural, and noncount nouns. A noun is specific—and therefore requires the article *the*—in the following cases:

- When it has already been mentioned once

  There was a fire today in our neighborhood. **The** fire destroyed the Smiths' garage.

  (*The* is used with the second mention of *fire*.)

- When it is identified by a word or phrase in the sentence

  The lights in the bathroom do not work.

  (*Lights* is identified by the words *in the bathroom*.)

- When its identity is suggested by the general context

  The coffee at Billy's Diner always tastes a week old.

  (*Coffee* is identified by the words *at Billy's Diner*.)

- When it is unique

  Scientists warn that there is a growing hole in **the** ozone layer.

  (Earth has only one ozone layer.)

- When it comes after a superlative adjective (*best, biggest, wisest*)

  Many of **the** best distance runners come from East Africa.

Omitting Articles

Omit articles with nonspecific plurals and nonspecific noncount nouns. Plurals and noncount nouns are nonspecific when they refer to something in general.

Lights were on all over the empty house.

Coffee should be stored in the refrigerator or freezer if possible.

Runners from Kenya, Ethiopia, and Tanzania often win world-class races.

Using *the* with Proper Nouns

Proper nouns name particular people, places, things, or ideas and are always capitalized. Most proper nouns do not require articles; those that do, however, require *the*. Following are general guidelines about when and when not to use *the*.

Do not use *the* for most singular proper nouns, including names of the following:

- *People and animals* (Rosa Parks, Skipper)
- *Continents, states, cities, streets, and parks* (Asia, North Dakota, San Diego, Rodeo Boulevard, Fairmount Park)
- *Most countries* (Thailand, Argentina, England)
- *Individual bodies of water, islands, and mountains* (Lake Tahoe, Prince Edward Island, Mount Saint Helens)

Use *the* for the following types of proper nouns:

- *Plural proper nouns* (the Jacksons, the United Arab Emirates, the Great Lakes, the Appalachian Mountains)
- *Names of large geographic areas, deserts, oceans, seas, and rivers* (the Northeast, the Gobi Desert, the Indian Ocean, the Mediterranean Sea, the Thames River)
- *Names with the format* "the _____ of _____" (the king of Sweden, the Gulf of Aden, the University of New Hampshire)

Activity

Underline the correct form of the noun in parentheses.

1. (A telephone, Telephone) is found in almost every American home.
2. Today Kim bought (a used car, the used car).

3. (The car, A car) Kim bought is four years old but in very good condition.

4. Thick (fog, fogs) blocked the plane's approach to the airport.

5. My grandparents and cousins all live in (New Jersey, the New Jersey).

6. Adults should have (patience, the patience) when dealing with children.

7. (Indian Ocean, The Indian Ocean) lies between the east coast of Africa and the west coast of Australia.

8. Cats are known for having a great deal of (curiosity, the curiosity).

9. Through the ages, (wine, the wine) has been made out of many fruits other than grapes, such as apples and blueberries.

10. (Water, The water) in the barrel outside is for watering the vegetable garden.

Subjects and Verbs

Avoiding Repeated Subjects

In English, a particular subject can be used only once in a word group with a subject and a verb. Don't repeat a subject in the same word group by following a noun with a pronoun.

Incorrect: My *friend she* is a wonderful cook.
Correct: My **friend** is a wonderful cook.
Correct: **She** is a wonderful cook.

Even when the subject and verb are separated by several words, the subject cannot be repeated in the same word group.

Incorrect: The *flowers* that are blooming in the yard *they* are called snapdragons.
Correct: The **flowers** that are blooming in the yard **are called** snapdragons.

Including Pronoun Subjects and Linking Verbs

Some languages may omit a pronoun as a subject, but in English, every sentence other than a command must have a subject. (In a command, the subject *you* is understood: [**You**] Hand in your papers now.)

Incorrect: The party was a success. *Was* lots of fun.

Correct: The party was a success. **It was** lots of fun.

Every English sentence must also have a verb, even when the meaning of the sentence is clear without the verb.

Incorrect: Rosa's handwriting very neat.

Correct: Rosa's handwriting **is** very neat.

Including *There* and *Here* at the Beginning of Sentences

Some English sentences begin with *there* or *here* plus a linking verb (usually a form of *to be: is, are,* and so on). In such sentences, the verb comes before the subject.

There are oranges in the refrigerator.

(The subject is the plural noun *oranges*, so the plural verb *are* is used.)

Here is the book you wanted.

(The subject is the singular noun *book*, so the singular verb *is* is used.)

In sentences like those above, remember not to omit *there* or *here*.

Incorrect: *Are* many good reasons to quit smoking.

Correct: **There are** many good reasons to quit smoking.

Not Using the Progressive Tense of Certain Verbs

The progressive tenses are made up of forms of *be* plus the *-ing* form of the main verb. They express actions or conditions still in progress at a particular time.

Iris **will be running** for student-body president this year.

However, verbs for mental states, the senses, possession, and inclusion are normally not used in the progressive tense.

Incorrect: I **am loving** chocolate.

Correct: I **love** chocolate.

Incorrect: Sonia **is having** a lovely singing voice.

Correct: Sonia **has** a lovely singing voice.

Common verbs not generally used in the progressive tense are listed in the box below.

Common Verbs Not Generally Used in the Progressive

Thoughts, attitudes and desires: agree, believe, imagine, know, like, love, prefer, think, understand, want, wish

Sense perceptions: hear, see, smell, taste

Appearances: appear, seem, look

Possession: belong, have, own, possess

Inclusion: contain, include

Using Gerunds and Infinitives after Verbs

A *gerund* is the *-ing* form of a verb that is used as a noun:

Complaining is my cousin's favorite activity.

(*Complaining* is the subject of the sentence.)

An *infinitive* is *to* plus the basic form of the verb (the form in which the verb is listed in the dictionary), as in **to eat.** The infinitive can function as an adverb, an adjective, or a noun.

We decided **to eat** dinner on the porch.

(*To eat dinner on the porch* functions as an adverb that describes the verb *decided*.)

Simon built a shelf **to hold** his compact disk collection.

(*To hold his compact disk collection* functions as an adjective describing the noun *shelf*.)

To have good friends is a blessing.

(*To have good friends* functions as a noun—the subject of the verb *is*.)

Some verbs can be followed by only a gerund or only an infinitive; other verbs can be followed by either. Examples are given in the following lists. There are many others; watch for them in your reading.

Verb + gerund (*dislike + studying*)
Verb + preposition + gerund (*insist + on + paying*)

Some verbs can be followed by a gerund but not by an infinitive. In many cases, there is a preposition (such as *for, in,* or *of*) between the verb and the gerund. Following are some verbs and verb-preposition combinations that can be followed by gerunds but not by infinitives:

admit	deny	look forward to
apologize for	discuss	postpone
appreciate	dislike	practice
approve of	enjoy	suspect of
avoid	feel like	talk about
be used to	finish	thank for
believe in	insist on	think about

Incorrect: Sometimes I *enjoy to eat* by myself in a restaurant.
Correct: Sometimes I **enjoy eating** by myself in a restaurant.

Incorrect: Do you *feel like to dance*?
Correct: Do you **feel like dancing**?

Verb + infinitive (*agree + to leave*)

Following are common verbs that can be followed by an infinitive but not by a gerund:

agree	decide	manage
arrange	expect	refuse
claim	have	wait

Incorrect: I *agreed taking* Grandma shopping this afternoon.
Correct: I **agreed to take** Grandma shopping this afternoon.

Verb + noun or pronoun + infinitive (*cause* + *them* + *to flee*)

Below are common verbs that are first followed by a noun or pronoun and then by an infinitive, not a gerund.

cause	force	remind
command	persuade	warn

Incorrect: The queen *commanded the prince obeying.*
Correct: The queen **commanded the prince to obey.**

Following are common verbs that can be followed either by an infinitive alone or by a noun or pronoun and an infinitive:

ask	need	want
expect	promise	would like

Jerry **would like to join** the army.
Jerry's parents **would like him to go** to college.

Verb + gerund or infinitive (*begin* + *packing* or *begin* + *to pack*)

Following are verbs that can be followed by either a gerund or an infinitive:

begin	hate	prefer
continue	love	start

The meaning of each of the verbs above remains the same or almost the same whether a gerund or an infinitive is used.

I prefer **eating** dinner early.

I prefer **to eat** dinner early.

With the verbs below, the gerunds and the infinitives have very different meanings.

forget	remember	stop

Nadia **stopped to put on** makeup.

(She interrupted something to put on makeup.)

Nadia **stopped putting on** makeup.

(She discontinued putting on makeup.)

Activity

Underline the correct form in parentheses.

1. The police officer (she gave, gave) me a ticket for speeding.

2. The telephone never stops ringing. (Is, It is) driving me crazy.

3. (Are paints and crayons, There are paints and crayons) in that cupboard.

4. That book (contains, is containing) photos of our wedding.

5. My midterm math grade persuaded me (getting, to get) a tutor.

6. After walking in the hot sun, we (very thirsty, were very thirsty).

7. The little girl (talked about to become, talked about becoming) a famous scientist.

8. Lucia (expects earning, expects to earn) a B in the class.

9. The pigeons on the sidewalk (pick up, they pick up) crumbs of food that people drop.

10. For lunch today I (want, am wanting) a big salad.

Adjectives

Following the Order of Adjectives in English

Adjectives describe nouns and pronouns. In English, an adjective usually comes directly before the word it describes or after a linking verb (a form of *be* or a "sense" verb such as *look*, *seem* and *taste*), in which case it modifies the subject. In each of the following two sentences, the adjective is **boldfaced** and the noun it describes is *italicized*.

> That is a **bright** *light*.
> That *light* is **bright**.

When more than one adjective modifies the same noun, the adjectives are usually stated in a certain order, though there are often exceptions. Following is the typical order of English adjectives:

Typical Order of Adjectives in a Series

1 **An article or another noun marker:** a, an, the, Joseph's, this, three, your

2 **Opinion adjective:** exciting, plain, annoying, difficult

3 **Size:** enormous, huge, petite, tiny

4 **Shape:** circular, short, round, square

5 **Age:** newborn, recent, old, new, young

6 **Color:** pink, yellow, orange, white

7 **Nationality:** Italian, Chinese, Guatemalan, Russian

8 **Religion:** Buddhist, Catholic, Jewish, Muslim

9 **Material:** plastic, silver, cement, cotton

10 **Noun used as an adjective:** school (as in *school bus*), closet (as in *closet shelf*), birthday (as in *birthday party*)

Here are some examples of the order of adjectives:

>**an interesting old** story
>**the long orange cotton** dress
>**your elderly Hungarian** cousin
>**Rafael's friendly little black** dog

In general, use no more than two or three adjectives after the article or other noun marker. Numerous adjectives in a series can be awkward: **the lovely little old Methodist stone** church.

Using the Present and Past Participles as Adjectives

The present participle ends in *-ing*. Past participles of regular verbs end in *-ed* or *-d*; a list of the past participles of many common irregular verbs appears on pages 461–463. Both types of participles may be used as adjectives. A participle used as an adjective may come before the word it describes:

>It was a **boring** *lecture*.

A participle used as an adjective may also follow a linking verb and describe the subject of the sentence:

>The *lecture* was **boring.**

While both present and past participles of a particular verb may be used as adjectives, their meanings differ. Use the present participle to describe whoever or whatever causes a feeling:

>a **surprising** *conversation*
>(The conversation *caused* the surprise.)

Use the past participle to describe whoever or whatever experiences the feeling:

>the **surprised** *waitress*
>(The waitress *is* surprised.)

Here are two more sentences that illustrate the differing meanings of present and past participles.

The mystery movie was **frightening.**

The audience was **frightened.**

(The movie caused the fear; the audience experienced the fear.)

Following are pairs of present and past participles with similar distinctions:

annoying / annoyed	exhausting / exhausted
boring / bored	fascinating / fascinated
confusing / confused	tiring / tired
depressing / depressed	surprising / surprised
exciting / excited	

Activity

Underline the correct form in parentheses.

1. It was so windy that we had to use stones to hold down the (yellow big plastic, big yellow plastic) tablecloth on the picnic table.

2. At the party, Julie sang a(n) (Vietnamese old, old Vietnamese) song.

3. For her party, the little girl asked if her mother would buy her a (beautiful long velvet, beautiful velvet long) dress.

4. The long walk home from the supermarket left Mira feeling (exhausting, exhausted).

5. The constant barking of our neighbor's dog is very (annoying, annoyed).

Prepositions Used for Time and Place

The use of prepositions in English is often not based on the prepositions' common meanings, and there are many exceptions to general rules. As a result, correct preposition use must be learned gradually through experience. Following is a chart showing how three of the most common prepositions are used in some customary references to time and place:

Use of *On*, *In*, and *At* to Refer to Time and Place

Time

On *a specific day:* on Saturday, on June 12, on your birthday

In *a part of a day:* in the morning, in the daytime (but *at* night)

In *a month or a year:* in November, in 1492

In *a period of time:* in a minute, in a couple of days, in a while

At *a specific time:* at 10:00 A.M., at dawn, at sunset, at dinnertime

Place

On *a surface:* on the dresser, on the porch, on the roof

In *a place that is enclosed:* in my bedroom, in the hallway, in the drawer

At *a specific location:* at the pool, at the bar, at the racetrack

---

Activity

Underline the correct preposition in parentheses.

1. Your next appointment is (on, at) Tuesday.

2. Class begins (on, at) 9 A.M.

3. I love to relax (on, in) a whirlpool bathtub.

4. Sonia is moving to Florida (in, at) a month.

5. The children's birthday party was held (on, at) the bowling alley.

■ **Review Test**

Underline the correct form in parentheses.

1. When I looked out the window, I was surprised by the deep (snow, snows).

2. (Are, There are) cockroaches in the kitchen.

3. When she did not get the job she wanted, Laura felt (depressing, depressed) for a few days.

4. Owls hunt (at, in) night and sleep most of the day.

5. Larry (postponed to go, postponed going) on vacation because he broke his foot.

6. My English teacher wears a (silver small, small silver) ring in his ear.

7. Marta (has, is having) a very bad cold.

8. (On, In) Valentine's Day, friends and lovers send each other affectionate cards.

9. (Turkey is, Turkeys are) the traditional main course at Thanksgiving dinner.

10. Before the camera was invented, (the paintings, paintings) were the only way to record how people look.

Appendix

Answers and Charts

Preview

This Appendix provides answers for the Sentence-Skills Diagnostic Test on pages 405–409 and for the Introductory Projects in Part Five. It also contains three useful charts: an assignment chart and a spelling list, to be filled in by the student, and a general form for planning a paragraph.

Answers to Sentence-Skills Diagnostic Test and Introductory Projects

Sentence-Skills Diagnostic Test (pages 405–409)

Fragments

1. X
2. C
3. X
4. X
5. C
6. X

Run-Ons

7. C
8. X
9. X
10. X
11. C
12. X

Standard English Verbs

13. C
14. C
15. X
16. X

Irregular Verbs

17. X
18. C
19. C
20. X

Subject-Verb Agreement

21. X
22. X
23. C
24. X

Consistent Verb Tense

25. X
26. C
27. C
28. X

Pronoun Agreement, Reference, and Point of View

29. X
30. C
31. X
32. C
33. X
34. C

Pronoun Types

35. X
36. C

Adjectives and Adverbs

37. X
38. X

Misplaced Modifiers

39. X
40. C
41. X
42. X

Dangling Modifiers

43. C
44. X
45. C
46. X

Faulty Parallelism

47. X
48. C
49. X
50. C

Capital Letters

51. X
52. X
53. C
54. X

Apostrophe

55. C
56. X
57. X
58. C

Quotation Marks

59. C
60. X
61. X
62. C

Comma

63. X
64. X
65. C
66. X
67. C
68. X

Commonly Confused Words

69. X
70. X
71. C
72. X
73. X
74. C

Effective Word Use

75. X
76. X
77. X
78. X

Introductory Projects

Fragments (page 419)

1. thought
2. subject
3. verb
4. subject

Run-Ons (page 435)

1. period
2. *but*
3. semicolon
4. *When*

Standard English Verbs (page 450)

enjoyed . . . enjoys; started . . . starts;
cooked . . . cooks

1. past . . . -*ed*
2. present . . . -*s*

Irregular Verbs (page 459)

1. crawled, crawled (regular)
2. brought, brought (irregular)
3. used, used (regular)
4. did, done (irregular)
5. gave, given (irregular)
6. laughed, laughed (regular)
7. went, gone (irregular)
8. scared, scared (regular)
9. dressed, dressed (regular)
10. saw, seen (irregular)

Subject-Verb Agreement (page 468)

The second sentence in each pair is correct.

Pronoun Agreement and Reference (page 475)

The second sentence in each pair is correct.

Misplaced Modifiers (page 493)

1. Intended: A young man with references is wanted to open oysters.
   Unintended: The oysters have references.
2. Intended: On their wedding day, Clyde and Charlotte decided they would have two children.
   Unintended: Clyde and Charlotte decided to have two children who would magically appear on the day of their wedding.
3. Intended: The students who failed the test no longer like the math instructor.
   Unintended: The math instructor failed the test.

Dangling Modifiers (page 497)

1. Intended: My dog sat with me as I smoked a pipe.
   Unintended: My dog smoked a pipe.
2. Intended: He looked at a leather-skirted woman.
   Unintended: His sports car looked at a leather-skirted woman.
3. Intended: A beef pie baked for several hours.
   Unintended: Grandmother baked for several hours.

Capital Letters (page 507)

All the answers to questions 1 to 13 should be in capital letters.

14. The   15. I   16. "That . . ."

Apostrophe (page 519)

1. The purpose of the *'s* is to show possession (Larry owns the motorcycle, the boyfriend belongs to the sister, Grandmother owns the shotgun, the room belongs to the men).
2. The purpose of the apostrophe is to show the omission of one or more letters in a contraction—two words shortened to form one word.